?.75 Barnes + Noble 1-67 (Swearingen)

THE COMMONS AND THEIR SPEAKERS
IN ENGLISH PARLIAMENTS
1376–1523

by the same author

The Commons in the Parliament of 1422

presented to

The International Commission for the History of
Representative and Parliamentary Institutions

(No. XXVIII)

The Commons and their Speakers
in English Parliaments
1376–1523

by

J. S. ROSKELL

MANCHESTER UNIVERSITY PRESS

© 1965, J. S. ROSKELL
Published by the University of Manchester
THE UNIVERSITY PRESS
316-324 Oxford Road, Manchester 13

Printed in Great Britain by Butler & Tanner Ltd, Frome and London

25894

Contents

v

Abbreviations

B.I.H.R.	*Bulletin of the Institute of Historical Research*
B.M.	British Museum
CCR	*Calendar of Close Rolls*
CFR	*Calendar of Fine Rolls*
CPR	*Calendar of Patent Rolls*
DKR	*Reports of the Deputy-Keeper of the Public Records*
DNB	*Dictionary of National Biography*
EHR	*English Historical Review*
HMC	Historical Manuscripts Commission
L. and P.	*Letters and Papers*
PPC	*Proceedings and Ordinances of the Privy Council*, ed. N. H. Nicolas
P.R.O.	Public Record Office
R.S.	Rolls Series
Rot. Parl.	*Rotuli Parliamentorum*
VCH	*Victoria County History*

Preface

THIS book is basically an examination of the origins of the office of Speaker for the Commons and an enquiry into the careers of the men who held it in the medieval period. The latter I have begun with the comparatively well documented appearance, in the Good Parliament of 1376, of Sir Peter de la Mare, the first Speaker known to have been chosen by the Commons from among themselves and to have acted for the duration of a parliament. I might have concluded my enquiry in 1533, with the first election to the Chair of a parliamentary burgess, all previous Speakers having been knights of the shire. The Speaker in question, however, was Humphrey Wingfield. A lawyer who was then M.P. for Great Yarmouth, Wingfield was one of the class from which earlier Speakers had been drawn: he was a member of an old family of substantial East Anglian landowners, a cousin of the Duke of Suffolk, and one of the chamberlains of Henry VIII's sister Mary. What is more, he was dubbed a knight at the very ceremony in which the King accepted him as Speaker. In fact, I have preferred to end my study with Sir Thomas More, Speaker in 1523. More is the first Speaker whose qualities of mind and spirit we know with some degree of intimacy and who can, from both verbal and pictorial portraiture, be evaluated as a person. He was a man of the Renaissance, with an international reputation as an exponent of the New Learning. In this respect, his career was important prospectively. In other respects, it compels a backward look. He was perhaps the morally greatest lay figure of the post-Conquest medieval English Church, against whose discontinuance as a part of Christendom under papal rule he made protest with his life. Again, he was both product and supporter of the best traditions of the medieval English Common Law. In being also a civil servant and royal administrator he was nothing exceptional, of course, among the medieval Speakers. But I have chosen to end this study of them with him, mainly because of his notable conduct in that office, where he showed himself deeply conscious of the medieval traditions of the Lower House. As Speaker he served the King. But he also did well by the Commons, not least by formulating a request for freedom of speech among them which made a new departure in the history of that important privilege. Incidentally, he was the first to be Speaker in one parliament for the Lower House and, as Lord Chancellor, Speaker in another for the Upper House.

It will, perhaps, be objected that in presenting an account of the careers of the Speakers over so long a period as a century and a half, I have related too much of the political and parliamentary background. It will, however, become very evident that most of the Speakers were important as men of affairs, involved in the practice of royal government and administration, implicated in politics, and often concerned, if only in a subsidiary capacity, with high matters of State. This being the case, a proper comprehension of the details of their careers and an understanding of their performance in the rôle of Speaker (if and when this can be discerned) seemed to demand a running commentary on political events and some statement about the circumstances in which parliaments met, continued, and ended. This is why there is so much of France, and also of finance. The period under review was, to use Professor Le Patourel's words, 'dominated by war: war in France, war in Scotland, war as a means of national livelihood'.[1] War inevitably meant large expenditure; this meant taxation; and taxation in turn meant meetings of parliament and an opening of opportunity to the Lower House to assert itself.

I have been able to say something about the careers of some of the Speakers *after* their tenure of office, in the footnotes. The later careers of some others, however, seemed to deserve a treatment too lengthy for mere footnotes, and so additional notes about these Speakers have been put into an Appendix, where the arrangement is in alphabetical order of names.

The arrangement of the material in Part II of the book—in chapters which run mainly according to reigns or (in the case of Henry VI's) to parts of a reign—is simply for the sake of convenience. Some division was necessary. But no special significance attaches to the mode used.

I wish to thank the staff of the Public Record Office for their great help over a number of years. I must also record my sense of obligation to Miss Hilda Lofthouse, Librarian of Chetham's Library in Manchester, for helping me to exploit the rich resources in the field of English local history held by that library. I want, too, to acknowledge my indebtedness to some other colleagues and friends who have given me help and encouragement. The discussions I had with Mr W. R. Fryer of the University of Nottingham in the early

[1] *History*, xlvi. 47. In their original context Professor Le Patourel's words referred only to the fourteenth century.

stages of composition were of great value to me. I have also benefited
from the advice of Dr J. M. W. Bean of the University of Manchester.
Professor E. F. Jacob and Mr K. B. McFarlane from time to time
have kindly supplied me with information about individual Speakers.
Professor V. H. Galbraith has ever been ready with sound advice
and warm encouragement. Then, too, I must thank my wife who
has shared in many discussions at home; she generally knows when
a thing makes sense and when it does not. Especially, however, do
I wish to say how very grateful I am to Professor Sir Goronwy
Edwards who generously undertook to read the whole book: his
constructive criticisms of it, arising out of a deep knowledge and
understanding of the whole subject of medieval parliamentary
history, have helped me to improve upon what I had written, often
in a very positive and vital way.

Lastly, I wish to thank Mrs Enid Lee of Narborough (Leics.) and
Miss Pauline Higgins of Manchester for their patient labours in
typing my manuscript, and Mr T. L. Jones, the Secretary of the
University Press, and his staff for their good offices.

J. S. ROSKELL

Manchester
1964

PART ONE

The Office of Speaker

CHAPTER I

The Origins of the Office of Speaker

AT the outset of this enquiry into the early development of one of the most important institutions of the English parliament, it may be stated quite categorically that the historical evidence is sparse and always inadequate. This is true of the medieval parliament in general. It is especially true of the medieval Commons. We know little of what they did, even less of how they did it. That central source, the *Rotuli Parliamentorum*, records little more of the Commons' doings than their formally stated results; regarding the internal proceedings of the Commons it records virtually nothing at all. Sir Goronwy Edwards, speaking of the evidence of the parliament-rolls, has remarked 'a certain quality of fortuitousness' which should put us on our guard. 'We must not assume', he says, 'that the earliest mention or the latest mention in the parliament-rolls of some method of procedure necessarily marks the earliest occasion or the latest occasion respectively on which that procedure was used; it may have been in use for some time and even for a long time, before (or after) it happens to be first (or last) mentioned in the parliament-rolls.'[1] This warning applies to such references as are made in the rolls to the election of the Speaker, the announcement of his name, his appearances before the King and Lords, his 'protestations', his oral statements, etc. The clerk of the parliament or his subordinates responsible for the actual compilation of the rolls were inconsistent and capricious in at least what they recorded of the details of parliamentary procedure, and it is, of course, in references or allusions to procedure where we should expect to find information bearing upon the Speaker's office. Although it would appear that at least as early as 1363 the Commons were being served by a royal clerk (their *commun clerc* alias *subclericus parliamenti*), he either kept no record of their proceedings or it has not survived. And, as is well known, the *Commons' Journals* were not to begin until 1547.

The chronicles of the later medieval period do not supply the deficiencies of the records when, so far as our subject is concerned, we would most wish them to do so. The writing of general English histories in the scriptorium at the abbey of St Albans petered out at

[1] *The Commons in Medieval Parliaments* (Creighton Lecture, 1957), p. 4.

the close of Henry V's reign; such other extant monastic chronicles as were being produced in the second half of the fourteenth century had already failed of continuance before its end. Almost all of these, moreover, discuss parliaments only haphazardly and, in any case, throw no light on parliamentary procedure. Fortunately, this latter characteristic is not shared by *The Anonimalle Chronicle* of the abbey of St Mary of York. This chronicle provides some remarkable and quite invaluable descriptions of certain sessions of the Good Parliament of 1376, including some of those held by the Commons meeting by themselves in the chapter-house of the abbey of Westminster. These, almost surely based on an eye-witness account, are unique. But even this narrative is brief and intermittent, and the writer never again repeated the particularity which he had devoted to the Good Parliament. All that helps to appraise the Commons' rôle in Elizabethan and later parliaments—records of their debates, diaries, letters, and such like—is almost totally absent from the evidence relating to medieval parliaments. One must make do with what there is, but also be ready to use evidence the bearing of which may sometimes be only indirect and inferential.

The office of Speaker for the Commons arose out of two basic circumstances. When the King summoned parliament, it was because he had certain demands to make of it, and parliament was called upon to give answers to certain 'points' put to it in the 'charge' (or articles officially selected for consideration) pronounced at the opening of parliament, normally by the Chancellor acting on the King's behalf. The Commons arrived at their share of these answers by means of discussions conducted in a room or place apart from that used by the King and the Lords, and therefore the answers they arrived at had somehow to be communicated to the King and Lords. These answers could, of course, have been communicated in writing, and sometimes they were; but many of the Commons' communications to the King and Lords were made orally, and in that case it was necessary and inevitable that someone should speak the Commons' answers on their behalf. The office of Commons' Speaker grew out of this function, and from the time when the Commons' Speaker first appeared, his performance of this function has been his primary duty.

In searching for the earliest of the Commons' Speakers, we need not look too remotely. In the parliament held at Lincoln in 1301, a knight of the shire for Lancashire, Sir Henry de Keighley, presented a bill of twelve articles to Edward I. But this hardly entitles Keighley to be distinguished as the first-known Speaker for the Commons. For, although present as a knight of the shire, he was also attending the parliament as one of the justices elected under the *Articuli super Cartas* to enforce the Charters, and it may have been in this latter capacity that he came to the front. In any case, and whether or not Archbishop Winchelsey was at the back of these demands which Keighley presented, they went forward expressly described as a *billa prelatorum et procerum regni*. Admittedly, the bill purported to be *ex parte tocius communitatis in parliamento*: but, such was the contemporary use of the term, the 'community' referred to here certainly included the 'lords' but by no means necessarily the elected Commons as well. It is safe to say that if Keighley did at all act for the elected Commons in 1301, it was not for them alone. His appearance perhaps indicates no more than that the 'lords' on this occasion had won over the Commons, or some of them, to their own point of view.[1]

When next, so far as we know, a parliament had recourse to the services of a single representative, it was in order that he should act for the whole community of the realm, the occasion being the renunciation of allegiance and homage to Edward II at Kenilworth in 1327. It was Sir William Trussell, *in cuius ore universitas Parliamenti sua verba posuerat*, who accompanied the deputation from parliament to the King and who, as *procurator totius parliamenti*, performed this corporate act, by which (in Maud Clarke's evocative words) 'renunciation of allegiance was transmuted from feudal defiance to the will of the commonalty . . . [so that] the king was rejected not by vassals but by subjects'.[2] A Lancastrian knight who had fought with

---

[1] T. Madox, *History of the Exchequer* (2nd ed., 1769), ii. 108; F. Palgrave, *Parliamentary Writs*, i. 104; Sir F. M. Powicke, *The Thirteenth Century, 1216–1307*, 704, 717n. Edward I so resented what was done on this occasion that even five years later he put Keighley in the Tower of London for a short time.

[2] M. V. Clarke, 'Committees of Estates and the Deposition of Edward II', *Historical Essays in honour of James Tait*, ed. J. G. Edwards, V. H. Galbraith, and E. F. Jacob, pp. 37, 42, 45. Trussell's title as proctor varies from source to source. In one text (Royal Historical Society, Camden Third Series, vol. li (1935), *Rotuli Parliamentorum Hactenus Inediti, 1279–1373*, ed. H. G. Richardson and G. O. Sayles, p. 101), he is described merely as *procuratour des prelatz, contes, et barons et autres gentz nomez en ma procuracie*. The editors suggest that Trussell may have been one of the two knights from north of Trent who, with two other representative knights from below this river, accompanied the deputation from London to Kenilworth. In view of Trussell's main residence being at Peatling (Leics.) and his appointment as royal escheator south of Trent a month after Edward II's deposition, it is just as likely that he was one of the two southern knights who joined the Kenilworth mission.

Earl Thomas of Lancaster against Edward II in 1322, for which he had incurred forfeiture, who had fled overseas and only recently returned with Queen Isabel, Trussell was not even a knight of the shire in this parliament which witnessed Edward II's deposition. Indeed, how Trussell came by a place in this parliament of 1327, or even whether he had any proper place there at all, is not known. But certainly his action at Kenilworth was not on behalf of the Commons alone, but rather for the larger community of parliament of which they were but a part. The Commons were as yet only slowly learning, and perhaps under direct suggestion from above, to deliberate together, and, even more slowly, realizing that their function as representatives of communities set them apart from the 'lords', who represented themselves and who, as peers of parliament, discharged a judicial function which the Commons did not share.

In this period even the 'parliament-roll' was only gradually moving towards having an identity of its own as a peculiar type of royal record. Its format was still experimental. Until recently its custody had been haphazard. Indeed, the decision as to which department of state should be responsible for its compilation had not long been taken. By the beginning of Edward III's reign the job of composition clearly belonged to the Clerk of the Parliaments, who was a Chancery clerk. But, far from being 'a detailed journal' (Stubbs), the roll was still largely made up of copies of petitions presented for consideration in time of parliament and not much else. Whatever narrative of parliamentary proceedings it contains is never more than 'meagre and altogether unworthy', and throws little light on the actual conduct of business.[1] This is true even regarding the doings of the Lords.

It is very seldom that we are vouchsafed a reference to the part taken by any individual prelate or magnate, unless he is a royal official and acting *ex officio*. Early in Edward III's reign, however, there are one or two occasions recorded when the peers needed a judgement, decision or opinion to be announced by one of their own number. When in 1330 Edward III invited the earls and barons to convict Roger Mortimer of treason because his crimes and offences were too notorious to be denied, they stated their agreement through a magnate whose name, however, was not recorded (*et disoient tres touz par un des Peres . . .*). In the first of the three parliaments of 1332 when the Lords were told to advise the King on the subject of local disorder and about a French proposal for a joint

[1] J. F. Willard and W. R. Morris, *The English Government at Work, 1327–1337*, vol. i, T. F. T. Plucknett, 'Parliament', p. 94.

crusade, the lay peers made answer *par bouche Monsr. Henri de Beaumont*, and during the same session this same magnate announced their award regarding an open quarrel in parliament between two of the lords (Grey of Rotherfield and Zouche of Ashby).[1] But declarations of this sort would appear to have been very unusual and were perhaps only necessary when the lay lords acted separately and had to inform the prelates as well as the King of their advice or decisions. Occasionally, individual answers were required of the lords to questions put by the King: for instance, in 1362 and 1368, when offers by David II of Scotland were being considered, and in 1366, when the lords' agreement was sought for the promotion to an earldom of the Seigneur de Coucy, who had married the King's daughter Isabel.[2] But only the general drift of their response was recorded, not the individual answers themselves, how much less the names of the individual lords supplying them. If the Lords acted together and agreed in concert, there was every reason for saying just that and saying no more. Being at the centre of parliament, in *the* parliament-chamber, the lords would not, however, normally require one of their number to speak for them. The King, even when present in parliament, usually spoke through a high administrative or judicial official, for instance, in declaring the causes for which parliament had been summoned; and if he needed to be told of some decision reached by the lords in his absence, the same line of communication was doubtless generally employed in the reverse direction. Edward III usually relied upon his Chancellor, the Chief Justice of his Bench, and his Chamberlain to forward his business.[3] But the Chancellor became especially responsible and eventually, certainly before the end of the Tudor period, perhaps because his functions had become analogous to those of the leader of the Lower House, he came to be called 'the Speaker of the higher house' or 'Lord Speaker'.

Parsimonious in their references to any part played in the transactions of the Upper House by individual lords (unless these were royal officials acting as such), it is hardly surprising that the parliament-rolls do not give the name of any individual acting either among or on behalf of the Commons until, in the roll of Edward III's last parliament, appears the first mention of a Speaker. There is one exception to this generalization. In the parliament which met at

[1] *Rot. Parl.*, ii. 53a; 64b, 66b.
[2] Ibid., 269a, 295a; 290b.
[3] H. G. Richardson and G. O. Sayles, 'The King's Ministers in Parliament, 1272–1377', *English Historical Review*, vol. xlvii, pp. 389–92.

B

Westminster in April 1343, after both Lords and Commons had been told about a truce with France, arranged in Brittany by papal mediation, they were instructed to deliberate separately and advise whether negotiations should continue for a peace-settlement. The answer of the Commons—that they preferred further negotiation but, if it failed, would support a resumption of the war—was declared to the King and the Lords by Sir William Trussell,[1] the same who had renounced homage to Edward II in 1327. It is most unlikely that Trussell was himself one of the elected Commons. In July 1340, he had been one of those sent by Edward III from Bruges to inform parliament of the military situation across the Channel. Now, in 1343, it was Sir Bartholomew Burghersh who had amplified the Chancellor's account of the diplomatic exchanges in Brittany. But it may well be that Trussell, as another expert in diplomatic affairs, had been entrusted with the job of enlightening the Commons in detail and apart, which done, they asked him to express their views to the King and Lords. There is no need to regard Trussell as having done more than act as spokesman for the occasion and on the topic in question. And when on the very next day the knights of the shire and others of the Commons came before parliament to report their advice on another problem—that of keeping the law *en son droit cours, en manere q'ele soit owele as Poures et as Riches*— there was no mention of Trussell acting for the Commons.

It evidently lay within the Commons' discretion to make convenient use of the services of some outsider when communicating with the King and/or the Lords. And the conveyance of information or the passing of demands and messages from above not unnaturally led to their bearer acting as a casual spokesman for the Lower House. Even during the Good Parliament of 1376 the Commons were not averse to communicating with the King through an intermediary who was not one of themselves. Thomas Walsingham of St Albans tells us that a knight of the King's Chamber, Sir Richard Stury, acted as a go-between for Edward III and the Commons: he carried the King's wishes to the knights and theirs to the King until, slandering the knights by reporting that they meant to depose the King like his father before him, Stury was banished from court. It is interesting to note that the term which Walsingham used to describe him was *referendarius*, a word later used in the records of Convocation

---

[1] *Rot. Parl.*, ii. 136b. There is just a possibility that Trussell was one of the knights elected for his own county of Leicestershire, as the name of only one of its shire-knights figures in the return.

as a synonym for the *prelocutor* of its lower house, who first appeared (although not then so designated) in 1399.[1] Even when the employment of a continuing Speaker chosen from amongst the Commons themselves became quite regular, communication with the Upper House was not of necessity restricted to the Speaker or even to members of the House. It is Walsingham again who informs us that when, early in 1382, William de Ufford, Earl of Suffolk, collapsed and died when climbing the stairs to the chamber in the palace at Westminster where the Lords were in session, he had just been chosen by the knights of the shire *ad pronunciandum ex parte illorum negotia reipublicae*.[2] And the Commons are known to have had an elected Speaker of their own number in this parliament, as indeed they had had in 1376. There was apparently a similar situation in the Coventry parliament of 1404 when, again according to Walsingham's account, Sir John Cheyne, a royal councillor, acted as *prolocutor* for the knights of parliament when they proposed a confiscation of the temporalities of the Church to augment the royal revenues, for Cheyne was not a knight of the shire on this particular occasion, and the Commons already had an elected Speaker of the usual kind in the person of Sir William Sturmy.[3]

Admittedly, these are pieces of chronicle rather than of record evidence, but there is at least some evidence from the parliament-rolls themselves which makes these stories credible. When, in the parliament which met at the end of September 1402, Henry IV allowed the Commons' request for the appointment of a delegation from the Lords, but sent both the Steward of the Household and his Secretary to protest to the Lower House that he only did so as a matter of grace, it was these officials who took back word that the Commons were well aware of this. In the next parliament (of January 1404), when certain of the King's plans for Household finance were first presented to the Lords and then to the Commons by Archbishop Arundel, it was the latter who on the Commons' behalf reported their agreement in the Upper House. When, in Henry VI's first parliament, in 1422, after a deputation from the Commons had asked for news about appointments to the offices of Chancellor,

[1] *Chronicon Angliae* (R.S.), ed. E. M. Thompson, p. 87; I. D. Churchill, *Canterbury Administration*, i. 378.

[2] *Chronicon Angliae*, op. cit., p. 333.

[3] *Thomae Walsingham Historia Anglicana* (R.S.), ed. H. T. Riley, ii. 265–6; and see *Transactions of the Bristol and Gloucestershire Archaeological Society*, vol. lxxv, J. S. Roskell, 'Sir John Cheyne of Beckford', 65–6.

Treasurer, and Keeper of the Privy Seal, it was the same few peers who had been chosen to inform the Commons who brought back their thanks. It was another group of peers who, having taken down to the Lower House a list of conditions upon which the new royal councillors were prepared to serve, reported an additional proviso demanded by the Commons. Again in the same parliament, when the Commons requested the Lords that those imprisoned for heresy and Lollardy in London and elsewhere should be delivered to the ordinaries for judgement in accordance with the canon law, it was the Bishop of London (perhaps the author of the petition in the first place) who explained it on the Commons' behalf. And it was on yet another occasion in the 1422 session that the new Chancellor conveyed the Commons' request that Thomas Chaucer, a former Speaker and then knight of the shire for Oxfordshire, should continue to enjoy the office of Chief Butler, to which Henry IV had appointed him (for life) twenty years before.[1]

From 1343, when Sir William Trussell escorted the Commons from the Painted Chamber to the White Chamber of the palace, there to inform Edward III and the peers of their agreement over the truce with France, no other individual, whether outsider (like Trussell himself) or proper member of the Lower House, is known to have acted as spokesman for the Commons until 1376. Then, however, we have the clear evidence of two important chronicles, *The Greater Chronicle* of Thomas Walsingham of St Albans, a southern Benedictine monastery, and *The Anonimalle Chronicle* of St Mary of York, a northern Benedictine house, for the Commons' employment in the Good Parliament of the services of Sir Peter de la Mare, one of the knights for Herefordshire, as their continuing Speaker.[2] Reference is made to De la Mare's prolocutorial activities in 1376 in two continuations of the *Polychronicon* of Ranulph Higden of Chester, both of which allude to his eloquence and one of them to his subsequent imprisonment in Nottingham Castle.[3] The English *Brut* notices Sir Peter's account in 1376 of the ill-doing of Dame Alice Perrers and some members of the royal council, and this description also refers to

[1] *Rot. Parl.*, iii. 486b, 529a; iv. 172a, 174a, 176b, 178b.

[2] *Chronicon Angliae*, op. cit., pp. 72–4, 76, 80; *The Anonimalle Chronicle*, ed. V. H. Galbraith (Manchester, 1927), pp. 82–94.

[3] *Polychronicon Ranulphi Higden* (R.S.), ed. J. R. Lumby, vol. viii, pp. 385, 426. The first of these two passages clearly depended upon one of the versions of the St Albans chronicle, some of whose phrases it copies word for word, e.g. in the note that De la Mare spoke *ac si esset coelitus inspiratus* (cf. *Chronicon Angliae*, p. 392).

his imprisonment at Nottingham.[1] Unfortunately, never again (except perhaps in 1397) do the extant chronicles supply so much reliable information of how a medieval Speaker comported himself in office. The *Anonimalle Chronicle* continues after 1376 to be of some value as a source for what transpired in parliament until its narrative comes to an abrupt end in 1381. But it makes not even a single reference to any of De la Mare's early successors in the Speakership. The *Greater Chronicle* of St Albans, in its account of the Bad Parliament of 1377 (Edward III's last), briefly notes the election, *ad pronunciandum verba communia*, of Sir Thomas Hungerford, *miles duci* [*Lancastriae*] *familiarissimus, utpote senescallus ejus, qui nil aliud voluit quod pronunciaret admittere, quam quod scivit oculis sui domini complacere.* But, although this chronicle has something to tell of the next parliament (Richard II's first) and even refers to Sir Peter de la Mare being among those knights of the Good Parliament who were now re-elected, it says nothing of his being once more chosen to be Speaker. (Which, according to the roll of this parliament, he certainly was.)[2]

Thereafter, no surviving chronicle mentions any Speaker until 1397. Then, however, because of the great interest in the proceedings of what proved to be Richard II's last parliament, the important part played in them by Sir John Bussy, the Speaker, drew the attention of a number of writers. Adam of Usk's chronicle and the *Historia vitae et regni Ricardi Secundi*, attributed to a monk of Evesham, have much to say of Bussy's activities on this occasion.[3] In terms almost precisely identical, they tell of the Commons being ordered by Richard II at the opening of the parliament to elect their Speaker there and then (*ante recessum eorum*). After referring to Bussy's acceptance by the King and his making of a 'protestation', they report his speech (in *oratio recta*) on the subject of the wrong done to the King in the appointment of the parliamentary commission of 1386, the blame for which fell upon Thomas of Woodstock, Richard,

---

[1] *The Brut or the Chronicle of England* (Early English Text Society, Orig. Series, vol. cxxxvi), ed. F. W. D. Brie, part 2, p. 330.

[2] *Chronicon Angliae*, op. cit., pp. 112, 171.

[3] *Chronicon Adae de Usk*, ed. E. M. Thompson (2nd ed., London, 1904), pp. 10–14; *Historia Vitae et Regni Ricardi II Angliae Regis*, ed. Thos. Hearne (Oxford, 1729), pp. 132–7. Despite an occasional difference in their details, there is a very close verbal correspondence between the narratives of these two chronicles for the year 1397. Either one of them was heavily dependent upon the other, or both repeated very faithfully some common source. But Adam of Usk, as he himself tells us, attended this parliament, so that, whether or not he was a plagiarist, his account still remains credible.

Earl of Arundel, and his brother Archbishop Arundel, whom Bussy also held responsible for the special pardon subsequently given to Earl Richard. They go on to relate his demand that this pardon should be repealed, his request that the Commons might make impeachments (followed by his prosecution of the primate), and his intervention in the trial of the Earl of Arundel. Much of this account of Bussy is amply confirmed in the full and independent narrative of *The Greater Chronicle* of Thomas Walsingham.[1] It also happens that no fewer than three chronicles refer to the election of Sir John Cheyne as Speaker at the beginning of the session of Henry IV's first parliament in October 1399. Adam of Usk speaks of his election and no more. But the other two refer to his election and supersession. A London chronicle says that he was discharged 'ffor dyvers infirmites and maladies that he hadde', being replaced by William (*rectius* John) Doreward, who then 'rehersed the protestacion'. The St Albans chronicler, Walsingham, goes further, however, giving us a fair idea of why the original election came to be controverted. He also mentions with approval the conduct of Sir Arnald Savage as Speaker in the second parliament of the new reign (in 1401).[2] But this is the last of Walsingham's allusions to any individual Speaker, which is hardly surprising if only because long before the end of Henry IV's reign his references to parliamentary affairs in general have become spasmodic and mostly jejune. Altogether, the extant chronicles covering the quarter of a century after the Good Parliament make reference to the Speaker in no more than five out of the twelve parliaments where he can be identified.

Fortunately, although the roll of the parliament of 1376 makes no mention of De la Mare, about whom the chronicle evidence is much fuller *in toto* than about any other later Speaker, the roll of the next parliament, the Bad Parliament of January 1377, confirms the notice of Hungerford's election in *The Greater Chronicle* of St Albans. And then the rolls of six out of the next ensuing nine parliaments which

---

[1] *Johannis de Trokelowe et Anon. Chronica et Annales* (R.S.), ed. H. T. Riley, pp. 209–15. Thomas Otterbourne's *Chronica Regum Angliae* (*Duo Rerum Anglicarum Scriptores Veteres*, ed. Thomas Hearne [Oxford, 1732], p. 192) has a brief note of Bussy's election. But, after speaking of him as *prolocutor parliamenti ex regis assignatione*, he describes him as *vir crudelissimus et ambitiosissimus supra modum*. These last words were 'lifted' from Walsingham's narrative, and Otterbourne's reference would seem, therefore, to possess no independent value.

[2] *Chronicon Adae de Usk*, op. cit., p. 36; *Chronicles of London*, ed. C. L. Kingsford (Oxford, 1905), p. 50; *Johannis de Trokelowe et Anon. Chronica et Annales*, op. cit., pp. 290, 302, 335.

met in Richard II's first six regnal years identify the Speaker and sometimes also disclose a little information about one or another of the formalities associated with his office. The value of the rolls appreciates when the value of the chronicles diminishes—from the point of view of our problem, of course. Reference is made in the roll of the parliament of October 1377 to Sir Peter de la Mare as again being Speaker; in the roll of 1378 to Sir James de Pickering; in both rolls of 1380 to Sir John de Gildsburgh; in the roll of 1381 to Sir Richard de Waldegrave; and in the first roll of 1383 to Pickering once again. The rolls of intervening parliaments—those of 1379 and of May and October 1382—make no mention of a Speaker. After Pickering's second election in the parliament of February 1383 there opens up a very serious gap: eleven parliaments went their way whose rolls neither record a Speaker's name nor refer to his existence or activity. Then, the roll of the 1394 parliament tells us that Sir John Bussy acted as Speaker. After an absence of evidence as to identity in the roll of the next parliament of 1395, so do the rolls of the two parliaments of 1397. Thenceforward, the name of the Speaker is supplied by the roll of every valid parliament.[1]

The failure of the Clerk of the Parliaments to identify the Speaker in 1379 and 1382 and for an unbroken stretch of ten years in the middle of Richard II's reign may perhaps be explained away as a lapse (if lapse is the right word) in his duty to engross the parliamentary record. It is surely unlikely that the Commons of their own volition, or for lack of initiative, would have suspended or discontinued in 1383 a practice which they are known to have recently employed no less than eight times. Happily, we are not left to rely entirely on speculation. The rolls of the parliaments of April 1384 and 1395 are like so many others of Richard II's reign in not disclosing the Speaker's identity. Both, however, record that the Commons were ordered to elect a Speaker.[2] It may reasonably be assumed, therefore, that from 1376 onwards, although for the next twenty years or so there are gaps, and sometimes wide gaps, in our information on this point, the Commons habitually elected a Speaker.

The first reference to a Commons' Speaker of the historic sort, that is, one who is elected by the Commons from among themselves,

---

[1] *Rot. Parl.*, ii. 374a; iii. 5b, 34b, 73a, 89b, 100a, 145b. We do not know the name of the Speaker in Henry IV's last parliament, which met in February 1413. Its proceedings were vitiated by the King's death in March following, and no parliament-roll has survived.

[2] Ibid., iii. 166a, 329a.

appears (as noted above) in the accounts furnished by a few contemporary chronicles of the Good Parliament of 1376. The first identification of such a Speaker made in the official record of a parliament occurs in the roll of the very next parliament which met early in 1377, an allusion confirmed by the account of this session in *The Greater Chronicle* of St Albans. This chronological coincidence of interest, private and official, however keenly (at first) this interest is expressed in the one type of record and however casually (at first) in the other, is a remarkably near coincidence. That the St Albans chronicler was captivated by De la Mare's activities as Speaker in 1376 may be explained by his own lively concern about the reforming zeal of the Commons in the Good Parliament and by his awareness of the hostility shown towards them on the part of the personage whom at this time he most detested, John of Gaunt, Duke of Lancaster. Likewise his interest in the Bad Parliament of 1377 was excited largely by the fact that it confirmed and regularized John of Gaunt's undoing of the work of its predecessor, hence his reference to Hungerford, Speaker in this parliament and also a valued servant of the Duke. (When Walsingham of St Albans takes a personal interest in a Speaker, it is always in one of whom he strongly approves or disapproves as a political figure.) The account in *The Anonimalle Chronicle* of York of De la Mare's activities as Speaker in 1376 was very likely prompted by its author's receipt of some windfall of information, perhaps a chatty newsletter from a government clerk who had attended the Good Parliament and had much to tell about what was remarkable in the session. Possibly the first reference to a Commons' Speaker in the parliament-roll of 1377 was due to a new interest in the keeping of parliamentary memoranda on the part of some subordinate of the Clerk of the Parliaments. And certainly, whether for that reason or because parliaments were at this time becoming politically much more exciting than before, the parliament-rolls at the very end of Edward III's reign and in Richard II's early years do become even generally much less stereotyped and formal both in what they record and how they record it: much more expansive, informative, and revealing, and especially in recording the outcome of the activities of the Commons. It is possible, none the less, that the chronological coincidence in these initial signs of interest in the Commons' Speaker is not to be explained away as accidental. The problem may be posed in two questions: in the first chronicle references to a Commons' Speaker in 1376 and in the first reference in a parliament-roll in 1377, are we meeting merely with the earliest allusions to an institution whose origins belong to an earlier time from which, however, unfortunately no evidence has survived? or are we meeting with the genesis of the office of Speaker itself? Might not this coincidence of interest be explained simply by the fact that a Commons' Speaker—one elected by the Commons from among themselves for the duration of a parliament—only made his first actual appearance in 1376?

When the Commons communicated or collaborated with the King and Lords in the course of a parliament, there is some evidence, even early evidence, to suggest that they frequently did so through a small group or deputation. In the parliament of March 1340 twelve knights of the shire and six burgesses were chosen to help a committee of lords and officials to deal with petitions.[1] In the following year, Edward III agreed that the commissioners ordered to investigate the conduct of royal ministers should submit their findings to him in the presence of the Lords and *certeynes persones des Communes*.[2] In 1348 a very select committee of six lords and justices was requested by the Commons to deal with unanswered petitions in company with four or six chosen from their own number.[3] When, in 1352, Chief Justice Shareshull had opened parliament with the usual declaration of the reasons for its meeting, he told the Commons to elect twenty-four or thirty from among themselves; these were to deliberate with some of the Lords in the Painted Chamber on the following day, after which they were to join their colleagues in the abbey chapter-house and tell them what had happened.[4] A request by the Lower House in 1373 for the assistance of an intercommuning-committee of lords was made by a deputation of *ascons de Communes*, who made their approach *en noun de touz*.[5] When, during the Good Parliament, on 9 May 1376, according to *The Anonimalle Chronicle*, Sir Peter de la Mare protested against the exclusion of many of his fellows from the parliament-chamber and insisted on *all* the Commons being admitted, the Duke of Lancaster is stated to have observed that there was no need for more than twelve or thirteen of the Commons to enter at any one time, in accordance with previous practice.[6] The Duke had clearly anticipated a small deputation. In 1378, at Gloucester, when the Lords made some observations upon the Commons' demand for a committee of the Lords to confer with them, they stated that it was customary for them and the Commons each to elect a small number of six or ten, and for these two parties

[1] *Rot. Parl.*, ii. 113a.   [2] Ibid., 131a.   [3] Ibid., 201a.
[4] Ibid., 237b.   [5] Ibid., 316b.   [6] *The Anonimalle Chronicle*, 84.

to meet for discussion, *en aisee manere, sanz murmur, crye, et noise*; the Commons agreed, and certain lords and members of the Lower House were chosen *en petite et resonable nombre, par manere come ent este usez d'ancienetee*.[1] It was again in a parliament at Gloucester, in 1407, when in the parliament-roll is recorded the first collision between the Lords and Commons over a constitutional issue—the question of the right to initiate money bills—that the Commons were ordered by the King to send to the Upper House *ascune certein noumbre des persones de leur compagnie, pur oier et reporter a lour compaignons ce q'ils aueroient en commandement de nostre Seigneur le Roy*; the Commons thereupon sent a dozen of their members who, being told the Lords' decision regarding a monetary grant, were then instructed to inform their fellows and secure their agreement, a proceeding to which the Commons took strong exception.[2] Such deputations as these can only have been constituted on an *ad hoc* basis. It is very likely that on most such occasions, before the establishment of the office of Speaker, one of the deputation would be either chosen by the Commons or nominated by the members of the deputation itself, to act as its foreman or 'speaker' just for that single occasion, that is, on an *ad hoc* basis, too. It was in 1376, so the evidence of *The Anonimalle Chronicle* at least seems to suggest, that the Commons first used the expedient of a speaker who, as one of themselves and privy to their counsels, headed their deputations and was responsible for representing them before the King and Lords whenever it was necessary to do so, continuously, that is, for the whole duration of a parliament, and not just temporarily or haphazardly. Or rather it was in 1376—so it would appear—that the Commons changed over from the type of spokesman who did no more than casually head an *ad hoc* deputation, to the type of Speaker who, once chosen by the Commons, acted on their behalf for the whole of a parliamentary session.

It will perhaps seem to require a great act of faith to accept the proposition that *The Anonimalle Chronicle*, which provides in its account of the Good Parliament of 1376[3] a narrative of the proceedings of the Commons in their own house of assembly unique until after the beginning of their own *Journals* in 1547, furnishes evidence for the actual creation of the historic office of Speaker; especially because neither this chronicle nor *The Greater Chronicle* of St Albans, which also has something to say about the activities of Sir Peter de

---

[1] *Rot. Parl.*, iii. 36b.   [2] Ibid., 611.
[3] *The Anonimalle Chronicle*, op. cit., pp. 80–94.

la Mare in 1376, makes any allusion to their novelty, and the very roll
of the Good Parliament makes no mention of even a Speaker, much
less of De la Mare himself. Even so, that 1376 marks the genesis of
the office of Speaker proper may fairly be maintained.

There can be hardly any doubt, of course, about the veracity of
the report of the Good Parliament given in *The Anonimalle Chronicle*.
Its editor, Professor Galbraith, is prepared to concede that the
author may *in general* have been 'not a very accurate worker', and
that 'the value of the York chronicle is very largely the value of its
lost sources'; but, regarding the part of the chronicle which deals
with the parliament of 1376, he is able to assert that 'the account as a
whole is unshaken by the closest criticism', and that 'the author's
language is the accurate language of a contemporary speaking with
an intimate knowledge of procedure'. As Professor Galbraith says,
'it may be that the report of proceedings in the Parliament [meaning,
the parliament-chamber where the Lords sat] is much more convincing than that of the Commons' speeches [in the abbey chapter-
house]'. But it is, in fact, precisely upon the narrative of what transpired in the parliament-chamber that we must largely depend for the
most significant evidence bearing upon Sir Peter de la Mare's rôle
as continuing Speaker.

The Good Parliament came together at Westminster on Monday,
28 April 1376, and lasted until Thursday, 10 July following. In this
unprecedentedly long session of over ten weeks, the Commons made
themselves responsible for initiating a programme of reform. As
well as a demand for the reconstitution of the royal Council, their
plan included a direct attack on a group of royal ministers and agents,
members of a Court camarilla who had laid themselves open to a
number of charges of financial corruption of one sort or another.
The attack took the form of a series of impeachments, the most important of which were eventually entertained by the peers acting in
their judicial capacity.

Although, from the account of *The Anonimalle Chronicle*, it seems
reasonably clear that early in the Good Parliament the Commons intended Sir Peter de la Mare to continue as their Speaker during the
session, an air of improvisation hangs over his initial prolocutorial
activities. The chronicle describes how, on the third day of the parliament (30 April), the Commons met in the chapter-house of Westminster Abbey to discuss Edward III's demands. First, an oath of
corporate loyalty was proposed and taken. Then, five or six un-
named knights rose in turn from their seats and made speeches at the

lectern in the middle of the chapter-house, drawing attention to a misuse of previous parliamentary grants and the embezzlement of public moneys, to an unwarranted removal of the Staple from Calais designed to profit the King's Chamberlain (Lord Latimer), Richard Lyons, and others, and to the need for a delegation of lords nominated by the Commons to intercommune with them. It is at this point in the narrative that Sir Peter de la Mare is first mentioned: speaking from where the others had spoken, he recounted with approval what had already been said, and then added his own counsel. There was, of course, no need to choose a Speaker, to bear what the St Albans chronicler calls the *onus verbi*, until the Commons were ready to go before the King and Lords in the parliament-chamber, if the Commons were not in the habit of electing a continuing Speaker who was to be there to act for the whole of the parliamentary session. And, in fact, over a week was spent in discussion before the Commons were prepared to answer the King's demands.

Already, because of his eloquence and his understanding of the Commons' requirements, Sir Peter de la Mare, by general assent of the Commons, had been asked to take the sole responsibility of stating their wishes to the Lords (*qil vodroit prendre la charge pur eux davoir la sovereinte de pronuncier lour voluntes en le graunt parlement avaunt les ditz seignours, coment ils furount avysez de fair et dire en descharge de lour conscience*). Seemingly on the understanding that the Commons went in a body (*sarrement*) before the Lords and supported what he should say on their behalf, De la Mare agreed. Prompted by a message from the King, delivered by Sir Alan Buxhill, a knight of the King's Chamber, on Friday, 9 May, the Commons presented themselves at the door of the parliament (*al huse de parlement*). Contrary to their intention, not all the Commons were allowed to enter the Lords' chamber: some got in, others were shut out and went away. We may note that De la Mare, in order to demonstrate that the Commons unanimously approved what he was about to say, refused to proceed until all were admitted; that the Duke of Lancaster, who in the absence of the Black Prince was presiding as the King's lieutenant, protested that this was unusual but finally allowed it; and that only then, after a waste of two hours while the absentees were being rounded up, did De la Mare make his speech, asking for the appointment of the Lords' delegation whose members he went on to nominate. Of greater significance for our immediate purpose, however, is the chronicler's brief but careful account of the introductory exchanges between Lancaster and De la Mare on this occasion. The Duke is reported to have asked the Commons who was to be their spokesman: *'Quel de vous avera la parlaunce et pronunciacion de ceo qe vous avez ordine parentre vous?'* Whereupon De la Mare made it clear that he was to be spokesman by answering and saying as much, but what he explicitly asserted was no more than an authority to speak just in that day's meeting: *Et le dit sire Peirs respondist qe par comune assent il averoit les paroles a la iourne.*[1] Clearly, although not formally apprised of any election, Lancaster had expected a spokesman to come forward. And it may be inferred from the terms of De la Mare's reply that the Duke was in ignorance, not because the Commons had neglected any duty to report the election of a Speaker, but because, since a spokesman's authority was normally only casual and ephemeral (merely for the day), any previous announcement was superfluous. No deputation sent by the Commons to the King and Lords could make an oral communication except through a spokesman of sorts. The absence of formality on this occasion, however, suggests recourse to a familiar contrivance rather than the employment of a regular Speaker, the recording of whose election, presentation, and acceptance in parliament-rolls happened still to be in fortuitous suspense.

That a hitherto casually discharged function was transformed in the Good Parliament into a recognized and regular office is at least suggested by the terms in which *The Anonimalle Chronicle* describes certain features of the next visit of the Commons to the parliament-chamber. This visit took place at their meeting with the Duke of Lancaster and the Lords on the following Monday, 12 May. It is possible that the problem of De la Mare's position during the remainder of the session had been discussed over the week-end, and that his retention as Speaker had been finally decided upon. However this may be, on 12 May the Commons conferred with the Lords' intercommuning-committee in the abbey chapter-house, reached

[1] I have taken the words *a la iourne* to mean 'in that day's meeting'. An alternative rendering, however, might be 'for the occasion', meaning 'for the whole meeting'. And this was, in fact, what De la Mare told Lancaster in their next encounter he had meant on the earlier occasion (only this time he used the expression *a cest fotz*). If this alternative rendering is accepted, what I have said about the enlargement of the scope of De la Mare's responsibility during the week-end between the Commons' visits to the parliament-chamber, stands wide open to correction. None the less, the main point to be established—that De la Mare was the first continuing Speaker—is unaffected: Lancaster's question at the outset of the second visit, *'Qi parlera?'*, depended on the possibility of the Commons having a fresh spokesman at their head.

agreement with its members, and once more went to meet the Lords in general in 'the parliament'. Again, the chronicle's report of the preliminary cross-talk between the Duke of Lancaster and De la Mare is instructive and, in its carefulness, perhaps significant. After an exchange of civilities between Lords and Commons and when all had settled down (*quaunt toutz furount en peas et saunz noys*), Lancaster once again demanded to know who was to speak for the Commons: '*Qi parlera?*' To which De la Mare replied by making a perhaps testy reference to his statement on the earlier occasion: '*Sire, come ieo vous dyse le tiercz iour passe, fuist ordine par comune assent qe ieo avera la parlaunce a cest fotz* [foitz].' It is possible that Lancaster's question was meant to imply that it would be more to his taste if the Commons' spokesman on this occasion were someone other than De la Mare. It is more probable, however, that, being quite prepared, or expecting, to find the Commons with a different spokesman at their head, Lancaster was simply asking the customary question. Whatever construction we put upon these brief words of question and reply, we cannot but notice, however, an enlargement in De la Mare's declared view of his authority: on 9 May, he had stated that he was to speak for that occasion, or rather, to be more precise, for that day's meeting; now, on 12 May, he stated that he had been authorized to speak for this time, meaning presumably for this time of parliament, for its duration. And, clearly, if we accept the account in *The Anonimalle Chronicle* of what happened in the Good Parliament during the next fortnight, De la Mare continued to act as the sole exponent of the Commons' complaints and demands, appearing and making speeches before the Lords certainly on no less than three other occasions (on 12, 24 and 26 May), until on the last of these recorded visits he petitioned for Lord Latimer's arrest and condemnation; and it was he who is expressly stated in the chronicle to have been responsible (along with the other knights of the shire) for marking the dissolution of the parliament by providing a feast for some of the Lords and others. If De la Mare came to the forefront in the Good Parliament as first of all merely an occasional spokesman of perhaps a traditional kind, but certainly chosen by the Commons from their own number, before the end of the parliament he was at any rate like his successors in the Speakership in another way, namely, in exercising this function on a basis of continuing responsibility. Once chosen Speaker, he remained Speaker for the parliament's duration.

According to *The Anonimalle Chronicle*, Sir Peter de la Mare's discharge of his duty as Speaker for the Commons in the Good Parliament was hedged about by conditions imposed by him and by them in both his interest and theirs. And here again may be detected in this chronicle an improvisation in the action and an informality in the record, which have already been noticed in its description of De la Mare's appearances, whether in the chapter-house of the abbey or in the parliament-chamber of the palace. The Commons and, presumably most keenly among them, their Speaker were determined that their impeachment of the King's unworthy ministers should take the form of a maintenance of their criminal accusations in common, in order to emphasize that they were based upon 'common clamour' and also, presumably, in order to avoid at all costs what Lord Latimer evidently desired, namely, that these accusations should appear to be made by an individual who could subsequently be treated as a false accuser open to the penalties of the statute of 38 Edward III. Certainly, on his earliest appearance in the parliament-chamber on Friday, 9 May, after objecting to the exclusion of many of the Commons and securing their admission, De la Mare had insisted that *'ceo qe une de nous dist, touz diount et assentount'*, and on his next appearance on Monday, 12 May, he meticulously adhered to the representative character of his rôle: *'fesaunt toutz vois protestacione devaunt toutz qe yssy sount, qe si ieo rien mesdy* [mis-say] *en ascune poynte qe ieo me sumet al coreccion et amendement de mes compaignouns, qar il ne ad si sage, ou ieo me ret pur fole, qe en une graunde mater ne purroit forfere'*. This is the first occasion on which *The Anonimalle Chronicle* records his making a 'protestation'. It was, in all substance, the 'protestation' which it became usual formally to allow to a Speaker when he was presented by the Commons and accepted by the King. As the Speaker himself is not mentioned in the roll of the parliament, there is naturally no reference to his 'protestation' in that record. And the claim De la Mare put forward in making it was, so far as *The Anonimalle Chronicle* discloses the facts, neither admitted nor even commented upon. Once the Speaker's 'protestation' became a formal act which required royal concurrence, it conferred upon the Speaker an obviously necessary right to speak in the parliament-chamber, but gave no privilege of freedom of speech to those for whom he spoke in their meetings outside the parliament-chamber. I shall have more to say about all this later on. But the 'protestation', in this earliest notice of its use, as a claim which apparently met with no response by way of either objection or acceptance, expressed something that was implicit in the function which De la Mare had undertaken at the

Commons' request, namely, a reciprocal safeguard for both himself and the Commons: it allowed the Speaker's utterances in the parliament-chamber, if uncorrected, to pass as statements agreed by his fellows and, at the same time, it gave a right to the Commons to challenge any divergence on their Speaker's part from what it was agreed he should say. In the circumstances in which it was uttered, on 12 May 1376, such a 'protestation' was highly necessary: it immediately preceded the Commons' first attack in the parliament-chamber on Lord Latimer and Richard Lyons. De la Mare's 'protestation' makes it quite clear that the very real dangers involved in their impeachment had been fully appreciated, not least by him and on his own personal account.

In considering whether in the last quarter of the fourteenth century the office of Commons' Speaker was in the earliest stages of its proper development, we must take into account other evidence than that provided by the narrative of the Good Parliament in *The Anonimalle Chronicle*: the evidence of the official rolls of the parliaments. Here we can observe how, from the last year of Edward III to the end of Richard II's reign, the Chancery clerks responsible for their compilation, after previously failing to record (save in 1343) the functioning of any spokesman of an occasional deputation from the Lower House appearing before the King and Lords and after even making no mention of Sir Peter de la Mare's activities in 1376, began to be concerned to record at any rate a simple fact or two about the Speaker and what he did. At first, their references to the Speaker, although recurrent, were only casual, haphazard, and spasmodic. At the same time, it may be noted that, when the effort was made to record anything relating to the Speaker and his actions, there is a variability, even spontaneity, in the manner in which this information is set out. The presentation is realistic, lively, and informal, and not at all stereotyped and colourless, which is what it eventually becomes when the Speakership was an established institution. (Especially, as we shall see, is this true of the record of the Speaker's 'protestations' of Richard II's reign, where it is possible that the Speaker's own phraseology was sometimes closely followed.) All of this does something to confirm the idea that when the Speaker and his activities began to be noticed in the parliament-rolls, a new departure in the procedure by which the Commons were represented in the Upper House had only just lately been made. The innovation in the composition of the record may well imply a recent formalizing and hardening of the Speaker's office. And the expansion of that record in relation to the Speaker may equally well reflect a growth in the importance of his functions.

Reference has already been made to the casual, even careless, way in which the parliament-rolls between 1377 and 1398 record even the Speaker's name: how, during these years, he is not identified for more than three successive parliaments running; in fact, for no more than ten out of the twenty-five parliaments which met in this period. Besides this, it may be noted that at first the rolls do not even use the name or title of Speaker, and that, even when they come to do so, it is for long enough with some variation in language. In each of the references to a Speaker which occur in the rolls of the parliaments of January and October 1377, October 1378, January and November 1380, October 1381, February 1383, and April 1384, he is described simply as one *qi avoit les paroles de par la Commune* [or *les Communes*], the only exception being an additional reference in the roll of 1381 to *cel office de Vant-parlour*.[1] Not until 1394, with the first known election of Sir John Bussy, do we encounter the term *commune Parlour*, which became the most general term in the early fifteenth century, when the narrative of the parliament-rolls was still mostly in French. When, after 1425, the narrative of the rolls was constantly in Latin, the word *Prelocutor* became normal. Other forms do occur, in some cases more than once and often in concurrent use: *Parlour pur les Communes* [or *la Commune*] (between 1397 and 1410), *Parlour et Procuratour* [*en Parlement*] (between 1397 and 1406), *Parlour de Parlement* (1406), *Commune Parlour pur les Communes* (1406), *prelocutor Communitatis in parliamento* (1406), *Purparlour de la Commune* (1407), *Speker for the Commune[s]* (1414, 1445), *Speker of the Parlement* (1447, 1454), *Speker of oure Parliament* (1485).[2] But most of these variants are exceptional. First *commune parlour*, then (early in Henry VI's reign) *prelocutor* became the regular designation. The English term, however, was evidently 'Speaker'.

In roughly the last two decades of the fourteenth century, those Chancery clerks whose duty it was to record what happened in parliament were being faced with a new (if minor) problem. The fitful uncertainty of even the simplest reference to the Speaker, together with the absence of any 'common-form' phraseology in recording his existence or activities in the parliament-rolls of that time, suggests that the Speakership was a new and immature office. So does the way

---

[1] *Rot. Parl.*, ii. 374a; iii. 5b, 34b, 73a, 89b, 100a, 145b, 166a; 100a.
[2] For most of these forms, reference is to the opening paragraphs of the appropriate parliament-roll.

c

in which the Chancery clerks recorded, if they happened to do so at all, the various formal elements or features of the procedure of the Speaker's appointment. When, in the fifteenth century, the references to the Speaker in the parliament-rolls achieved a large measure of formal consistency or sameness, these elements were as follows: the order to the Commons to elect a Speaker given at the opening of a parliament by the Chancellor or (if, as very occasionally, there was no Chancellor in office or he was unable to officiate) by some other prelate or dignitary who had declared the causes of summons; the Commons' presentation of their Speaker-elect, and the acceptance of the election by the King or his lieutenant holding the parliament; the Speaker's formal plea to be excused, and the King's formal refusal of this request; the Speaker's petition for the allowance of his 'protestation'; his further request for the enactment of the 'protestation' on the roll of the parliament; and, finally, the royal answer to both of these last two petitions. Whether even many (how much less all) of these different formalities were in concurrent use from when the Speakership first emerged, cannot be known for sure. But it is very doubtful. Certainly, it was only towards the end of Henry VI's reign (in 1453) that each and all of these procedures began to be recorded in the parliament-rolls with an entire regularity and without intermission, although the most significant of them—the official order to elect, the presentation, and the 'protestation'—had been continuously present together in the record since early in Henry IV's reign (from 1401). So far as the fourteenth-century history of the Speakership is concerned, it will be evident from the analysis which follows that, although each one of all the various elements of procedure had at some time or another made its appearance in the parliament-rolls before the end of Richard II's reign, never more than two of these elements appear together in the record of a single late fourteenth-century parliament, and that often there is only one recorded (namely, the 'protestation').

The first reference in a parliament-roll to the fact of the Speaker's being actually elected by the Commons does not occur until January 1380, when Sir John de Gildsburgh is described as having been *eslit par la Commune d'avoir pur eulx les paroles*.[1] The first notice of the Commons' being commanded to choose a Speaker does not appear until April 1384: then, when the Salisbury parliament was adjourned at its outset for five days, an order was given to the Commons (by whom is not stated) that they should use the interval profitably and

[1] *Rot. Parl.*, iii. 73a.

tretassent de la persone qi auroit les paroles en cest Parlement pur la Commune, to the end that *pur l'election de tielle persone le Parlement my fuist tariez, come ad este devaunt ore*.[1] The roll, however, unfortunately does not go on to give the result of any election. No note of such an injunction to elect re-appears until 1395, when the roll records how the Chancellor, after opening the parliament with the customary *pronunciatio*, told the Commons to assemble on the following day in either the chapter-house or the refectory of the abbey of Westminster *et y faire election de celuy q'aueroit les parols de par les Communes*.[2] Again, the roll does not give even the Speaker's name. No further order to the Commons to proceed to elect a Speaker is recorded before 1401 when, after declaring the causes of summons, Chief Justice Thirning gave the Commons a command from the King that they *facent election entre eux de leur commune Parlour, et luy presenterent devaunt luy* [the King], *come le manere est, Samedy ensuant* [the next day] *a dys del clocke*.[3] After this time, except for a chance aberration in 1406, the parliament-rolls quite consistently allude to a royal order being given to the Commons at the beginning of each parliament to choose their Speaker.

The first reference in the rolls to the Commons' formally presenting their Speaker-elect does not occur until 1394: on this occasion the roll does not record any official injunction to elect, but states that on the third day of the session the Commons presented Sir John Bussy as *lour commune Parlour* to the King *en plein Parlement*.[4] In the very short roll of the next parliament of 1395, as we have seen, nothing is said of any Speaker except that the Commons were told to elect one on the second day of the parliament. The roll of the following parliament of January 1397, after omitting all reference to any order to elect, records that on the second day the Commons once again presented Bussy, *a qui le Roy s'agrea bien*.[5] This notice of the

---

[1] Ibid., 166a.   [2] Ibid., 329a.
[3] Ibid., 454b.   [4] Ibid., 310a.
[5] Ibid., 338a. The terms in which the King's (or in his absence his Lieutenant's) approval of the Commons' Speaker was expressed were fairly uniform. From 1397 until 1423 the words used were *a qui le Roy* [or *Gardein*] *s'agrea bien*, except that in 1407 and 1410 the phrase *et luy chargea q'il l'emprendroit sur luy* was added, and that in 1411 the King simply replied to the Speaker's plea to be excused his office that he *s'agrea bien a ce qe les Communes avoient fait touchant leur election*. When in 1425 the narrative of the parliament-rolls began to be kept in Latin, the formula of acceptance became *de quo idem Dominus Rex de avisamento Consilii sui se bene contentavit* (in 1426, *de avisamento et assensu Dominorum Spiritualium et Temporalium in presenti Parliamento existencium*); and so it remained until 1447, except in

King's acceptance of the result of the Commons' election is the first of its kind, but from this time forward the rolls record both the Commons' presentation of their Speaker and the act of royal recognition, with utter regularity.

The first reference to the Speaker's formal plea to be exonerated from his duty, made at the time of his presentation, does not properly appear until 1404. It is true that in the parliament of 1381-2 Sir Richard de Waldegrave endeavoured to be discharged (*s'afforceast de lui avoir excusez de cel office de Vant-parlour*), only to have his request turned down (*mais le Roy luy chargeast de le faire par sa ligeance, depuis q'il estoit a ce esluz par ses compaignons*). Although Waldegrave then went on to make his first recorded 'protestation', his attempt to escape from office had not taken place until the beginning of the third week of the parliament; and, moreover, there is clear evidence that the Commons had been having an uncomfortable time amongst themselves, almost certainly over the problem of Richard II's grants of manumission to serfs during the recent Peasants' Revolt; so that it would seem that, unlike most of the later Speakers' pleas to be excused, this one of Waldegrave's was quite seriously meant.[1] No other plea to be exonerated is recorded until 1399, and here again the circumstances were exceptional: Sir John Cheyne, after being presented by the Commons and recognized by Henry IV, and even after having made his 'protestation', on the very next day came into the parliament at the head of the Commons to report that they had realized that he was in no fit state of health to do his office and had already elected his successor, so anticipating the King's answer to the request, which he then went on to make (successfully), that the King would excuse him and accept the new Speaker-elect.[2] The roll of the parliament of January 1404 relates that, at his formal presentation as Speaker on the second day of the session, Sir Arnald Savage asked to be discharged (*se vorroit avoir excusez de celle occupation par diverses voies*), a request which the King declined (*nostre Seigneur le Roy ne luy vorroit avoir acunement pur excusez, mais s'agrea bien a la election faite par les ditz Communes sur le dit Monsr. Arnald*).[3] The roll of the

---

1431 (*de quo idem Custos se bene contentavit*) and in 1432, 1433, 1435 and 1437 (when agreement with the Commons' choice of a Speaker simply took the form of a refusal to excuse him). From 1449 onwards the phrase *de quo idem Dominus Rex se bene contentavit* was common form, the only exceptions being in 1460 and 1478 when it was omitted and acceptance once again took shape as a refusal of the Speaker's request to be discharged.

[1] *Rot. Parl.*, iii. 100a.   [2] Ibid., 424b.   [3] Ibid., 523a.

next parliament (October 1404) makes no mention of any attempt on the Speaker's part to be excused. But the rolls register Sir John Tiptoft's request for discharge in 1406 (*si bien par cause de sa juvente, et pur defaute de seen* [sense] *et discrecion, come par plusours autres voies*), the requests of Thomas Chaucer in the successive parliaments of 1407, 1410, and 1411, and the request of William Stourton in 1413 (*a cause de son petit estat, noun sufficiantie de science, et infirmitee de corps*).[1] There was perhaps some ground for Stourton's petition, because he was actually superseded during the single session of 1413 on the ground of ill-health, and, certainly, he died later in the same year. But all of these requests for exoneration (save Cheyne's) were rejected. And so were all later ones, with one single exception: Henry VI admitted the 'excusation' of Sir John Popham in the parliament of November 1449 (expressly, *debilitate sui corporis guerrarum fremitibus, ipsius Domini Regis et Patris sui obsequiis, ac diversarum infirmitatum vexationibus, necnon senii gravitate multipliciter depressi, considerata*).[2] The constant disallowance of the Speaker's excusation suggests that at least in time the plea had become merely an act of 'common-form' modesty on his part. The general emptiness of the formality may account for the Clerk of the Parliaments' occasional failures to record it and, if he recorded it, his occasional omission of the royal rejection. After Henry V's first parliament the excusation was not again noticed in the rolls until 1425. From 1427, however, it became the regular practice to record it, and there is no later instance of its omission in the medieval period, save only in 1450. No record of the King's normal refusal to allow it appears in the rolls of the successive parliaments of 1433 and 1435, but on these occasions he obviously turned it down all the same.[3]

---

[1] Ibid., 568a, 609a, 622b, 648a; iv. 4a.   [2] Ibid., v. 171b.

[3] Once the excusation had come under steady notice in the rolls, a typical formula would run as follows: *Qui quidem A.B., post excusationem suam notabiliter factam, pro eo quod ipsa sua excusatio ex parte Domini Regis admitti non potuit, eidem Domino Regi humiliter supplicavit* . . . [for allowance of his protestation]. But now and then there might be variations in the form of words. In 1437 (when the narrative, for once in a while, happened to be in French) Sir John Tyrell *humblement supplia au Roi pur luy avoir excuser de cell occupation, et de doner en commaundement as ditz Communes, pur renoveller lour election, et de presenter autiel Persone qe savoit ministrer et declarer au Roy le vrai et noble entent de les ditz Communes, issint qe par son due report, iceste Parlement purroit le pluis tost prendre bone esploit* (Rot. Parl., iv. 495b). In February 1449, John Say *se de onere occupationis predicte excusare volens, plura de sui insufficientia reportans prefato Domino Regi, instanter deprecebatur de tam magno onere expediri* (ibid., v. 141b). In 1460, John Green *plura de sui insufficientia proponens, prefato Domino Regi instantissime supplicabat ipsum de*

The most important single part of the procedure by which a Speaker-elect was entitled to discharge his primary function was his formal request to be allowed his 'protestation', in other words, to be given the right to speak in the parliament-chamber in accordance with the terms of his 'protestation'. These terms were as necessary to the Commons as to himself. For the Speaker's demand was at least partly designed, as we have already seen in *The Anonimalle Chronicle*'s account of Sir Peter de la Mare's Speakership in the Good Parliament, to make clear that the Speaker's main rôle was essentially that of a delegate, that he was the mouthpiece of the Commons and no more, and that the Commons should be allowed to correct whatever he might say amiss on their behalf. From the beginning of Richard II's reign, it is in connexion with this 'protestation' that the Speaker is usually mentioned in the parliament-rolls. In fact, except in the last parliament-roll of Edward III, where Sir Thomas Hungerford is referred to as speaking for the Commons on the last day of the session and is referred to in no other way, the earliest references in the rolls to a Speaker are references simply to his making his 'protestation', nothing at first being recorded there (as we have seen) of any election and presentation by the Commons or of acceptance by or on behalf of the King. Except that in the roll of the parliament of November 1380 the Speaker (Sir John de Gildsburgh) is mentioned as requesting a clearer statement of the demands made of the Commons by the Crown (*lour charge*), including the amount of taxation required, and as later announcing a continuation of the wool-subsidy, no allusion at all being made here to any 'protestation', the reference in the roll of the parliament of October 1377 to Sir Peter de la Mare as Speaker is typical of the references made to his immediate successors in Richard II's reign: *Et puis apres les Communes y vindrent en Parlement devant le Roi et illoeqes Monsr. Peres de la Mare, Chivaler, q'avoit les paroles de par la Commune, faisant sa Protestation qe . . .* (words followed by the terms of the protestation used on this occasion).[1]

---

predicte occupationis onere excusari; cui, de mandato Regis, per prefatum Dominum Cancellarium extitit responsum quod prefatus Dominus Rex, electionem dicti Prelocutoris fore unitatis et concordie intelligens, quam ipse inhabilem se reddiderit, ipsum habiliorem reputavit, firmiter injungendo eidem ut onus predictum super se assumeret (ibid., 374a).

[1] *Rot. Parl.*, iii. 5b. Cf. the roll of the Gloucester parliament of 1378 (ibid., 34b): *Et puis apres les Communes y revindrent devant le Roi, les Prelatz et Seigneurs en Parlement, et illoeqes Monsr. James de Pekeryng, Chivaler, q'avoit les paroles de par la Commune, faisant sa Protestation si bien pur lui mesmes come pur toute la Commune*

In 1394 all that the parliament-roll says of the protestation is that the Speaker, Sir John Bussy, made it *en manere accustume*.[1] Otherwise, the parliament-rolls of the period of the Speaker's emergence and early development, when they make allusion to his protestation— and, if they mention the Speaker at all, they practically always do so —never fail to define its terms. A parliament-roll of this early period gives at least their substance. But often it provides a detailed and seemingly complete rehearsal of them. Among these first protestations there is a general, basic identity of content, and occasionally there are traces of the phraseology becoming stereotyped; but there are enough dissimilarities of content and wording to suggest that the form of the protestation itself was in an early stage of its development and even susceptible to political shifts. After 1394, it is not until 1411 that a parliament-roll omits from its record of the protestation a reference to the Commons' right to amend the Speaker's utterances if in any way he said more or less than instructed. The particular clause embodying this requirement is again omitted in the roll of Henry V's last parliament in 1421 and in the rolls of a number of Henry VI's earlier parliaments (those of 1423, 1425, 1426, 1427 and 1431), but afterwards it is only very exceptionally absent. Eventually, the Clerk of the Parliaments or other Chancery clerks responsible for drafting the rolls moved almost inevitably towards the adoption of a stereotyped formula for the protestation, one which expressed its basic content more economically than once had been the case; and its enrolled form, after 1439 generally, and after 1460 quite consistently for the rest of the fifteenth century, achieved a large measure of even verbal uniformity.

Although the parliament-rolls from 1377 onwards, if and when they mention the Speaker, refer to his protestation and generally record its terms, there is nothing recorded of its approval by the King until 1394: *et a cause qe la dite protestation sembla honeste et resonable, le Roi l'accepta.*[2] From then on, however, the fact that it was

---

d'Engleterre illoeqes assemble . . . Cf. the roll of the parliament of January 1380 (ibid., 73a): *Item, les Communes, apres q'ils furent advisez de lour dite Charge, retourn- erent en Parlement en presence de ñre Seigneur le Roi, et Monsr. Johan de Gildesburgh, Chivaler, q'estoit eslit par la Commune d'avoir pur eulx les paroles, faisant sa protesta- tion qe . . .* Cf. the roll of the parliament of February 1383 (ibid., 145b): *Item, quant mesme la Commune s'avoient longement deliberez et entrecommunez avec les Prelatz et Seigneurs dessuisditz de lour Charge avantdite, ils vindrent en Parlement en presence de ñre Seigneur le Roi et des Seigneurs de Parlement, et illoeqes Monsr. James de Pikeryng, Chivaler, q'avoit les paroles pur la Commune, dist, en faisant sa protestation, qe. . . .*
[1] *Rot. Parl.*, iii. 310a.   [2] Ibid., 310a.

both made and formally allowed was always recorded. The manner
in which the concession was expressed in the record varied according
to the terms in which the request had been made. For instance, when
after 1406 for a time it became usual for the Speaker to add to his
protestation a request that he might enjoy any such privileges as his
predecessors in office had been allowed, the King was described in
the rolls as granting those privileges enjoyed by previous Speakers
in the time of his predecessors (alternatively, *ante hec tempora*), a concession which continued to be recorded as the stock answer long
after this additional request had itself ceased to be noticed.

A further demand which came to be formally made by the Speaker
was for the 'enactment' or, in other words, the enrolment of his
protestation. Such a request, which evidently became superfluous in
practice, was for long enough exceptional or at any rate only exceptionally recorded. First mentioned in the parliament-roll of September 1397,[1] it was referred to in the rolls of 1399, 1401, and 1406,
and again in those of 1425-9, but it was not until after it had once
more re-appeared in 1437 that it became common form.

[1] *Rot. Parl.*, iii. 348b.

The Speaker's Protestation, and the problem of freedom of speech in the Lower House

IT should be realized that the Speaker's protestation was not alto-gether *sui generis*. The Speaker's protestation of his right to correct himself or be corrected, was similar to the protestation which a party or his learned counsel was entitled to make before pleading orally in any royal court, including the high court of parliament. For instance, the Earl of Suffolk, the ex-Chancellor, when in 1386 impeached by the Commons and required by the Lords to answer for himself, made protestation that he might add to or withdraw from his replications whatever his counsel advised.[1] And upon occasion those acting as counsel in private suits entertained by the Upper House might also use a protestation very like that of the Commons' Speaker. For example, when the Earl Marshal claimed precedence of the Earl of Warwick in the parliament of 1425, the latter's counsel, Sir Walter Beauchamp (who had been Commons' Speaker in 1416), requested that he might be allowed to speak under protestation so that, *if he faied lesse then he had in commaundement or of his dulle remembraunce or soryetfulled lesse than was profitable to my lordes title, or if he of his folie, which God defende, seide more than he had in commaundement*, his principal might be free to correct it at his discretion. He requested too that this protestation might be recorded. Similarly, on this same occasion, the Earl Marshal's counsel, Roger Hunt (who had been Commons' Speaker in 1420 and was to be so again in 1433), made a request that he might *resort ayein to reformation of his seid lord Erl Mareshall*, that whatever he said should not turn to the displeasure of any of the lords or of Warwick, and that this protestation might be enacted.[2] The fact that such protestations were couched in terms roughly parallel to those of a Speaker's protestation in no way detracts, how-ever, from the latter's importance.

That the Speaker's protestation was no mere formality is clear from the significant variations in its early content and from the incidental but important uses which it could be made by the Com-mons to serve. It is also clear from the frequency with which, at

[1] *Rot. Parl.*, iii. 216b. [2] Ibid., iv. 267b, 268b.

certain times in the reigns of Richard II and Henry IV, the Speaker
resorted to his protestation in the course of a single parliament or
even during a single session, a procedure which culminated in Sir
John Tiptoft, Speaker in the long parliament of 1406, appealing to
his protestation no fewer than six times, once in the first session, four
times in the second, and once in the third and last session.[1] Further,
and of especial significance, there were occasions when the protestation obviously attracted an interest that was properly political. In
1410, when Thomas Chaucer, Bishop Beaufort's cousin and as such
closely attached to the party of the Prince of Wales, was re-elected
Speaker and made his protestation, it was Henry IV himself who
allowed it, but only as was usual and on the express understanding
that the Commons, realizing the need for unity and agreement, would
act and speak not dishonourably but rather so as to nourish the
friendship and harmony of all parties.[2] And then, in the next parliament of 1411, when, being a second time re-elected Speaker, Chaucer
again made the habitual request for his privilege, the King stated that
he should enjoy no more than the customary protestation, *qar il* [the
King himself] *ne ne vorroit aucunement avoir nulle manere de Novellerie en
cest Parlement* but would maintain his own royal liberty and franchise
as intact as ever it had been under his predecessors; whereupon,
Chaucer requested a day's adjournment to allow his protestation (or
rather, as he put it, the Commons' protestation) to be set out in a
written and more detailed form (*pur mettre en escript leur dite Protestation plus en especial*), the outcome of which proved acceptable in the
end.[3] Although the substance of the protestation was obviously a
matter of some moment both to the Commons and the King, the
available evidence unfortunately does not even hint at the reason for
the royal caution on this particular occasion.

It is to the general question of the content of the protestation, as
recorded in the parliament-rolls, that we must now turn. The first of
the Speaker's protestations to be officially recorded is the one in-

---

[1] As in the parliaments of 1381–2 (ibid., iii. 100b), 1397–8 (357a), 1399 (427b),
1401 (466a), October 1404 (547a), 1406 (569a, 572a, 573b, 574a, 577a, 579b), and
1407 (609a). It may be suspected that protestations were made much more frequently than the records made by some clerks actually indicate, and the making
of a protestation may well have been the rule followed by spokesmen of deputations from the Commons to the parliament-chamber before the days of Speakers.
It may be noted, however, that *The Anonimalle Chronicle* does not refer to any
protestation being made by Sir Peter de la Mare when first he appeared before
the Lords in the Good Parliament on 9 May 1376.
[2] Ibid., iii. 622b.   [3] Ibid., 648a.

cluded in the roll of the first parliament of Richard II. In October 1377, the Speaker, Sir Peter de la Mare, made his protestation, we are told, in these terms: *qe ce qil y avoit a dire nel'* [ne le] *dirroit del soen propre moevement, einz del mocion, assent, et voluntee expres de toute la Commune illoeqes esteante; et s'il avenist q'il y forveiast* [offended] *de rienz, ou par cas y deist chose qe ne fust de l'assent de ses compaignons, q'il ent fuist par mesmes ses compaignons tantost amendez illoeqes, et devant q'il*[s] *y partissent de la place.*[1] It was unusual for the Speaker to be recorded as laying quite so particular an emphasis on his freedom from personal responsibility as appears in this protestation. The circumstances were peculiar: De la Mare himself had not long been freed from imprisonment for the part he had taken as the Commons' leader and Speaker in the Good Parliament of the previous year and perhaps felt it necessary to make a specially clear and candid disclaimer of personal accountability. A similar submission, the next and the only other disclaimer of this special sort, was made in Henry IV's first parliament in 1399 by John Doreward. The latter added to his protestation a request to the King *qe ceo q'il deust ensi parler en cest Parlement pur les ditz Communes ne serroit pris q'il le face de son propre motif ou voluntee singulere, ainz q'il est et serra le commune assent et accord de toutz ses Compaignons suisditz.* On this occasion the circumstances were again exceptional: Doreward had been elected to follow Sir John Cheyne when the latter withdrew on the day following his acceptance.[2] The Speaker's right to be corrected by his fellows, which is recorded in De la Mare's protestation of 1377 (and incidentally contained, according to *The Anonimalle Chronicle* account, in the protestation he had made in the Good Parliament) and which henceforward was habitually a part of the protestation, was seemingly thought to afford sufficient protection as a rule.

It would appear that the original and primary object of the protestation was to safeguard the Speaker. He was entitled to say to the King and Lords no more and no less than what the Commons had agreed and authorized. Accordingly, if the Speaker's protestation allowed for the possible desire of the Commons to correct his utterances, and they chose not to invoke it, it would follow that they tacitly approved of the way in which the Speaker had expressed their proposals and *ipso facto* assumed responsibility for all that he had said; if so, then he would be protected. The Speaker was no more than the Commons' agent. But obviously, as the Commons' proper accredited channel of communication with the King and Lords, he

[1] Ibid., 5b.   [2] Ibid., 424b.

was so important an agent that in their interest, as well as in his own, the discharge of his duty must be subject to limitations. The Commons must be safeguarded against their Speaker (or rather against his potential indiscretions), as he is against them (or rather against the possible consequences of his acting on their behalf). The clause in the protestation which permitted the Commons to object or take exception to any personal imprudence (or under- or over-statements on their Speaker's part) supplied this need. The privilege it conveyed was in practice as much a privilege granted to the Commons as it was one allowed to their Speaker. Not personally responsible *vis-à-vis* the King for whatever he did in parliament on the Commons' behalf, provided that it was demonstrably with their approval that he did it, the Speaker was subject to correction by the Commons for any mistakes, deficiencies or excesses, and failures to do their will. If they were to be regarded as responsible for him, he must be made responsible to them.

The Speaker's subjection to the Commons' control was indispensable to the proper working of parliament. For what really mattered, of course, was that the Commons should not be misrepresented, especially not to their own disadvantage and also, if possible, not to the King's or the Lords' discomfiture either. But supposing the Commons' views were not misrepresented but very faithfully represented by their Speaker to the King and Lords, and nevertheless gave rise to the annoyance and misliking of these superior estates, what then? At least some of the protestations allowed to Speakers under Richard II, Henry IV, and Henry V, throw an important light on this question, containing as they do an apology from the Speaker for whatever in his speeches might seem to be, in matter or form, derogatory to the King and/or the Lords.

The earliest of the protestations of this particular kind is the one made by Sir James de Pickering when first he was Speaker in the second parliament of Richard II which met at Gloucester in October 1378. This protestation is expressly recorded as being made *si bien pur lui mesmes come pur toute la Commune d'Engleterre illoeqes assemble*. It begins, *Et primerement pur la dite Commune, qe si par cas il y deist chose qe purroit soner en prejudice, damage, esclaundre, ou vilanie de n̄re Seigneur le Roi ou de sa Coroune, ou en amenusement de l'honour et l'estat des grantz Seigneurs du Roialme, qe ce ne feust acceptez par le Roi et les Seigneurs, einz tenuz pur nul, et come rienz n'ent eust este dit: desicome la Commune n'est en autre volentee, mais souvrainement desirent l'oneur et l'estat de nostre Seigneur le Roi et les dreitures de sa Coroune estre maintenuz et gardez en touz pointz,*

et la reverence d'autres Seigneurs estre duement gardez toutz partz. And it
goes on, *Et pur sa propre persone demesne, faisant sa Protestation, qe si
pur meins bone discretion, ou en autre manere, il y deist chose qe ne fust del
commune assent de ses compaignons, ou par cas forvoiast* [offended] *de rienz
en ses paroles, q'il feust par eulx susportez* [withdrawn] *et amendez, ore
devant lour departir, ou en apres quant lour pleust.*[1]

The second part of this protestation of 1378 does little more than
paraphrase the more significant part of the protestation made in the
previous parliament. It is the striking first clause of Pickering's
request which commands attention. Another comparable apology to
both King and Lords, similarly offered beforehand, was also made in
the protestation next to be recorded in the parliament-rolls: the one
made in January 1380 by Sir John de Gildsburgh, who then asked,
however, that anything which he happened to say which displeased
the King or the Lords should not even be attributed to the Commons, but be put down to his own ignorance or negligence and so
discounted.[2] Thereafter, no protestation which included an apology
to the Lords as well as to the King is ever again recorded.[3] Indeed,
the parliament-rolls do not again record even an apology to the King
as part of the Speaker's protestation until 1397 (although it should be
remembered that in the intervening period protestations in any form
were seldom enrolled).[4] In the parliament of 1397–8, however, Sir
John Bussy as Speaker made two protestations, one in the first
session at Westminster in September 1397, the other in the brief
second session at Shrewsbury in January 1398, both of which included apologies in advance for what, out of ignorance or negligence,
he might say which displeased the King or was contrary to his estate
and regality.[5] In each of Henry IV's parliaments and in the first
parliament of Henry V in 1413 a similar request to be excused if
offence was taken by the King was preferred by the Speaker either

---

[1] *Rot. Parl.*, iii. 34b.   [2] Ibid., 73a.

[3] In the second session of the parliament of 1406, however, the Speaker (Sir
John Tiptoft) requested that he be allowed recourse to his protestation *en cas
q'il avoit riens parlez qe serroit displesance a nostre Seigneur le Roy ou a Seigneurs du
Parlement,* which suggests that in his *original* protestation (which on this occasion,
oddly enough, the parliament-roll does not provide) Tiptoft had made some
allusion to the Lords (ibid., 573b).

[4] In the concluding words of the protestation made by Sir James de Pickering
in 1383—*la Commune . . . feust de si bone volentee envers lour Seigneur lige come nulle
Commune mieultz purroit estre*—there is some suggestion that an apology to the
King in advance had actually been made on that occasion (ibid., 145).

[5] Ibid., 348b, 357a.

at his presentation or later (as in 1406).[1] After this time, however, it became usual for the Speaker to demand no more than the privileges of his predecessors in office *plus* the right of appeal to the Commons for correction; and the only plea to be excused by the King, if his declarations displeased him, advanced by any other later Speaker was that made by John Say in February 1449.[2]

Regarding the Speaker's care to disclaim any desire on his own or the Commons' part to give offence to the Lords, there is evidence to suggest that, although it is recorded as part of his formal protestation on only two occasions (in 1378 and 1380), on at least those occasions this apology to the Lords was every bit as seriously intended as the apology that was then (and later) made to the King. To be properly appreciated, the apology to the Lords should be seen against the background of those political circumstances which also prompted the re-affirmation and expansion, in 1378, of the terms of the Statute of 1275 touching the crime of *scandalum magnatum*.[3] In the Good Parliament two peers (William Lord Latimer, acting-Chamberlain to Edward III, and John Lord Neville, Steward of the Household) had been successfully impeached by the Commons of certain offences which implied grave misgovernment of affairs of State and mis-behaviour about the person of the King. The Duke of Lancaster had not been directly implicated, but that his own conduct in the closing stages of his father's reign had given rise to suspicion in certain quarters is apparent from a significant incident at the beginning of Richard II's first parliament in 1377. Then, following a request by the Commons to the Lords for a delegation to intercommune with them, of which delegation Lancaster was to be one, he protested that the Commons had defamed him and that *l'en avoit parlez si malveise-ment de sa persone chose qe droitement serroit entenduz apperte Traison si ce fust voir, qe Dieu defende*. He refused to do anything further until these slanders were investigated and, when both Lords and Commons tried to mollify his feelings, went on to say that any *trouvour de tielles paroles par quelles l'en moeveroit legerement debat parentre les Seigneurs du Roialme si fust appert et verroi Traitour*, and to demand an ordinance providing for the future punishment of such *parlours et trovours de me[n]songes*.[4]

[1] *Rot. Parl.*, iii. 424b (1399); 455a (1401); 486a (1402); 523a (January 1404); 546a (October 1404); 573b, 577a (1406); 609a (1407); 622b (1410); 648a (1411); iv. 4a (1413).

[2] Ibid., v. 141b.

[3] Statute of Westminster I (1275), c. 34; Stat. 2 Richard II, c. 5. Cf. T. F. T. Plucknett, *A Concise History of the Common Law*, pp. 429 et seq.

[4] *Rot. Parl.*, iii. 5.

In 1377 nothing seemingly was done, but in the next parliament (at Gloucester a year later) the Chancellor drew attention to the fact that in different parts of the kingdom there were ill-disposed persons, worthy of the name of *bachyters*, who *moelt communement s'afforcent a dire et controver et conter fauxes, horribles, et perilouses mensonges des Seigneurs et autres, grantz Officers et bones gentz del Roialme, et les font privement notefier et semer entre les Communes et autres et ne les poent ne ne* [sic] *veullent avouer en appert*.[1] The Statute of 1275, whose purpose was to make words (which would not otherwise be defamatory) actionable if derogatory to magnates, was confirmed in this Gloucester parliament. There are, however, some interesting and significant differences between the old and the new Statute. The former referred to the danger of discord *entre le Rey e son pople ou aukuns homes de son reaume*; the latter drew attention to the risk of debate and discord *parentre les . . . seigneurs ou parentre les seigneurs et Communes*, and added to the magnates protected by the provisions of the act the Chancellor, the Treasurer, the Keeper of the Privy Seal, the Steward of the Household, the Justices of both Benches, and other (unspecified) great officials of the Crown. That this extension was seriously intended—perhaps as a deterrent to impeachments—was soon demonstrated by the use to which the reformed Statute was put when the Chancellor (Sir Michael de la Pole) was unsuccessfully impeached, by a London fishmonger in the Salisbury parliament of 1384, of accepting bribes in the conduct of his office. (The fishmonger was adjudged to pay 1,000 marks damages for defamation.) Certainly the problem which the framers of the new Statute had in mind in 1378 was still a very real one ten years later, for in 1388 the Statute was again re-enacted so as to allow the punishment of offenders to lie within the Council's jurisdiction.[2] The inclusion of an apology to the Lords in a few of the earliest protestations of the Speaker may be regarded as at least related to the re-enactment and amplification of the Statute of *Scandalum Magnatum*.

From the fact that the Speaker's apology to the Lords soon ceased to be made, it might be inferred that the Commons' behaviour became so unobjectionable to the peers as to make such an apology unnecessary. Admittedly, there were times when the political attitude of the Lower House admirably suited the magnates, as in 1386, when they combined to bring down Richard II's Chancellor, De la Pole, in 1388 when they united to destroy Richard II's first 'tyranny', and in the later 1390's when both Lords and Commons were at one if

[1] Ibid., iii 33b.   [2] Stat. 12 Richard II, c. 11; *Rot. Parl.*, iii. 168–70.

only in being equally supine under the threat of the King's absolutist
tendencies. But this agreement or absence of friction in the second
half of Richard II's reign was by no means always maintained under
his successor. In Henry IV's reign there were several uncomfortable
incidents in the relations between the two Houses which suggest that
they were far from having maintained any earlier cordiality. Indeed,
the Lords were at times as irritated as the King himself was by the
forwardness of the Commons, and not without reason. In the first of
the two parliaments of 1404, after drawing attention to the need for
repairs in the royal castles and manors, where what should have been
the King's profits were granted away, and also noticing the great cost
of the royal Household, the Commons requested the King to charge
the Lords to give their advice *sanz dissimulation ou aucune adulation*
and, when this was done, themselves requested the Lords to act
diligently and loyally without being over-nice towards one another
(*sanz curtosie faire entre eux en ascune manere*), affirming their own intention to do the same.[1] Here are signs of disharmony, or at least of
distrust. This lack of sympathy was still present in 1406, witness the
evidence of the St Albans *Greater Chronicle*;[2] and it culminated in the
ensuing parliament at Gloucester in 1407 in the first proper collision
between the two Houses on a straight constitutional issue of first-
rate importance (the question of initiating money bills), when what
the roll of the parliament refers to as *altercation moeve entre les Seigneurs
et les Communes* was serious enough to require a written *cedule de
Indemnitee* for the protection of both parties.[3] All this implies that, in
Henry IV's reign at least, the Commons were capable of 'going it
alone' as opponents or critics of the government, whether or not this
suited the Lords and whether or not it involved the two Houses in
discourteous or acrimonious exchanges. And much later still, in
1425, there was *moche altercacyon bytwyne the lordys and the comyns* (so a
London chronicle tells us) over the conditions attached to the Commons' grant of tunnage and poundage.[4] Admittedly, the word
'altercation' need signify no more than the colourless word 'debate',
but, on the occasions referred to, the issues were seen to be so
important that 'contentious dispute' seems a more likely meaning.

---

[1] *Rot. Parl.*, iii. 524a.

[2] *The St Albans Chronicle, 1406–1420* (from Bodley MS. 462), ed. V. H.
Galbraith, pp. 2–3.

[3] *Rot. Parl.*, iii. 611a.

[4] Camden Society, *The Historical Collections of a Citizen of London*, ed. James
Gairdner (1876), p. 157.

One further observation of a general kind may perhaps be made on this topic of the apology to the King (and, if more rarely, to the Lords as well) that was sometimes made beforehand by the Commons in their Speaker's protestation. An apology is usually made for some act already committed and because it is advisable to offer it, whether or not the act in question was voluntary. To make an apology in advance for some act is, however, to admit *ipso facto* that the act is conceivable, that it is already known that it will give offence, and, therefore, that if the act is committed the offence which it occasions will be aggravated: such an apology may even go some way to create a presumption or expectation that some offensive act will occur. Did the Commons, when they offered such an apology in advance, regard it as unlikely or likely to be needed? If the latter, which seems the more probable, the apology suggests that the Commons were not so timid or abject that offensive conduct on their part could be regarded as unlikely, and that the Commons needed to be circumspect only because they knew that they were very liable to offend.

In connexion with this matter of the Speaker's inclusion in his protestation of an apology to the King and Lords, it has been noticed that the request to be excused from blame for utterances which were regarded as derogatory to their dignity and estate was sometimes made expressly on behalf of all the Commons. This was so in 1378. It was so again in 1398, when Sir John Bussy's apology was made explicitly *pur luy et ses compaignons* and covered what should be said by them.[1] In 1411, too, Thomas Chaucer, when making the same disclaimer of any intention to displease the King, asked him to excuse the Commons as well as himself.[2] In these instances the request for the Commons to be excused was obviously no more than a request that they as well as their Speaker should be exonerated if he, when acting on their behalf, overstepped the limits of discretion. Privilege of speech in the Lower House itself was hardly in question. And yet reference could sometimes be made by the Speaker at his presentation to the Commons' possession of parliamentary liberties of their own. Both in 1399 and 1401, after making his own protestation, the Speaker asked that the Commons might have *lour libertee en Parlement* as before.[3] Such a reference to the Commons' enjoyment of any liberty in parliament is, however, very rare. In fact, it is not until the last parliament to be summoned in Henry VI's name in 1460 that any further allusion is made in the Speaker's requests at his acceptance to the Commons' own liberties. On this occasion the Speaker

[1] *Rot. Parl.*, iii. 357a. [2] Ibid., 648. [3] Ibid., 424b, 455a.

asked that the Commons might freely use *omnes libertates et liberae consuetudines* enjoyed by them in the time of the King's progenitors; and seven years later, in 1467, Sir John Say asked that both he and his fellows might have *talia et tanta Privilegia et Libertates* as any past Speaker or the Commons had customarily enjoyed.[1] What precisely were these liberties, free customs, and privileges allowed to the Commons on these few occasions when they are mentioned, is not defined. It is most likely that the liberties in question included immunity for individual members of the Commons from being arrested or detained if they were impleaded of any personal action while coming to, attending, or returning from parliament, special security against assault or molestation to protect them and their servants at such a time, and perhaps also exemption from being appointed to collect whatever parliamentary taxes they should grant.[2] Must freedom of speech be excluded?

In his conviction that the Commons in the medieval period enjoyed the privilege of freedom of speech, Henry Elsynge, Clerk of the House of Commons between 1632 and 1648, was confirmed by his reading of the case of Thomas Haxey in 1397.[3] In this next to the last of Richard II's parliaments Haxey promoted a bill in the Commons complaining *inter alia* of excessive expenditure in the royal Household, a bill to which (as offensive to his own regality, majesty, and liberty) the King took such violent exception that he caused the Lords to declare its promotion an act of treason; in Henry IV's first parliament an annulment of the judgement against Haxey was requested by the Commons, *si bien en accomplissement de Droit come pur salvation des Libertees de lez ditz Communes* and also on the ground that it was *encontre droit et la course quel avoit este use devant en Parlement, en anientisment des Custumes de lez Communes*.[4] It is important to observe how the Commons' liberties are here equated with their customs.

[1] *Rot. Parl.*, v. 374a, 572a.
[2] In 1478, when the Commons petitioned on behalf of one of their members for respite of a writ of execution in a personal action until after the parliament, they actually pointed out that what they were requesting was one of those liberties and franchises confirmed to them by royal authority at the beginning of this parliament (*Rot. Parl.*, vi. 191b). In 1407, however, the Commons' right to give a proper consent to taxation was referred to as a liberty of theirs, and the initiation of a financial grant in the Lords in that year was regarded by the Commons as such a breach of this liberty that it was agreed that this incident should not prejudice it (ibid., iii. 611b).
[3] Henry Elsynge, *The Ancient Method and Manner of holding Parliaments in England* (London, 1660), pp. 139–42.
[4] *Rot. Parl.*, iii. 434a.

But when it is considered that objection was most likely being made to the irregularity of the Lords' trial of Haxey, to the definition of his offence as a new form of treason outside the limits defined by statute, to the retrospective application of this definition in Haxey's case, and to interference with the normal procedure of petitioning, and when, especially, it is also realized that Haxey, a cleric and civil servant, had not himself been a member of the Commons when he promoted his bill and that, even if he had been, no privilege could be pleaded where treason was involved, it will be evident that the reversal of the judgement against him in 1399 cannot be regarded as even implying (how much less as containing) an official admission that the Commons were entitled to the privilege of free speech amongst themselves.[1] It is true that when in 1455 Thomas Young, a lawyer and later on under Edward IV a royal judge, complained that in 1451 (when he was M.P. for Bristol), *for matiers by him shewed in the Hous accustumed for the Comyns* (namely a proposal to have the Duke of York recognized as Henry VI's heir), he had been imprisoned in the Tower, he supported his petition for compensation with a claim that the Commons, *by the olde liberte and fredom of the Comyns of this Lande* whom they represented, were entitled to have *theire fredom to speke and sey in the Hous of their assemble as to theym is thought convenyent or resonable withoute eny maner chalenge, charge, or punycion therefore to be leyde to theym in eny wyse*.[2] It may be said that, by forwarding Young's petition to the Lords, the Commons implicitly, and by granting compensation, the King's Council effectively, acknowledged the substantial justice of Young's plea for redress. But that is not to say that, in acting as it did, the Council necessarily committed itself to recognizing Young's claim that the Commons enjoyed the privilege of free discussion amongst themselves; and, so far as the record of the case discloses the facts, Young's statement on the subject of privilege passed as a private notion which attracted no comment one way or the other. It is difficult to imagine the Commons themselves at this time actually repudiating such a theory. But the claim was Young's, not theirs. Moreover, as Sir John Neale once remarked, it was 'a claim unique in the Middle Ages'.[3] Perhaps it can be said that it showed the set of the current of opinion. None the less, the privilege

[1] *Tudor Studies presented to A. F. Pollard* (ed. R. W. Seton-Watson), J. E. Neale, 'The Commons' Privilege of Free Speech in Parliament', p. 259.
[2] *Rot. Parl.*, v. 337a.
[3] *Tudor Studies*, op. cit., pp. 264–5; and cf. T. P. Taswell-Langmead, *English Constitutional History*, 10th ed. (1946) by T. F. T. Plucknett, p. 218.

which Young claimed for the Commons was never so formally recognized before the Tudor period as to be recorded.

It was not until Sir Thomas More's election in the parliament of 1523 that a Speaker is known to have added to his protestation a clear request for liberty of speech for the Commons in their own deliberations. The kernel of this particular petition to the King was as follows: [that] *it may therefore like your most aboundant grace, our most benigne and godly kinge, to give to all your comons heare assembled your most gracious licens and pardon, freely, without doubte of your dreadfull displeasure, every man to discharge his consciens, and boldlye, in every thinge incident among* [us], *to declare his advise; and whatsoever happen any man to say,* [that] *it may like your noble maiestye, of your inestimable goodnes, to take all in goode parte, interpreting every mans wordes, howe unconingly soever they be couched, to proceed yeat of good zeale towardes the profit of your realme and honor of your royall person.* . . .[1] Even this demand we know only from a draft of the speech quoted in the biography of More written by his son-in-law, William Roper. And a request of such import did not, in fact, appear in the Speaker's protestation as formally registered in the *Lords' Journals* until 1542. Early in Elizabeth's reign, however, such a request had already become formalized. And by then certainly, freedom of speech in the Lower House itself was recognized as 'an undoubted privilege'. That is not of course to say that the liberty was limitless. As Sir John Neale puts it, 'liberty was not licence, which still remained punishable; and the danger was that while the Crown retained the right to enforce discipline in parliament, it necessarily defined licence'.[2] And this would seem to be a fair statement.

That the Commons had to wait until the Tudor period for a formal concession of the privilege of free speech in their own House, cannot then be gainsaid. But just as there are 'some sinister hints' afforded by sixteenth-century evidence that 'formal tolerance' of bold speech in the Commons now and then degenerated into 'informal coercion' (Neale), so is there some evidence afforded by medieval sources that the Commons were by no means constantly, and evidently sometimes not at all, embarrassed by their lack of possession of any formal

[1] William Roper, *The Lyfe of Sir Thomas More, Knighte*, ed. E. V. Hitchcock (Early English Text Society, Original Series, no. 197), p. 16. It is interesting to note that More's expression, *every man to discharge his consciens* had been anticipated in *The Anonimalle Chronicle*'s account (p. 83) of the Commons' appointment of Sir Peter de la Mare to be their Speaker in the Good Parliament, when they empowered him to announce in the parliament-chamber *coment ils furount avysez de fair et dire en descharge de lour conscience.*

[2] *Tudor Studies*, op. cit., pp. 267-8, 274.

privilege of free speech. It has already been suggested that the apology made beforehand to the King and (sometimes) the Lords in the Speaker's protestation, for anything which he might say to their displeasure, rested on an assumption on the Commons' part that they were liable and perhaps very likely to offend in 'discharging their conscience'. If the Commons were even liable to offend in what their Speaker, choosing his words, said on their behalf in parliament in the King and the Lords' presence, how much more prone must they not have been to lapse into appalling frankness in their own meeting-place out of parliament?

Henry Elsynge, Clerk of the Commons between 1632 and 1648, in his treatise, *The Ancient Method and Manner of holding Parliaments in England*, made a point worth noting: 'The Commons did oftentimes, under Edward III, discuss and debate amongst themselves many things concerning the King's prerogative, and agreed upon petitions for laws to be made directly against his prerogative, as may appear by divers of the said petitions, yet they were never interrupted in their consultations, nor received check for the same, as may appear also by the answers to the said petitions.'[1] Professor Plucknett's comment on this statement is that 'things tolerated by Edward III under political pressure . . . might seem inexpedient to his successors', and it would be readily conceded that in the later phases of Richard II's reign, the King, out of concern for his royal estate and prerogative, so exercised his *regimen parliamenti* as to render the Commons complaisant if not even cowed and subservient. But this rather shabby passage in the history of the medieval Commons was a violent reaction from quite dissimilar conditions in the period of Richard's own minority, when the Commons had been developing a proper political independence. And there was soon to be an almost equally violent counter-reaction under Henry IV, whose political difficulties gave the Commons ample opportunity to re-assert their influence upon affairs of State. It is difficult to imagine their impeachments during the Good Parliament and in 1386 and 1388 emerging from sessions that were orderly and provided models of respectful speech. And in the first half of Richard II's reign the chapter-house or refectory of the abbey of Westminster, when the Commons met there, must frequently have been a place disturbed by *murmur, crye, and noise*.[2] When parliament met at Gloucester in 1378, there would

---

[1] Henry Elsynge, op. cit., pp. 139–40. The passage is cited in T. P. Taswell-Langmead, op. cit., p. 217.

[2] *Rot. Parl.*, iii. 36b.

appear to have been no dearth of free speech in the Lower House: even in the Upper House itself the Commons responded to the Council's suggestion that if they now made a grant of taxation it would not need to be soon repeated, by observing that this was what they had been led to think and hope when making their last large grant (of a double subsidy) in the previous year, a subsidy which they had only made (they *now* said) following a promise just to that effect; after the Steward of the Household (Lord Scrope) had denied all knowledge of any such undertaking and also refused to admit that funds remained in the Treasury (which the Commons asserted), they demanded an audit of accounts; and the audit was conceded on the understanding that it should not be regarded as a right exacted *par coartacion* [coercion] *parmi la dite requeste*![1] Later, even after being told to get on with their proper business and reminded of the large expense to which a prolonged attendance would subject their local communities, the Commons demanded a copy of their last previous financial grant and also asked for a delegation from the Lords for the purpose of intercommuning which itself caused some further agitation in that quarter (although, admittedly, for quite specific procedural reasons). *The Anonimalle Chronicle* tells us besides that there was more trouble among the Commons in this session over the question of the recent sacrilege and breach of sanctuary in Westminster Abbey, especially after the King's Council sent down Dr John Wyclif and a doctor of law to put the royal case on ecclesiastical immunities, a proceeding which resulted in these experts being exposed to *plusours malicouns de les communes et circumesteauntz*.[2]

Complaints of royal expenditure, abuses in the Chancery, Exchequer, and the Courts, misgovernment of the Household, and other administrative inadequacies, complaints of the sort to which Richard II was so vehemently to object at the time of Haxey's case in 1397, continued to be made in successive parliaments of the royal minority. In 1380, at Northampton, the Chancellor, when opening the parliament, went so far as to instruct the Commons *qe pur Dieux ils lessessassent toutes foreines matires dont rancour ou brige* [dispute] *purront sourdre, et effectuelment tretassent de ceste lour charge;*[3] but, for all

---

[1] *Rot. Parl.*, iii. 35–6.   [2] *The Anonimalle Chronicle*, op. cit., p. 124.

[3] *Rot. Parl.*, iii. 89b. The word 'foreign' in this quotation means 'external' or 'outside', that is, outside the points of the 'charge'. The Lord Keeper used exactly, in effect, the same adjuration to both Houses in 1566: 'to spare superfluous things and which needeth not' (J. E. Neale, *Elizabeth I and her Parliaments, 1559–1581*, p. 135).

that, they still went on to complain of *pluralitee des guerres* and *coustages importables*,[1] and the government's statement that it needed £160,000 was received by the Commons as so *moelt outrageouse et oultrement importable* that they instantly demanded its reduction.[2] If we had not this sort of evidence, it would still be reasonable to suppose that, when direct royal demands for money grants were met with direct refusals on the Commons' part, there was at least plain speaking in the Lower House. And such refusals are expressly recorded of the parliaments of 1378 and 1381;[3] while in 1381 and 1385 the Commons even suspended indirect taxation for brief periods to demonstrate and underline the reality of the need for their assent. In the meantime, in the autumn and winter parliaments of 1382-3, when there was dispute between the Commons and the Lords over the merits of the *voie de Flandres* (the expedition by Bishop Despenser which the Commons supported) and the *voie d'Espagne* (an expedition by John of Gaunt which the Lords had accepted) it was the Commons' view which prevailed, though obviously only with difficulty.[4] At Salisbury in 1384 the Chancellor (Sir Michael de la Pole), opening parliament, again urged the Commons to consider the related problems of peace and defence, *entrelessantz de tout chescune autre foreine matire en le moien temps: qar par foreins matires . . . ont delaiez les Parlementz devaunt ceste heure moelt oultrageousement.*[5] When, performing the same function later in the same year, the Chancellor ended by noting that the parliament's business would be expedited if *omnis materia melancholie et invidie* were omitted, the Commons were among his audience, and it is likely that he had them in mind as well as his peers.[6] So troublesome were the Commons in 1386, when not only was Suffolk impeached after being dismissed from the Chancellorship but also the King was compelled to accept government by parliamentary commission, that in the next year Richard II asked his sheriffs about the possibility of direct royal interference in elections[7] and was thought to be intending to raise war in order to destroy certain knights of the shire as well as some of the magnates.[8]

Even from the period in which Richard II rode his parliaments on a tight rein, there is some evidence of a sort that the Commons could still occasionally erupt: the evidence from a passage in Passus IV of

[1] Ibid., 93b.   [2] Ibid., 89b.   [3] Ibid., 35b, 104a.
[4] Thomas Walsingham, *Historia Anglicana*, ed. T. H. Riley (R.S.), ii. 84.
[5] *Rot. Parl.*, iii. 167a.   [6] Ibid., 184b.
[7] *Historia Anglicana*, ii. 161; cf. *Rot. Parl.*, iii. 235 (art. XXXVI).
[8] *Rot. Parl.*, iii. 243a.

the poem *Mum and the Sothsegger*. It is true that the satirist, who wrote this poem shortly before Richard II's deposition, was discontented with the Commons' performance in their traditional rôle, which he defined as *to shewe the sores of the royaulme*; but even in his disappointment with the many he makes clear that there were a few among the Commons who were eager to the point of rashness and others who, though in reality good friends to the King, were misrepresented to him by informers as hostile.[1] Such tale-bearers were a recurrent phenomenon, and we may reasonably assume that their insinuations were not without basis, and that these drew attention to discussions in the Commons that had passed the limits of respectfulness or discretion. There is a more substantial reference to such informers in so impeccable a source as the roll of Henry IV's second parliament (of January 1401): on the sixth day of the session the Commons asked the King that, if it happened that one of their number, to please him and do themselves a bit of good (*pur faire plaisance au Roy et pur avauncer soy mesmes*), gave him news of matters that were still only pending, as a result of which he might be angry (*moevez grevousement*) with them or with some individual member, he should not listen to or credit it.[2] Three years later, in the next parliament but one (January 1404), there was a repetition of this request or rather complaint, Sir Arnald Savage adding to his protestation as Speaker a demand from the Commons that, if they complained of his administration, the King would not take umbrage at what they said by reason of any *sinistre information d'aucune persone*.[3] This request was clearly no idle one, for the Commons soon went on to make in this parliament such a virulent attack on the conduct of the royal Household as no parliament had witnessed since 1397, when Richard II had caused even the initiation of such criticism to be defined as treasonable; demands were now made by the Commons for the removal from the Household of aliens and others concerning some of whom Henry IV himself said that he knew no reason why this should be necessary. The Commons' proposal was, however, accepted, and the King gratuitously volunteered to dismiss any who had incurred the resentment of his people. All of this is reported in the parliament-roll itself.[4]

In the same parliament the Lower House is known to have been loud in its objection to the demand for a large subsidy made by

[1] *Mum and the Sothsegger*, ed. M. Day and R. Steele (Early English Text Society, Original Series, no. 199).

[2] *Rot. Parl.*, iii. 456a.   [3] Ibid., 523a.   [4] Ibid., 525a.

Henry and his Council. According to a Canterbury chronicle,[1] the Commons drew attention to the normal revenues of the Crown, the King's possession of the Duchy of Lancaster, his continuance of the increases in taxation on trade made by Richard II, and the profits from royal wardships; and when the King persisted, saying that not in his day should the lands of his ancestors be lost, they suggested that he should meet them half-way by reducing the customs, which the King refused.

Then, in an anonymous newsletter sent from London to Durham in the course of the same session,[2] we are treated to a uniquely circumstantial account of a series of verbal exchanges between the Speaker and King Henry himself in the Upper House, which can only have resulted from very plain speaking in the Lower House. It appears that Sir Arnald Savage countered the royal request for fresh taxes by drawing attention to improvident expenditure; not only did he demand an audit of accounts, but pointed to specific causes for the drain on royal funds. Grants by letters patent of £1,000 a year to various ladies (presumably of the Queen's Breton following) and of £8,000 to an anonymous Lombard were so unjustifiable as to have brought the Commons, so the Speaker said, to the end of their patience. At this point the King himself intervened, and he and the Speaker soon fell to open wrangling: Henry's protest that for him to repeal his letters patent would be shameful and scandalous drew from Sir Arnald Savage a suggestion that the grants should be reduced to a tenth of their original amount, and when the King confessed himself amazed at the Commons' ill-will and discontent, the Speaker recalled that parliament had so far voted him a subsidy of a tenth and fifteenth every year, in addition to which there had been expeditions into Wales and elsewhere that were still unpaid for, not to mention excessive purveyances for the Household (one purveyor alone owing £6,000 and more). These, said Savage, were the facts accounting for the Commons' attitude, and he not only went on to add that the King was ill-served by the malicious advice of some of his Council, but promised particulars. Evidently, Henry was much put out by all this and, the Durham newsletter tells us, kept away from parliament for five or six days. But even when he re-appeared (on 28 January), the Commons resumed their badgering: Savage asked him to order the Lords to state their policy. Archbishop Arundel indignantly (*ove*

---

[1] *Eulogium Historiarum*, ed. F. S. Haydon (R.S.), iii. 399–400.

[2] Constance M. Fraser, 'Some Durham Documents relating to the Hilary Parliament of 1404', *B.I.H.R.*, xxxiv., pp. 197–9.

graunt ire) demanded the Speaker's reasons for his request, only to be told that it would be more honourable for the lords to speak their minds than to be discovered disloyal later on. And so, doing as the Commons wished, the King commanded all the lords to speak out openly, piously observing that this was what parliament was for, and that it was by the lords' election that he had acquired the crown. No sooner satisfied on this point than the Commons raised another awkward matter: the question of the Earl of Northumberland, who in the previous summer had raised forces in the north-east to support the rebellion, led by his son and brother, which was crushed at the battle of Shrewsbury. Speaker Savage asked that the earl should be allowed to explain himself before parliament and, if proved only to have committed a trespass (not treason), should be given a charter of pardon and restored to all his previous estates. When Henry demurred to this, saying that he would need to be advised by his Council, the Commons reacted by threatening to refuse a financial grant, only consenting, when the King proposed an adjournment, to think it over before they returned to parliament. During a brief visit to Windsor the King did in fact pardon Northumberland, and together they came up to London on the day the newsletter was written (4 February), the earl well attended and in good heart. The Commons' proposals had in effect carried the day. Eventually the Lower House did succumb to the government's demand for a subsidy, but their grant was a novel levy on landed income, and they made it only after much disputation, at the end of a long and therefore expensive session (20 March), and on condition of the appointment of special treasurers for the tax.

The Coventry parliament in the autumn of the same year was similarly a stormy session, resulting in a bitter quarrel between the knights of the shire and some of the prelates and temporal lords, led by Archbishop Arundel, who keenly resisted the knights when they pressed for a temporary confiscation of the temporalities of the Church in addition to a general resumption of royal grants.

In 1406 there was again a reference made by the Speaker (and recorded in the parliament-roll) not to the possibility of tale-bearing (as in 1404), but to the fact that the King had already heard spiteful stories (*sinistre report*) of disloyal speech among the Commons, for which his heart was heavy towards them.[1] In this same parliament of 1406, so the St Albans historian, Thomas Walsingham, informs us, the parliamentary knights' resistance to taxation, together with

[1] *Rot. Parl.*, iii. 569b.

the Lords' resistance to the conditions upon which the Commons finally agreed to make a grant, eventually provoked the King to an open show of really violent ill-temper (*et rex furibundus irascitur contra omnes*) and into threatening to resort to force in order to get his way.[1] Five years later, the roll of the parliament of 1411 records (in its notes of the last day's session) the presentation of a petition calling attention to the great general disquiet (*grand murmur en vostre poeple*) at the King's reported heaviness towards some of those who had attended this and the previous parliament, and asking him to recognize the loyalty of the estates.[2] These various references combine to suggest that, if at times the Commons felt embarrassment, it was not embarrassment at being *prevented* from declaring their mind by any lack of a formal privilege of freedom of speech.

For the rest of the fifteenth century it seems difficult at first to question the Commons' general subordination to the government of the day and their occasional subservience to particular aristocratic, or even royalist, interests and parties. But this may be only on the face of things. As the century progresses, the parliament-rolls become very much less revealing of details of the Commons' activities than they are for the last quarter of the fourteenth century and the first decade or so of the fifteenth. The decline, or rather suspension, of the writing of full-scale annals of the type which the monastic *scriptorium* at St Albans was still able to produce in Henry V's reign, means, too, that there is little that can be used to eke out the slender information of the official records of parliamentary proceedings. Nevertheless, from time to time there are indications that the Commons were still able to take an independent and critical line of their own which sometimes put them into serious disfavour with the royal administration, a circumstance which suggests that they continued to enjoy a large measure of freedom of discussion in practice. In the sessions of 1439–40 there were difficulties between the Commons and the government over its mercantile policies, especially with regard to the 'hosting' of alien merchants; and the Commons won the day in spite of an adjournment to Reading and in the face of strong resistance from the Court.[3] Again, in the parliament whose three sessions (the first two at Westminster, the third at Leicester) lasted (with roughly a month's break between them) from 6 November

---

[1] *The St Albans Chronicle, 1406–1420*, ed. V. H. Galbraith, pp. 2–3.
[2] *Rot. Parl.*, iii. 658b.
[3] *The Cambridge Medieval History*, vol. viii., K. B. McFarlane, 'England: The Lancastrian Kings', p. 401; *Chronicles of London*, ed. C. L. Kingsford, p. 153.

1449 to about the end of the first week in June 1450, this hostility between Commons and Court was repeated with even greater passion. The Commons, perhaps encouraged on the quiet by Lord Cromwell, not only contrived the impeachment of the King's chief adviser, the Duke of Suffolk: when the King demanded a subsidy for the defence of Normandy, they withstood, so (in his *Dictionarium Theologicum*) says Dr Thomas Gascoigne, sometime Chancellor of the University of Oxford, *plures minas et a rege et a suis juvenibus consiliariis*; they refused to be intimidated by the rumoured prospect of parliament's indefinite continuance (with all its entailed expense), and in the end voted not a normal subsidy but a graduated income-tax, and even then only in return for an unwelcome Act of Resumption. Moreover, probably as a result of their protests against the cession of Maine and Anjou or, maybe, against the conduct of the war itself, the Commons (according to the same authority) drew from the King the demand, *quod communitas Anglie non intromitteret se de factis regis et dominorum.*[1] Obviously this was a parliament when there was commotion and bitterness among the Commons. And so, evidently, was the next, in 1450–51, out of which came the case of Thomas Young. All that need now be said about this matter is that Young certainly acted in 1451 as though he himself believed in that claim for customary freedom of speech which he was to advance in 1455.[2]

Taking this evidence as a whole, however varying in reliability the sources, and however wide the chronological gaps, it may be suggested that, although there is no clear categorical indication that the Commons in the pre-Tudor period enjoyed free speech *de jure*, certainly there were times when they seem to have practised it *de facto*. Indeed, with especial regard to what is reported of Henry IV's parliaments (of which our records are less incomplete than usual), it may be asked, what more could the Commons have done, had they enjoyed a formal privilege of free speech, than they were able to do, as it seems, without it? Before government measures in the form of official bills superseded the petitions of the Commons as the normal basis of legislation in the late fifteenth and early sixteenth centuries,

---

[1] William Worcester says, *In eodem Parliamento, domino de Cromwell secrete laborante, dux Suffolchiae per communes in Parliamento de alta et grandi prodicione appellatus est* (*Liber Niger Scaccarii necnon Wilhelmi Worcestrii Annales Rerum Anglicarum*, ed. Thomas Hearne, (London, 1771) vol. ii., pp. 467–8); Thomas Gascoigne, *Loci e Libro Veritatum*, ed. J. E. T. Rogers, pp. 189–90.

[2] See above, p. 41.

when, in consequence, the offence of displeasing the King 'must have undergone a sinister extension' (Neale),[1] it seems likely that the Commons enjoyed freedom of speech in practice and as of custom, although not as of right. (And yet, what medievalist would ever be happy in making any strict division between custom and right?) What also contributed to the demand for the formal privilege of free speech, made by Sir Thomas More in 1523, may well have been not any new-found sense of corporateness in the Commons or promise of a fresh career, but a realization of the fragility of custom and long-user in face of the ruthless temper informing this new monarchy of Henry VIII's in its attitude to political opposition. More's request, whatever it may now be regarded as eventually leading to, may perhaps be seen to have been, at the time it was made, something of a rearguard action on the Commons' part.

Some of the earliest protestations of the Commons' Speaker were designed to protect him and his fellow-members from suffering any effect of disapproval on the part of those superior estates which met in the Upper House of parliament. A more important and long-lasting feature than the inclusion of any apology to the King and/or the Lords was, however, that part of the protestation which gave the Commons a right to correct the Speaker if he said more or less than instructed. This requirement was clearly regarded by the Commons themselves as *the* vital part of the protestation. It established the point that their Speaker, elected by them from their own number, was not entitled to speak except as they allowed him, that he was responsible to them, and that, in fact, he was strictly their own agent. It cannot be categorically stated that the medieval Speaker invariably did as he was told by his colleagues and no more. Such discoverable evidence as bears on this question suggests, however, that the Commons habitually allowed him little latitude (which is not to imply that he desired more). The Speaker in the parliament of January 1404, Sir Arnald Savage, referred in the parliament-chamber to reports reaching the King to the effect that on an earlier visit he had presumed, on his own authority and without the assent of the Commons, to petition for the *entire* abolition of liveries. These reports he now went on to deny. He explained that he had requested no more than the enforcement of the recent statute against liveries (the terms of which allowed liveries to be given by the King and the Prince of Wales). He then asked those of the Commons who were present

[1] *Tudor Studies*, op. cit., p. 273.

(presumably a deputation) whether or not they assented, and, when they agreed, again demanded the execution of the statute, on the understanding that, if any clarification, abridgement or enlargement of this or any other statute were needed, the Commons should be informed and should discuss it before they communicated their intention or assent, as was customary.[1] Whether or not Savage had actually overstepped the mark by acting without the Commons' approval is beside the point: the incident clearly shows that he was not entitled to do so, and knew it.

There is only one other relevant piece of evidence that I know of. It is of greater significance, however, than the last. Four days after being presented as Speaker in Henry V's first parliament (which met on 15 May 1413), William Stourton pointed out that, under Henry IV, the Commons had petitioned for good governance and been favourably answered, but to what effect the present King knew well (*en ad bone conisance*); and so now he repeated the request, drawing special attention to the needs of the Scottish border, Wales, Ireland, Calais, and Guienne, and to disturbances at Cirencester and in other localities. The official answer was no more than an order to the Speaker to consult with his colleagues and put these complaints into writing, which apparently there and then he agreed to do. But how touchy were the Commons regarding their right to correct, and so snaffle their Speaker, is made evident by what followed. Three days later (25 May) a deputation from the Lower House, headed not by the Speaker but by another knight of the shire, John Doreward (who had been Speaker in Henry IV's first parliament), explained to the King and Lords that, in undertaking to put the Commons' complaints into writing, the Speaker had acted without their approval. Doreward went on to ask that to save time the Commons might submit no more than a schedule giving the headings of the articles in question (*briefment appoyntez*). The King, to show them his good lordship and goodwill, recognized their objection to the Speaker's promise and excused them; whereupon Doreward requested the acceptance and enactment of Stourton's protestation, which also was allowed. The Commons here had successfully insisted on their right to control the Speaker's acts in parliament, that right being embodied in his own protestation. It is probable that, when, nine days later still (on 3 June), the Commons presented Doreward himself as Speaker, it was not altogether because Stourton was ill in bed and unable to act, as was alleged, but because his unsatisfactory conduct still

[1] *Rot. Parl.*, iii. 523b.

rankled and also because the Commons wished to turn the incident to political account.[1]

Beginning as a safeguard for the Speaker himself, his right to be corrected by the Commons could evidently be used, as this incident of 1413 shows, to control him. It is possible that the Commons also saw in this right of correction a means of acquiring certain additional procedural advantages of a different sort. Might they not already have begun to regard this right to correct or amend what the Speaker had said in their name as affording them opportunity, within the limits of a single parliament, to go back on, or revise in detail, conclusions which they themselves indeed had reached? Some such intention may just conceivably be read into one or two of the earliest Speaker's protestations (as we have them). In the protestation which De la Mare made in 1377 he asked that, if ever he happened to say more than the Commons had agreed, they should correct him there and then (*devant qil*[s] *y partissent de la place*).[2] But his successor in 1378 (Pickering) asked for correction either then or later and as the Commons liked (*ore devant lour departir, ou en apres quant lour pleust*),[3] and in January 1380 Gildsburgh as Speaker requested that any necessary amendment of his speeches should be made at whatever time it suited the Commons (*a quelle heure qe leur pleust*).[4] There were doubtless occasions when the Commons wished to 'think again', regretted petitions they had already preferred, or woke up to the fact that petitions which were undesirable had got through to the King (perhaps because there was no adequate procedure for checking them) and wanted to disavow them: for example, when the parliament of 1410 had been in session only eleven days they asked to have one of their petitions, a petition regarding the recent statute relating to the Lollards, returned to them; this was allowed, but only, however, on the understanding that it was exceptional, granted of the King's special grace, and not to be regarded as constituting a precedent.[5]

Henry IV had not always seen fit to be so severe as this: the long parliament of 1406 had been sitting some three weeks when the Speaker, Sir John Tiptoft, came into parliament to ask for the customary privileges of his office and to request that if he said more

---

[1] Ibid., iv. 4–5. This incident has some procedural interest: it suggests that the Commons preferred oral to written communications, a fact which has a direct relevance to the rise of the office of Speaker.

[2] Ibid., iii. 5b. My interpretation of the words quoted seems preferable to such an alternative as 'before they depart from the parliament then sitting'.

[3] Ibid., 34b.   [4] Ibid., 73a.   [5] Ibid., 623b.

than was agreed by the Commons he should be allowed to correct and reform it *par bone deliberation de ses . . . compaignons*, adding, however, on behalf of the Commons the further demand that if they preferred anything in writing they might have it back whenever they wished in order to amend it, even in substance if necessary: *qe si riens serroit deliverez par eux en escript, q'ils purront re-avoir mesme l'escript, a quel heure qe lour plerroit durant le dit Parlement, a l'entent qe la matire comprise en ycel escript purroit par eux estre refourmez et amendez s'il embosoigneroit.* These requests the King allowed, saying that he wished Tiptoft to have as comprehensive a protestation as previous Speakers had enjoyed.[1] As it happened, the King himself was able to profit by his own concession later in the parliament. On 7 June 1406, during the second session, the Speaker appealed to his protestation and then submitted a petition from the Commons asking that a statute of 1404, 'recognizing' the succession to the Crown as vested in Henry IV's sons and their issue, should be altered to restrict it to the heirs-male of his body. On the last day of the third and final session of the parliament (22 December 1406), following another petition, the arrangement of June was cancelled and the Crown settled on the King and the heirs of his body as before. Although this new petition was proposed in the name of the Lords and Commons together and presented not by the Speaker but by Archbishop Arundel, the Speaker's original protestation was invoked permitting the amendment: *et considerantz qe, par force de la Protestation fait par la dit Commune en cest present Parlement devaunt le . . . dit vij jour [de Juyn], par vous, soveraigne Seigneur, grante et ottroie, le suisdit Act fait sur la continue de le vaunt dit Supplication par le dit Commune en cest present Parlement baille, purra estre changiez, amendez, et en meillour fourme redigez.*[2] The amendment was, of course, as these words make clear, one not simply of a Commons' bill that was pending, but of a Commons' bill that had actually passed. But Tiptoft's earlier demand in this parliament that the government should allow the Commons to retract written petitions for their own further scrutiny and amendment was not only unusual, but obviously a demand for something which was not regarded as implicitly conceded in the Speaker's usual protestation as it stood. The concession of 1406 cannot be paralleled, and how exceptional it was is further illustrated by the incident of 1410 touching the petition about Lollards. The Commons' control of their own written bills, once these had left the House, was normally severely limited.

[1] *Rot. Parl.*, iii., 568b.   [2] Ibid., 577a, 581a.

The petitions of the Commons were as a rule submitted in this form of written bills. It was, however, possible for their petitions to be made in the form of oral requests. But the government obviously preferred an approach taking the form of a written bill. And there are times when this official attitude was actually expressed in the record. On the last day of the first session of the parliament which met after the Peasants' Revolt (13 December 1381), when the Commons asked to see the form of the proposed royal general pardon, they were told not only that such a pardon depended on their voting a subsidy, but also that their petition would not be allowed unless they put it into writing, and that this was reasonable if only because the King was wont to give his answers in writing and not by word of mouth.[1] Again, on one occasion early in Henry IV's second parliament (of January 1401), when the Commons made several requests *par bouche*, they were told to put them, along with others preferred at the same time, among their *communes petitions*, to which the King would reply by the Lords' advice.[2] There was, of course, good reason, and sometimes it was accidentally supplied by the Commons themselves, why the government should be so reluctant to entertain verbal requests: we need only revert to the incident in January 1404, when Speaker Savage drew attention to his verbal request on the subject of the Statute of Liveries and explained that he had been completely misunderstood.[3] If such mistakes and ambiguities were to be avoided, it is no wonder that the King now and then set his face against the entertainment of oral petitions. Requests made by the Speaker *par bouche*, however, continued to be made side by side with those preferred in writing,[4] and in Henry V's first parliament (in 1413), as we have seen,[5] the Commons objected, and successfully, to their Speaker's undertaking at the King's behest to have their verbal requests put into writing, unless they themselves consented. The reason stated in 1413 was that the drawing up of 'especial' complaints in writing would delay the work of parliament, and the Commons agreed to supply written 'headings' of their complaints and did in fact do so. But one reason why the Commons sometimes preferred to petition by word of mouth instead of by written bill may well have been that the former procedure might in

[1] Ibid., 104b.   [2] Ibid., 456b.
[3] See above, pp. 51-2.
[4] E.g. on the last day of each of the three sessions of the parliament of 1406 (*Rot. Parl.*, iii. 569, 577-8, 583 et seq.).
[5] See above, p. 52.

E

a sense commit them less definitely to the detailed content of a request than did a written bill. Once a request had gone forward, it was difficult for the Commons to recover it, whether in order to annul it (as in the case of the bill about the Lollard Statute in 1410), or whether to alter it by amendments of their own. Inevitably, it was even more difficult for the Commons to control the passage of a bill to the further extent of checking any amendments made by the Lords and/or the Crown. That the Commons were sometimes concerned about these difficulties, especially regarding the problem of their consent to external amendments to their bills, is quite clear from the well-known petition which they presented in Henry V's second parliament. In relation to this problem it is important to bear in mind the connexion, illustrated in the bill itself, between the written bill, the oral request, and the right of amendment as contained in the Speaker's protestation.

In the parliament which met at Leicester in April 1414, the Commons made an important demand regarding their petitions, or rather (choosing a narrower front) regarding those petitions which, if agreed by the Lords and accepted by the King, were then turned into statutes. In a petition, significantly couched in English (the first extant bill from the Lower House written in the vernacular), the Commons asserted that, since the *Commune of youre lond*, whose representatives they were, was *a membre of youre Parlement* and therefore *as well Assentirs as Peticioners*, it was their *liberte and fredom* that no statute or law should be made without their assent; they then requested that in future no complaint of theirs calling for remedy, whether made *by mouthe of their Speker for the Commune* or by written petition, should result in an enacted statute which either by *addicions* or *diminucions* changed *the sentence and the entente axked by the Speker mouthe or the petitions . . . yeven up yn writyng*, unless they assented; finally they disclaimed any intention of impugning the royal prerogative right to refuse or grant any petition made *by spekyng* or *by writyng*. The King, in his reply, allowed that they should not be bound without their assent to any enactments, based on their petitions, which were *contrarie of hir askyng*.[1]

H. L. Gray has shown that the legislation passed in the previous parliament of 1413 warranted the criticism implied in the request of 1414, but that the legislation of Henry IV's reign (and of an even earlier time) did not; and from this he inferred that the request had resulted from the Commons' irritation at a very recent

[1] *Rot. Parl.*, iv. 22b.

departure from normal practice.[1] Even more significantly, it has been asserted (by S. B. Chrimes) that Henry V's answer [provided we construe the word *contrarie* as meaning 'opposite to' and not 'different from'] left the Commons' claim unconfirmed or even quite rejected.[2] What has perhaps not been sufficiently noted is the distinction in terms, drawn by the Commons in this petition of 1414, between oral and written petitions. The Commons did not otherwise discriminate on this occasion between these two petitioning procedures. But it seems probable that behind the terminological distinction there lay a procedural difference of some importance.

In the nature of things, the content of an oral request was not likely to be so definitively expressed as that of a written bill. It might need clarification by the Commons themselves. And in the process of clarifying, the Commons were likely to be given opportunity to make alteration. Indeed, regarding a verbal request made by their Speaker, the Commons were entitled to make emendations under the terms of his protestation. It was, then, perhaps in order to make possible or facilitate emendations of their own that the Commons sometimes preferred petitioning by oral request. But just because the oral request was at least potentially less conclusive than the written bill, the government frequently refused to entertain this type of petition and, if ever it allowed its use, did so only with reluctance. Therefore, while the Commons' control over their verbal petitions was more real than over their written petitions, the value of this control was limited as long as this method of approach to the government was itself precarious. It would seem, then, that in 1414 the Commons wished to establish their right to assent to external amendments to their petitions (the amendments made by the Lords and the King), whether their petitions were either written or oral. But since this was only possible if oral petitions were unquestioningly accepted by the government, it would also appear that, under cover of the major requirement (acknowledgment of their right to assent to all amendments), the Commons were seeking governmental recognition of a claim to make requests by whatever procedure they themselves thought appropriate, either verbal request or written bill. In other words, they wanted recognition of an equal validity as between the one type of petition and the other. In view of the long

[1] H. L. Gray, *The Influence of the Commons on Early Legislation* (Harvard Historical Studies, xxxiv.), pp. 261 et seq.

[2] S. B. Chrimes, *English Constitutional Ideas in the Fifteenth Century*, pp. 159–64. The *caveat* within the square brackets is mine, not Professor Chrimes'.

governmental discouragement given to the verbal petition, this was a demand of some considerable (even if, on this occasion, subsidiary) importance. Henry V's answer to the Commons' claims in 1414, however, ignored the Commons' distinction between verbal and written petitions, and so gave nothing away on the lesser claim, which was certainly lost along with, as it appears, the greater one.

CHAPTER 3

The Speaker's Election

AS early as 1384, as we have seen,[1] the Commons were actually being instructed by the Chancellor to elect their Speaker promptly at the beginning of parliament, so that its business should not be unnecessarily retarded and its duration prolonged. It is this official order, coupled with the Speaker's formal acceptance by the King, which allows us to say that his function was soon exalted into the office of Speaker. The government was obviously not long in coming to regard the Speaker's office as important to the conduct of parliament's business. It may also have discovered in this early period that the Speaker could perform on its behalf useful services in the Lower House itself as a political leader and possibly even as a manager of some of the business of the House. (The part played by Sir John Bussy in the impeachments of 1397 is especially worth recalling here.) If the Speaker's duties were a matter of concern to the government, then it would naturally take an interest in his election and perhaps even impose its own candidate for the office. The fact that the government did either of these things could be regarded as a sort of tribute to the growing importance of the Commons in the structure and working of parliament. But it could also, of course, be regarded as a threat to undermine their independence. The question how far the medieval Commons were able to elect their Speaker freely, or whether he was foisted on them from above, is an important problem, which must be faced by anyone who wishes to examine the larger issue of their political independence.

That, in the sixteenth century, the Speaker was generally a governmental nominee, and his election therefore no more than a formality, seems fairly settled. The remark with which Cardinal Wolsey ended his complaint against Sir Thomas More's conduct as Speaker in 1523, *'Would to God you had been at Rome, Master More, when I made you Speaker'*, whatever else it suggests, quite clearly implies that More's election had been arranged by the Lord Chancellor.[2] From Elizabeth I's reign there is no safe example of a contested election to the

---

[1] See above, p. 13.

[2] *The Life of Sir Thomas More, by William Roper*, ed. H. V. Hitchcock (1935), p. 19.

Chair. One Elizabethan Speaker's election, however, provided the occasion for a division: in 1566, after the death of the existing Speaker during a recess, the nomination of the official candidate (Richard Onslow, the Solicitor-General) was challenged, and he was elected only by a quite narrow majority. Otherwise, the Elizabethan Commons normally chose a Speaker already decided upon by the government, following his nomination by the senior Privy Councillor present in the House, cries or murmurs of approval being all that usually marked the moment of election. In fact, what Sir John Neale suggests is that the election was no more than a brief act of pantomime, followed by polite applause of varying volume. When parliament met in February 1589, the official choice of Serjeant Thomas Snagge as Commons' Speaker had been cut-and-dried for nearly half a year, a postponement of the opening of the session having made no difference to the Queen's original decision.[1] As late as 1571, in John Hooker's *Order and Usage howe to keepe a Parliament*, service could still be paid to the principle of freedom from royal intervention in elections of members of parliament and Speaker alike: *that the King* [sic] *ought not to make any choise or cause anie choise to be made of any knight, cittizens, burgesses . . .* [or] *speaker of the common house . . .; but they must be elected and chosen by the laws, orders, and customs of the realm, as they were wont and ought to be.* The next clause, however, gives the game away, or at least suggests that much of this was mere lip-service: *and the Kinges good advise yet not to be contemned.*[2] And in his *Institutes* (1628), Sir Edward Coke (formerly, in 1593, himself a Speaker) could declare quite simply regarding the Speaker's election that *the use is* (*as in the congier de eslier of a bishop*) *that the King doth name a discreet and learned man whom the Commons elect.*[3] And apparently in some such wise it was until 1679, the last instance in which the King took steps to impose his own nominee upon the Lower House.[4]

But what of pre-Tudor times? Was the Speaker's election then also a 'put-up' job? Pollard seems to have thought it was. Commenting on the circumstances of De la Mare's election in 1376, he acknowledged that in this case, at least, there was no 'concealed nomination' by the Crown. He was, however, of the opinion that afterwards this

[1] J. E. Neale, *The Elizabethan House of Commons* (1949), pp. 354, 356; *Elizabeth I and her Parliaments, 1559–1581* (1953), p. 134; *Elizabeth I and her Parliaments, 1584–1601* (1957), p. 201.

[2] B.M., Harleian MS. no. 1178, fo. 23v.

[3] Sir Edward Coke, *Institutes of the Laws of England*, Fourth Part (London, 1797), vol. vii, p. 8 (cited by Neale, *The Elizabethan House of Commons*, p. 355).

[4] A. E. Dasent, *The Speakers of the House of Commons*, p. 226.

became 'the almost invariable method of determining the Speaker's election', and he suggested that even as early as 1397 the Speaker 'became—and remains—a government nominee elected by the Commons'. There may be some ground for Pollard's assurance that Richard II imposed Sir John Bussy upon the Commons as their Speaker in September 1397, in the statement made by Thomas Walsingham, the St Albans chronicler, that on account of Bussy's worldly prudence, guile and eloquence, *Rex constituit eum Prolocutorem praesentis Parliamenti*.[1] It must none the less be stated that it is impossible to settle this question with so much confidence for the medieval period as a whole. Only the most tentative of opinions can be put forward. For we know next to nothing of the procedure of the Speaker's election during that time.

Contemporary chronicles rarely even allude to the Speaker, much less do they notice his election or describe the manner of it. The St Albans chronicler does, indeed, briefly mention the election of the Speaker in the Bad Parliament of 1377. He says that Sir Thomas Hungerford was elected by a majority of the knights of the shire (*electus . . . a majori parte*).[2] We cannot rule out the possibility that at this very early stage in the history of the Speakership the knights, as the most important members of the Lower House, not merely took the lead in but even arrogated to themselves alone the election of its Speaker. Certainly then, and for over a century and a half, he was chosen from within their ranks. We cannot, therefore, just brush aside this St Albans reference. Again, among the *objectus* or charges justifying Richard II's deposition, Sir John Bussy, Speaker in the last of his parliaments (1397–8), is described as *unus de militibus comitatuum . . . vocem habens eorum in Parliamento*, a phrase which, if it means what it says, might be taken to suggest that since the Speaker represented the knights it would be they who chose him.[3] We cannot afford, in this connexion, to ignore the attempted reform of certain elements of Scottish parliamentary practice by James I in 1428. This was only four years after his return from a long exile in England, and the reform may perhaps have owed something to English practice. James's ordinance, after providing for the election of two or more commissaries from each shire, went on to propose that it should be left to these counterparts of the English shire-knights to elect *a wise and ane expert man callit the common spekar of the parliament quhilk sal*

---

[1] *EHR*, lii (1938), 600, 602; *Annales Ricardi Secundi*, 209.

[2] *Chronicon Angliae*, op. cit., 112.

[3] *Rot. Parl.*, iii. 421b.

propone all and sundry nedes and causes pertening to the commonis in the parliament or generall consal.[1]

Unfortunately, the direct evidence of the rolls of the parliaments on this whole question of the Speaker's election is most scanty and inadequate. The rolls do no more, in fact, than record the Chancellor's order to elect and mention the ceremony in which the Speaker was presented to the King after his election. But they do at least appear to settle one important point. Normally, the order to elect is merely recorded as given to 'the Commons'. Occasionally, however, as in 1395, 1404, throughout Henry V's reign, and again in 1422 and 1427, it is the knights, citizens, and burgesses who are expressly stated in the roll to have been told to make the election. We may, therefore, at any rate tentatively conclude that the Speaker's election was a proceeding to which all the Commons were in some way party, although the knights' influence upon the election is likely in practice to have been powerful if not even decisive.

But, of course, the real question is not whether the knights alone elected the Speaker and the rest of the Commons acquiesced, but whether the election was normally determined by an official nomination which, however blandly it was conveyed, the Commons had no option but to accept. Because of the paucity of direct evidence, a consideration of the nature of the Speaker's election to some extent depends upon attention being given to a number of subsidiary questions. If the government was normally able to make a decisive nomination, so that the Speaker was in effect appointed by the Crown, would there ever be a contested election for the Speakership? would the election take more than a very short time to accomplish? would an ex-Speaker, especially one who had acted very recently, be passed over and not re-elected? would the Commons' choice of Speaker ever be unwelcome to the government? and would a Speaker have anything to fear in official circles if the Commons misbehaved themselves? Furthermore, would not the Speaker probably be a royal civil servant or official, an inmate of the King's Household, or a friend of some great minister of state or other influential member of the King's Council? and might he not receive a personal reward from the government expressly for his work as Speaker? We shall return to these questions later.

[1] *The Acts of the Parliament of Scotland* (1814), ii. 15, § 2. This ordinance of 1428 did not take effect, and the intended reform of Scottish representation was not made effective until 1585 and 1587 when fresh acts were passed (R. S. Rait, *The Parliaments of Scotland*, 195, 518–20).

But first of all let us examine such direct evidence as can be found for supposing that the medieval Commons were able, in electing their Speaker, to exercise a real choice. It must at once be said that all such evidence is most depressingly meagre. The St Albans chronicler's allusion to Sir Thomas Hungerford's election in Edward III's last parliament (1377) has already been noticed. He describes this Speaker as not only chosen simply by the shire-knights, but also as *electus . . . a majori parte ad pronunciandum verba communia*. We are not entitled to lay much store by these few vague words. Their author, Thomas Walsingham, may have meant no more than that most of the knights were in favour of Hungerford being Speaker. Perhaps there was an election 'by voices', but it would certainly be very risky even to imagine that Hungerford's nomination had been actively opposed by a counter-nomination, resulting in a contested election settled by a majority-vote. There is, however, one piece of evidence of a contested election to the Speakership in the medieval period. It appears in the Gildhall Roll, 8–9 Henry V, in the archives of the borough of King's Lynn. Not evidence of record in the strict sense, it is none the less a piece of record evidence. Its origin is unimpeachable, its value beyond dispute. Being unique and coming from the formal record of a report about the doings of the parliament of 1420 made to his fellow-townsmen by one of the two parliamentary burgesses for Bishop's Lynn on their return home from the parliament, it merits, in the context of this discussion, a full rehearsal on the point in question: *Et [Thomas Brygge] dicit quod Rogerus Hunte et Ricardus Russell nominati fuerunt ibidem prolocutores, tamen dicit quod, examinacionibus inde factis, Rogerus prevaluit, et habuit plures voces iiij etc. et optinuit officium prolocutoris parliamenti.*[1] Roger Hunt was in fact elected, according to the parliament-roll itself. Here, in 1420 at any rate, the Speaker's election was so real a proceeding as to result in a contest between two nominees, neither of whom had previously been Speaker; the competition was evidently close, indeed so close that a count or scrutiny (*examinacio*) of votes was needed to decide between

[1] This passage was discovered by Professor May McKisack and is cited in her book, *The Parliamentary Representation of the English Boroughs during the Middle Ages*, p. 142. As Miss McKisack suggests, it is much more likely that the unsuccessful nominee was John Russell, a lawyer and knight of the shire for Herefordshire in 1420, who had previously sat in 1414, 1417, and 1419, and was to be Speaker in 1423 and 1432, and not the only Richard Russell sitting in 1420, who was returned from the unimportant borough of Dunwich and for the first known time at that. The use of *etc.* in the memorandum of the report is a pity! It would be interesting to know what it covers.

them. Perhaps only when competition was keen, were the Commons likely to resort to a division. But they were clearly able to do so in such a circumstance. The Lynn memorial is a chance survival, and it would be unreasonable to imagine that the Commons had never used this procedure before and did not do so again. We may in this connexion also notice the fact that, in the roll of the parliament of 1427, the Speaker's election is expressly reported as made by the Commons *unanimiter*.[1] That need not at all imply that a contested election was the more common occurrence. But it may well suggest that it was not altogether rare.

If the government usually decided in advance who was to be Speaker, we should not expect to hear of any official anxiety lest his election might be a protracted affair. The only evidence from the roll of a late fourteenth-century parliament bearing on this point does in fact indicate official concern about the Commons frittering away time over the Speaker's election. At Salisbury in 1384, as we have seen, the Commons were told to take advantage of a short adjournment of five days at the beginning of parliament by 'treating' about their Speaker. It is important to notice that this was proposed expressly in order to avoid such delays as had previously occurred, and also that the word used was 'treat' (*tretassent*), a word suggestive of mature consideration, negotiation even.[2] So far as is recorded in the parliament-rolls, it was not until Henry IV's reign that, at the opening of parliament, the Chancellor fixed a time-limit for the Speaker's election by arranging when he should be presented in the Upper House. In 1401 and 1402 the Commons were instructed to present at ten o'clock and in 1404 (January) at nine o'clock at the latest, in each case on the second day.[3] And thereafter, habitually, they were told to be ready on the second day.[4] Later on, the Chancellor even regularly laid down when the Commons should meet for the election itself. In 1407[5]

---

[1] *Rot. Parl.*, iv. 317a.   [2] Ibid., iii. 166a.

[3] Ibid., iii. 454b, 485b, 522b.

[4] The only known exceptions to this rule between 1401 and 1432 are in May 1421 (fifth day), 1425 (when the Commons were merely told to present *absque dilationis diffugio*), 1426 (second or third day), and 1432 (third day). After 1432 the day for the Speaker's presentation was stipulated only spasmodically until finally, after 1459, all notice of such a requirement disappears from the parliament-rolls. In 1433 and 1435 the Commons were instructed to present with all despatch (*cum ea celeritate qua commode poterant*); in 1447, on the fourth day (a Monday); in 1455 and 1459, on the third day.

[5] So far as is known from the parliament-rolls, the first time when the Commons were given a particular day on which to elect their Speaker was in 1395 (*Rot. Parl.*, iii. 329), after which there is no further mention of such an order

they were told to meet on the afternoon of the first day; in 1410 and 1413, early on the second day; for the greater part of Henry V's reign, that is from 1414 to 1420, on the first day again; afterwards, quite invariably on the second day. In 1410 and 1413 the Chancellor actually specified at the outset both the very hour at which the Commons were to elect and the very hour at which they were to present their Speaker: in 1410, they were to elect on the second day *a oept de clok* and present *a noef del clok a pluys tard*; in 1413 they were to elect, again on the second day, *al sept del clokke a matyn* and to present *a oept del clokke mesme le jour*.[1] Evidently, on these occasions the official view was that an hour ought to suffice for the Commons to elect and be ready to present. Whether this was always long enough, we do not know. What we do know is that, although in 1410 the Commons presented their Speaker at least sometime on the second day, in 1413 it was not the second, nor even the third, but the fourth day of the session when they did so. We also know for sure that, although orders of such particularity do not thereafter re-appear in the records,[2] the Chancellor at any rate continued to emphasize the necessity for a speedy election and an early presentation.[3] But oftener than not the order for the time of the presentation was not punctually observed. In 1426, although the second or third day was appointed, it was actually the eleventh when the Speaker was presented.[4] So long a deferment as this was, however, quite exceptional, and, whenever the Commons were unpunctual, they were rarely more than a day late. After 1427 the Commons are frequently reported as sending a deputation to the Lords to communicate their Speaker's name (at the same time requesting the Lords to seek the King's consent to postpone formal presentation[5] or, as after 1460, to ask him to appoint

---

until 1407. After 1407 the only parliament-rolls not recording the command are those of 1411, 1421 and 1422.

[1] *Rot. Parl.*, iii. 622b; iv. 3.

[2] On only one occasion after 1413 did the Chancellor specify the hour at which the Commons were to present their Speaker: in 1437 he told them to elect him on the second day before eight o'clock (*octavam horam*), when they were to present him (ibid., iv. 495b).

[3] In 1414 (twice) and 1416 the Commons were ordered to elect on the first day and present before dinner (*avaunt manger*) on the second. In 1421 (twice) and in 1422 they were simply told to elect in haste; in 1423 and 1425, to elect on the morning of the second day and present as soon as possible on that same day (*sy tost come ils purroient; absque dilationis diffugio*).

[4] *Rot. Parl.*, iv. 295–6.

[5] The Lords are recorded as being asked to arrange this respite in 1427, 1429, 1431, 1439, 1442, 1445, 1449 (February), 1463, and 1483.

a time suitable to himself[1]), all this on the very day officially appointed for the Speaker's election. This indicates that any unpunctuality in the presentation was by this time not due to a delayed or protracted election.

These facts may be used to argue that in the later fourteenth century the Commons' choosing of their Speaker was sometimes not so promptly accomplished as was officially desired; that in the early fifteenth century the government still felt it necessary to insist on the need for despatch, but that by the beginning of Henry VI's reign the Commons no longer needed to be quite so firmly prodded into expediting their Speaker's election, and that any delay in his presentation was not their fault. Regarding the main question, whether the Speaker's election was a cut-and-dried affair, this evidence regarding the chronology of election and presentation seems to indicate that it was not so in the late fourteenth and early fifteenth centuries. The later evidence on this aspect of the problem is quite indeterminate and really of no value, one way or the other. We are not compelled to believe that when the Speaker's election was promptly made, this promptitude depended on any prior decision or arrangement on the government's part. After all, it was in everybody's interest, the Commons' own included, to get a parliament off to a good start.

We may next consider whether, in the medieval period, the government actually had ample or even sufficient time, between the local election of the knight of the shire who became Speaker and the opening of parliament, in which to decide that he in particular should

[1] The Chancellor and/or the Lords were notified by the Commons of their Speaker's election and asked to secure the appointment of a day on which he might be presented to the King for formal acceptance in 1460, 1467, 1472, 1478, 1484 and thereafter under Henry VII. In 1460 the parliament-roll merely says that the Chancellor was informed; in 1472, that the Lords were informed and that the Chancellor told the Commons that the King would send them word (*verbum transmitteret*) about the presentation; in 1478, that the Chancellor told them when it was to take place; in 1483 and 1495 that the Chancellor and Lords were notified. At other times the roll simply states that the Commons informed the Lords. A further variation appears in the roll of 1478 when the Commons, although notifying the Lords that they had made an election, did not there and then disclose the name of the Speaker-elect (*non nominando personam*): this deviation from earlier practice was common form under Henry VII. The roll of 1495 relates that the Chancellor and Lords, on the King's behalf, congratulated the Commons on their speed of action (*de eorum celeri expeditione*) and then told them to meet in their own House two days later at the tenth hour, when the King would let them know the time for the Speaker to be presented.

be Speaker. If it could be shown that the local election of the knight
who became Speaker generally took place far too late for the government to decide upon his election to the office, this might weigh
against the supposition that the government normally intervened in
this matter. We may then enquire how frequently a former Speaker
was again elected to the Chair, and, more especially, how frequently
the Speaker in one parliament was re-elected as Speaker in the
immediately succeeding parliament. The point here, of course, is that
the Speaker for one parliament, if he had then been the government's
nominee, might well be the government's first preference for the
Chair of the new House of Commons, if the government entertained
such preferences. We may further ask whether, if such an ex-Speaker
was not elected to the Chair—and, for the purpose of argument, let
us assume that this meant failure to be nominated by the government
—this was because the government could not have known that he
was available.

It can be stated quite safely that there was generally plenty of time
for the government to decide whom to nominate for the Speakership, had it wished to make a nomination. On only three occasions
in the fifteenth century is it clear that the Speaker-to-be was elected
to parliament less than a week before it began: in 1413 (when William
Stourton was elected for Dorset only six days before parliament
met), in 1422 (when Roger Flore was elected for Rutland four days
before), and in 1426 (when Sir Richard Vernon was elected for
Derbyshire five days before). It is also clear that, on the not very
frequent occasions when a Speaker in one parliament was re-elected
as knight of the shire to the next, there was similarly time for the
government to make up its mind that he should again be Speaker.
And yet in the fifteen cases[1] in the fifteenth century where the last
Speaker was re-elected to parliament, only seven times did it happen
that he was re-elected Speaker: in 1410 (Thomas Chaucer), 1411
(Thomas Chaucer again), 1417 (Roger Flore), 1419 (Roger Flore
again), 1442 (William Tresham), 1467 (Sir John Say), and 1478
(William Allington). After Roger Flore was first elected Speaker in
October 1416, on each of the three subsequent occasions on which
he was returned as knight of the shire (in 1417, 1419 and 1422) he was
made Speaker. Especially because he was a Crown lawyer and one of

[1] In 1402 (Savage), 1410 (Chaucer), 1411 (Chaucer), 1413 (Chaucer), April
1414 (Doreward), 1417 (Flore), 1419 (Flore), May 1421 (Hunt), 1429 (Tyrell),
1433 (Russell), 1442 (Tresham), February 1449 (Tresham), 1467 (Say), 1478
(Allington), 1495 (Empson).

the two Chief Stewards of the Duchy of Lancaster, it is conceivable
that he was a government nominee for the Chair; although it could
be supposed with equal confidence (but with equal lack of supporting evidence) that he was chosen simply because he was acceptable
to the Commons. Let us, however, take the case of another Crown
lawyer, William Tresham, who was elected Speaker in four[1] of the
six parliaments which met between 1439 and his assassination in
1450. If on these occasions Tresham had been the direct nominee of
the Court, and if such a nomination had been a normal proceeding,
the Commons' freedom of election being virtually non-existent or
non-effective, it is rather difficult to understand why he was not also
made Speaker in the two other parliaments which met in these
years.[2] On these two occasions he was returned as knight of the shire
for Northamptonshire as usual and was therefore equally available to
be nominated and chosen as in the four other parliaments.

The sort of evidence which we have just discussed proves on
examination to be very indeterminate at best. That the government
had as a rule plenty of time in which to arrange a Speaker's nomination need not mean that it made use of it for this purpose. On the
other hand, if the time available was short, it need not have been
insufficient to do what was necessary. The main argument, then, is
neither advanced nor retarded by these considerations.

We next turn to the more significant and interesting question,
whether the Commons' election of a Speaker at any time proved
unwelcome or even unacceptable to the government or to some
interest powerful in official circles. Again, the evidence is fragmentary, but less insecure in character. Such as it is, it seems in the
main to substantiate the Commons' independence in the matter of
their Speaker's election. There are a few instances of the Speaker's
being changed in the course of a parliament. The first occurred in
1399. After Richard II's resignation of the crown and Henry of
Bolingbroke's claim to it had been accepted on 30 September, parliament, being formally re-summoned, met on 6 October, only to be
adjourned until 14 October, the morrow of Henry IV's coronation.
It was then that the Commons presented Sir John Cheyne as their
Speaker-elect. He was accepted by the King, who also agreed to his
'protestation'. On the very next day, however, Cheyne sought and
secured exoneration ostensibly on the grounds of illness and in-
firmity, the Commons having already chosen John Doreward to

[1] In 1439, 1442, 1447, and November 1449.
[2] In 1445 and February 1449.

replace him.[1] The roll of the parliament, which is our source for this information, gives away nothing as to the underlying causes or circumstances of this withdrawal and substitution. Fortunately, the St Albans chronicler felt moved to say more. He tells us that when parliament met on 6 October, Archbishop Arundel, a firm political ally of the new King and newly reinstated in the primatial see, instructed the Commons to proceed to elect a Speaker, and that right away (the narrative implies) they chose Cheyne. On the next day, the southern Convocation met in St Paul's. In the course of its proceedings, Arundel alluded to the anti-clericalism of many of the parliamentary knights; especially dangerous, he said, were the *sensus et opiniones* of Sir John Cheyne, already the Speaker-elect, an apostate clerk who had long been an enemy of the Church.[2] It looks very much as though Cheyne's abandonment of his office as Speaker a week later was due to pressure exerted on the Commons from behind the scenes by the restored Archbishop, possibly through the King. (From the ecclesiastical view-point, Cheyne's successor, Doreward, was a 'safe' man and, moreover, had connexions with Canterbury, with Christchurch priory as well as with Archbishop Arundel himself; he was also, even by the time of his Speakership, a member of the King's Council.) So far as we know, the Commons were insensitive (or pusillanimous) enough not to challenge Cheyne's displacement. But that is hardly the point. Although Cheyne was a member of the royal Council by the following spring and enjoyed at this time royal favour in other ways, it is difficult to conceive that he was not in the first place the Commons' own free choice for the Speakership in Henry IV's first parliament. If Cheyne's choice had been officially dictated, surely he must have been acceptable to the government. The only alternative is to regard the change as a *volte-face* on the part of the government itself. Such a change is conceivable. A more plausible explanation, however, is that, although the proprieties were observed and ostensibly Cheyne backed out voluntarily, the Commons' own free choice was in effect overruled.

Whereas the first Lancastrian reign began with a virtual rejection by the government of a Speaker freely chosen by the Commons, the second began with the rejection of their Speaker by the Commons themselves. As has been seen in another context,[3] this was because, at Henry V's behest, the Speaker in question, William Stourton, had exceeded his powers as their agent in the Upper House. In other

---

[1] *Rot. Parl.*, iii. 424b.   [2] *Annales Henrici Quarti*, p. 290.
[3] See p. 52.

words, in 1399 the Commons succumbed to pressure from above when official objection was taken to the person of their Speaker: in 1413, it was the Commons themselves who took exception to their Speaker because, in the conduct of his office, *he* had given way to pressure from above. Doreward's election in Henry IV's first parliament suggests a rather subservient or complaisant attitude on the Commons' part; his election to follow Stourton in Henry V's first parliament conceivably may suggest that, in the meantime, the Lower House had developed stronger nerves or acquired a greater measure of independence. But that, though important, is by the way. That the freedom of the Commons to choose their Speaker for themselves was at this time a reality is shown, firstly, by the fact that, having elected one Speaker and found him too amenable to royal influence for their liking, they were able to make another election, and again, and more especially, by the fact that their second choice, John Doreward, had himself actually led their opposition to his predecessor. It was formally alleged in the parliament-roll of 1413 (as in Cheyne's case in 1399) that Stourton needed to be superseded because he was ill and keeping to his bed, but, although he died in the autumn of the same year, it is quite possible that his illness at this juncture was a diplomatic one. Sir John Tyrell's replacement in 1437 may perhaps be more safely attributed to illness, as was also formally alleged, for not only did he too die during the year of his Speakership, but the parliament lasted for no more than a week after his supersession. The replacement of Thomas Thorpe in 1454, the outcome of his imprisonment by contrivance of the Duke of York, whose political enemy he was, is similarly unhelpful in relation to the problem under discussion.

It is well known that the medieval Speaker-elect, when presented to the King for his acceptance, made a sort of 'disabling speech' and asked to be excused from office. This, it is true, quite soon became a formality. Yet, for our present enquiry, this request to be excused becomes on one occasion the turning-point of an important and significant incident. Just once in our period the excusation of the Speaker-elect was actually allowed. This happened in November 1449 when Sir John Popham asked to be exonerated, and was. Ill-health from war-wounds was the professed basis of Popham's plea. But it must surely have been his long connexion with the House of York which prompted the government to discharge him, or rather to disembarrass itself. It seems unlikely that this contretemps could have occurred except as the result of Popham's being freely elected by the Commons, whose membership showed how discredited the government was in the country at large and whose political activities reflected their own hostility to the régime. And in the next parliament (1450), it was again a Yorkist partisan who was elected Speaker, only this time without any suggestion of his supersession: the Duke of York's own head of household, his Chamberlain, Sir William Oldhall, a man who (like Popham) was a veteran of the French war and, in his dissatisfaction with its conduct, was as truly representative of the Commons' temper in 1450 as that temper was of the feelings of the nation. Neither the Commons' first election of Speaker in November 1449 nor their one and only choice in November 1450 is likely to have rested upon a government nomination. If either of these two elections was in any way 'rigged', it was hardly the government which would be likely to do the 'rigging'.

It is also perhaps worth bearing in mind the circumstances in which, according to Abbot Wheathampstead of St Albans, his own local enemy, Sir Thomas Charlton, a member of the royal Household, came to be elected in 1454 following Speaker Thorpe's imprisonment. The abbot represents the election as a move privately made by Charlton to secure his own private ends: *totum suum nisum apposuit quomodo in Parliamento Prolocutor fieret, taliterque apud suos notos affines et consanguineos mediavit quod, laboribus eorum et instantiis, Prolocutor inter Communes effectus est.*[1] It must, of course, be pointed out that neither the direction in which this influence was exerted by Charlton's kinsfolk, whether upon the government or in the Lower House itself, nor indeed who were these kinsfolk who pressed for his election, is indicated. Charlton had a family connexion with the Countess of Salisbury, whose husband was the brother-in-law and a supporter of the Duke of York (then soon to be made Protector). But he certainly had relatives among the Commons themselves: his fellow-knight of the shire for Middlesex was his cousin, Henry Frowyke, and this cousin's two brothers-in-law, Roger and Richard Lewkenore, were sitting for Sussex and Bramber respectively. Inconclusive though this evidence may be, it has a certain slant: the situation seems hardly to consort with a Court nomination.

Much earlier than this, there had been other occasions when the personal career of the Speaker suggests that, whatever manœuvres lay behind his election by the Commons, it was not the influence of the government of the day which secured him his place of distinction in the Lower House. We need not go quite so far back as Sir Peter

[1] *Registrum Abbatiae Johannis Whethamsted,* ed. T. H. Riley (R.S.), vol. i, p. 136.

F

de la Mare who as Speaker in 1376 had led the Commons in their hostility to some of the highest officials of the Court of Edward III. Let us however take the cases of Sir James de Pickering (Speaker in 1378 and 1383) and Sir John de Gildsburgh (twice Speaker in 1380). Neither of these was a royal retainer when acting in the capacity of Speaker, although Pickering was afterwards to become one. Gildsburgh, it is true, was well known to men who had been in the retinue of the Black Prince and were well to the fore in Richard II's Household, and also to Archbishop Sudbury who became Chancellor during Gildsburgh's first Speakership and was still in office when he was re-elected; but Gildsburgh's closest connexion, as tenant and retainer, was with Thomas of Woodstock, about whose French expedition (of 1380–1) the Commons in both the 1380 parliaments showed much concern. So that, if we were able to search for any political machination behind Gildsburgh's election, it would be among the friends of this youngest of Edward III's sons rather than in government circles proper. Again, we must consider Thomas Chaucer (successively Speaker in 1407, 1410 and 1411) who, although in the strict sense a Crown official as Chief Butler of England, was more intimately involved with his cousin, Henry Beaufort, Bishop of Winchester, and with Beaufort's political ally, the young Prince of Wales, Henry of Monmouth, than with Henry IV. Chaucer's Speakerships may therefore be regarded as evidence of the challenge of this group within the royal family which came to be constantly at odds with the ageing King: Henry IV's angry rejoinder early in the parliament of 1411, that he would have none of Speaker Chaucer's 'novelties', may or may not be symptomatic of the tension to which this disagreement in the royal House gave rise; certainly, however, it strongly suggests that Henry IV had not had much to do with Chaucer's elections as Speaker.

The medieval Speaker was none the less in most cases a man who was attached to the Court, maybe as an ordinary retainer of the King, more likely as holding an office in the royal Household or in some other administrative service of the Crown, perhaps even a member of the King's Council, or, in a period of minority government and conciliar control, as a man who was associated with one or more of the lords of the Council. Our account of the careers of the Speakers will disclose that they almost all fit this description.

Of course, even if we were to suppose that the Speaker could always be relied upon to bring pressure to bear on his fellows, we should be unwise to rest content with the assumption that his own opinions were 'fast-dyed' in the tincture of his official or aristocratic connexions (which themselves might well be mutually conflicting). Mr McFarlane has warned us of the danger of regarding members of the professional administrative class, so many of whom frequently sat among the parliamentary Commons, as mere pawns or subservient hangers-on, whose careers depended entirely on the 'good lordship' of a single great magnate or the favour of the King. These men played their own game, seeking interest and fees where they could find them, so that the only uncomplicated, exclusive loyalty which their unquiet minds knew in this time of unrest and strain and generally unstable government was to their own prospering and security. In any case, the Commons would have been hard put to it to elect as Speaker any one of their more influential and experienced members who did not occupy some royal office or was not attached to some great lord. Why the Commons chose the Speakers they did was probably often for the same general reasons which actuated the King or a magnate when he retained the services of members of that class of 'men of business' to which so many of the medieval Speakers belonged: just as the King and great lords required the best counsel available for the conduct of their public and private concerns, so presumably the Commons also wanted their business to be put through with efficiency; and where emphatic speech was needed when their answers or petitions were laid before the King and Lords, they would wish it to be made with a maximum of relevance, cogency, and eloquence. What recommended 'the man of business' to Kings and magnates would also recommend him to his fellows in the Lower House. Moreover, if their Speaker were employed in the royal service or had associations with others of high place, the Commons were likely to think this to be to their own greater advantage. For, however critical the Commons might be of government policy or finance, and however distasteful to the royal executive might be the pressure they exerted upon it, their demands would not lose point by being presented through an intermediary who was acceptable on personal grounds. The occasional nervousness of Speakers, some of the early Speakers in particular, exemplified (as we have seen) in their 'protestations', is a clear indication that, whatever their official complexion, they did not always feel so confident of being treated with that consideration or sympathy which would have been their due had they been simply royal employees set up temporarily to manage the Lower House on behalf of the Crown.

But eventually the medieval Speaker did in some sense become a government agent. As we shall later have cause to notice in greater detail, from 1435 onwards there is clear evidence, at first only now and then but later (under the Yorkists) fairly regularly, that the Speaker was paid an honorarium or gratuity expressly for his diligence and services in the office, the amount of which varied and so, presumably, depended to some extent upon the official estimation of the value of those services; and that, in the second half of the fifteenth century, he sometimes appears to have been simply a royal official openly seconded to just another paid post, the office of Commons' Speaker.

We must conclude this review of the rather scanty and disappointing evidence on a very important topic by alluding to two incidents, both of which are unsatisfactorily reported and yet which seem to bear directly on the question. In 1485, the Chief Justice of the King's Bench, arguing Henry VII's right to summon his first parliament though himself under attaint, is reported in the *Year Books*[1] as referring to the case of Sir Thomas Tresham who, when under attaint, had at some unspecified date been proposed for the Speakership: *qui fuit intend que il sera Speaker de le Parlement*, words which, ambiguous though they are, seem to imply that Tresham had been a government nominee for the office of Speaker. The occasion of this obscure affair would appear to have been the parliament which met during the Lancastrian Readeption of 1470-1. The circumstances of the other incident are a little clearer. It seems that Sir Thomas Fitz-William's election as Speaker in Henry VII's third parliament in January 1489 was arranged well in advance. Being then Recorder of London, FitzWilliam was in the usual course elected to parliament for the City on 2 December 1488, but sometime in the next five weeks got himself elected and returned for his own county of Lincolnshire. If this was in order that, as now a knight of the shire, he might qualify for the Speakership, which seems very probable, he may already have been considered for the Chair and informed of the proposal to nominate him.[2]

What all this maddeningly fragmentary and tantalizingly indecisive evidence means, it is difficult to say. It is like trying to determine the

[1] J. C. Wedgwood, *History of Parliament, 1439-1509, Register*, p. 384.

[2] Ibid., *Biographies*, p. 337; A. B. Beaven, *Aldermen of the City of London*, p. 273. According to the *Journal* of the City, FitzWilliam did not at first 'choose for which to sit', London or Lincolnshire, nor was a new writ issued for the City, but a substitute was elected for London on 7 January 1489, six days before parliament met.

direction of the wind on a gusty day from occasional glimpses of a weather-vane in a state of disrepair. However, regarding the first half-century of the history of the Speakership, a period in which the Commons frequently showed a sense of the importance of their own political independence, the direct and indirect evidence seems to be convergent and to indicate that, in electing their Speaker, the Commons were normally left with freedom to act in accordance with their own devices and desires, even though it was not impossible for their choice to be rejected. Under Henry VI and the Yorkists there are signs of an enhanced official appreciation of the value of the Speaker in the conduct of business in the Lower House, and the lawyerly, 'civil servant' type of Speaker came to predominate. Whether this evolution, alone, converted the Speaker's election into a merely formal confirmation by the Commons of an irresistible royal nomination, is another matter. For there were certainly occasions in mid-century when, the government's credit being low, the Commons were able to elect as Speaker one whose political outlook was identified with the cause of hostile critics. None the less, as time went on, the signs point to a growing practical restriction of the Commons' independence of action. The question of the Commons' freedom in the election of their Speaker ultimately resolves itself into a technical quibble. His and their normal subservience to the New Monarchy emerges as a significant feature in the changed pattern of relations between the King and Parliament.

CHAPTER 4

The Speaker's Functions

THE Speaker's first and, certainly in the medieval period, his ever
most important duty was to do what his name suggests: to act
as spokesman for the Commons when they had communications
—whether 'answers' or requests—to make to the King and Lords.
If the Commons appeared in the Upper House to make a report,
submit a verbal petition or complaint, make one of their 'recommendations' of princes or peers, or present a grant of taxation, it was
usual for them to do so *by mouthe of their Speker*. Whatever the short-
comings of the parliament-rolls, they were put together in sufficient
detail for this at least to be quite clear. (In the roll which covers the
three sessions of the long parliament of 1406 there are no fewer than
two score references to Sir John Tiptoft, the then Speaker, appearing
in the Lords.) The Speaker was the Commons' agent. Indeed, Tiptoft is actually referred to as 'Parlour *et Procuratour*'. Once the Speaker
had been elected and accepted, there could seldom be any reason
why the Commons should not use his services in the parliament-
chamber. And there was at least one very powerful reason why his
services alone should be so used: as we have seen, the royal allowance
of his protestation secured him a formal privilege of speech and at
the same time enabled the Commons to control his utterances, in
their interest as well as his own. Admittedly, there were occasions
(and very probably more than the few reported in the rolls of
fifteenth-century parliaments) when the Commons despatched to the
Lords a deputation without their Speaker at its head.[1] But, undoubtedly, it was he who was the normal leader on visits to the Upper
House and the Commons' accredited spokesman once they were
there.

A gift of lucid speech, as well as a capacity clearly to understand
what the Commons had decided among themselves and wished to be
expressed in the presence of the King and Lords, was obviously
an important quality to be looked for in any Speaker. Contemporary
evidence definitely states that many of the medieval Speakers possessed it. It was an ability to speak well which, together with some
other qualifications, brought Sir Peter de la Mare to the forefront in

[1] *Rot. Parl.*, iv. 199, 296; v, 284-5.

the Good Parliament of 1376. Both the St Albans chronicler, Thomas Walsingham, and the author of *The Anonimalle Chronicle* are clear enough on this point. For the former, not the least important of the signs that the knights of the shire in this session were inspired by the Holy Ghost was their recognition that De la Mare possessed the gift of tongues and the boldness to use it. It was his *audacia proferandi quae mente conceperat atque facundia insperata* which impressed the St Albans chronicler just as, presumably, it had done his informant, Sir Thomas de la Hoo, knight of the shire for Bedfordshire on that occasion.[1] Similarly, the compiler of *The Anonimalle Chronicle* believed that the Commons requested De la Mare to be Speaker because he *fuist si bien parlaunt et si sagement rehersaunt des maters et purpose de ses compaignons et les enfourmaunt pluis avaunt q'ils mesmes ne savoient* (putting them into shape before they themselves had quite realized what they were).[2] According to the St Albans chronicler, it was not only the exceptional worldly prudence and guile of Sir John Bussy which qualified him for the Speakership in Richard II's last parliament (1397–8), but also that he was powerful in eloquence (*pollens eloquentia*) and so able to praise the King with what the chronicler, himself at a loss, called indescribable words of flattery (*inenerrabilibus verbis adulationis*), which proved much to the King's taste none the less.[3] That Bussy *in cunctis suis propositionibus non humanos honores exhibuit Regi sed divinos, adveniens verba adulatoria et insueta*, naturally aroused in Walsingham only feelings of disgust. For Bussy's early successor, Sir Arnald Savage, Speaker in Henry IV's second and fourth parliaments, however, Walsingham had nothing but praise. And, in his account of the 1401 parliament, he particularly noticed that Savage's rhetoric (and sentiments) deservedly met with a favourable reception: *tam diserte, tam eloquenter, tam gratiose declaravit communitatis negotia, praecipue ne de cetero taxis gravarentur, aut talliagiis, quod laudem ab universis promeruit ea die.*[4]

There is no cause to doubt Walsingham's judgement, for certain speeches made on the Commons' behalf in 1401 were obviously impressive enough to be reported in the parliament-roll itself with a quite extraordinary fullness. (The orations are not actually attributed to Savage, but there can be little question that they are in fact samples of his style of declamation.) In the first to be noted were defined the three prerequisites of good government, these being *seen* [sense], *humanite, et richesse*: with the first of these qualities

[1] *Chronicon Angliae*, op. cit., 72.   [2] *The Anonimalle Chronicle*, op. cit., 83.
[3] *Annales Ricardi Secundi*, 209, 211.   [4] Ibid., 335.

Henry IV was stated to be well-endowed in his own person and in the persons of his lords; they and others of the knighthood and gentility of his realm possessed the second; and the third was to be discovered in the King's possession of the heart of his people.[1] On another occasion in the session, when deploring the existence of discord between some of the lords (especially between the Earl of Rutland and Lord FitzWalter) and emphasizing the need for unity between the estates, Savage delivered a speech which likened the estates to a Trinity, comprising the King, the Lords Spiritual and Temporal, and the Commons. Finally, and on the last day of the session, he ingeniously demonstrated how the progress of a parliament was like the Mass: the Archbishop of Canterbury began the office and read the Epistle and the Gospel; the King, in the middle at the offertory, undertook to uphold the Faith as affirmed by Holy Church, her Doctors, and Holy Scripture (a reference, perhaps, to the passage during the session of the Statute *De haeretico comburendo*), and also to ensure the maintenance of just law to poor and rich alike; and then, to conclude the Office, the Commons came to say *Ite missa est* and *Deo gratias*, this last for three reasons, namely, that God had granted them a gracious King, just, wise, and courageous to resist his enemies, that the King had taken steps to meet the threat of perverse and subversive doctrine, and that he had a good and whole heart towards Lords and Commons, and they towards him.[2] As to the verbal brilliance of these orations, we have no proper means of judging. We may suspect that they lacked nothing less in prolixity than in unctuosity. (This is not to say that Savage's audience would have found anything distasteful in these characteristics, which were still quite fashionable in Elizabeth I's time.)

The Clerk of the Parliaments, who was responsible for compiling the roll, was naturally more concerned as a general rule to register the substance of a verbal communication from the Lower House than the form and manner of its delivery. What the Speaker said to reinforce a complaint or request, it was not necessarily the business of the Clerk to record in detail. When required to convey the Commons' special approval of some individual or group of magnates (and the Commons not infrequently resorted to this practice in the fifteenth century[3]), the Speaker was given an obvious oppor-

---

[1] *Rot. Parl.*, iii. 456a.   [2] Ibid., 466a.

[3] Commendations made by the Speaker on the Commons' behalf are recorded in the rolls of the following parliaments: 1404 (October), on one occasion for Henry IV's sons, the Duke of York, and the King's half-brothers, John and

tunity to make a show of his rhetorical accomplishments and doubtless sometimes availed himself of it; but a brief note of the names of those he commended was all that was usually made in the roll. At least some of these 'recommendations' and other orations, *pièces d'occasion*, were however considered important enough to warrant a relaxation of the normal reticence of the record, so that we are able to judge, to some extent, of their verbal quality. In 1406 the Clerk of the Parliaments let himself go and devoted nearly two hundred words to what was presumably a *précis* of Tiptoft's speech telling of the Commons' high regard for Prince Henry of Monmouth, the royal heir-apparent, their approval of his filial humility, courage, and readiness to forego his own will and adhere to the advice of his council, and their prayer that he would continue to express these qualities.[1]

For the set oration in English which Speaker Russell delivered on 17 November 1423, on the great occasion in the first session of the parliament of 1423–4 when Henry VI, then nearly two years old, made his earliest appearance before the estates, we have to rely on the version reported in a London chronicle. This account, however, seems to reproduce the speech in full. In it, on the Commons' behalf, the Speaker thanked God for His gift of the King, coupling their gratitude with a prayer that Henry of Windsor might reign *with long*

Thomas Beaufort, and at another time for the Duke of York again (regarding his services as Lieutenant of Guienne), Sir Thomas Erpingham, Sir Thomas Rempstone, John Norbury *et les autres vaillantz Chivalers et Esquiers qi leur mystrent en aventure ovesqe nostre Seigneur le Roy a son venue en Engleterre*; 1407, for the good service performed against the Welsh rebels by Prince Henry and those with him; 1410, on behalf of Prince Henry and other members of the King's Council appointed in the previous parliament and, at the end of the parliament, for the Queen and the King's other sons; 1417, for Lord Charlton of Powys, who had captured Sir John Oldcastle, *heretik et traitour a Dieu et a Roy*, and brought him to London; 1429, on behalf of Cardinal Beaufort at the end of the first session, and of the lords of the Council at the end of the parliament; 1437, regarding the action of the Duke of Gloucester and other temporal lords in the previous year in rescuing Calais and resisting the Duke of Burgundy, and also in recognition of the diligence of Cardinal Beaufort, and the Chancellor, the Treasurer, and other lords of the Council *pro complemento Justicie*; 1483, in support of Richard, Duke of Gloucester, the Earl of Northumberland, Lord Stanley, and other barons and knights who had been on active service in the Scottish war. In the consecutive parliaments of 1422, 1423, 1425, 1426 and 1427, the Speaker conveyed the Commons' commendations, but the rolls do not specify for whom these were made.

[1] *Rot. Parl.*, iii. 574.

perseveracion and vertuous contynuaunce; he also went on to refer to Henry V as *the Rote, Welle and shelde of our worldly conforte and suerte*, to the King's uncles of Bedford and Gloucester as *ful largely endowed of high trouth, Justice, and Wisedome, and also manhod*, and to the lords of the Council and *here assistence, cotidian labour, and diligent besynes*.[1]

The record of the well-known speech, addressed on the Commons' behalf to Henry VI ten years later (on 24 November 1433), in which Speaker Hunt extolled the military conduct of the Duke of Bedford in France but advised his retention in this country, is inscribed on the roll of the parliament itself.[2] Set out in English and at length, it quite possibly contains Hunt's oration in its complete form. Having described the King's hold on France at the time of his accession as *right tendre, right yong and grene*, the speech had gone on to admire the chivalrous behaviour of the Regent who *frely fro tyme to tyme when the case requirid it, exposid his persone to the labour and to the aventure of the Werre, as the poueryst Knyght or Gentilman beyng there in the Kyngs service, and chevid many greet and faire thinges worthi to be had in perpetuell remembraunce*, especially, the battle of Verneuil, *the which was the grettest dede doon by Englissh men in our dayes, save the Bataille of Agyncourte*. Equally telling is the wording of the later passage in which Hunt proceeded to speak of Bedford's tranquillizing influence on affairs at home in England.

Similarly, the roll of the parliament of 1445–6 seems to hold much, if not all, of the speech in which, *in the most humble and tendre wyse*, Speaker Burley recommended the Marquess of Suffolk and the *ryght grete and notable werkys whiche he hathe don to the pleasir of God, of oure saide Soveraigne Lord, and of his people* (especially his contribution to a peace with France and the arrangement of Henry VI's marriage) and then went on to urge the Lords to ask the King to take Suffolk into his royal favour and secure the enactment of the Marquess's *declarations, laboures, and demenyng . . . to his true acquitail and discharge, and honour of hym in tyme to come*.[3]

The longest record of an oration made by any of the medieval Speakers is that of the speech made by Sir James Strangeways on the ninth day of Edward IV's first parliament (12 November 1461), when he gave thanks for the King's victories in the field and assertion of his rights, praising the *noble and condigne merites, Princely and Knyghtly corage . . ., the beaute of personage that it hath pleased Almyghty God to send you, the wysdome that of his grace is annexed therunto, and the*

---

[1] *Chronicles of London*, ed. C. L. Kingsford (Oxford, 1905), pp. 280–1.
[2] *Rot. Parl.*, iv. 423.   [3] Ibid., v. 73–4.

blissid and noble disposicion and application of youre seid Highnes, *to the commyn wele and policie of youre seid Reame and to Godds Chirch of the same*. Strangeways went on to petition for the acceptance of Edward's title to the throne as justified by his lineage, stating that the Commons were well aware that Edward was King by divine, human, and natural law; and he further asked that the Lancastrian régime should be stigmatized as usurpative and that the compromise of 1460, under which Henry of Windsor had been allowed to retain the crown for life, should be annulled because he had broken its terms.[1] What the roll enacts is expressly the *cedula inscripta* of Strangeways' speech itself. This is presumably the case, too, with the *magna declaratio per modum requeste* made on the last day of the first session of the parliament of 1472–5 by Speaker Allington: after recalling that God (during the time of the Lancastrian Readeption) had empowered the King *to reduce* [lead] *this youre Reame, and youre true Subgetts of the same, oute of the daungerous chaunces of Bataill, into the prosperous and moost desired estate of peas, which peas in no wyse may persevere or contynue theryn, or in any pollitique body, withoute due execution of the Lawes within the same used and approved*, Allington drew attention to crimes *committed and doon by such persones as eyther been of grete myght, or elles favoured under persones of grete power, in such wise as their outeragious demerytees as yet remayn unpunysshed*, and went on to ask for the execution of all those beneficial statutes made in and since Edward I's time, which aimed at the suppression of crime and riot, especially those relating to the abuses of livery and maintenance.[2] The important speech in which, on 10 December 1485, in Henry VII's first parliament, Speaker Lovell expressed the Commons' proposal that the King should marry Elizabeth of York, was quite differently recorded: on this occasion merely a few lines of formal Latin were made to suffice.[3]

The Speaker is unlikely to have been afforded much scope for declamation in discharging what was, legally and from the government's point of view, the most important single one of his duties: the delivery of subsidy bills. In 1407 Henry IV had conceded that financial grants, when once agreed by both Lords and Commons (but not until then), should be announced to him *par bouche de Purparlour de la dite Commune pur le temps esteant*—a provision intended by the Commons to leave the last word on such matters with them.[4] After 1407 it is not until Henry VI's reign that the parliament-rolls actually

[1] Ibid., 462–3.   [2] Ibid., vi. 8–9.   [3] Ibid., 278.
[4] Ibid., iii. 611.

state that it was the Speaker who communicated the grants of taxes: but from 1422 onwards they generally do so, and there is no reason to doubt that the concession of 1407 was always observed in this respect. What was allowed in 1407 had in fact been then described as already customary; indeed, as early as 1380 (in the Northampton parliament) it had been the Speaker who informed the King that the Lords and Commons had concurred in extending the current grant of the wool-subsidy from Martinmas 1381 to Christmas following.[1] Since grants were as a rule embodied in indentured schedules, their presentation by the Speaker would be largely a formal ceremony, except perhaps when a new type of subsidy was voted (there were a few such experiments in the first half of the fifteenth century) and an explanation proved necessary. This may sometimes have been the case with appropriations, although these were normally written into the subsidy bills themselves.

The Speaker's work did not always end with the dissolution of the parliament in which he had served. He was an obvious choice for inclusion in any committee set up to deal with business left over from a parliament, upon which representation of the Lower House was considered necessary or desirable. Sir John de Gildsburgh, Speaker in the January parliament of 1380, was one of the three knights of the shire appointed to be members of a commission of prelates, magnates and commoners authorized by the parliament to investigate the state of the King's Household and all the branches of the royal administration, especially from the point of view of income and expenditure.[2] No commoners were appointed to the great parliamentary commission set up to rule the country in 1386, and in any case we do not know who was Speaker in that parliament; but, when, in 1398, in order to have parliamentary sanction for his own arbitrary policy in certain of its aspects, Richard II himself adopted the device of a parliamentary commission, he added to a group of his closest supporters among the peers six knights of the shire with the Speaker, Bussy, at their head.[3] At the end of the parliament of 1406, during which Sir John Tiptoft, expressly as the Commons' Speaker, had appended his own personal seal of arms to the patents exemplifying two Acts regulating the royal succession,[4] he was the first-named of the twelve members of the Lower House assigned by the Commons to attend, along with a number of the Lords, the engrossment of the roll of the parliament.[5] Such procedures seem not to have been used

---

[1] *Rot. Parl.*, iii. 90.   [2] Ibid., 73.   [3] Ibid., 360b.
[4] Ibid., 574b, 582a.   [5] Ibid., 585a.

in later parliaments of the fifteenth century. And the only later medieval instance on record of the Speaker being employed in completing the business of a parliament after its dissolution was in 1467. On this occasion the Commons had entertained a complaint (of excessive charges for coining bullion) without having the time to examine it thoroughly, so that a commission of oyer and terminer was appointed at their request: they themselves nominated ten *persones of the Comen House*, chief of whom was Sir John Say, their Speaker, to join a group of lords, officials, and judges.[1]

Although the Speaker's primary function was to speak for the Commons in the Lords, some attempt must be made to discover when he assumed functions in the Lower House itself, particularly the rôle of chairman, exercising control over the Commons' own domestic proceedings. Since 1363 the Commons had had their own clerk (*subclericus parliamenti*), but even when once they had also acquired a Speaker there are still sufficient indications, especially in the occasional lack of efficiency in dealing with their own petitions and those originating elsewhere, that their business was not so well organized as to make a chairman's services redundant. It is, however, not until 1571, the date of John Hooker's *Order and Usage howe to keepe a Parliament*, that a proper description of the Speaker's duties in the Lower House itself becomes available.[2] By that time his office is described as being *to direct and guyde that house in good order and to see that ordinances, usages, and customs of the house to be firmely kept and observed*. More particularly, Hooker notes that the Speaker must keep a register of attendance, a requirement which recalls the statute of 1515 forbidding any member of the Commons to depart or absent himself during a session of parliament (on pain of loss of wages) unless he had the licence of the Speaker and the House, and providing for such licences to be recorded.[3] During debate, it is the Speaker's duty to decide which member shall speak, if more than one rise to do so. He must ensure that speeches are relevant, and he alone may remind a member *to come to his matter*. He is entitled to correct and, with the advice of the House, punish any member who misbehaves. If the liberties of the House are infringed by the arrest of a member, he is to see to the punishment of whoever is responsible, and he has the power to commit an offender against privilege into the custody of the Serjeant-at-arms or elsewhere. It is the Speaker's

---

[1] Ibid., v. 634a.
[2] B.M., Harleian MS. 1178, fol. 22 et seq.
[3] Stat. 6 Henry VIII, c. 16 (*Statutes of the Realm*, iii. 134).

place to ensure that a true record of the proceedings of the House is kept, and he is to provide for the custody of this journal as well as for the safe-keeping of bills. Unless the whole House makes special order just how and when bills are to be read, the choice is his. He must read the bills and may briefly explain them. (This function was elucidated in the formal ruling of the House in 1604 that *if any doubt arise upon a bill, the Speaker is to explain, but not sway the House with argument or dispute*.) After a second reading, the Speaker is responsible for ordering a bill to be engrossed; after another reading he is to put the question and, if a division is demanded, appoint the tellers. Should there then be a tie, he has a casting vote, but otherwise no vote at all. It is his duty to hold aloof from interfering in public and private affairs, and to keep himself to himself where parliamentary matters are concerned. These customary usages governing the Speaker's conduct, as set out by Hooker in the reign of Elizabeth I, are to some extent known to have been a developing tradition that may have stretched back over two centuries. Some of them can confidently be presumed to have developed in pre-Tudor times. But the Commons' own *Journals* do not begin until 1547, and it is therefore difficult to punctuate their emergence. It is sometimes hard to do so even roughly. To do so precisely is generally not possible.

It seems doubtful whether the Speakers were ever the mere exponents of the Commons' views in the Lords. It is clear from the narratives of the Commons' doings in 1376 supplied by *The Anonimalle Chronicle* of York and (to a lesser degree) by the St Albans chronicle that Sir Peter de la Mare was very active in shaping the views of the Commons during their deliberations in the Lower House itself. Indeed, it was because he had already emerged as their political leader that he was chosen Speaker. He makes his first appearance in the story of *The Anonimalle Chronicle* simply as a knight of the shire speaking from the lectern in the middle of the chapter-house of Westminster abbey, as a few others had already done before him, recapitulating the points they had made and adding his own counsel.[1] At that early stage in the session the Commons were without a Speaker, but if, after as before he had been chosen Speaker, De la Mare exercised some control over the Commons, there is nothing in *The Anonimalle Chronicle* to suggest that he did so in other than a political sense. There is nothing in the narrative to suggest that he acted as chairman in the Commons, controlling their procedure; and if De la Mare, the first continuing Speaker, did not act in this way, at

[1] *The Anonimalle Chronicle,* 82.

any rate no previous spokesman is at all likely to have done so. From evidence in the rolls of some of the early parliaments of Richard II's reign themselves, taciturn though they are, it seems, however, at least possible that the Speaker soon became something more than a channel of communication with the Upper House, that he had in fact already become involved in the conduct of the business of the Lower House in certain of its aspects.

If, as occasionally happened, the Commons were left in some doubt of the substance of their official agenda (their *charge*) as declared in the Chancellor's exposition of the causes for which parliament had been summoned, it was the Speaker who asked for it to be repeated or elucidated. Presumably, this was to help him to tell them accurately what the *charge* contained and perhaps to hold them to its consideration. When, at the beginning of the North-ampton parliament in November 1380, the Chancellor demanded a subsidy, and the Commons had deliberated for a day, it was the Speaker (Gildsburgh) who came back into the Upper House to ask for a clearer statement of what they had been told, especially regarding the minimum total sum needed.[1] In the next parliament of 1381, the first after the Peasants' Revolt, it was again the Speaker (Waldegrave) who, when parliament had been in proper session for over a week and the Archbishop of Canterbury's address had already been supplemented by a statement from the Treasurer, said that the Commons were *en partie de variance entre nous* touching the *charge*; to make for a better understanding, Waldegrave went on to ask for it to be repeated, with the result that a further statement, particularly emphasizing the question of the repeal of the letters of manumission granted by Richard II to the villeins during the recent insurrection, was supplied by Lord Scrope, the new Chancellor.[2] Now and then, even the Speaker himself might rehearse in the Lords the points made in the speech opening parliament. In September 1397, on the day of his presentation, Sir John Bussy prefaced the Commons' proposal for the annulment of the parliamentary commission of 1386 (*come chose fait traiterousement*) with an outline of the Chancellor's *pronunciatio*.[3] Again, in Henry IV's second parliament of 1401, Sir Arnald Savage, following his acceptance, clearly and in few words gave the gist of (*declara en substance*) the causes of summons as pro-pounded by Chief Justice Thirning, to help him remember the

---

[1] *Rot. Parl.*, iii. 89.   [2] Ibid., 100a.

[3] Ibid., 349a. For the Speaker to rehearse the Commons' *charge* may have been the normal procedure, though it is not often recorded.

speech (*pur avoir en memoire la pronunciation du Parlement*), after which he went on to ask that the Commons might have sufficient time to discuss important questions so that they did not have to give 'snap-answers' at the end of the parliament, which was what had some-times happened.[1] The Speaker's preoccupation with the Commons' *charge* on these occasions quite possibly suggests that his office had even then come to embrace a responsibility to control, from the outset of a parliament, the Commons' discussions of their official agenda. That as early as 1384 the Commons were being officially ordered to elect their Speaker promptly, so as not to hold up parlia-ment's business, does nothing to weaken the supposition. Further, when evidence appears for the Speaker's concern with the passage of bills through the Lower House, this suggests that his interest in the conduct of the Commons' business extended beyond that part of it which was imposed by the government.

By the end of the fourteenth century the Commons had for some time played a part in the preferment of petitions calling attention to public abuses which required remedy by statute. Although the Commons by no means monopolized the promotion of common petitions, statutes were in fact frequently based upon common petitions either formulated or adopted by them, and the theory that laws for which they did not themselves petition must receive their assent, was generally acknowledged in practice. In 1399 the special function of the Commons as *petitioners et demandours* was formally recognized.[2] And in 1414 the Commons themselves asserted a claim to be considered (where statute and law were concerned) *as well Assentirs as Peticioners*,[3] which was especially important in the case of bills originating in the Upper House either by the Lords' own motion or by governmental initiative. In the fourteenth century it was not at all uncommon for private petitions (*singuleres petitions*) to be promoted in the name of the Commons and then masquerade in the guise of public bills. (If promoted in this way, they would not only seem to be more important than they really were, but would also enjoy, as the Commons' own bills did, the advantage of delivery through the Clerk of the Parliaments to the King and Council, instead of passing, more circuitously, *via* the panels of receivers and triers.) Sharp practice of this sort was frowned upon, not least by the

---

[1] *Rot. Parl.*, iii. 455.

[2] Ibid., 427b. (This reference is not, of course, to the most telling part of the document.)

[3] Ibid., iv. 22b.

Commons themselves. Openly to canvass the Commons' support for private bills (frankly presented as such) was soon realized to be an equally valuable and not so dubious a method. Before the end of the fourteenth century private petitions were being actually addressed as well to the Commons as to the King and Lords; and a few petitions of this sort were even addressed, in the first instance, to the Commons alone. This last practice was soon followed with greater frequency under the Lancastrians. The consideration of bills, public and private together, occupied an ever greater part of the Commons' attention and time.[1]

How soon the Speaker came to exercise control over bills entertained by the Lower House cannot be precisely stated. It may be noticed that, when, in the parliament of January 1397, Richard II expressed himself offended by a bill already brought by the Commons to the Lords' notice (more particularly by its final article of complaint against excessive expenditure in the royal Household), it was the Speaker (Bussy) who was charged by the Duke of Lancaster to divulge the identity of its promoter, with the result that on the next day the bill itself was surrendered in the Upper House together with the name of Thomas Haxey, the Commons making full apology.[2] Haxey's bill had been considered at a meeting of Lords and Commons, presumably at a joint committee for the purpose of 'intercommuning'. But, because the Commons corporately asked the King's pardon for promoting the bill, this promotion had evidently been corporately undertaken. We could hardly infer from this incident, however, that the Speaker was already regarded as responsible for the discipline of the Commons. And it would be even less justifiable to infer that the Speaker was involved *ex officio* in regulating the Commons' entertainment of bills. None the less, since it was undoubtedly the Speaker's normal place to present petitions agreed by the Commons—witness, for example, how in 1406 Speaker Tiptoft *en noun des ditz Communes myst avaunt en parlement une peticione contenante diverses articles* (demanding the expulsion of aliens and a resumption of royal grants)[3]—it is hardly surprising that the Speaker soon came to be concerned with the Commons' own treatment of bills: his effective presentation of them in the Lords would to some

---

[1] A. R. Myers, 'Parliamentary Petitions in the Fifteenth Century', *EHR*, vol. lii, pp. 398-9; Doris Rayner, 'The Forms and Machinery of the "Commune Petition" in the Fourteenth Century', *EHR*, vol. lvi, pp. 213-15.

[2] *Rot. Parl.*, iii. 339.

[3] Ibid., 578b.

extent depend upon his being aware of the manner of their reception in the Lower House as well as upon his knowledge of their content and significance.

What evidence can be discovered to illustrate the medieval Speaker's connexion with the passage of bills through the Commons relates in the main to private petitions. A few such have survived from the fifteenth century which actually include the Speaker in the address. In either December 1420 or May 1421 the *pore liege men and soudeors in the town of Caleys*, complaining of arrears of pay for over five years amounting (if the debt to the Captain of Calais, the Earl of Warwick, be included) to £28,718 odd, directed their petition to *the worthy, wise, and discrete persons, Speaker of this present Parlement and to alle the Knyghtes of the shires*. They requested that it *like unto youre high discrecions to have recomaunded amonge alle youre other Peticions the aforeseid Town*, and (to conclude) that *youre gode and graciouse mediacion so to be preferred that the pore Soudeours may have, in partie of paiement, the somme that is received of the assignment last apointed be oure . . . soveraign lord, as far as hit wold strecche, and for the remenent that is due unto hem to ordeigne as best liketh to youre gode and graciouse Lordship*.[1] Another petition on the same subject in 1437, but this time presented as a personal bill by Humphrey, Duke of Gloucester, then Captain of Calais, was addressed *Unto the Speker and all the wise and discrete Comunes assembled in this present Parlement*. Referring to the Commons' deliberations over the partial appropriation of the wool-subsidy (up to £1 per sack) to the payment of the Calais garrison, the petition asked that, if this should be found insufficient, the Treasurer might have parliament's authority to make up the difference. Approved by the Commons, read in parliament two days before the dissolution, Gloucester's petition was agreed by the Lords and received the royal assent.[2] Both these petitions relating to the payment of the Calais garrison, though by strict definition private petitions, were petitions of public import. Since they had a direct bearing on the royal finances and were connected, clearly at least in the case of the second, with the Commons' appropriation of taxation, they perhaps ought to be regarded as evidence not so much for the Speaker's relation to private petitions in general, as for his relation to subsidy-bills in particular. This, however, was certainly not the case with the petition submitted in 1424 by Edward Lord Hastings and similarly addressed *To the worshipfull Speker and to all the Knyghtes and Communes of this*

[1] *Rot. Parl.*, iv. 159b.
[2] Ibid., 499a.

present parlement.[1] This was a private petition proper, as well in content as in form.

How useful and practically important the Speaker's influence on the passage of private bills through the Commons was likely to be, is confirmed by other evidence, not so meagre in amount and of more positive significance. When, in February 1454, Sir Thomas Charlton was elected Speaker in place of Thomas Thorpe, Abbot Wheat-hampstead of St Albans, with whom at this time Charlton was embroiled over his claim to the abbey's Hertfordshire manor of Burston, went so far as to state in his *Register* that Charlton had been advised by his counsel to get himself made Speaker, so as to be able, *vigore dicti officii, trahere ad se Communes ac ita suum promovere intentum juxta desiderium cordis sui* or, in other words, so that, *regimen domus inferioris in se suscipiens*, he might promote his own petition for parliamentary authority to be given to his recovery of the estate in question. Even though, as this account goes on to say, a warning letter from Lord Cromwell came along in sufficient time for the abbot to ensure the failure of Charlton's petition, clearly it was thought possible for a Speaker to exploit his office to the extent of expediting a bill and to stand at least a good chance of pushing it through the Commons. It is conceivable that Charlton's petition passed the Commons, only to fail elsewhere: the abbot's account of the business merely says that Charlton failed of his purpose in the end (*finaliter*).[2]

In appreciating the Speaker's influence on the promotion of private petitions, we need not rely solely on this evidence provided by the St Albans *Register* about Speaker Charlton. From the parliament-rolls themselves, and from a time long before as well as after Charlton's alleged pursuit of his own self-interest, come certain indications that the Speaker could take advantage of his office to assist himself and his friends. These indications are seldom more than pointers. Just how the Speaker acted is nowhere revealed by the record. But the occasions on which he had an immediate, personal interest in a petition sponsored by the Commons, are numerous enough to suggest that his office put him in a favourable position to steer private bills, and especially his own, through the Lower House.

In 1410 Thomas Chaucer evidently profited by his position as Speaker to secure the Commons' adoption of a petition preferred by

---

[1] P.R.O., Ancient Petitions, no. 9883.
[2] *Registrum Abbatiae Johannis Whethamsted*, ed. H. T. Riley (R.S.), vol. i, pp. 136-7.

him in his capacity as Chief Butler of England. After himself showing the Lords the adverse effects of certain admissions to the franchise of the City of London on the exercise of his official rights of prisage of wines, he asked the King and Council to send for the mayor and aldermen and the masters of the gilds and order them to confine the franchise to resident citizens and to repeal any acts of enfranchisement already made that were contrary to this restriction.[1] When again he was Speaker, in the second parliament of 1414, Chaucer once more took advantage of his office to get the Commons to accept and present a bill asking parliament on behalf of himself, his friend Lewis John, and John Snipston, to authorize Henry IV's executors to repay them for wines purveyed for the late King's Household. (Chaucer himself was owed £523 odd.) The petitioners pointed out that their Exchequer tallies had been rendered ineffective by the discharge of the particular customs-officials upon whose revenue the tallies were drawn and because of the inadequacy of this revenue itself, and that in any case the executors were unnecessarily demanding debentures under the seal of Henry IV's Treasurer of Household as proof of purveyance. Read in parliament, the bill was allowed on condition that non-payment was confirmed by the customs-officials' accounts. In the very same parliament the Commons presented, again successfully, another petition on their Speaker's behalf, a request that Henry V should, with the Lords' assent, confirm all charters and patents of John of Gaunt, Richard II, and Henry IV, by which Chaucer held offices, annuities or lands, and that the petition itself and the royal response should be enacted on the parliament-roll.[2] Whether, when, in the spring of 1421, Chaucer was Speaker for the fifth and last time, he had a personal interest in the bill by which the Commons secured the restoration of Thomas Montagu, Earl of Salisbury, to the inheritance forfeited for treason by the earl's father twenty years before, is a matter for mere speculation: it is not known for sure (although it is possible) that Chaucer's only child, Alice, had already married the earl as her second husband.[3]

There can be little doubt that, by utilizing his office for his own ends, Sir Thomas Waweton, Speaker in 1425, secured the successful presentation of a personal petition in the form of a bill from the Lower House—to be paid the half-yearly (Easter) instalment of his annuity of forty marks due out of income from the late Earl of March's manor of Ryhall (Rutland) but not disbursed by the royal

[1] Rot. Parl., iii. 646.   [2] Ibid., iv. 37, 39.
[3] Ibid., 141–2.

officials who had taken possession of the estate.[1] Waweton's hand
can perhaps also be seen behind the Commons' presentation, in the
same parliament, of the petition for livery of dower (parcel by
parcel, without waiting for a writ of general livery) made by Anne,
the Earl of March's widow: it was at the Commons' special request,
as well as by the advice of the Lords, that the petition was granted,
on condition that the countess made oath in Chancery not to re-marry
without royal licence. In this connexion, it is certainly worth noting
that on 7 March 1426 livery of the manor of Ryhall, from which the
Speaker was entitled to draw his own annuity, was given to the
countess as part of her dower.[2]

Another instance of the Speaker having a particular interest in a
petition made by the Commons occurs ten years later, in 1435, when
the Nottinghamshire lawyer, John Bowes, was in office. This
petition, which was recorded in the roll of the parliament, was put
forward on behalf of a neighbour of Bowes, Sir Thomas Rempstone,
a former chamberlain of the late Duke of Bedford who had been
taken prisoner by the French at the battle of Patay in June 1429. One
half of Rempstone's ransom (which totalled about £3,000) was to
be paid in cash, so the petition stated, and the rest commuted by
the release of one of the hostages of the Duke of Orleans (a French
esquire then, as surety for Orleans's debts, in the custody of the
executors of the late Thomas Beaufort, Duke of Exeter). The
exchange had been long delayed, and now, in 1435, the King was
being petitioned to allow Beaufort's executors (with parliamentary
authority) to deliver the hostage to Rempstone's mother and some
of his neighbours, so that the arrangements for his ransom and
exchange could be completed, the Earl of Suffolk and other of Rempstone's friends guaranteeing the executors' satisfaction. The petition
passed the Lords, and the King agreed. Speaker Bowes himself was
one of the guarantors. His connexion with the Rempstone family,
it is in any case clear from other evidence, was of the closest.[3] It
appears very likely that the Commons had adopted the petition at
their Speaker's soliciting.

[1] Ibid., v. 399b. Although this petition is described by the editors of the *Rotuli
Parliamentorum* as being *de incerto anno*, there can be no doubt that it belongs to
the parliament of 1425, when only one Exchequer term had elapsed since the
death of the Earl of March in January 1425.

[2] *Rot. Parl.*, iv. 285–6.

[3] Ibid., 488–9. For Bowes's connexion with the Rempstone family, see my
paper, 'John Bowes of Costock', in *Transactions of the Thoroton Society of Nottinghamshire*, vol. lx (1956), pp. 16–17.

It is perhaps worth noting that in the next parliament of 1437, when the Commons' as well as the Lords' assent was procured for a royal patent licensing Humphrey, Duke of Gloucester, and his wife to empark 200 acres and build towers at their manor of Greenwich, the Speaker was Sir John Tyrell, who had long been closely connected with the Duke.[1] If it was at all necessary to smooth the bill's passage through the Lower House, Tyrell is likely to have done what he could. Another petition presented in this same session by Gloucester, in his capacity as Captain of Calais, was even expressly addressed to the Speaker and Commons. This bill, however, did not happen to be read until after Tyrell had resigned the Speakership for reasons of ill-health.[2]

When, at Bury St Edmunds in 1447, the Northamptonshire lawyer, William Tresham, was acting as Speaker for the third time, it seems that he was able to use special influence to promote a petition, addressed in the first instance to the Commons and presented by them to the King, on behalf of himself and his fellow-executors of the will of John Brokley, late alderman of London. The testator's widow and executrix, who was now re-married, had received some £8,000 from her former husband's estate but, it was alleged, had done little for his soul, and so the other executors were requesting that she and her present husband should be summoned before the Chancellor, who would then use his discretion.[3] The petition succeeded. In the next parliament but one, the parliament of 1449-50, Tresham's fourth term as Speaker 'paid off' rather more directly. Certainly, he all but completely escaped the Act of Resumption passed at Leicester in the parliament's third and last session. In the course of this session, a petition was submitted by a group of prominent esquires of the royal Household, of whom Tresham himself was one, claiming a general exemption from the Act (except for some specified items of income from royal sources which the petitioners were evidently resigned to losing). The outcome was a proviso to the Act which exempted *inter alia* all of Tresham's fees, annuities and offices, saving a single annuity of £20.[4] The Speaker also used his influence to secure for the collegiate church of St Mary at Leicester a proviso continuing its grant of a tun of wine from the

---

[1] *Rot. Parl.*, iv. 498-9.   [2] See above, p. 88.

[3] *Rot. Parl.*, v. 129. One of Tresham's co-executors, Thomas Burgoyne, a lawyer and the under-sheriff of London, was sitting for Bridgwater in this parliament.

[4] Ibid., 189a.

royal prisage at Hull: the college's request for exemption is actually subscribed *per Willelmum Tresham*, his being the only commoner's name appearing on any of these petitions submitted to the Lords for their consideration and later approved by the King.[1]

The alleged exertions made by Sir Thomas Charlton in 1454 to secure the Speakership and avail himself of its opportunities for promoting his own interests, have already been noted. The Speaker in the ensuing parliament (1455–6), Sir John Wenlock, also seems to have done his best to exploit his position. During the third and last of its sessions two Acts were passed confirming an arrangement to repay the merchants of the Calais Staple their advances of cash, for the defence of the town, out of the customs and subsidies. It was, however, agreed that this proposal should not prejudice the repayment, from the Southampton customs, of a loan of 1,550 marks made by Wenlock to the Crown sometime before the end of 1449, the whole of which was so far unpaid. It was further allowed that Wenlock should now receive preferential treatment. Moreover, in the Resumption Act passed during this same session, one of the Commons' own provisos safeguarded these arrangements on their Speaker's behalf. Incidentally, the Lancastrian government's later attitude to the business, for Wenlock was still unsatisfied even three years later, may well have been one factor eventually disposing him to transfer his support to the Yorkists.[2]

The opening and only proper session of Edward IV's first parliament in 1461 proved far more satisfactory to the Commons' Speaker on that occasion, Sir James Strangeways, and for more reasons than one. He certainly derived some advantage from the Commons' adoption as their own of a private, family petition addressed to the King by the Speaker himself, his son Richard, his late wife's sister, and her husband, Sir John Conyers.[3] A problem had arisen over certain Irish estates of Lady Strangeways' family (the Darcys) leased to one Sir Thomas Bathe, who had forfeited these and other lands of his own in accordance with a judgement made by the King's late father (Richard, Duke of York) in a parliament held at Drogheda in February 1460. The petitioners represented that the leaseholds were

[1] Chancery, Parliament and Council, P.R.O., C 49/58/11. (I am indebted to Dr B. P. Wolffe for this reference.)

[2] *Rot. Parl.*, v. 300b, 302b. For further particulars, see my article on Wenlock in *The Publications of the Bedfordshire Historical Record Society*, vol. xxxviii (1958), p. 32.

[3] *Rot. Parl.*, v. 485. Speaker Strangeways' first wife, Elizabeth Darcy, had died some time between June 1459 and the beginning of this parliament of 1461.

not rightfully forfeit, since the lease had provided for their re-entry if the rent fell into arrears, which had indeed been the case when the forfeiture was imposed. The petition went on to state that unfortunately Sir James Strangeways and Conyers had been then *driven to such streitnesse* because of their service to the new King, his father, and other *true Lordes of his blode*, as to be unable to take proper action and see to their interests in Ireland; and so it was now requested that parliamentary authority be given for the petitioners to re-enter their property and recover the mesne issues, and for Strangeways senior, the Speaker himself, to enter that share of the estates which was his *by the curtesie*. The petition was granted.

That, in these instances of a Speaker presenting a petition of his own or for friends, he was taking advantage of an office giving him peculiar opportunities, seems the more likely if it is noted that none of the Speakers in question (so far as is known) presented such a petition at any other time.

That the Speaker could bring his official influence to bear upon the passage of private bills and could use it to do himself some service is further illustrated by one or two incidents which occurred during the long, multi-sessioned parliament of 1472–5, when the lawyer William Allington was Speaker for the first time. During the opening session, in the autumn of 1472, two Acts were passed relating to the royal heir-apparent: the first ratified his titles of Prince of Wales and Earl of Chester; the second confirmed his endowment with the Duchy of Cornwall. It was in this latter Act that the Speaker had a particular interest, for one of its provisos safeguarded any grant or office already held by him in the Duchy.[1] Allington was, however, only one of several beneficiaries, and the proviso was in any case probably so nearly 'common form' as hardly to require any special influence at all on his part. But that Allington was able, and did not scruple, to exert pressure on the passage of private bills when they happened to involve his own interest is made perfectly clear in a remarkable account of a quite different case which came up much later in the same parliament. On 12 March 1475, two days before the end of its seventh and final session, an indenture was drawn up between William Hussey of Sleaford, the King's Attorney-General, and Thomas Daniel, a former Esquire of the Body to Henry VI, who had taken part against Edward IV at the battle of Towton and so had incurred forfeiture by Act of Attainder in the first Yorkist parliament of 1461. Some time during the parliament of 1472–5, but before

[1] *Rot. Parl.*, vi. 16a.

the summer session of 1474, Daniel and Hussey had agreed that if Hussey secured the annulment of Daniel's attainder (and a royal grant to him of certain manors in Ireland), he himself should within a month be given an annuity of 10 marks from Daniel's manor of Burton Pedwardine (near Sleaford). On 6 June 1474 (the first day of parliament's sixth session) Daniel's petition for the reversal of his attainder had been exhibited and allowed. (Earlier sessions of this parliament had witnessed similar annulments, and the political climate was therefore generally favourable.) But it had been necessary to 'square' the Speaker not to oppose the bill: in the indenture itself the Attorney-General represented that he had only performed his promise, to have the attainder revoked, after interceding with Speaker Allington, this being necessary because the Speaker was incensed with Daniel for having once been the cause of his father's imprisonment in one of the London gaols. Finally, to complete the story, in March 1475, on the eve of parliament's dissolution, for £8 paid by Hussey to Daniel and in consideration of another bill, endorsed by the King, granting two more manors in Ireland to Daniel, the latter released to the Attorney-General all his title in Burton Pedwardine, binding himself in a bond of £500. The whole covenant (chicanery and all) was enrolled on the Close Rolls of the royal Chancery itself.[1]

John Hooker's treatise of 1571 states that the Speaker was entitled to an established fee of £5 for every private bill passed by both Houses and enacted. William Lambarde's tract of about 1587 says that this fee was due for such a bill even before its first reading, but confirms the amount. On the basis of this recognized tariff, Sir John Neale is able to estimate that the Speaker in a later Elizabethan parliament might receive between two and three hundred pounds for his handling of private bills alone.[2] But he might also receive additional payments in consideration of favours shown, or even hoped for, and from London such gifts were already quite usual and tending to rise in value.[3]

That in the medieval period the Speaker's power over private bills amounted to life or death as (on Neale's authority) we may say was the case under Elizabeth I, cannot be asserted. None the less, there is clear evidence from the second half of the fifteenth century that the Speaker's goodwill towards private bills needed to be rewarded, and at least sometimes even to be purchased in advance. In 1454 a pipe

---

[1] CCR, 1468–76, 411–12.
[2] J. E. Neale, *The Elizabethan House of Commons*, pp. 335–8.   [3] Ibid., 337n.

of red and two barrels of sweet wine came the Speaker's way as a
reward from the City of London. In 1472 the Court of Aldermen
granted £7 to one of the City M.P.s, £5 of which was to go to the
Speaker, leaving no more than £2 to be spent at the member's discretion entertaining any others for their favour. The Brodhull of the
Cinque Ports allowed their representatives in Edward IV's last
parliament (1483) fourteen shillings for a present of fish to the
Speaker (only a shilling less than they voted for a similar gift to the
Lord Warden of the Ports).[1] In 1487, when, unsuccessfully in the
event, the London Pewterers' Company presented a petition for
parliamentary authority to be given for the suppression of hawkers
and pedlars, one item of expenditure for promoting the bill which
appeared in the Company's accounts was for the purchase of *a gar-
nysshe large vessell newe fascioned Counterfeit* worth 27s. 4d. for *Maister
Speker of the parliament*. The cost of this gift compares very favourably with the 6s. 8d. which the Pewterers paid in this same year to
the Clerk of the Parliaments *to spede our billes to be redde*.[2] On his
election as Speaker in 1489 Sir Thomas FitzWilliam was voted ten
marks by the Chamber of the City of London. FitzWilliam was,
however, perhaps a special case, for he was the City's own Recorder
at this time.[3] On the other hand, although Sir Robert Sheffield,
FitzWilliam's successor in the Recordership, resigned a few years
before he became Speaker in 1512, the pension he still enjoyed as
ex-Recorder was then increased from 3 to 5 marks, *to thentent that he
shall shew his lawful favor and counsell in the maters of this Citie*; and,
moreover, the Court of Aldermen later voted him a special reward
of £5 for his services in parliament, *pro certis causis Civitatis expediendis*.[4] Mainly restricted to London and few though they are, these
notices of payments and gifts to the Speaker suggest that already his
services in expediting the passage of bills were a matter for serious
calculation on the part of civic, corporate and (we can hardly doubt)
private petitioners.

That this was so need cause no surprise if we accept the estimate
of the Speaker's authority among the Commons succinctly made in
the sermon which the Chancellor, Bishop Russell of Lincoln, prepared in 1483 for Edward V's first parliament (which, of course,

---

[1] I am indebted to Mr Keith Houghton for these pieces of information.

[2] A. R. Myers, 'Some Observations on the Procedure of the Commons in
dealing with Bills in the Lancastrian Period', *The University of Toronto Law
Journal*, vol. iii, p. 66.   [3] J. C. Wedgwood, *Biographies*, 337.

[4] Ibid., 760. Sheffield was Recorder of London from 1495 to 1508.

never sat). Comparing the English constitution with that of ancient Rome, the bishop stated in his discourse that *the peuple* [of Rome] . . . *obteigned a specyalle magistrate called* tribunus plebis *to be ther president in ther consultacions, lyke as yn the senate the one of the consuls proposed and diffined alle that was amonges them* . . .; and, he went on to say, *lyke as in this house* [the Lords] *one* tanquam consul *makithe the questions, soo yn the lower house in like wyse alle ys directed by the speker* quasi per tribunum.[1] By this time at the very latest, the Speaker was evidently discharging functions that were at least analogous to those of a chairman. And evidence is soon forthcoming to confirm this conclusion: the report of the Colchester burgesses on their return home from the first of Henry VII's parliaments in 1485 describes how, at the election of Sir Thomas Lovell, *it pleased the Knyghts that were there present for to ryse from ther sets and so for to goo to that place where as the Speker stode and set him in his sete.*[2] Surely this 'seat' can have been none other than the Speaker's Chair.

For want of even the most formal journal of the Commons' doings in the fifteenth century, it is not possible to say just how the Speaker's direction of the Commons had come to be translated into terms of procedure. But from his obvious antecedent connexion with petitions presented to the Commons, it may fairly be assumed that for some time he had handled the passage of bills generally through the House. How often the Commons were likely to divide over bills, we do not know. There is, however, no question that before the end of the fifteenth century they had at least accepted the principle of a majority vote, for they applied it in electing the Speaker himself in 1420, and in 1475 Justice Littleton (in a purely legal discussion) stated that if a bill were agreed by *le greindre party des Chivallers des counties* . . . *al feasans d'un acte du Parliament,* this would make it a statute even if *le meindre party ne voille my agreer a cel act.*[3] We know

---

[1] Cited by S. B. Chrimes, op. cit., p. 174.

[2] *The Red Paper Book of Colchester,* ed. Sir W. Gurney Benham, p. 62. The first use of the word 'Chair' in a formal record is in the Commons' own *Journals.* It is made there on the earliest possible occasion, that is, in the first reference to the election of a Speaker appearing in the *Journals:* when, in March 1553 (at the beginning of the last parliamentary session of Edward VI's reign), Serjeant Dyer had been nominated by the Treasurer of the Household and chosen by the Commons, he was promptly (before being presented to the King) 'set in the Chair'. And we are also told that the third of the Speakers of Mary's reign, Sir Clement Higham, was (again as soon as elected) 'brought to the Chair by Mr Treasurer and Mr Controller' (*The Commons Journals,* vol. i, pp. 24a, 37a).

[3] S. B. Chrimes, op. cit., p. 373.

that, when petitions were considered by the Lower House of Convocation, it was already usual by 1433 for the *prolocutor* of the clergy to test their feeling by taking a count of votes (*facto . . . vocum scrutinio per circuitum, ut est moris*).[1] In what fashion a division in the Lower House of parliament was conducted in pre-Tudor times cannot be stated. According to the Commons' *Journals*, when they begin under Edward VI, divisions were still, however, very unusual.

Some consideration has been given to the medieval Speaker's influence over the Commons' own business, including their treatment of bills introduced by private petitioners. An attempt must now be made to face the problem posed by the following questions: how useful did the Speaker make himself to the government? how far in practice did he promote the King's business and act as his agent among the Commons? to what extent did he act as a go-between for the King as well as the Commons? In considering this problem we cannot afford to discuss again the question of the Commons' freedom in electing their Speaker. But that question and the question of the government's employment of the Speaker as agent in the Lower House, although not identical, are surely related: if the Commons ever had their Speaker foisted on them by the King, it must have been in order that he should attempt to manage them in the royal interest. What has been said on the subject of the Commons' election of their Speaker must therefore be borne in mind.

In examining the question of the Speaker's usefulness to the government, we must also bear in mind that, ideally, a parliament was a demonstration of a community of interests between the government and the governed. Henry IV himself put this point into words when, approving the Speaker's protestation in 1410, he stated that all the estates of the parliament were there to consult the common weal, his own and the kingdom's advantage, and to achieve unity and union with one assent and accord, so that on this occasion, as he hoped, the Commons would not wish to attempt or express anything that was not honourable, but rather would wish to nourish love and concord between all parties.[2] Whether relations between King and Commons were good or bad—and there were clearly many times when there was at least tension between them—the Speaker's part was potentially important.

To ensure that the Commons tackled their official agenda promptly would seem to have become one of the Speaker's obligatory func-

---

[1] *Annales Monasterii Sti Albani*, ed. H. T. Riley (R.S), i. 359.
[2] *Rot. Parl.*, iii. 623a.

tions very early in the history of his office. Gildsburgh's concern
with the financial demands of the Crown at the very outset of the
Northampton parliament of 1380 suggests this. The Chancellor's
order to the Commons at the beginning of the Salisbury parliament
of 1384, to take advantage of a temporary adjournment by electing
their Speaker, makes it clearer still. On this occasion, the Chancellor
urgently expressed to all present the Council's need for advice about
negotiating peace with France or, alternatively, about providing for
defence, and said that these matters must be considered immediately,
*entrelessantz de tout chescune autre foreine matire en le moien temps, qar par
foreins matires quelles n'ont de riens profitez au bien de Commune, ont
delaiez les Parlementz devaunt ceste heure moelt oultrageousement.*[1] This
warning to expedite the King's *charge* and eschew diversions was not
given to the Commons alone; but it certainly affected them, and
perhaps them particularly. It was an old complaint of the King's
administration that parliaments were only too ready to discuss grievances and private suits to the neglect or detriment of official business; and sundry devices had been adopted in the past to ensure
adherence to the proper order of parliamentary action, to secure
respect for that *regimen parliamenti* which (as Richard II elicited from
his judges at Nottingham in 1387) was his to determine as a matter
of indisputable, prerogative right. That a Speaker elected for the
duration of parliament could do much to hold the Commons to an
order of business officially laid down is not likely to have escaped
the notice of the government for very long; indeed, the Speaker's
potential usefulness as a manager of the Commons' deliberations,
and not simply his significance as one who transmitted their outcome, seems to have been appreciated quite early in official circles.
Perhaps the 'continuing Speaker' appeared to be an advantage to
both sides, King and Commons alike.

There can be no doubt at all that Richard II found Speaker Bussy
an extremely valuable agent among the Commons, especially in
his last parliament of 1397–8. Richard's achievement in securing a
complaisant Lower House (matching his success in constructing a
party among the Lords) owed much to Bussy's influence over the
Commons. Bussy's Speakership was, in fact, characterized on this
occasion by a remarkable servility on his own and the Commons'
part.[2] That we can discern so much of the personal domination

[1] Ibid., 166–7.
[2] See my biography of Bussy in *Lincolnshire Architectural and Archaeological
Society, Reports and Papers*, vol. vii, part 1 (1957), especially pp. 38–41.

exercised by their Speaker over the Lower House in Richard II's last parliament is largely owing to the bitter account of it given by Thomas Walsingham of St Albans. When, and if so with what effect, Bussy's successors acted as royal agents, we are unfortunately nothing like so well-informed. In the parliaments of Henry IV there was an inevitable reaction against the political subservience of Richard II's later years, a reaction which was evidently very strong in the Commons. This was a time in which the King's difficulties, beset as he was for so long with rebellions and unrest, provided the Commons with opportunities to re-assert their proper and independent influence on affairs of State, some of which opportunities, certainly, they did not neglect. And that more than one of the early Lancastrian Speakers was required by the Commons to play an important part in their recovery of a more significant rôle in parliamentary affairs, can be just as confidently stated, however close occasionally may have been the personal association of the Speaker with the King and his administration. If, during Henry's reign, the Speaker acted as a channel for royal directives, it is likely that he did so only very discreetly and when it was agreeable to the Commons.

In the first half of Henry IV's reign (down to 1406) the Commons' elections to the Speakership were invariably of men acceptable to the King on personal grounds, sympathetic to his difficulties, and likely to have inside knowledge of his policies: three of the five who filled the office in the six parliaments meeting in these years were actually members of his Council. And yet the relatively copious information we possess concerning these parliaments does nothing to suggest that the Speakers in question were able to take the King's part and intervene effectively in the Lower House on his behalf. Indeed, there were times when the Speaker was clearly at one with his colleagues in their expression of views which the King can only have found a source of discomfort and irritation, and when the Speaker himself found it necessary to rely on the protection given him by his protestation. The atmosphere in the Commons in 1401, when Savage first was Speaker, was very uneasy: it was then that Savage won much esteem for suggesting with all the power of his eloquence that an end be put to excessive taxation;[1] and the Commons' own awareness of the King's dissatisfaction with their conduct was such that, on the last day, they asked his pardon in case they had offended him. In the next parliament, in 1402, the Commons had a

[1] See my paper, 'Sir Arnald Savage of Bobbing', in *Archaeologia Cantiana*, vol. lxx (1956), p. 77.

brush with the King over a matter of procedure, in which Speaker
Retford's influence might have been expected to serve the King's
interest: when the Commons requested an 'intercommuning' committee from the Lords, their demand was allowed, but only after the
King had made a protest (communicated by a deputation which
included his Steward of the Household and Secretary) that such a
committee for 'intercommuning' between the two Houses was conceded as of grace, which shows how suspiciously the King regarded
this device and its possible use on this occasion.[1] Savage's rôle as
Speaker in the violent attack on the extravagance of the royal
Household during the Westminster parliament of 1404 was such as
to suggest one of two things, or perhaps both: that there was nothing
to prevent a royal councillor (which Savage then was) from offering
criticism when a member of the Commons, or that the Commons'
Speaker could act in that capacity only as the Commons required
or permitted.[2] The next parliament which met in the following
autumn at Coventry, where Sir William Sturmy was Speaker, was
just as turbulent. This, however, was because of an attack made by
the parliamentary knights on the possessions of the Church, and,
although the King can have derived no satisfaction from the resulting quarrel, he himself secured from the parliament what was to
prove the largest financial grant of his reign. The parliament of 1406,
which met on 1 March 1406 and continued (with two adjournments)
to within three days of Christmas, lasted so long mainly because of
the Commons' resistance to the royal demand for taxation. That Sir
John Tiptoft, a Knight of the King's Chamber and the Speaker in
this parliament, did not neglect his duty to the King is very likely.
But his frequent apologies and resort to his protestation when confronting the Upper House suggest that he hardly played much of a
rôle as a royal agent in the Lower House.[3]

In the parliaments of the second half of Henry IV's reign—those
of 1407, 1410 and 1411—it was Thomas Chaucer who was always
Speaker. If he acted as agent for anybody in the Commons—and
there is no doubt that he was acceptable to his cousins, the Beauforts,
and to their political ally, the royal heir-apparent, Henry of Monmouth—it was certainly not on behalf of the King who, at the beginning of Chaucer's last Speakership of his reign, testily objected to

---

[1] *Rot. Parl.*, iii. 486b. (The reason for Henry's acting as he did is unknown.)
[2] *Archaeologia Cantiana*, op. cit., vol. lxx, p. 80.
[3] It is of course possible that the clerk recorded Tiptoft's protestations more
fully than was usually done.

his *novelleries*. If the Speaker was ever something of a marionette, most of the evidence relating to early Lancastrian parliaments goes to show that, however sympathetic may have been his own personal attitude to the King, it was the Commons who pulled the strings controlling his movements in parliament.

Presumably the Speaker would have some difficulty in acting as a royal agent among the Commons if relations between them and the King happened to be strained. This was almost generally the case under the first Lancastrian King. When relations between the Lower House and the government were easier, there was doubtless more room and opportunity for the Speaker to act openly and successfully on the King's behalf. There was some irritation evidently felt by the Commons at certain royal actions in Henry V's first parliament.[1] During the rest of his reign, however, this single-minded, energetic and fortunate ruler learned how to play on the Commons' sympathies, and there was never anything approaching a crisis between him and them. All the Speakers under Henry V were men acceptable to him and, because of the Commons' confidence, were probably able to act as much as his agent with them as theirs with him (or, during his absences abroad, with his Lieutenant).

During the minority of Henry VI there was no shortage of unrest, and parliament was often the scene of it. The main causes of political tension were the personal ambition and policy of the Protector, Humphrey, Duke of Gloucester, against which most of his fellow-members of the Council, led by Bishop Beaufort of Winchester, closed their ranks and secured the support of a majority in the Lords: the competing parties were generally of unequal strength. Since many of the knights of the shire were the retainers of the most influential of the lords of the Council, the Commons were not at all apathetic to the struggle for power; but, partly for the same reason, their relations with the Council as a whole were usually cordial. This circumstance may none the less have owed something to the small demand for direct taxation made by the Council during the earliest years of Henry VI, and to the fact that even when, in 1429, the exaction of tenths and fifteenths was resumed, this did not become excessive. (The burden of direct taxation, always a possible cause of trouble with the Commons, was not allowed to become half so heavy under Henry VI as it had been under Henry V.) Generally speaking, the Commons were ready to fall into line behind the government of the day. The Speakers of the period of Henry VI's minority were

[1] See above, pp. 52, 56.

frequently men personally attached to one or more of the members of the Council, although variable in their political complexion; and it seems likely that, as probably had already been the case under Henry V, they were often able to act as government agents in the Lower House. As we shall see, there is proof that this was so on at least one occasion.[1]

If the growth of local faction and disorder in England did not itself make clear the general ineffectiveness of the royal administration under Henry VI, the failure of the long struggle to retain Henry V's territorial conquests in France brought it home at last. Here Lancastrian diplomacy had proved as unfortunate as the declining military effort. By 1450 the Court party was utterly discredited. Soon the dynasty itself was threatened. Faction deteriorated into civil war, spasmodic in its occurrence, but eventually, in 1461, resulting in the displacement of the House of Lancaster by the House of York. If sometimes driven underground, the possibility of armed commotion remained alive under the Yorkists and, when Henry VII ousted Richard III, under him as well. In these circumstances, in the second half of the fifteenth century parliament had to some extent degenerated into a machine for registering the very triumphs of faction. And it sometimes provided opportunity for trials of the political strength of the parties. On these occasions, control of the Commons was at least an important consideration. Their manipulation by the Speaker was one approach to the problem. In the last decade of Lancastrian rule, the Speaker had been a supporter of one of the contending parties, more usually that of the Court. After 1461 he was almost automatically a Crown employee, a servant of the King. Precisely how the Speaker operated as an agent of the government and regulated its business in the Lower House is still largely hidden from us, but the evidence that he did so becomes more positive and distinct than ever before. Not only did the Commons now become generally much more amenable than they had sometimes previously been. It was under Edward IV that the Speaker first came to be paid by the Crown, with a fair regularity, a proper, substantial cash-reward, assessed in round figures, just for his services as Speaker.

[1] In 1435. See below, p. 108.

H

CHAPTER 5

The Speaker's Rewards

T O occupy the Speakership was in some sense a reward in itself.
The office certainly dignified its holder. This may be gathered
from the notice given to the Speaker in the *Book of Nurture* composed
about the middle of the fifteenth century by John Russell, sometime
uschere in chambur and *mershalle also in halle* to Humphrey, Duke of
Gloucester (as Russell described himself). The treatise gives a precedence list of all estates *after theire degre*, showing carefully *in what
place aftur theire dignitye how they owght to sytte* at table in hall. In this
list *the Spekere of the parlement* is said to be entitled to sit side by side
with no less than barons, mitred abbots, *the iij chef Justicez* and the
Mayor of London, and the author goes on to say that *alle these
Estates are gret and honorable*.[1] The *Boke of Kervynge* printed in 1513 by
Caxton's former apprentice, Wynkyn de Worde, follows and confirms Russell's placing of the Speaker in its order of precedence.[2] No
later than the beginning of Edward IV's reign the Speaker's official
dignity was both magnified and safeguarded by the appointment of
a royal serjeant-at-arms who, *chosen by the Commons of England . . . to
entend to the same Commens in tyme of every Parlement*, was more particularly required to wait upon their Speaker.[3] By that time, how-

---

[1] *Early English Text Society*, vol. 32, 188. (The date of the book is not known,
but it was probably written within a decade or so, either way, of the middle of
the fifteenth century.)

[2] Ibid., 285.

[3] That particular one of the King's serjeants-at-arms *chosen by the Commons of
England aforetymes to entend to the same Commens in tyme of every Parlement* is first
mentioned only in 1467 when, being so described, John Bury was exempted
from the Act of Resumption of that year (*Rot. Parl.*, v. 574b). But the patent of
29 July 1471 by which his successor, Maurice Gethyn, was granted for life the
office of King's serjeant-at-arms with the special duty of attending upon the
Speaker, states that his fee of a shilling a day and livery of the suit of an esquire
of the Household were to be as John Bury lately had them (*CPR, 1467–77*, 265),
and the patent by which John Bury first received this fee and livery is dated
16 July 1461 (ibid., *1461–7*, 125). On 10 October 1471 the office (with its special
duty) was given to Richard Siddale (ibid., *1467–77*, 281). On 20 July 1474 a
grant of it was made to Nicholas Brytte as from the time of Siddale's appointment (ibid., 452), and on 28 December 1483 Brytte was confirmed in the office
for life, by Richard III, as from Michaelmas 1483 (ibid., *1476–85*, 413). Brytte's

ever, there were much more tangible rewards attached to the Speaker's office than a temporary enhancement of his personal dignity. And these were then more than personal presents received by him from parties seeking preference for their private petitions.

That the Commons had enough confidence in one of their number to choose him to act as their intermediary with the Upper House and to conduct their own domestic business, was in itself a potentially valuable testimonial. Most Speakers had already made something of a reputation for themselves before their election. But by being singled out in this special way, if only for a short space, a man was generally given a chance to better himself. A few Speakers seem not to have been able to make much use of it. Occasionally, their career had passed its zenith, and it was too late to exploit the opportunity. It might, however, appear that a fair number of the Speakers used the office as a stepping-stone to greater things. But in the case of at least some, especially those whose career was already well founded, their term of office as Speaker need not necessarily be regarded as more than an incident with no very significant bearing on their future prospects.

Certainly, we should guard against attributing, automatically, a Speaker's later appointment to an office of State or Household, or other position of importance in the royal administration, to his having gone up in the King's estimation simply because of political services rendered as Speaker. How much more should we take care not to interpret any such promotion as a mere reward for his tenure of the Chair. If advancement or a profitable grant came a Speaker's way at the time of his Speakership or very shortly afterwards, there might seem to be some ground for connecting them with it. But even then, unless his prolocutorial services were specifically mentioned,

---

appointment evidently ended with Richard III's death; and the office, now described as that of 'the sergeant-at-arms of the noble mansion of parliament', was granted for life on 28 September 1485 by Henry VII to John Harper, yeoman and 'harbeger' of the Household, in recognition of services to the King in Brittany and France and 'at the victorious field' (of Bosworth) (ibid., *1485-94*, 6). Harper was exempted from the Resumption Act of 1485 in two of its provisos: in the one he is described as serjeant-at-arms *chosen by the Comons of England to entend to the same Comons in tyme of every Parlement*, in the other, as *specially attending upon the Speker of oure Parlement* (Rot. Parl., vi. 339a, 344a). In his renewed grant of the same office on 7 March 1489 he is referred to as 'one of the King's serjeants-at-arms, specially attendant upon the King out of time of parliament, and during the time of parliament upon the Speaker elected by the Commons in each parliament' (CPR, *1485-94*, 260-1).

we could never be sure that he did not come by this preferment for some other, external reason. Sir Richard de Waldegrave, within eight months of being Speaker in the parliament of 1381-2 was steward of the estates of Richard II's young Queen, Anne of Bohemia;[1] it would, however, be risky to assume that this office was a reward for his work in the Commons, especially because, as one of 'the King's knights' since 1377, he was already qualified to fill it. Sir John Bussy, after being Speaker in the January parliament of 1397, had his royal annuity of 40 marks raised by half to £40 and, when Speaker again during the September session of the same year, commuted this enlarged annuity at first for a life-tenancy free of rent, and then (a day later) for a grant in tail-male, of three Suffolk manors recently forfeited by one of Richard II's attainted enemies, simultaneously receiving other sequestrated lands and property;[2] any or all of these acquisitions might have come his way as a firm supporter of the King's policy and member of his Council. John Doreward, Speaker in Henry IV's first parliament, five days before its dissolution was granted an Exchequer lease of the alien priory of West Mersea (Essex), and three weeks after the dissolution of parliament he received as an annuity the whole of the fee-farm of Colchester (worth £35);[3] but these were concessions he could reasonably have expected to acquire as a member of the King's Council, to which he had already been appointed before the parliament ended. Only three days after the dissolution of the parliament of 1401 in which Sir Arnald Savage first was Speaker, the annuity of £50 granted him by Richard II in 1396 was renewed (although not increased);[4] but Savage was already a member of the council of the young Prince of Wales and as such quite entitled to the fee. After Savage's next term as Speaker, three years later, there is nothing to show that his services were officially appreciated (which, in view of the rôle he had played in the parliament, is hardly surprising); indeed, the annuities Savage enjoyed as a member of the King's Council were already running into arrears. A fortnight before the end of the third and final session of the parliament of 1406, the then Speaker, Sir John Tiptoft, was nominated Treasurer of the Household. His conduct as Speaker during this difficult parliament may well have been quite exemplary from Henry IV's standpoint; but, as a Knight of the King's Chamber, Tiptoft was already qualified for this Household post,

[1] *CFR, 1377-83*, 330.   [2] *CPR, 1396-9*, 84, 198, 217, 253, 277, 289.
[3] *CFR, 1399-1405*, 28; *CPR, 1399-1401*, 154.
[4] *CPR, 1399-1401*, 444.

which in any event was far too important to be given as a reward for
a Speaker's services merely. In fact, the appointment was part of the
newly constituted Council's plan to reform the King's Household.
The grant which Tiptoft received on the same day as his Household
appointment—£150 and the forfeited estates of Rees ap Griffith (an
adherent of Owen Glendower) in Carmarthenshire, Cardiganshire
and elsewhere in south Wales, together with the royal forests of
Waybridge and Sapley (Huntingdonshire)—was obviously made to
support his new office and not in respect of his Speakership.[1] Thomas
Chaucer's resumption of his office as Chief Butler on the day after
the dissolution of the next parliament, the Gloucester parliament of
1407,[2] was similarly a political manœuvre which could have had
little, if anything at all, to do with his recent service as Speaker in
that session. So, in all probability, was Roger Flore's appointment
as Chief Steward of the Duchy of Lancaster lands north of Trent
less than a fortnight after his first Speakership ended in November
1416,[3] for he was already in Henry V's confidence as a trustee in the
estates with which the King had recently endowed his Bridgettine
nunnery at Syon. Flore's successor in the Duchy Chief Stewardship,
John Tyrell, was appointed in December 1427, two days after the
end of the earlier of the two sessions of the parliament of 1427–8 in
which he acted as Speaker for the first time.[4] With at least another
session still to run, this promotion of Tyrell's was hardly a reward
for his parliamentary services, and the timing of it was doubtless
conditioned solely by the vacancy in the office brought about by
Flore's death a month or so before. On the last day of the next
parliament but one (1431), in which Tyrell again acted as Speaker,
an Exchequer payment of £100 in his favour was warranted by the
Council; but this was expressly an advance of fees to which Tyrell
was entitled as one of the councillors accompanying Henry VI on his
visit to France.[5] The lawyer, John Russell, Speaker (for the second
time) in the next parliament of 1432, seemingly got nothing for
himself out of his tenure of office. His successor in 1433, Roger
Hunt, another lawyer, did no better: in fact, towards the middle of
the second session (on 5 November), he was made sheriff of Cambridgeshire and Huntingdonshire, an appointment from which he

[1] J. H. Wylie, *The Reign of Henry IV*, ii. 475–6; *CPR, 1405–8*, 313, 318; *Rot.
Parl.*, iii. 586, 591.
[2] *CPR, 1405–8*, 380.
[3] R. Somerville, *History of the Duchy of Lancaster*, i. 419.
[4] Ibid., 420.   [5] *PPC*, iv. 82.

more than once petitioned (through a large deputation of his fellow-M.P.s headed by Sir John Tyrell) to be discharged, but with no other result than a promise to compensate him for any financial loss.[1]

What I have tried in the last paragraph to make clear is that, unless a royal grant to a Speaker is made to him expressly for his services to the King in that office, it is not safe to assume that it is such services that are in fact being rewarded by any grant which is made to him. That royal grants to a Speaker coincided with, or followed shortly after, his period of office does not in itself establish any connexion between grant and conduct in office. On the other hand, when recompense is attached to work done by a Speaker on the King's behalf, it may safely be implied that the Speaker's office has come to include functions in the Lower House itself and, moreover, that these are now so significant as to enable him, as Speaker, to serve the King's interests among the Commons.

So far as is known,[2] the first reference to a Speaker being rewarded by the King for services in that office appears on the Issue Roll of the Exchequer for Michaelmas term 1435. Here it is recorded that, on 16 December (a week before the dissolution of the parliament which had met in the previous October), John Bowes, *pronunciator presentis parliamenti*, was paid £13 13s. 4d. *de regardo speciali pro labore et diligentia per ipsum habita in diversis materiis specialibus tunc temporis ibidem expediendis, per cuius labores multum domino Regi prevalebat.*[3] A fortnight earlier, the Lower Exchequer had paid out to seven other lawyers, who almost to a man were members of the Commons, various sums ranging from £1 to £6 13s. 4d., similarly for their promotion of the King's business in parliament; and on the very day that Bowes was paid his reward, three of them and another lawyer-member received £3 each for laboriously 'engrossing' divers grants made by the Lords and Commons.[4] We need have no doubt that

[1] *CPR, 1441–6*, 150.

[2] I have scrutinized all the medieval Issue Rolls of the Exchequer from before the end of Edward III's reign and all Privy Seal Warrants for Issue relating to the medieval Speakers.

[3] P.R.O., E 403/721, mem. 11. The payment is erroneously noted as made to *William* Bowes.

[4] On 2 December 1435 William Tresham (M.P. Northants.), John Hody (M.P. Somerset), and John Vampage (the King's Attorney-General, summoned to parliament by individual writ) were paid at the Lower Exchequer £6 13s. 4d. each; William Burley (M.P. Shropshire) and Nicholas Metley (M.P. Warwicks.), £3 6s. 8d. each; Nicholas Ayssheton (M.P. Helston), £2; and John Chamberlain, £1. The payment was made to each recipient as *in presenti parliamento laboranti circa diversa negocia et materias necessarias ipsius domini Regis ibidem*

Bowes's services had been performed in parliament and, unlike some of theirs, had been of a political nature. Since the Commons had granted a tenth and fifteenth,[1] a supplementary grant of a graduated income-tax on freehold lands and offices, and a renewal of customs-dues until November 1437, which together may well have exceeded the Council's original hopes, the Commons' Speaker had evidently deserved his higher fee. It was small enough compared with Speakers' fees later on. And for long this is an isolated case.

No payment similar to that which John Bowes received in 1435 was made to any of his successors for a generation. A fortnight after the parliament of 1439–40 came to an end at Reading, the lawyer-member for Shropshire, William Burley, was paid by the Exchequer £5 expressly for his labour and diligence in expediting in the parliament matters which had specially touched the King's profit, a payment made to him by the hand of Richard Blyke, then M.P. for Bridgnorth, who himself was granted one mark (13s. 4d.) for the same reason;[2] but Speaker Tresham got nothing for his toil. Of course, Tresham was not doing at all badly on other counts, and in May 1440 acquired an annuity of 40 marks from the royal manor of King's Cliffe (Northants.): this last, however, was for good service generally, including service to Henry V as well as to Henry VI.[3] Some three months after acting as Speaker for a second time running (in 1442), Tresham got the promise of the Chancellorship of the Duchy of Lancaster for life on the next vacancy.[4] But, even if it safely matured, an appointment of this sort was one likely to come the way of any well-established lawyer already retained as counsel to the Duchy, such as Tresham was; and the same might be said of his appointment in December 1447 as Chancellor for those parts of the Duchy enfeoffed to fulfil Henry VI's will,[5] a promotion made at the end of the year in which at Bury St Edmunds, he had acted as Speaker for the third time. Although a week before that parliament began, Tresham was given a reward at the Exchequer for special

---

expedienda pro commodo Regis (P.R.O., E 403/721, mems. 6, 7). On 16 December, Tresham, Burley, Hody, and Robert Rodes (M.P. Newcastle-on-Tyne) were each paid £3 as a special reward *pro laboriosis scripturis et ingrosacione diversis concessis* [sic] *tam dominorum quam communitatis regni Anglie in presenti parliamento Regi concessis pro commodo ipsius domini Regis per ipsos sic ingrossatis* (ibid., mem. 10).

[1] Admittedly this subsidy was subject to a reduction of £4,000, as in 1433, and to a collection spread over the next two years.

[2] P.R.O., E 403/737, mem. 17.   [3] *CPR, 1436–41*, 430.

[4] R. Somerville, op. cit., i. 390.   [5] Ibid., 211.

work,[1] there is no record that he later received any payment particularly for his services as Speaker. Those services are hardly likely
to have stood in his way. But to say that they resulted in his later
promotion is to fall under the spell of the old fallacy, *post hoc, ergo
propter hoc*. Tresham was in fact in continuous receipt of favours of
one sort or another. The same may be said of other Speakers who
later came into royal grants or offices. John Say, Speaker in the
earlier of the two parliaments which met in 1449, on 3 April, the day
before the end of its first session, was granted an additional annuity
of 50 marks (as from Christmas 1448) and on 10 June, nearly a week
before the third session began at Winchester, was awarded the reversion of the Chancellorship of the Duchy of Lancaster for life when
Tresham gave it up or died.[2] The timing of these grants hardly
suggests that they were rewards for Say's activity as Speaker; in any
case, they were even singly disproportionate to the service rendered.
No reward came Tresham's way when, for the fourth and last time,
he was Speaker in 1449–50. The Yorkist, Oldhall, Speaker in 1450–1,
stood no chance of one. It is just possible that the gift of £200 made
by Henry VI *for certain causes and considerations moving him* to Thomas
Thorpe, Speaker in 1453, and dated little more than a week after the
end of the second session,[3] was on account of Thorpe's recent services in the Lower House. It was at least a cash-grant, comparable
in amount with what some later Speakers were to get. But it has to
be remembered not only that these later emoluments were generally
paid after a parliament was over and done with, but that Thorpe was
a favoured courtier and the King's servant in various other capacities
—a Baron of the Exchequer and member of the royal Council, no
less—and the gift need not have been made for his work as Speaker.
Thorpe's successor in the same parliament, Sir Thomas Charlton,
got nothing resembling a reward, monetary or other. Nor, strictly
speaking, did Sir John Wenlock for his services in the 1455–6 parliament. It was not so, however, with Thomas Tresham, Speaker in the
parliament which met at Coventry on 20 November 1459 to register
the recent Lancastrian victory at the Rout of Ludford by attainting
the Yorkist leaders and their foremost supporters in arms, and to
guarantee the Lancastrian dynasty in its possession of the throne. At
Northampton, in his own county, on 5 February 1460, nearly seven
weeks after the dissolution of the parliament, Tresham was granted

[1] P.R.O., E 403/765, mem. 15.
[2] *CPR, 1446–52*, 246; R. Somerville, op. cit., i. 391.
[3] P.R.O., E 403/793, mem. 8.

for life £40 a year from lands and rents at Stamford and Grantham
forfeited by the Duke of York, on the understanding that if these
proved inadequate he should have a fresh patent charging the
annuity to another source: the writ itself mentions Tresham's services in the Coventry parliament, presumably in the office of Speaker
(although this is not stated in terms). But they were not the only
reason for the grant: it was made, also expressly, on account of
Tresham's losses in Henry VI's service.[1] It was not in fact until
after Edward IV's accession that the Speaker began to receive a
substantial payment solely in respect of his conduct in office.

Under Edward IV the Speaker was given a gratuity for his parliamentary work with a regularity which was only broken at the end of
his reign, after the parliament of 1483. But, not surprisingly, the
amount itself of the Speaker's grant from the Crown did not as yet
become uniform. Sir James Strangeways was Speaker in Edward's
first parliament which sat from 4 November to 21 December 1461,
when it was prorogued until 6 May 1462 only to be then instantly
dissolved. Although there was no vote of taxation, signal proof of
the King's satisfaction with Strangeways' conduct was forthcoming
three weeks after the dissolution: on 27 May 1462, at Leicester (where
Edward had stayed since before Easter), the late Speaker was granted
200 marks, *quas dominus Rex, de gratia sua speciali, eidem Jacobo liberari
mandavit, consideracione boni, veri ac fidelis servicii necnon diligenciae eidem
domino Regi per dictum Jacobum in parliamento suo ut prolocutor* [sic]
eiusdem impensi, habendas de regardo.[2] Not until over a year later, on
18 June 1463, did the Exchequer make payment and, even then, in
the somewhat dissatisfying form of a grant by assignment. This was
on the last day of the first session of the next parliament, which
Strangeways perhaps attended, although he was not re-elected
Speaker. The office was now held by John Say. The parliament had
only been in session a fortnight when (on 13 May 1463) Say was
granted 200 marks, but this was for special work as Under-Treasurer

---

[1] *CPR, 1452–61,* 577; Patent Roll 38 Henry VI, part 2, P.R.O., C 66/489,
mem. 21, where the grant of the annuity was made *consideracione boni et fidelis
servicii quod humilis et fidelis serviens noster Thomas Tresham armiger nobis impendit ac
grandium dampnorum et deperditorum que ipse in persona sua in servicio nostro sepe
sustinuit, necnon fidelis servicii quod idem Thomas nobis in parliamento nostro ad suos
grandes labores impendit.* If the grant failed, the Chancellor was to make other
letters patent providing for it to be paid from a different source without need
of a fresh approach to the King.

[2] P.R.O., E 403/829, mem. 5. Strangeways was certainly authorized to
receive 200 marks, not £88 6s. 8d., as noted in Wedgwood, op. cit., *Biographies.*

of the Exchequer on different occasions. On 22 June, five days after
the session, he was however given an additional £200, to be paid
by assignment at the Lower Exchequer, and, although this was a
reward for his service as Under-Treasurer from the beginning of the
reign until then, all the labour and costs so far borne by him in the
parliament were also now expressly taken into account.[1] This recompense had probably been well earned, for during their first session
the Commons had granted £37,000 for defence (although they were
to ask in the next that £6,000 should be deducted and that the levy
of half of the truncated grant should be postponed). The last session
of the parliament, early in 1465, saw the Commons give tunnage and
poundage and the wool-subsidy to Edward IV for life, but there is
no evidence that John Say received any further financial recognition
for his Speakership. By then, however, he was in regular receipt of
his fee of £40 a year as a member of the King's Council and, two
months after the dissolution of the parliament, he was created a
Knight of the Bath in the honours-list for the Queen's coronation
(at Whitsuntide 1465). In the next parliament, which met on 3 June
1467, Say was re-elected Speaker. During its first session, which
ended as early as 1 July, no grant of funds was demanded, and the
chief financial item of business was an Act of Resumption; the
second proper session, from 12 May to 7 June 1468, when the
parliament was dissolved, resulted in a grant of two whole tenths
and fifteenths. Once more Say's work had evidently been highly
esteemed, for again, as in 1463, he was allowed £200. On this
occasion the Privy Seal warrant for the reward (dated 25 July 1468)
followed the parliament and, moreover, was exclusively *in consideracion of the great costes, charges, and expenses born and had* by Say during
the recent parliament *by occasion of the office of Speker for the Commons
of this our Reaume in the same assembled.*[2]

The fairly close sequence of Edward IV's parliaments was broken
by the disturbed political conditions which came to a climax in the
Lancastrian Readeption of 1470–1. Although Edward IV was restored to his throne by his military victories at Barnet and Tewkesbury in the spring of 1471, parliament did not meet until October
1472. But, once met, it lasted longer than any previous parliament:
its seven sessions were spread over two and a half years and together
totalled over three hundred days. Especially from the King's point
of view it worked to a purpose: by the end of its sixth session on

[1] P.R.O., E 403/829, mems. 2, 5.
[2] Privy Seal Warrants for Issue, P.R.O., E 404/74/1, no. 53.

18 July 1474 its votes enabled him to engage with the Duke of Burgundy to invade France in the following spring. Edward clearly did
not fail to realize the important part played by the Speaker, William
Allington, in persuading the Commons to accept the necessarily
heavy financial burdens; and on 16 July 1474, two days before the
end of this sixth session, a Privy Seal warrant was issued authorizing
the Lower Exchequer to pay Allington £100 *in redy money* and on
sight of the warrant, on the ground that he *hath doon his true and due
diligence in awaityng and attending upon our . . . parlement to his grete
costis, charges, and expenses*, without reimbursement of any sort; the
same warrant further provided that the Speaker should have *at
thende of the said parlement an othir £100 withouten prest or eny othir
charge to be sette upon him, . . . eny statute, act, ordenance, or restraint to
the contrary notwithstanding*. Whether Allington was able to lay hands
on all that was made immediately due to him, and also realize the
promise of more, is doubtful: his warrant was endorsed by the
Under-Treasurer (his predecessor as Speaker, Sir John Say) with
only two notes of payment, they being for no more than £20 and
20 marks respectively.[1] But Allington was ready to be re-elected
Speaker when the next parliament met on 16 January 1478. Although
it sat for only one short session of six weeks, during which its chief
business was to attaint the Duke of Clarence and the King asked for
no financial grant, three days after its dissolution on 26 February, in
a Privy Seal warrant dated at Greenwich, Allington was granted
£100 for *good and laudable service* as Speaker. By the end of the current
Exchequer term, however, he had been allowed no more than half
of this sum, and even that was not in ready money but by assignment.[2]

It is reasonably certain that the Speaker in Edward IV's last and
shortest parliament of 1483, John Wood, then Under-Treasurer of
the Exchequer, was not authorized to take any special reward for his
parliamentary services, although, since he was knighted by the King
when parliament rose, there is no question of a fall from grace. Nor,
seemingly, was Catesby, Speaker in Richard III's only parliament of
the following year, recompensed in cash, perhaps because he had
recently done so well out of grants of land forfeited by those who
had joined the unsuccessful revolt of the Duke of Buckingham and
from other available sources of royal bounty. Neither has there

[1] P.R.O., E 404/75/4, no. 29.
[2] E 404/76/3, no. 37. To be paid by assignment of Crown revenue at source
was, of course, a common experience among royal creditors.

survived any warrant to pay Sir Thomas Lovell for his services as
Speaker in Henry VII's first parliament of 1485–6.

There is, however, clear evidence that Edward IV's usual practice
was soon taken up again. Moreover, payments now appear to have
been made at more of a flat rate, although as yet irrespective of the
duration of a parliament or the number of its sessions. Even the
terminology of the warrant seems now to have achieved a brief
common form—payment was being made to the Speaker simply *in
consideracion of the laudable service to us done.* Henry VII's second parliament (1487) sat for no more than one session, which lasted for less
than six weeks; but the Speaker, Sir John Mordaunt, three days after
the dissolution, received a Privy Seal warrant for a reward of £100,
payable in the Exchequer either in cash or by tally.[1] This same sum
was ordered to be paid to Sir Thomas FitzWilliam, the next Speaker
(in 1489–90), although his service had been given in a parliament
which ran to three separate meetings comprising in all nearly eighteen weeks of session.[2] Thereafter until the Reformation Parliament
whenever there is a Privy Seal warrant for issue of a Speaker's fee *at
the Exchequer*—and this is more frequently the case than not—the
grant is for the round sum of £100, whether the parliament ran to
a single short session (as in 1510, when a month sufficed to do parliament's business) or to two sessions of longer duration (as in 1523,
when together they took up more than fourteen weeks).[3]

All of the Yorkist and early Tudor warrants of Privy Seal for payment of a Speaker's fee or reward were directed to the Exchequer,
and the resulting payments appear as eventually achieving both
regularity and uniformity. But certainly no later than early in Henry
VIII's reign, it is clear that the Speaker might be given an additional
bonus paid, not at the Exchequer, but out of the funds of the King's
Chamber. This extra reward makes its first appearance in the *King's*

---

[1] E 404/79, no. 46.   [2] E 404/80, no. 642.

[3] £100 in each case is known to have been paid at the Exchequer to Sir Richard
Empson, Speaker in the parliament of 1491–2 which ran to two sessions totalling
eight weeks (E 404/81); to Robert Drury, Speaker in the parliament of 1495
after a single session of under ten weeks (B.M., Harleian MS. no. 1777, fo. 75);
and to Thomas Englefield, Speaker in the parliament of 1497 which was dissolved after one session of eight weeks (E 404/82). No Privy Seal warrant has
survived for any fee of Edmund Dudley's in 1504. Englefield's reward at the
Exchequer in 1510, for his services in Henry VIII's first parliament, whose single
session was limited to a month, was the usual £100 (E 404/87, no. 120), and this
is what More was authorized to collect at the Exchequer in 1523 (E 404/94,
no. 97).

Book of Payments in January 1513 when, after the second session of Henry VIII's second parliament, Sir Robert Sheffield was given £200 by the Treasurer of the Chamber; and the same account-book records a payment of £100 to Sheffield's successor, Sir Thomas Neville, after even the first of the two sessions of 1515.[1] That by the time of the next parliament, in 1523, this supplementary fee from the Chamber was itself regarded as customary and normally fixed at £100 is made clear by the terms of a brief but illuminating correspondence relating to the payment of Sir Thomas More for his services as Speaker in that year.[2]

Notwithstanding the displeasure felt by Wolsey over More's conduct in office, on 24 August 1523, eleven days after the dissolution, the Lord Chancellor was magnanimous (or prudent) enough to give the ex-Speaker a letter for him to take to the King recommending payment of the usual fee. The letter says that 'it hath been accustomed that the Speakers of the parliaments, in consideration of their diligence and pains taken, have had, though the parliament hath been right soon finished, *above the £100 ordinary*,[3] a reward of £100 for the better maintenance of their household and other charges sustained in the same'. And that this testimonial or warrant from Wolsey was referring to a reward of £100 additional to another of the same amount, is confirmed by the terms of the letter of thanks written by Sir Thomas two days later: here he alluded to £100 as the Speaker's fee to be taken at the Receipt of the Exchequer, and to the extra £100 as coming 'out of his [the King's] coffers by the hands of the treasurer of his Chamber'. The variability of Exchequer remuneration under the Yorkists and its occasional absence altogether under them and Henry VII suggest, however, that the generosity implied in a supplementary payment out of the King's Chamber is unlikely to have been common form in 1523 for very long. Nor is there evidence of a continuance of double reward. The Speaker's recompense was soon afterwards to be stabilized at a single fee of £100, but at £100 per session. This was the basis of Speaker Audley's reward of £200, paid him for the first two sessions of the Reformation Parliament, and it was at this rate that Sir John Baker was paid for his work in the 1547–52 parliament. £100 for each session is what Hooker's treatise of 1571 says was the Speaker's due. And although there is a possibility that Elizabeth I paid 'double hire' if a session lasted over two legal terms—which, as Sir John Neale says, was 'a

---

[1] *L. and P., Henry VIII*, vol. ii, part 2, pp. 1459, 1468.
[2] R. W. Chambers, *Sir Thomas More* (1938), pp. 207–8.   [3] My italics.

reasonable convention for Speakers who were practising lawyers'
—John Puckering, grasper though he was, himself laid claim to no
more than £400 for the four sessions he served as Speaker in the
course of the two successive parliaments of 1584–5 and 1586–7.
With this rate, Puckering's own assertion that the official allowance
was 'never certain' but always dependent on the duration of parliament, is strictly not at variance.[1]

If the steep inflationary spiral of the sixteenth century is taken into
account, the value of the fees conferred upon Speakers in the second
half of the preceding century, when the habit of governmental
remuneration took proper root, seems substantial, even handsome,
by comparison with Tudor practice. These monetary rewards to the
Speaker, especially because in the later fifteenth century they were
not invariably made and were slow to become uniform in amount,
suggest a realistic appraisal by the Crown of the services rewarded.

Before the end of the fifteenth century the Speaker may even normally have worn the appearance of a civil servant seconded, as it
were, to additional special duties as the King's agent in the Lower
House of parliament. This is not, however, to say that in consequence the Commons came to be at the King's mere beck and call.
The story of Sir Thomas More's tenure of the Chair in 1523 should
restrain us from drawing any such conclusion.[2] For his failure to do
all that was required by the Crown on that occasion, More soon had
to bear the Cardinal's anger. Clearly, there were limits to what a
Speaker could perform among the Commons for his Prince. And
none knew this better than More. Nominated and paid by the Crown
though he might be, the Speaker was not only still one of the
Commons himself, but in his office was responsible, first and foremost, to them. All that we may say with confidence of the late
fifteenth and early sixteenth century Speaker in this connexion, is
that the balance of his responsibility was in course of being gradually redressed. The story of his payment by the Crown, especially in
the initial stages of the practice, helps considerably to illuminate this
development.

[1] J. E. Neale, *The Elizabethan House of Commons*, pp. 332–3.
[2] See Chapter 11, pp. 327–30.

PART TWO

The Speakers and their Parliaments

CHAPTER 6

Under Edward III, Richard II, and Henry IV

THE earliest known Speaker was Sir Peter de la Mare who acted in the Good Parliament of 1376 when knight of the shire for Herefordshire.[1] The most important feature of his career was his connexion with Edmund Mortimer, Earl of March, husband of the heiress of the late Duke of Clarence, Lionel of Antwerp, Edward III's third son. March was one of a number of magnates who on this occasion shared the Commons' dissatisfaction with the mis-management of the war against France and their sense of outrage at what were popularly regarded as the peculations of a small group of highly placed courtiers, especially Lord Latimer (Edward III's Chamberlain), Lord Neville (Steward of the King's Household, and Latimer's brother-in-law) and certain London financiers, chief of whom was Richard Lyons. It was the impeachment of these men by the Commons which De la Mare instigated and successfully conducted. John of Gaunt, Duke of Lancaster, now the most prominent of the King's sons, was clearly hostile to March, even taking steps to exclude the claim of the earl's wife or heir to a place in the line of succession to the throne. He also detested De la Mare and the Commons' proceedings under his leadership, regarding them as an indirect attack on himself. But from the St Albans chronicles and *The Anonimalle Chronicle* of York, there is enough evidence to suggest that the Commons were nevertheless successful in persuading the peers in general to back their plan for halting corruption in high places. The Prince of Wales himself, though he died during the session, had been supporting them. De la Mare's own association with the Earl of March is likely to have been a factor of even considerable importance in assisting the Commons to mount their attack. The Speaker's connexion with March was personal and close: Sir Peter was a Mortimer tenant in his manor of Yatton in Herefordshire; he was already one of the earl's feoffees-to-uses in the most important of his estates in the Welsh border shires and was to become, in 1380, one of the executors of his will; at the time of the Good Parliament itself he was the earl's seneschal. In view of De la

[1] For references and a fuller treatment of Sir Peter de la Mare's career, see my paper, 'Sir Peter de la Mare, Speaker for the Commons in Parliament in 1376 and 1377', *Nottingham Mediaeval Studies*, vol. ii (1958), pp. 24–37.

Mare's influence in the Lower House, it is hardly surprising that March was one of the committee of peers chosen by the Commons to help in framing their demands for reform, and was also one of the royal Council newly set up in accordance with their demands.

In their hostility towards certain members of the Court, the Commons had done no more than stand upon accepted constitutional proprieties. They acted throughout expressly on the King's behalf, and with due deference to the royal prerogative. But before Edward III's death most of what the Good Parliament had done was obliterated. Indeed, by the dismissal of the new Council, the restoration of Lord Latimer to the King's favour, the impeachment of Bishop Wykeham of Winchester (March's old guardian and an enemy of the Duke of Lancaster) in a Great Council in the autumn of 1376, and the exclusion of March from his office as Marshal of England, the Court party had carried the war into the opposition's camp. The imprisonment of De la Mare himself in Nottingham castle towards the end of the year was part of this reaction. Despite this, Sir Peter had made such an impression that, even in the Bad Parliament (which met in January 1377 to ratify and carry further what had been already done to undo the work of its predecessor), he was not forgotten in his misfortune: a few of the knights of the shire, who had also sat in the Good Parliament, tried, at great risk to themselves (so the St Albans chronicler tells us), to get the Commons unanimously to demand his liberation, on the ground that he was prepared to answer all charges and submit to the judgement of the Lords. These efforts, however, did not succeed.

Early in 1377 hostility to John of Gaunt was growing among the lay magnates, but more especially among the prelates. The latter refused to do business in Convocation until Bishop Wykeham was allowed to take his place there. A more popular disaffection came to a head in the City. Here the Londoners rallied to their bishop (William Courtenay) when Lancaster threatened him during the investigation of the theological doctrines of his protégé, John Wyclif. None the less, in what proved to be the last of Edward III's parliaments, Lancaster had matters nearly all his own way. He contrived to place a number of his retainers in the Commons. Moreover, the Commons elected Sir Thomas Hungerford, knight of the shire for Wiltshire, as their Speaker.[1]

[1] For details of Sir Thomas Hungerford's career and references, see my article, 'Three Wiltshire Speakers', *Wiltshire Archaeological and Natural History Magazine*, vol. lvi, pp. 274–300.

By inheritance, marriage, purchase and lease, himself owner or possessor of numerous manors in Wiltshire, Somerset, Gloucestershire, and Berkshire, Hungerford was a great estate-agent and governor of franchises, acting concurrently for a number of influential patrons. In 1377 these included Ralph Erghum, Bishop of Salisbury, and until recently John of Gaunt's chancellor, in whose cathedral city Hungerford was the bishop's steward for life. They also included William Montagu, second Earl of Salisbury, to whom Hungerford was steward, also for life, in the estates of his earldom, as well as his counsellor. But the most important of Hungerford's connexions was undoubtedly with John of Gaunt himself. The precise date of its origin is not known. In 1372, however, Sir Thomas had been given a newly created appointment in the administration of the Duchy of Lancaster, the office of chief steward and surveyor of all the duke's estates in Wales and in the English counties below Thames. Then, in 1375, only two years before his Speakership, he had been made chief steward of all the duchy lordships south of Trent. This office, which he was to retain until 1393, gave Hungerford an automatic membership of the ducal council and carried with it the handsome remuneration of 100 marks a year plus a generous expense allowance. Simultaneously, he was appointed to the local duchy stewardships of Monmouth and the Three Castles, in both cases for life. The St Albans chronicler, referring to Hungerford's election as Speaker in 1377, was able to describe him as *miles duci familiarissimus, utpote senescallus ejus; qui nil aliud voluit quod pronunciaret admittere, quam quod scivit oculis sui domini complacere*. In the following year Hungerford became one of the duke's executors. His eldest son Thomas was also a member of the Lancastrian retinue.

During the last illness of Edward III, Lancaster largely controlled the royal government. But that the King's death would at least modify the duke's ascendancy had been made clear before that event. Edward III died on 21 June 1377; three days earlier, Lancaster's enemy, Wykeham, had been pardoned, and the temporalities of his see were also restored. Former supporters of the Black Prince now joined Richard II's Council, and members of his retinue took up station in the royal Household. When the first parliament of the new reign met in October following, the reaction against the old régime continued. At the request of the Commons the constitution of the royal Council was modified, Lord Latimer being one of those now excluded, the Earl of March continuing as a member. This petition and the Commons' other demands, for a greater responsibility of ministers to parliament, were a reversion to proposals made by the Lower House in 1376. The attack made in the Good Parliament on Alice Perrers, Edward III's mistress, was also resumed. None of this is at all surprising when it is noted that nearly half (22) of the large number of knights of the shire with previous parliamentary experience (51 out of the total of 74) had served in the Good Parliament, and that the Commons' Speaker was again Sir Peter de la Mare. Nor is the latter's election surprising.

Released from Nottingham castle a week or so after Edward III's death, De la Mare was now riding high in popular esteem. Hastening to the capital to thank the new sovereign for his clemency, he had received, according to the St Albans chronicler, a welcome recalling that given to Thomas Becket on his return from exile; the Londoners especially made much of him with presents and feasts. Official favour soon found expression more positive than mere pardon: the order to let Sir Peter go free had spoken of the King's remission of his contempt; but when, at the Exchequer on 5 August 1378, he was given a *donum* of 50 marks, this was stated to be not only on account of services to Richard II but *in exoneracione anime Regis Edwardi*; moreover, his detention at Nottingham was now said to have resulted *certis de causis irracionabilibus*. More than an acquittal: rather a reversal of the *onus*. De la Mare did not, however, act again as Speaker. In fact, when the second parliament of the reign met at Gloucester in October 1378, he was not even re-elected as knight of the shire.[1]

Already the record of the new reign was tarnished. Richard's nonage was in itself a great weakness to the government. Lack of confident and efficient leadership, disillusionment with a stale and discredited policy of war with France, dissatisfaction caused by burdensome (yet inadequate) taxation, all helped to generate an uneasy atmosphere when parliament met. Especially was this so among

[1] De la Mare was again M.P. for Herefordshire five times between 1380 and 1383. In the meantime he had been absent in Ireland preparing for the visit of the Earl of March who, appointed as the royal Lieutenant of Ireland in October 1379, went there in the following spring and remained until his death in December 1381. Sir Peter served the earl as one of his attorneys in England and, after his death, both as a feoffee and as an executor of his will. Made a J.P. in Herefordshire (for the first time) in May 1380, he was appointed to a number of royal commissions set up to deal with local disorders following the Peasants' Revolt, but did not act as a J.P. after 1382. How long he survived is not known, but he was dead by 1400, leaving no issue.

the Commons. There was every prospect of acrimonious exchanges when parliament came together at Gloucester in the autumn of 1378, and in fact the session was a particularly disturbed one. The administration presented far too many targets for attack. John of Gaunt's expedition to Brittany had failed. Parliament was being asked for fresh supply less than a year after the grant of a double subsidy. There was the scandalous breach of sanctuary at Westminster, in which Lancaster himself was rumoured to have been implicated. For the first time for forty years, parliament had been convened in a place other than Westminster (presumably because the renewed vendetta between Lancaster and the Bishop of London threatened fresh disorders in the City). The choice of the abbey of Gloucester as the seat of the parliament perhaps added to the embarrassments of the government. For there stood the tomb of Edward II, the centre of his flourishing cult, but the reminder of a royal disaster. The Commons, incredulous that all of the previous subsidy could have been so vainly spent, demanded a view of its accounts. But although the government allowed this concession, the ill grace with which it did so hardly improved its case for fresh direct taxation, and the Commons refused to grant any. There had already been trouble with the Lords, who objected to recent novelties in the working of 'intercommuning' committees of the Houses. The Commons were also disturbed about the business of the Westminster rights of sanctuary, regarding which the abbot had made a personal appeal for their support against the royal Council.

During this stormy session of four weeks the Commons' Speaker was Sir James de Pickering of Killington in Lonsdale, knight of the shire for Westmorland. Their choice seems perhaps a strange one. Pickering had been mainly notable for his connexion with Sir William Windsor of Grayrigg, his powerful neighbour, chiefly when the latter was first employed as the King's Lieutenant in Ireland in 1369. Pickering, as 'Chief Justice of the Pleas following the Lieutenant and the principal person of the Lieutenant's secret council', had been intimately involved in the oppressive policy, particularly exemplified in complaints by the Irish parliament, which resulted in Windsor's recall in 1372. Although Pickering remained closely associated with Windsor, being eventually appointed by him as one of his executors, he had not been implicated in Windsor's second Irish administration between 1374 and 1376, when the local opposition to it came to a head and became part of the general attack on the Court party in the

Good Parliament. In any case, the formal investigation of the conduct of both Windsor and his subordinates had soon petered out. In electing Pickering to be Speaker, the Commons may well have been chiefly motivated by the fact that he was a man of law and one of the few knights at Gloucester who had sat in the previous parliament. They may also have had in mind the interest he was likely to take in the relief of local disorder. He and his tenantry had recently suffered from it, and important proposals on the subject were to be made during the session.[1]

When parliament met again, at Westminster in April 1379, Pickering sat once more for Westmorland in what was his third Parliament running. It is possible that he was re-elected Speaker. But, since the roll of this parliament makes no reference at all to a Speaker, this is mere conjecture. The parliament had been summoned chiefly in order to secure funds with which to repay Crown loans already contracted. On this occasion, following the precedent of Edward III's last parliament, a grant was conceded in the form of a graduated poll-tax. But when parliament was next convened, in January 1380, the burden of the Chancellor's tale when he declared the causes of summons was as in recent sessions: still further financial aid was needed on account of the war and the perilous state of all that was left of Edward III's conquests in northern France. Despite the fact that the government actually offered, as in the previous parliament, to furnish the accounts of its income and expenditure, the Commons were not appeased. Through their Speaker they asked for the dismissal of the existing Council, demanded the nomination in parliament of those principal officials who, if their suggestions were adopted, would compose the new Council until the next parliament, and also required the appointment of a commission of general enquiry into the royal finances, consisting of fifteen members. Three were to be knights of the shire (including the Speaker), and another three, townsmen, one of the York M.P.s and two from London (these last, both of them, former Treasurers for the War).

The Speaker on this occasion was Sir John de Gildsburgh of Wennington who, although he was nearly fifty years of age, was sitting for the first time as knight of the shire for Essex. A frequent

[1] M. V. Clarke, *Fourteenth Century Studies*, 186, 206, 220–9; and see my article, 'Two Medieval Westmorland Speakers', *Transactions of the Cumberland and Westmorland Antiquarian and Archaeological Society*, New Series, vol. lxi, part 1 ('Sir James de Pickering of Killington'), pp. 79–103.

campaigner in France in the previous reign,[1] he had been a retainer
and also a feoffee and executor of a friend of the Black Prince,
Bartholomew Lord Burghersh, who had died in 1369.[2] He had then
joined the retinue of Humphrey de Bohun, Earl of Hereford, Essex,
and Northampton, and hereditary Constable of England, who made
him one of the executors of his will not long before he died in 1373.[3]
Gildsburgh shared this responsibility with Simon Sudbury, then
Bishop of London but soon (in 1375) translated to Canterbury. (It
is not without interest that Gildsburgh's first election as Speaker
roughly coincided with Sudbury's appointment as Chancellor of
England.) Gildsburgh held of Humphrey de Bohun an important
group of estates near his castle of Pleshey and also in Hertfordshire,
and after the earl's death was tenant of the dowager countess and also
of Eleanor, the elder of the earl's two daughters and coheirs, and
her husband, Thomas of Woodstock, Edward III's youngest son.
Evidently, this new contact with Woodstock, who was created Earl
of Buckingham at Richard II's coronation, proved very important
to Gildsburgh; when he was knighted in 1378 it was as a member of
Woodstock's retinue, then engaged in an unsuccessful expedition to
Brittany. And it is worth noting that when the Commons voted a
subsidy and a half for the French war early in 1380, during the first
of Gildsburgh's Speakerships, they asked that this grant and the
revenues from the tax on wool exports should be earmarked to pay
for the army that was soon to be sent to Brittany again, this time
under Woodstock's leadership.

During 1380 Earl Thomas's political stock was rising: in April he
was admitted (rather belatedly) into the Order of the Garter; in May,
he was given the custody of his wife's younger sister's share of their
inheritance; in June, he was formally appointed to command the
expedition to assist Duke John IV of Brittany. In the late autumn he
was safely nearing the end of a long but unchallenged march to
Brittany, from Calais via Troyes and through the heart of France.
On 1 June 1380, when this expedition was still only in process of
organization, Gildsburgh had been appointed to act along with two

---

[1] Born in 1331 or thereabouts, Gildsburgh went to school at Oxford, was
present as a page or young esquire at the battle of Crécy (1346), took part in the
battle of Poitiers (1356), and served in Edward III's campaign which ended with
the treaty of Brétigny (1360) (N. H. Nicolas, *The Scrope and Grosvenor Con-
troversy*, i. 159, 217).

[2] *CCR, 1364–8*, 178; ibid., *1369–74*, 41–2, 74–5, 281; *CPR, 1364–7*, 160;
N. H. Nicolas, *Testamenta Vetusta*, i. 106.

[3] Ibid., 89.

Exchequer officials and the London mercer, John Philipot, as receiver of the income from the parliamentary subsidies appropriated for distribution as wages among the magnates and captains under Woodstock's leadership. In view of these circumstances it is perhaps not surprising that, when parliament met again, at Northampton in November 1380, Gildsburgh, re-elected for Essex, was again appointed Speaker.

Despite the fact that the financial concessions in the first parliament of 1380 had been accompanied by a request from the Lower House that no parliament should be summoned for the purpose of making a grant before Michaelmas 1381, it was again the same old story of heavy military expenditure, inadequacy of supplies, and treasury exhaustion. Archbishop Sudbury, opening the session as Chancellor, could give no more creditable a financial statement than had been furnished at the beginning of the year; rather, drawing attention to the government's obligation (under indenture) to pay Woodstock's military expenses for the next half-year, the Chancellor told the Commons that another grant was unavoidable and admonished them to put aside all irrelevances (*foreines matires*) likely to give rise to rancour. When, as Speaker, Gildsburgh asked for a clear statement of what total minimum grant was required, no less a figure than £160,000 (equivalent to upwards of four tenths and fifteenths) was given out. The Commons did not hesitate to refuse this amount as out of the question and, although they offered to raise as much as £100,000 by a poll-tax, only did so on condition that the clergy subscribed a third of this sum. The prelates objected to the threat to ecclesiastical freedom contained in this proviso; but the Commons, although only after long discussions with the Lords Temporal, finally granted a poll-tax of three groats (one shilling) and further extended the wool-subsidy from Martinmas to Christmas 1381. In view of their Speaker's connexion with Thomas of Woodstock, it is important to note that, after first petitioning that this *tallage* should be used to 'refresh' the leaders of the expedition to Brittany and to honour the military covenants between the King and Woodstock, the Commons ended by actually stipulating as a formal condition of their grant that it should go towards the expedition and other measures of defence exclusively. Unfortunately for Woodstock's enterprise, Duke John of Brittany came to terms with Charles VI of France. And the English army, having idled away the winter in the Breton ports, returned to England in the spring of 1381 with nothing accomplished: another costly and futile undertaking. A further demand of the Commons was for the revival of the commission of administrative enquiry set up (so far without result) in the previous parliament. Otherwise, the Commons were content with the current distribution of the higher executive offices of State, although Bishop Brantingham of Exeter was to yield place at the Treasury to Sir Robert Hales, head of the Hospitallers in England, in February 1381. As Tout noted, 'this harmony between the parliament and the administration is the more remarkable since it was the poll-tax voted at Northampton which led to the great cataclysm of the Peasants' Revolt of 1381'. Evidently, the peasants of Essex, where (very near to Gildsburgh's own place at Wennington) the rising began, did not forget his share in the concession. Being a member of the inspectoral commission appointed to detect tax evasions in Essex, he was all the luckier to come through the commotion with his life. Certainly his property did not escape unscathed. Two years went by before he again sat in parliament.[1]

The first parliament to meet after the *tragedia rustica* (Walsingham) did so in November 1381. When once the recent quarrel between the Duke of Lancaster and the Earl of Northumberland had been composed and the ugly threat of further internal conflict was thus averted, parliament's next business was to allay the effects of the recent rebellion. It was felt legally necessary to rescind all those concessions which Richard II had made to pacify the peasants at the height of the crisis, especially the grant of royal letters of manumission to all villeins. And it was doubtless hoped that to bring about this repudiation all men of property in parliament, Lords and Commons alike, would come together on common ground.

It is just possible, however, that the Commons were not of one mind over this issue. Their Speaker was Sir Richard de Waldegrave,[2] a knight of the shire for Suffolk, one of the counties most dangerously affected by the recent rising. There is no evidence that Waldegrave himself had suffered in person or estate, but Bures St Mary in the Stour valley, where he resided, had not entirely escaped trouble. On 18 November, more than a fortnight after the beginning of the session, he asked to be excused from his office as Speaker. Such a request was soon to become common form, but only when the Speaker was being presented, and it is conceivable that on this

---

[1] For further particulars regarding Gildsburgh, see the Appendix.

[2] For references and a more detailed treatment of Waldegrave's life, see my paper, 'Sir Richard de Waldegrave of Bures St Mary', *The Proceedings of the Suffolk Institute of Archaeology*, vol. xxvii, part 3 (1957), pp. 154–75.

occasion the request was seriously meant. When ordered to continue, Waldegrave demanded a repetition of the government's programme for the session, because, he said, the Commons were disputing what it was (*en partie de variaunce entre nous touchant mesme la charge*). And when the new Chancellor, Lord Scrope, recapitulated the Commons' 'charge', the Speaker was told to pay special attention (so states the parliament-roll) to the question of the repeal of the royal grants of manumission to the peasants. It may be simply that the Commons had questioned Waldegrave's guidance through their programme. But it is possible that behind their doubts about the agenda, there was dispute among them about official policy towards the peasantry, and that Waldegrave had been genuinely embarrassed by the state of feeling in the Lower House. Certainly, what followed was unusual: regarding the repeal of manumissions, it was asked of the whole parliament together—prelates, lay lords, knights, citizens, and burgesses—what was their attitude to it? They all replied that the repeal was well done, requesting the annulment of the manumissions by authority of parliament; this was then agreed *de touz a une voice*. Had the Commons none the less been internally divided on this point? Had opposition in some quarters, perhaps among the townsmen, been at first with difficulty overruled by the shire-knights of the landlord class, only to be finally swamped in a mass declaration in full parliament? No categorical answer is possible. But certainly, later in this first session, the Commons generally were to express dissatisfaction about other aspects of the subject, for example, over the proposed terms of the pardons for those implicated in the revolt in varying degree. They asked leave to inspect these terms. The government countered this demand by one of their own: if the King was to allow a general pardon, then he was entitled to a financial grant; moreover, if he allowed a general pardon, the Commons were not entitled by custom to see it in advance; it would be shown them in writing only on the last day of the session. But it was in return for no more than a token extension of the wool-subsidy for a month that the terms of the general pardon were read to them. To direct taxation, the Commons had refused to be party, saying that it would be too dangerous.

The session was otherwise noteworthy for the Commons' successful requirement of an 'intercommuning' committee of Lords (seemingly in abeyance since 1378), and for their unsuccessful claim to receive a report of the Lords' advice to the King before they put forward their own. Parliament then went into recess for Christmas (the first adjournment of the reign). The Commons had themselves advised this step. Ostensibly, it was to give them an opportunity to induce their constituencies to be more generous regarding taxation. The King agreed because his bride-to-be, Anne of Bohemia, was expected to arrive in the near future and the lords would wish to welcome her and pay their respects.

It is possible that little of what had so far transpired during the parliament had been personally congenial to the Commons' Speaker. Aged about forty-three in 1381, Sir Richard de Waldegrave had once been a retainer of William de Bohun, Earl of Northampton, serving with him in France in 1360 (the last year of the earl's life), and then a retainer of his son Humphrey, Earl of Northampton, Hereford and Essex, whom he accompanied on expeditions to the Baltic and the Near East, and also into France after Edward III had resumed hostilities in 1369. There is, in fact, a remarkable resemblance between Sir Richard's career and that of the knight of the prologue to Chaucer's *Canterbury Tales* (which may not have been entirely adventitious). After Earl Humphrey's death in 1373, Waldegrave remained in contact with the dowager countess, Joan. But, unlike so many of the Bohun retainers (including Gildsburgh, his predecessor in the Speakership), he was not drawn into the circle of Thomas of Woodstock. Instead, in 1377, helped perhaps by the King's chief chamberlain, Lord Brian, whose heir married Waldegrave's daughter, and by his own kinsman Warin de Waldegrave, who was a personal squire to the King's half-brother, John Holland, Sir Richard had been retained as a knight of the royal Household. More significantly, he was appointed in the year of Richard II's marriage as steward of the lands of Queen Anne, and eventually (in 1393) became a member of the King's Council. Fifth on the list of the known Speakers, Waldegrave is the first to have been a proper royal retainer.

When, following the royal wedding and the Queen's coronation in January 1382, parliament reassembled, it sat for nearly a month. But, although it then renewed the wool-subsidy for an even generously long period (until midsummer 1386), it persisted in making no grant of direct taxation, and economy continued to supply the keynote of suggestions for governmental reform. The leading questions now facing parliament were, however, in the sphere of international policy: should hostilities against France be resumed? if so, directly by attack against France herself, or indirectly by attack against her allies? and, if the latter, then in what quarter, Flanders or Spain? The

last of these options was canvassed by John of Gaunt, who needed
support for his claim to the Castilian throne, whereas what the Commons favoured was an attack through Flanders, where the great
manufacturing towns had been in revolt against their count since
1379. Over this problem, even the roll of the parliament says there
was much argument and wrangling.

That the Commons' attitude to the Lancastrian panacea remained
unfavourable for the next three years meant that parliamentary
sessions continued to be occasions of great difficulty and even tur-
moil. During that time parliament was frequently convened. Two
more parliaments met in 1382, the first (in May) admittedly for only
a fortnight and the second (in October) for less than three weeks.
Waldegrave was re-elected for Suffolk to both sessions. But the
parliament-rolls do not refer to any Speaker, and it would be idle
to speculate whether Waldegrave again acted as the Commons'
spokesman.

When the next parliament met in February 1383, it again proved
to be for little more than a fortnight. During this short session the
Commons' Speaker was Sir James de Pickering, the same who had
been Speaker at Gloucester in 1378. In the autumn of 1382 he had
been returned for Westmorland, but was now sitting for the first
time for Yorkshire where he had just been appointed as royal
escheator. Although there is no certain evidence that Pickering was
a regular retainer of John of Gaunt, it is very probable that he was
now connected with the duke. The Peasants' Revolt had been
savagely hostile to Lancaster, so much so that, happening at the time
of the outbreak to be engaged in negotiations with the Scots, the
duke had finally taken refuge over the northern border. Still ignorant
that the rising had spent itself, he wrote from Edinburgh on 25 June
1381 to his local receiver in Lancashire instructing him to send all
his available cash and as much as he could raise by loan to Carlisle.
Here the money was to be handed over to Sir James de Pickering and
then taken, presumably by Pickering or an agent of his, to the duke
himself.[1] Perhaps this connexion had matured into an even closer
relationship. But, if so, there is no sign that Pickering was able as
Speaker to affect the Commons' continued preference, more positively asserted in this parliament, for the foreign policy to which
Lancaster was hostile: the 'way of Flanders'. It is possible that

[1] Royal Historical Society, Camden Third Series, vol. lvi, *John of Gaunt's
Register, 1379–83*, ed. E. C. Lodge and R. Somerville, vol. i, p. 184.

Pickering may not have wished to do so. One of the Commons' arguments—that the truce with Scotland was due to expire and that this made it even dangerous for Lancaster (or his brothers) to be out of the kingdom—was one which the Speaker, as a north country knight whose main estates were in Westmorland and Cumberland, was himself likely to sympathize with and support.

Excluding the parliament of February 1383, in the ten years between 1383 and 1393 there met eleven parliaments, the records of which vouchsafe no reference to any Speaker's name or activities. This was a time of feverish political activity, which reached a critical culmination in the years 1386-8. In the parliament of 1386, taking advantage of the departure of John of Gaunt for Spain and the panic of a threatened French invasion, a powerful group in the Upper House, led by Thomas of Woodstock (now Duke of Gloucester), the Earls of Arundel and Warwick, and Arundel's brother Thomas, Bishop of Ely, and supported by the Commons, swept the Court party from its control of the royal administration: the Earl of Suffolk was deprived of the Chancellorship and then impeached; simultaneously, changes were made in the offices of Treasurer and Keeper of the Privy Seal; and the exercise of the royal authority was virtually handed over to a parliamentary commission made up of peers. The leaders of the aristocratic party, feeling themselves threatened by Richard II's violent reaction to these proceedings, late in 1387 combined (as the Lords Appellant) to bring charges of treason against the chief of the King's friends, menaced Richard himself with deposition, and in the 'Merciless Parliament' of 1388 procured the execution of some and the disinheritance and banishment of others of the King's supporters, including the royal judges, again with the co-operation of the Lower House. In this bitter and ferocious struggle for political control, the attempt was being made—and temporarily it was successful in an anti-royal sense—to determine an important question. This was not, indeed, whether King or Parliament should be supreme (which in theory could hardly be in doubt), but rather which of two views of parliament should prevail, the King's conception or parliament's own conception of itself. In the royal view, parliament should be an instrument of government. In parliament's view, it should be an organ of control. By 1389, however, the administration of the Appellants had shown their personal incapacity, and Richard II was able to re-assert his own authority, at the same time repudiating all responsibility for the past conduct of his government. He now went on to act moderately, appointed officials acceptable to the country, and ruled through them and his Council; for the time being he hid his ambition to be revenged on his enemies for the loss of so many of his friends, with the result that his relations with parliament became more cordial than at any earlier time. In the years between 1389 and 1397 Richard often convened great councils of magnates instead of parliaments, so that parliaments came to meet less frequently and even tended, when they did meet, to be of shorter duration. General satisfaction being expressed with officials and councillors alike, and taxation being lighter than before (an average of little more than half of a tenth and fifteenth a year), parliaments were no longer the noisy meetings they had lately been. In fact, they seem to have gone out of their way to show their loyalty to the King.

One such parliament was that which met in January 1394. Politically, it was marked by a strengthening of the carefully fostered friendship between the King and the eldest of his uncles, the Duke of Lancaster, who was a source of great support to the Crown in these years. The Earl of Arundel's violent attack on John of Gaunt during the parliament, when resisted by the King, petered out in a shamefaced apology. That on this occasion the Commons elected as their Speaker Sir John Bussy of Hougham in Kesteven, knight of the shire for Lincolnshire in his sixth consecutive parliament, suggests that they appreciated the realities of the situation and exercised their choice in a way bound to be equally agreeable to the King and the most powerful magnate in the Upper House. For Bussy was both a royal and a Lancastrian retainer.[1] Although in 1387–8 he had given active support to the Lords Appellant, in December 1391 he was retained for life as a 'King's knight' with an annual fee of 40 marks. On the other hand, by 1394 his membership of the Lancastrian entourage as a knight-bachelor was over ten years old, having developed into a much closer and more personal connexion, which had perhaps already taken him into the higher administrative service of the Duchy of Lancaster. Certainly, by the summer of 1394 he was occupying the important office of chief steward of John of Gaunt's vast estates north of Trent, a post which carried with it *ex officio* membership of the duke's council. Bussy was to occupy his chief stewardship during the rest of his parliamentary career.

---

[1] For references and a fuller discussion of Bussy's career, see my article, 'Two Medieval Lincolnshire Speakers: 1. Sir John Bussy of Hougham', *Lincolnshire Architectural and Archaeological Society, Reports and Papers*, vol. vii, part 1 (1957), pp. 27–45. See also the Appendix.

Parliament met again for a short session in January 1395 at a time when Richard II was in Ireland and John of Gaunt away in his newly granted Duchy of Aquitaine. Although the parliament-roll says that the Commons were officially ordered to elect a Speaker, it does not go on to record his name. But, if (as there is good reason to believe) it was as a member of a deputation to the King from the Lower House that Bussy, less than a fortnight after the parliament, moved up from Westminster to the Dee estuary to take passage to Ireland, it is very likely that this was because he had again served as Speaker during the recent session. Quite as a matter of course, he had represented Lincolnshire there, as he continued to do in the next two parliaments. In both of these parliaments of 1397-8 Bussy was again Speaker.

Richard II now began to abandon the policy of moderation and to indulge more freely his natural inclinations towards absolute rule. In Bussy he found a willing supporter of the royal prerogative in its extremest and most dogmatic forms: references to the 'busch' in political songs of the time suggest that the Speaker was generally detested on this account. In the January parliament of 1397 his ability to handle the Commons was apparently at first in some doubt, for example, over the question of an expedition to Milan with which the King intended to assist his new father-in-law and ally, Charles VI of France. But after Haxey's bill of complaint had been surrendered, Bussy's capacity for managing the Lower House evidently re-asserted itself. Richard did not press his advantage to the point of demanding more than a renewal of the subsidies on trade and, although he now recalled his former judges (banished to Ireland by the 'Merciless Parliament'), this dangerously suspicious move was accompanied by a declaration that the acts of 1388 were otherwise to be regarded as still valid. The parliament also witnessed a registration of the royal act legitimizing the Beauforts, John of Gaunt's children by Katherine Swynford, his now middle-aged mistress whom he had married in the previous year. A few days prior to the end of the short session of three weeks, Bussy was one of the feoffees made party to a settlement of certain Duchy of Lancaster estates on the duke and duchess and the duke's heirs.

Between the January and September parliaments of 1397, Richard II determined to nullify all the opposition acts of the years 1386-8, including the statutes and judgements of the 'Merciless Parliament'. He also meant to have his revenge on such of the Lords Appellant of 1388 as were still hostile to him and on those surviving members of the parliamentary commission of 1386 whose fidelity he doubted.

Re-elected for Lincolnshire as usual, Bussy was re-elected Speaker in the second parliament of the year. He was clearly designed to be as much the King's agent among the Commons as theirs with the King. Since the procedure used against Gloucester, Arundel and Warwick was initiated by such a bill of appeal as they themselves had used in 1388, the Commons were excluded from any proper share in it. But Bussy, who as a member of the royal Council had advised Richard in July to take the step of arresting these three great lords, now moved the Commons to petition for the repeal of the royal pardons behind which they had previously sheltered. During the trial of Arundel itself, he clamoured with his supporters for the earl to be judged as a traitor, so much so that Arundel rounded on him and threw back the charge in his teeth: '*Non fideles communes hoc petunt, sed tu quis sis, novi satis bene*' (St Albans chronicle) or '*Et fideles plebei regni non sunt hic . . . Et scio, quia tu semper falsus fuisti*' (Evesham chronicle): a charge for which there is some justification, as is shown by Bussy's later receiving a royal pardon for having supported Gloucester and Arundel in 1387–8. Bussy was also largely instrumental in getting the Commons to demand that the clergy should authorize a proctor to assent to any judgement of blood made in the parliament. Further, he successfully incited the Commons to impeach of treason Arundel's brother Thomas, now Archbishop of Canterbury, for his share in the happenings of 1386–8. The Commons had already petitioned for the annulment of the parliamentary commission of 1386; and they now proceeded to be party to a wider definition of the law of treason than had been made in the Statute of Treasons of 1352. All went well for the royalist party: Lords and Commons alike proved servile; Gloucester was condemned (posthumously, having been already murdered at Calais); the Earl of Arundel, also condemned, was executed; Archbishop Arundel and Warwick were both sentenced to forfeiture and exile. When the Lords and the knights of the shire had sworn oaths to maintain the acts of the parliament, it disbanded on 30 September, having been told that it must meet again on 27 January 1398 at Shrewsbury. After no more than a fortnight's session, Richard II had 'emerged a despot in fact as well as in theory' (Tout). His aristocratic supporters were recompensed with titles of greater dignity. And, as we have already seen, Bussy's management of the Commons, exemplary from the viewpoint of the King, certainly did not stand in the way of his being also rewarded with some share of the forfeitures.

The recess was a busy time for the Speaker; he was a regular member of the King's Council, and he was also one of those few councillors specially appointed to assess the fines of those exempted from the general pardon. It was during the late autumn that he secured for himself a grant for life of the office of under-seneschal in the great liberty of the abbey of Bury St Edmunds.

When parliament reassembled at Shrewsbury, Bussy continued, of course, to act as the Commons' Speaker. At the outset of this session all the proceedings of the 'Merciless Parliament' of 1388 were annulled at the request of the new Appellants, the Commons affirming that they had meant to petition in the same strain themselves. This decision was followed by a general acceptance of the conclusions agreed by the judges at Nottingham in 1387 regarding the royal prerogative in its relation to the conduct and competence of parliaments. Meanwhile, the Commons moved for the conclusion of certain political trials left over from the earlier session including that of Lord Cobham. Further, under Bussy's guidance, they took no longer than four days to agree on their financial grant: one and a half tenths and fifteenths were voted; and then the wool-subsidies were renewed for the King's lifetime, an extension which was an act of parliamentary generosity quite without precedent. (We must not, of course, forget that previous grants had in fact been pretty continuous.) Then, after fresh oaths to maintain all the acts of the parliament, the session ended on 31 January 1398. But before the dismissal, parliament set up a commission at the Commons' request, empowered to deal with unanswered petitions. For this, there were precedents. More importantly, it was also to terminate the recent quarrel between the only two Lords Appellant of 1388 who still remained unpunished—Henry of Bolingbroke, the Duke of Lancaster's heir, now Duke of Hereford, and Thomas Mowbray, now Duke of Norfolk—and to deal with the consequences of that dispute (principally, the charge of treason against Norfolk for having slandered the King). This parliamentary commission included from among the Commons six knights of the shire, at the head of whom was their Speaker. Still one of the ordinary royal Council, Bussy was to be the most active commoner-member of the parliamentary commission, being certainly party to some of its most important decisions, including the judgements of banishment against Bolingbroke and Mowbray in September 1398 and their disinheritance in March 1399. The depth of Bussy's complicity in Richard's tyranny requires no further test than his execution by Bolingbroke at Bristol in July following, two months before Richard's deposition.

K

When parliament was next called together, it was in order to witness the termination of Richard II's reign. After Richard's deposition and the recognition of Henry IV had been accomplished on 30 September 1399, not by parliament but by the 'estates of the realm', the writs of summons were deemed to have been invalidated by Richard's prior cession of the crown so that it was necessary formally to re-summon parliament. The Houses met afresh on 6 October, only to be adjourned on the same day until 14 October, the morrow of the new King's coronation. Told, however, at their first meeting on 6 October, to elect a Speaker (so the St Albans chronicler says), the Commons evidently did so forthwith.

Their choice had fallen on Sir John Cheyne of Beckford, one of the Gloucestershire knights.[1] Cheyne had been a royal retainer in the latest years of Edward III and had continued as a member of the royal Household under Richard II, eventually (no later than 1389) becoming one of the select group of knights of the King's Chamber. None the less, in the parliament of 1397–8 he was condemned for treason (on charges unknown) and sentenced to life-imprisonment, from which he had probably not been freed until Bolingbroke's return from exile. Previously to all this, Cheyne had been employed as a diplomatic envoy: to the Duke of Brittany in 1380 (over the delicate question of his allegiance to England); to Wenzel, King of the Romans, in 1381 (shortly before Richard II's marriage to Wenzel's sister Anne); and to the Roman Curia in 1390 (to present royal letters to Pope Boniface IX explaining the second Statute of Provisors). These appointments suggest that he was a man of considerable intelligence. Cheyne had in fact originally intended a career in the Church and had even taken minor orders. His abandonment of this course, especially because it was done without dispensation, seriously discredited him in the eyes of some churchmen who even after the turn of the century still regarded him as a renegade and apostate.[2] But since all this had happened in his youth, it is almost certain that there were other and more serious grounds for this ecclesiastical dislike. Not only had he been very ready to take his fees as a royal retainer in the form of revenues from the estates of the English dependencies of certain French abbeys and priories, but also

[1] For references and an extended treatment of Cheyne's career, see my paper, 'Sir John Cheyne of Beckford', *Transactions of the Bristol and Gloucestershire Archaeological Society*, vol. lxxv (1956), pp. 43–72. See the Appendix for additional details.

[2] Thomas Walsingham, *Historia Anglicana*, op. cit., ii. 266.

had long been very friendly with some former members of the Black Prince's household who adopted, or at least favoured (as he himself did), the Lollard heresy. Now, in 1399, Archbishop Arundel, speaking in Convocation, was able to allude to the dangerous opinions held by the Speaker-elect and said that he had long been an enemy of the Church. And although, when parliament properly began its business on 14 October, Cheyne was presented by the Commons to the King, who even then agreed to his election, on the very next day Cheyne asked leave to resign. His formal excuse was ill-health. There can, however, be little doubt that what caused his withdrawal was the primate's objection. (And though Cheyne was soon to be made a member of Henry IV's Council, Arundel's hostility continued.)

When Cheyne asked to be exonerated, the Commons had already chosen his successor. This was John Doreward of Bocking, knight of the shire for Essex.[1] Far from being an anti-clerical, Doreward was of the type of conventionally pious layman especially acceptable to the English prelacy at a time when Lollardy was seeking to popularize its appeal to the gentry by promoting schemes for ecclesiastical disendowment, in particular at the expense of the *possessionati* among the monastic clergy. Earlier in the 1390's Doreward had been steward of the great franchise of Bury St Edmunds (the office to which Sir John Bussy had succeeded in November 1397).[2] Bocking, his main residence, was the centre of a deanery in which Archbishop Arundel exercised large powers of ecclesiastical jurisdiction. Here, in the parish church, in 1397 Doreward had been the founder of his family's second chantry, the primate himself being on its bede-roll. He had also connexions with the cathedral priory of Christchurch, Canterbury.[3] Besides, he was clearly *persona grata* with the new King, having been made 'caretaker' sheriff of Essex and Herts as recently as

---

[1] Doreward had previously been M.P. for Essex in the parliaments of 1395 and January 1397. He was a J.P. in Essex almost continuously from 1386 until his death in 1420, but he was not a J.P. when elected M.P. in 1399, having been excluded from the commission in July 1397.

[2] *CCR, 1389-92*, 268, 374; *CPR, 1388-92*, 485; ibid., *1391-6*, 305. In 1401 Doreward was received into the confraternity of the abbey of Bury St Edmunds (B.M., Arundel MS. no. 68, fo. 57).

[3] I. D. Churchill, *Canterbury Administration*, i. 64n.; *CPR, 1391-6*, 285; *CCR, 1392-6*, 238, 254, 258; *Literae Cantuarienses*, ed. J. B. Sheppard (R.S.), iii. 52; *The Register of Henry Chichele*, ed. E. F. Jacob, i. 162; *Archaeologia Cantiana*, xxix. 68. Doreward founded other chantries, at Stanway and in the house of Austin canons at Colchester.

22 August, that is, for the last few weeks of Richard's reign.[1] He
was also temporarily deputy to the Chief Butler at Colchester until
elected Speaker.[2] Now, during the actual course of this parliament,
he was appointed a member of Henry IV's Council with the high
fee of 100 marks a year plus expenses;[3] and this fee was shortly to be
augmented by a grant of £35 a year from the fee-farm of the borough
of Colchester,[4] together with the right to farm the alien priory of
West Mersea, a dependency of the abbey of St Ouen at Rouen.[5] (He
was to remain a member of the Council until 1406, frequently acting
as its intermediary with the King.) Sir Thomas Erpingham, now
Henry IV's Chamberlain and Warden of the Cinque Ports, had for
some time been one of Doreward's feoffees.[6] Very probably a lawyer, Doreward was himself in great demand in Essex as a feoffee-to-
uses, and in this and other ways he was intimately connected with
members of the family of the late Duke of Gloucester, revenge
for whose murder was a powerful emotional demand in this first
parliament after Richard's fall. Doreward was a feoffee of Eleanor,
the duke's widow and Henry IV's first wife's sister, who had
not long outlived her husband, and also of Eleanor's mother, the
Dowager Countess of Hereford. The duke himself had valued his

[1] P.R.O. *Lists and Indexes*, ix (List of Sheriffs), p. 44. Doreward duly made
appearance in the Exchequer as ex-sheriff in Michaelmas term, 1399, but *nihil
tulit* (K.R. Memoranda Rolls, P.R.O., E 159/176).

[2] *CPR, 1396–9*, 590.

[3] Doreward was appointed as a member of the Council on 1 November 1399
and, confirmed in the parliament of 1404, he continued in office until 22 May
1406 (*PPC*, i. 100–1, 144, 146, 155, 168, 222; J. F. Baldwin, *The King's Council in
the Middle Ages*, pp. 150, 154, 399, 413; *Rot. Parl.*, iii. 530a; Privy Seal warrants
for issue, P.R.O., E 404/16/72; 17/280; Exchequer, Issue Rolls, P.R.O., E 403/
569, mems. 2, 21; E 403/571, mem. 8; E 403/573, mems. 9, 13; E 403/585,
mem. 2).

[4] This sum of £35 was all of what Colchester was liable to pay in the Exchequer. Doreward surrendered the grant on 22 October 1404 in favour of
Henry IV's youngest son, Humphrey.

[5] Doreward was granted a lease of the estates of the alien priory of West
Mersea on 24 November 1399, at a rent (payable in the Exchequer) of 140 marks
a year. In May 1400 the abbey of St Ouen was licensed by royal patent to grant
the priory to Doreward for life. In March 1401 the rent was cancelled. Doreward
retained these estates until his death and his widow until 1423 (*CFR, 1399–
1405*, 28; *CPR, 1399–1401*, 284, 293, 308, 480; ibid., *1416–22*, 441; *PPC*,
i. 194, 199; *CCR, 1422–9*, 300 ff.; *Monasticon*, viii. 1425; *Rot. Parl.*, iii. 491, 499;
iv. 319).

[6] For Doreward's relations with Erpingham, see *CFR, 1399–1405*, 47, 233;
CPR, 1401–5, 104; ibid., *1405–8*, 330.

services.[1] Doreward also had close relations with Lord FitzWalter,[2] an Essex peer who was especially prominent in this parliament among the challengers of those who were popularly held responsible for Gloucester's death. It may be particularly noted here that this parliament of 1399 resulted in the annulment of the measures of Richard II's last parliament of 1397-8. The reversals included the forfeitures of that time, and a special concession was made in the case of Archbishop Arundel, who was allowed damages from Roger Walden, intruded into the primatial see by Richard II. No details are known of the part individually played by Doreward as Speaker. But the Commons may not have been always easy to manage: they were said to have objected to the King's mildness towards his predecessor's closest friends among the Lords.

When Henry IV first summoned his next parliament, his intention was that it should meet at York in October 1400. But by then a quarrel on the Welsh border between Owen Glendower and Lord Grey of Ruthin had swiftly grown into a full-scale Welsh national rising, so that parliament was ordered to meet at Westminster instead and not until 20 January 1401. The Commons now elected as their Speaker the forty-two-year-old knight of the shire for Kent, Sir Arnald Savage of Bobbing.[3] His parents had both been intimate members of the Black Prince's household, his mother having been nurse to Richard of Bordeaux, and when Richard came to the throne, Sir Arnald himself soon joined the royal Household. In 1390 he was rewarded with an annuity of 40 marks, and by 1392 had so far advanced as to be one of the eight knights of the King's Chamber. He was constable of the royal castle of Queenborough in the Isle of Sheppey from 1393 until 1396 when, in lieu of this office and his existing fees, Richard II granted him for life a fresh annuity of £50 charged on the London customs. Although Savage was then still a Chamber-knight, he seems not to have gone with the King to Ireland in the spring of 1399, and it would appear that he was not long in accepting and acclimatizing himself to Richard's deposition. Within two months of Henry IV's accession he was confirmed in his office of J.P. in Kent. Precisely when he became a member of the

---

[1] For the Gloucester connexion, see R. Gough, *The History and Antiquities of Pleshy*, App., 80; CPR, *1391-6*, 533; ibid., *1399-1401*, 366; ibid., *1408-13*, 158; ibid., *1416-22*, 105; CFR, *1399-1405*, 74; *Catalogue of Ancient Deeds*, iii. C 3007.

[2] For the FitzWalter connexion, see CPR, *1377-81*, 601; CCR, *1405-9*, 446.

[3] For references and a closer view of Savage's career, see my article, 'Sir Arnald Savage of Bobbing,' *Archaeologia Cantiana*, vol. lxx (1956), pp. 68-83.

council of the royal heir-apparent, Henry, Prince of Wales, and also steward of his household is not known; but he was already holding the former office by May 1401, and the latter by December following. It is not at all improbable that he was closely connected with Henry of Monmouth when serving as Speaker from 22 January to 10 March 1401. If this were so, it would be a fact of some significance. For, although Henry IV had himself personally intervened in the effort to crush the Welsh rebellion, the immediate responsibility rested on the Prince of Wales along with Henry Hotspur, Justice of Chester and North Wales. Moreover, the Commons in the 1401 parliament took a keen interest in the Welsh situation: they asked for an enquiry about Welsh-born officials of the Crown, the King answering the request by ordering his own council and the council of the Prince of Wales to examine the statutes of Edward I prohibiting the employment of Welshmen in the royal administration, and to revise them with the advice of both Lords and Commons. The financial demands which the King made of the parliament—to the tune of £130,000—were pitched too high for the Commons to be entirely comfortable; and, in fact, they took advantage of the King's predicament to press some important claims of their own. They demanded, for instance, ample time to deliberate questions of policy upon which they were asked to advise; they protested against the King's listening to premature reports of their proceedings; and they requested to be told of the King's answers to their petitions before they made their financial grant. Most of these points were favourably dealt with by Henry IV, but what the last and very striking request demanded he eventually turned down as uncustomary. Even so, the Commons voted a tenth and fifteenth and renewed the subsidies of tunnage and poundage. Although Savage is reported to have won esteem by warning the government against future taxation, the fact that the King now confirmed his annuity of £50 (granted him in 1396) suggests royal satisfaction with his conduct as a Speaker in this parliament.

With Wales in revolt and Scotland and France both threatening war, Henry IV was reluctant to call a second parliament in 1401. Glendower continued successful, and in 1402 discontent in England was such as to give rise to unhealthy rumours that Richard II was still alive. In August the King himself mounted a heavy attack against the principality, having already summoned parliament for the end of September. If Henry was anticipating a personal triumph, his hopes were entirely disappointed; and the great victory of the Percies against the Scots at Humbledon Hill, although encouraging in itself, provided an unhappy contrast with his own failure. The appearance in parliament of the son of the Regent of Scotland and other captives from the recent battle on the northern front only emphasized the disparity in the outcome of the two campaigns. The Commons' request for an 'intercommuning' committee of Lords, although successful, was treated by the King as if unwelcome. But otherwise the session passed off reasonably well, ending with a fairly liberal, if somewhat grudgingly conceded, grant of a tenth and fifteenth, together with a continuation of the wool-subsidy and tunnage and poundage until Michaelmas 1405.

The Commons' Speaker on this occasion was Sir Henry de Retford of Castlethorpe, who had been re-elected for Lincolnshire.[1] Not far short of fifty years old, Retford was a knight with some military experience: he had served in the army which Richard II had led to Scotland in 1385, accompanied John of Gaunt's force to Spain in 1386, and been a member of Richard's first expedition to Ireland in 1394–5. Before this, in 1393, Richard had retained him for life at an annual fee of 40 marks. In 1397, following the conclusion of the long truce with France and Richard's marriage with Isabel of Valois, Retford had been a member of the joint Anglo-French embassy which went to Avignon and Rome to demand the resignation of the two contending popes (Benedict XIII and Boniface IX). This diplomatic employment and his appointment as sheriff of Lincolnshire about the time of his return from Italy and soon after Richard's parliamentary triumph of 1397[2] suggest that Retford at that time had good prospects under Richard's absolute rule. He was not, however,

[1] For references and a fuller treatment of Retford's life, see my article, 'Two Medieval Lincolnshire Speakers: 2. Sir Henry de Retford', *Lincolnshire Architectural and Archaeological Society, Reports and Papers*, vol. vii, part 2 (1957–8), pp. 117–25.

[2] Before his Speakership Retford had already been sheriff of Lincolnshire, but for no more than a month, in 1389 and then again, for the normal term, in 1392–3. He was first appointed a J.P. in Lindsey in November 1397. He was M.P. for Lincs. in the parliament of 1401 and was one of the four knights from the county commanded to attend a Great Council summoned to Westminster for 15 August 1401. He was not immediately re-elected to parliament after his Speakership, but was summoned to another special Great Council in 1404 and then elected as M.P. for the last time to the Coventry parliament of October 1404. Retford secured no additional rewards from Henry IV, or at least none required to pass the Great Seal. But he loyally supported the régime, for example, on the occasion of the rebellion of Archbishop Scrope and the Earl Marshal in Yorkshire in 1405, when he was a member of the court-martial set up to try the rebel leaders. In 1406–7 he was sheriff of Lincs. for the first time under Henry

among those sheriffs whom Richard re-appointed for a second year running. And after the revolution of 1399 he lost little time in show-ing active support for Henry IV: confirmed as J.P. in Lindsey within two months of the new King's accession, he followed him into Scot-land in August 1400. It was in consideration of this service that the royal annuity which Retford had enjoyed as a retainer of Richard II was confirmed. It is clear that he was now regarded as quite trust-worthy by the new régime: in May 1402 he was one of the Lincoln-shire commissioners authorized to arrest those charged with sedi-tious talk and, in August following, when Henry IV began to prepare for an all-out effort to put down the Welsh rebellion, he was one of only two commissioners appointed to supervise all the Lincoln-shire militia and ensure their junction with the royal forces at Shrewsbury, reporting there in person to the King himself. This was, of course, within a month or so of the meeting of the parliament in which Retford served as Speaker: his awareness of Henry's military, and consequently financial, problems must surely have been a factor of some importance governing his election. That he knew at first-hand something of the ecclesiastical situation in Europe may also have had an effect on the choice of the Lower House: at the opening of the session, the Chancellor (Bishop Stafford of Exeter) had drawn attention to the seemingly good prospects of restoring a single papal obedience; and at the end of the parliament Henry IV was asked by the Commons themselves to do his best to heal the Schism.

1403 was another year of trouble and distress. Henry IV's mar-riage to Joan, widow of Duke John IV of Brittany, achieved little of its diplomatic purpose, and the Queen's foreign entourage became an added source of popular grievance. A great rising of the King's former friends, the Percies, in alliance with Welsh and Scots, was crushed at the battle of Shrewsbury on 21 July; and the Earl of Northumberland, his son and brother dead, submitted. The King had some further military success in south Wales. But discontent re-mained. And when parliament, having been inadvisedly summoned to Coventry for 3 December 1403, eventually met at Westminster in mid-January 1404, dissatisfaction reached a climax.

The Commons' Speaker now was again Sir Arnald Savage, who three years before had shown that he knew how to speak out. It is

---

IV. He died shortly before the middle of June 1409. His widow survived him by half a century, in the meantime (somewhen between 1420 and 1428) marrying William Lord Clinton of Maxstoke (as his third wife) and, when he died, Sir John Heron of Northumberland.

not, however, unquestionably correct to represent his election as 'in itself a challenge to the king' (Stubbs). The date of Savage's super-session by Sir John Stanley of Knowsley (Lancs.) as steward of the household of Henry of Monmouth is not precisely known; but this change almost certainly only took place in order that Savage should be able to join the royal Council itself, and this he had done by Michaelmas 1402 at the latest. Enjoying a handsome recompense of £100 a year, and with his old annuity of £50 on the London customs (first given him in 1396) raised by a third in June 1403 to help him to meet his additional expenses in attending on the King's person, Savage was still a member of the Council when parliament met early in 1404, and moreover an active member. But that Savage did not allow his rôle as councillor to stop him from acting effectively as Speaker is clear from what happened during the session.

The Lower House was not long in expressing its concern about the dangerous state of the north after the Percy rising, and it also drew attention to the abuses of livery. Complaint was made, too, of excessive royal expenditure. More especially, the Commons attacked the royal Household as being extravagantly organized and overrun with aliens, in particular by those of the Breton following of the Queen. This resulted in a novel appropriation of royal income, amounting to some £12,000, to Household use and, perhaps in order both to guarantee payment and to clinch the restriction, in the appointment of special treasurers of the yield from the taxes parliament voted. Moreover, at the Commons' special and insistent request, the King was prevailed upon to nominate his Council, part of whose duty it would be to provide remedy for all the complaints and grievances disclosed during the session. And twenty-two lords, knights, and esquires were appointed in parliament to act as councillors until it should meet again: among the seven commoners now on the Council were three knights of the shire, the Speaker himself being continued in office. From a chronicle of Canterbury provenance and more particularly from the evidence of a newsletter sent to Durham in the course of the parliament, it is clear that there were difficulties over taxation between the King and the Lower House in this session, the Commons demanding a reduction of the customs in return for a direct subsidy.[1] They held out for ten weeks (which

[1] *Eulogium Historiarum*, ed. F. S. Haydon (R.S.), iii. 399–400; Constance M. Fraser, 'Some Durham Documents relating to the Hilary Parliament of 1404', *B.I.H.R.*, xxxiv, pp. 197–9. For a fuller reference to the Durham newsletter, see p. 47.

made this parliament the longest since 1388); and, when eventually they did give way, it was to make only a provisional grant of a novel tax of 5 per cent on income from land, which was likely to be quite inadequate and in any case was made to depend on the appointment of the special treasurers for the fund. Regarding Speaker Savage, it is perhaps worth noting that, although during the parliament of 1406 he was re-appointed a member of the King's Council and was also considered for the office of Controller of the Household, he never again sat as knight of the shire after 1404.[1]

The situation at home and abroad in 1404 continued to give such cause for anxiety as to require another parliament in the autumn. To assist its concentration on matters of State, this meeting was to take place at Coventry, where the members would be far from the distractions of private litigation in the courts at Westminster. Even the writs of summons themselves prohibited the election of lawyers, and it is likely that Henry IV sought to affect the composition of the Lower House more positively, by ordering the sheriffs to return official nominees.[2] By the time parliament met on 6 October, there was an immediate threat of French invasion from both Harfleur and Sluys. English trade relations with Flanders were dislocated. A breach had also occurred with the Prussian and other Baltic towns of the Hanseatic League over the claims of the cloth-merchants of the east-coast towns of England to reciprocity of treatment: as recently as May 1404 Danzig had prohibited the annual voyage from the Baltic to England, and an embargo had been placed upon imports of English cloth.

It may well have been the Commons' appreciation of these mercantile problems which chiefly prompted them to elect Sir William Sturmy of Wolfhall (Wilts.) as their Speaker in this Coventry parliament.[3] He was already a diplomatist with a considerable range of continental experience, and it was to be by the advice of parliament itself that he was included at the end of the session in an embassy to the High Master of the Order of the Teutonic Knights, which was still the principal force in Baltic politics. Although Sturmy had been retained by Richard II as a 'King's knight' in 1392 with an annual fee of 40 marks, had served on Richard's first Irish expedition of 1394-5,

---

[1] For more facts relating to Savage, see the Appendix.

[2] *Eulogium Historiarum*, iii. 402.

[3] For references and a more detailed biography of this Speaker, see my paper, 'Sir William Sturmy', *Transactions of the Devonshire Association for the Advancement of Science, Literature and Art*, vol. lxxxix (1957), pp. 78-92.

and had been a member (like his recent predecessor in the Speakership, Retford) of the joint Anglo-French mission sent to the rival
papal *curiae* in 1397 to try to end the Schism, his career received no
long-term set-back as a result of the revolution of 1399. The royal
annuity given him by Richard II was not confirmed until March
1401, but just before this was done Henry IV had made him a member of his Council with an annual fee of 100 marks. This appointment was probably made in anticipation of Sturmy's employment in
an important drive to secure foreign recognition for the House of
Lancaster. For, although he continued to be paid his stipend as a
royal councillor until July 1402, he was in fact absent in Germany on
diplomatic business for most of the time: first, in 1401, to treat for
the homage of the Duke of Guelders and probably to get him to
recognize the new King of the Romans, Henry's ally, Rupert III of
Bavaria, who had recently been elected in place of Wenzel of
Bohemia (Richard II's brother-in-law); second, in 1402, to negotiate
the marriage of Henry IV's elder daughter, Blanche, to Rupert's
eldest son, Lewis, Count Palatine of the Rhine and Duke of Bavaria.
(Until the marriage took place at Heidelberg in July 1402, Sturmy
was steward of household to the young princess.) More recently,
early in the very year of his Speakership, Sturmy had been over in
Rotterdam, trying to iron out claims and counter-claims to compensation for losses from acts of piracy committed against one
another by Flemish and English merchantmen in the Narrow Seas.

During the Coventry session, which lasted from 6 October to
14 November 1404, the Commons were at first every bit as difficult
as in the preceding parliament, the embarrassing state of the royal
finances being once again their chief concern. Obliged to find some
means of aiding the King, but anxious that he should at least do
everything possible to live of his own, they demanded a resumption
of royal grants since 40 Edward III (1366). Meanwhile, because this
would take time to administer, they extracted from the King, as 'an
immediate stop-gap measure', an undertaking that he would require
the surrender of a year's income from all royal lands leased out at
farm and enforce a year's stoppage of all pensions conferred by
Richard II and himself.[1] In addition to making these proposals,
some of the knights even went so far as to press for the appropriation, for one year at any rate, of the temporalities of the Church. It

[1] For this question, see the valuable article of B. P. Wolffe, 'Acts of Resumption in the Lancastrian Parliaments 1399–1456', *EHR*, vol. lxxiii (1958), pp.
586–90.

was this demand that led Archbishop Arundel to invoke the Great Charter and, carrying the attack into his enemies' camp, to rate the knights for their cupidity in securing for themselves alone, and to the neglect of the King, all the profits of the alien priory estates sequestrated by the Crown. The St Albans chronicler, upon whom alone we must rely for evidence of this anti-clerical movement among the Commons, says that the spokesman for the knights on this matter was Sir John Cheyne, the rejected Speaker of 1399. Cheyne was not even elected to the parliament, but it is possible that Sturmy, the Commons' accredited Speaker, had dissociated himself from this insolence. The session at least ended satisfactorily. It is true that when the Commons made a grant of subsidies, it was again on condition that two special treasurers were appointed (one of them being Sir John Pelham, a knight of the King's Chamber and M.P. for Sussex), that their accounts of expenditure should undergo in the next parliament an audit of which the Commons were to be informed, and that anybody who made drafts on the subsidy-revenues, even by a royal warrant, for purposes other than those of defence, should suffer the penalty appropriate to treason. The size of the Commons' grant, however, was more than decent: in addition to a continuation by the Lords of the tax of 5 per cent on landed incomes (admittedly now restricted to incomes of more than 500 marks a year), they extended the wool-subsidy, tunnage, and poundage for two years (to Michaelmas 1407) and granted two tenths and fifteenths, payable by instalments but all within a twelvemonth: the largest parliamentary subsidy of the whole reign. Henry IV had evidently no real cause for complaint of Sturmy's conduct as Speaker, and it is worth noting that Sturmy continued to be employed now and then as a diplomat and before the end of the reign was appointed chief steward of the estates of the Queen, Joan of Navarre.

Although no parliament met in the following year, 1405, it was quite the most critical of Henry IV's reign. The general unrest reached its most dangerous culmination in the north. Here, the old Earl of Northumberland plotted fresh treasons, and Archbishop Scrope and Thomas Mowbray, the Earl Marshal, indicted the King as a usurper and oppressor and in May led a great rising in Yorkshire. Mainly thanks to the Nevilles this rebellion failed, and its promoters, including the northern metropolitan himself, were executed out of hand. Henry IV drove the Percy into Scotland and then, in the autumn, turned against Wales. This Welsh campaign was as usual inconclusive. None the less, the King had now overcome his

main difficulties. But whether or not his execution of Archbishop
Scrope is to be regarded as 'the sign of a mind and moral power
already decaying' (Stubbs), the fact remains that Henry's physical
health was now breaking down under the accumulated strain of the
past few years. Before the end of 1405 it was decided to summon
parliament to meet in mid-February 1406 and once again at Coventry.
In view of the expedition to be led by Prince Henry into Wales,
Gloucester was chosen instead, but then (less than a week before it
was due to meet) parliament was postponed for a fortnight and
ordered to assemble at Westminster after all. By this time fresh opposition to Henry IV's administration was growing, now even within
the Council itself and with his half-brothers, the Beauforts, at its
centre. When parliament came together on 1 March 1406, the
political situation was in an uneasy state of flux.

This parliament of 1406 turned out to be the longest which had so
far met: with two adjournments, it continued to within three days of
Christmas, its three sessions comprising nearly twenty-three weeks.
It lasted so long mainly because of the Commons' obstinacy over
taxation and redress of grievances, which they insisted on treating as
related questions. Constitutionally, it involved indeed several important points: the King was made, however reluctantly, to concede
an audit of the accounts of the War Treasurers (the committee including members from the Lower House); once again he was prevailed upon to nominate the members of his Council in parliament;
further, he was subjected to severe restrictions designed to prevent
his evasion of this Council's surveillance; moreover, the councillors
themselves were constrained to acknowledge their responsibility to
parliament, and to swear to observe certain conditions laid down for
their conduct which were to last until the next parliament. Not until
this last concession was granted, did the Commons finally vote a
modest supply—a single tenth and fifteenth. It was the knights of
the shire who played the largest part in all this stiff bargaining and
opposition to the King.

The Commons' Speaker, judging from the many times he renewed his 'protestation', can have little relished his duties as exponent of their views. He was Sir John Tiptoft, a young and still
unmarried knight of the royal Household, who, having attended
both the parliaments of 1404, was now (as before) sitting for
Huntingdonshire. A member of a cadet branch of a family whose
representatives had been parliamentary peers under each of the three
Edwards, he had been attached to Henry IV's personal retinue from

no later than the spring of 1397.[1] It is very probable that Tiptoft had actively supported Bolingbroke from the moment of his return from exile in the summer of 1399. Certainly, he was one of the forty-six esquires knighted by Henry at the Tower on the eve of his coronation and was soon afterwards retained for life as a 'King's knight' with the large annuity of 100 marks.[2] By September 1402 (if no earlier) both he and his father (Sir Payn) had been recruited into the select group of twelve knights of the King's Chamber and were still members in 1406.[3] Young Tiptoft would have found it difficult to complain of lack of generosity on Henry IV's part, but he had always been at hand during the campaigns against rebels in England and Wales. Nor can there be any doubt of his administrative ability. In fact, on 8 December 1406, when the third and last session of the parliament in which he acted as Speaker had still a fortnight to run, Tiptoft was appointed Treasurer of the King's Household and so became the first layman to hold this office.[4] It is inconceivable that Henry did not approve of this appointment of his henchman; and it is fair to presume that, however unwelcome to the King had been the attitude of the Commons in this parliament, Henry was not dissatisfied personally with Tiptoft. At the same time, it may perhaps also be allowed that, since Tiptoft's and other major promotions in the royal Household were being made by the new Council and to ensure 'moderate governance', his recent conduct as Speaker had by no means alienated the exponents of administrative reform. Tiptoft was to remain Treasurer of the Household until his appointment as Treasurer of England in July 1408. That his dismissal from this post in December 1409 was closely followed by that of Archbishop Arundel from the Chancellorship, and that it was a close friend of the Prince of Wales (Lord Scrope) who followed Tiptoft at the Exchequer, suggests that Tiptoft adhered to the party at Court which so far had resisted the ambitions of the Prince and his supporters,

[1] Duchy of Lancaster, Accounts Various, Account Books of the Treasurer of the Household of Henry, Earl of Derby (later Henry IV), P.R.O., D.L. 28/1/9; 1/10.

[2] *The Great Chronicle of London*, ed. A. H. Thomas and I. D. Thornley (London, 1938), p. 73; *CPR, 1399–1401*, 98.

[3] Exchequer, Accounts Various, Wardrobe Accounts, September 1402–3, P.R.O., E 101/404/21, fo. 44v.

[4] J. H. Wylie, *The Reign of Henry IV*, ii. 475–6. Tiptoft's account as Treasurer of the Household covers the period from 8 December 1406 to 17 July 1408; the first reference to him acting in this capacity on the Issue Rolls of the Exchequer is dated 13 December 1406 (P.R.O., E 403/589, mem. 11).

Henry IV's half-brothers, the Beauforts. We need follow Tiptoft's long and influential career no further here, save to notice that he was the earliest Speaker to attain the peerage (in 1426).[1]

When the Lancastrian dynasty had been in greatest danger, the royal family as a whole had stood together. Once the dynasty was at least safe, tensions began to develop within its own ranks. But when parliament next met, at Gloucester, for an autumn session in 1407, the royal executive was nevertheless able to follow its bent with a greater assurance than before. From certain incidents during the session, it is also clear that the Lower House had lost something of its earlier temper. There is no record that the Commons protested against the waiving of the oath of responsibility as imposed upon the Council in the previous parliament, and a complaint made through their Speaker against illegal purveyance was easily shelved. It is true that the Commons were able to resist a peremptory demand from the King to endorse the grant of a subsidy upon which only the Lords had reached agreement; but it is noteworthy that the Commons' outcry was directed against the Lords, not the King, and that in any case what the Lords had recommended was finally accepted just as it stood, parliament voting as much as a subsidy and a half.[2]

That the leadership of the Lower House at Gloucester fell to Thomas Chaucer of Ewelme (the son of the poet, Geoffrey), knight of the shire for Oxfordshire,[3] perhaps suggests that the Beaufort party was anxious to make use of the Commons to embarrass the government and that the Commons were willing to be so used, even though what happened makes it obvious that neither derived much strength from the alliance. At least, there can be no doubt that Speaker Chaucer's connexion with the Beauforts had been and still was a very close one: he was their cousin, his mother and theirs (Philippa and Katherine Roet) being sisters; and as recently as June 1406 the most able and politically active of the Beaufort family, Henry, Bishop of Winchester, had made Chaucer constable of his

---

[1] For Tiptoft's later life, see the Appendix.

[2] The King showed his relief at this outcome by undertaking not to ask for more tenths and fifteenths between Lady Day 1408 and Lady Day 1410 (*Rot. Parl.*, iii. 612b).

[3] Thomas Chaucer had been M.P. for Oxfordshire in 1401, 1402, and 1406 and sheriff of Oxfordshire and Berkshire in 1400–1 and 1403–4. He was escheator in the two counties in 1406–7, the year of his first Speakership. His place at Ewelme in the Chilterns together with estates in Hampshire and East Anglia came to Chaucer by his marriage with Maud, a daughter and coheir of John Burghersh and a cousin of the Duchess of York (wife of Edward of Norwich).

castle at Taunton and overseer of his episcopal estates in Somerset, with a substantial annual fee of £40.[1] Geoffrey Chaucer had owed much to the help of his sister-in-law's lover, John of Gaunt, and it had been quite natural for his son to begin his career in the Lancastrian retinue. Thomas evidently accompanied John of Gaunt to Spain in 1386: it was at Bayonne in 1389 that the duke retained him for life at an annual fee of £10. This pension was doubled in 1394, and at the time of Lancaster's death in February 1399 Thomas was constable of the Lancastrian stronghold at Knaresborough and chief forester in that lordship. It is true that, after being removed from these offices when Richard II deprived Henry of Bolingbroke of his inheritance, he was compensated by a grant from the fee-farm of the royal borough of Wallingford (close to his own place at Ewelme).[2] None the less, at the beginning of his reign Henry IV had every reason to trust in Thomas Chaucer's support, and the latter was soon confirmed in all the grants made to him by John of Gaunt and Richard II. In even the first month of his reign, the new King appointed Chaucer as constable of Wallingford castle and steward of the honours of Wallingford and St Valery and of the four and a half hundreds of Chiltern, in each case for life. Since these estates (as parcels of the Duchy of Cornwall) had already been assigned to the eldest of the King's sons, Henry of Monmouth, it was most likely he who had initiated Chaucer's appointment. But the grant passed the Great Seal.[3] Moreover, although these offices brought Chaucer into relationship with the prince, the King's own continued confidence in him is convincingly attested by his appointment as Chief Butler of England in November 1402. And this office was given to Chaucer for life. In May 1407, however, Sir John Tiptoft, then Treasurer of the Household, superseded him; and, although Chaucer was re-instated immediately after his 1407 Speakership, it was on different terms from before: no longer for life but only at the King's pleasure.[4]

Chaucer's successive appointment, removal, and re-instatement on

[1] *CPR, 1405–8*, 406.

[2] J. H. Wylie, *The Reign of Henry IV*, iv. 313; *CPR, 1396–9*, 490, 494; H. A. Napier, *Historical Notices of Swyncombe and Ewelme*.

[3] *CPR, 1399–1401*, 15, 33–4; *1413–16*, 157; P.R.O., D.L. 28/4/3; *Rot. Parl.*, iii. 667.

[4] *CPR, 1401–5*, 170; *1405–8*, 327, 380. In the summer of 1402, not long before he was appointed by Henry IV as Chief Butler, Chaucer went to Germany in the entourage of the Princess Blanche, Henry's elder daughter, to attend her marriage to Lewis of Bavaria.

inferior terms may perhaps be regarded as minor indications of the tension building up in the royal family itself. The discharge of Henry IV's close friend, Archbishop Arundel, from the Chancellorship (in which, because of the King's physical weakness, he had virtually acted as viceregent since his appointment in January 1407) marks a clearer stage in the deterioration of relations between the King and the Prince of Wales and his friends, who included the Beauforts and their cousin Chaucer. Arundel's surrender of the Great Seal took place on 21 December 1409. This event and Sir John Tiptoft's slightly earlier dismissal from the Treasury together augured an important shift in the control of the authority of the Crown.

Nearly two months before these changes, parliament had been summoned to Bristol for 27 January 1410. Perhaps to make it easier for the King to attend, only three days before Arundel relinquished the Great Seal the place of meeting was altered to Westminster. Of the likely trend of events, some indication had already been given by the appointment (on 6 January) of the Prince of Wales's intimate friend, Henry Lord Scrope of Masham, to the headship of the Exchequer. Still clearer signs could be seen when parliament met: there being as yet no Chancellor to open parliament, this service was performed by Bishop Beaufort; four days later, his brother, Sir Thomas Beaufort, assumed custody of the Great Seal; in between times their cousin Chaucer had been re-elected Speaker.[1]

The first session, which lasted until the end of Passion Week (15 March), was chiefly remarkable for the Commons' promotion of a Lollard bill planning a confiscation of the temporalities of bishops and greater abbots. But the King would have nothing to do with it. In the second session (7 April–9 May) the Commons showed greater realism and addressed themselves to the related needs of greater financial strictness and administrative probity. After roughly a fortnight (on 23 April) they proposed a scheme of reform, which included the now 'common form' demand for the nomination in parliament of a royal Council whose members should take an oath of office there. The King spent over a week in coming to his answer, and when (on 2 May) he produced a brief list of seven councillors, it

---

[1] Chaucer himself seems to have exerted pressure on the burgesses of Taunton (where he was the Bishop of Winchester's steward) to elect a friend of his own: one of the two originally elected M.P.s was William Motte, one of Chaucer's co-feoffees for Robert James of Boarstall (Bucks.), and when Motte's name was erased from the return it was only to allow the substitution of Thomas Edward, Chaucer's co-feoffee for John Golafre of Fifield (Berks.). James and Golafre were both returned as M.P.s for Berkshire.

L

can have given him little personal satisfaction: the royal heir and his friends were preponderant. For the first time in the reign, the Council now included no commoner. Moreover, the new councillors went so far as to bring pressure upon the Commons to make an adequate grant by exposing their reluctance to serve unless one were voted, and also by making difficulties about their official oath. The Lower House evidently agreed to support the new administration. But it is doubtful whether it did so with much enthusiasm. Certainly, it did not do so with alacrity. Two sessions were required to elicit a grant of funds. It is true that, finally, the Commons extended the wool-subsidy, appropriated three parts of it to the defence of Calais, of which the prince had lately been made Captain, and placed no more than 20,000 marks at the King's own personal disposal. But the extension was for no longer than two years, and the appropriation to Calais had first been proposed by the Lords before ever the grant was made. It is also true that the Commons granted one and a half tenths and fifteenths. Their collection, however, was to be spread over two years: a cold response to the original royal demand to be allowed a tenth and fifteenth in each year no parliament met. None the less, the parliament of 1410 represented something of a victory for the Prince of Wales, and at the dissolution (on the day after the Commons had announced their vote) he made it more complete when, taking advantage of the Commons' demand for a final list of the councillors and their full and straightforward repetition of the official oath, he secured the replacement of Henry IV's old friends, Bishop Langley of Durham and the Earl of Westmorland, by two of his own, Bishop Chichele of St Davids and the Earl of Warwick. That at least some credit for the prince's success can be given to Thomas Chaucer may reasonably be assumed. That his rôle in the parliament of 1410 had been a positive one, is clear from the very record of the next.

This last effective parliament of Henry IV met on 3 November 1411 and sat until 19 December. Early in the year Chaucer had strengthened his local power in Oxfordshire by leasing from the Queen a number of her dower estates in the north of the county, including Woodstock,[1] and was now returned as knight of the shire for the fourth consecutive time. At Westminster, he was once again re-elected Speaker. This in itself suggests that the Prince of Wales and the Beauforts still commanded support in the Lower House.

[1] *CPR, 1408-13*, 283, 298. Chaucer paid the Queen £127 odd per annum for this lease, which was his for life.

None the less, the ascendancy of this party was already threatened, and its demand that Henry IV should abdicate (recorded in some of the chronicles as made during this session) was in fact an act of desperation. Even the King, ailing though he was, took advantage of Chaucer's request for privilege of speech to tell him that he would not submit to any sort of 'novelty' or fresh restraint on his liberty in this parliament, and Chaucer had to remodel his petition in more discreet and acceptable terms. Moreover, when the prince and his colleagues on the Council received their *congé* during the session, it was not suggested that their successors should be nominated and sworn in parliament as they themselves had been. Parliament ended very uneasily: on the last day the Commons had to agree to the King's demand for the annulment of a statute of 1410 which infringed his prerogative; Lords and Commons alike humbly petitioned the King to declare himself satisfied with the loyalty of the members of this and the previous parliament; but the vote of supplies —a mere year's extension of the wool-subsidy and a tax of 6s. 8d. on every £20 of annual income from lands and rents—fell so far short of liberality as hardly to suggest great confidence in the old régime now newly restored. Henry of Monmouth's opponents were soon, however, clearly in control: Sir John Pelham, an executor of the King's will, the chief steward of the Duchy of Lancaster estates south of Trent, and a friend of Archbishop Arundel, became Treasurer of England; early in 1412 the primate himself once more became Chancellor. The prince was followed as chief of the Council by his next younger brother, Thomas, whom the King soon afterwards created Duke of Clarence. The conduct of affairs rested with this ministry until the end of the reign.

Another parliament met on 3 February 1413. It continued in session for over six weeks, but Henry IV's death on 20 March both ended and nullified its proceedings. Of these no normal record was kept, and the name of the Speaker is unknown. Especially since the electoral returns have not survived either, it would be idle to speculate on his identity, but Thomas Chaucer may be regarded as the most unlikely of possibilities. None the less, he remained of some account: not only did he continue in office as Chief Butler, but in 1412 Bishop Repingdon of Lincoln, a friend of Henry IV, appointed him as constable and seneschal of the castle and town of Banbury for life.[1]

[1] J. W. F. Hill, *Medieval Lincoln*, 258n.

CHAPTER 7

Under Henry V

ON the first day of his reign (21 March 1413) Henry V appointed
Bishop Beaufort as Chancellor and the Earl of Arundel (Archbishop Arundel's nephew, but an old friend of his own) as
Treasurer. On the following day Henry summoned his first parliament, which was to meet on 14 May. So far as the new administration was concerned, the session passed off well enough: it came to an
end in under four weeks (on 9 June) with a grant of a tenth and
fifteenth (payable within the year), an extension of the wool-subsidy
for no less than four years and of tunnage and poundage for one, and
an appropriation of £10,000 for expenditure by the royal Household.
The Commons, however, when announcing their grant, had expressed a hope that taxation in all its forms would soon be alleviated
by good government. At the end of the first week of the session,
they had already complained of Henry IV's failure to provide a more
competent administration (despite his approval of their requests for
bon governance), a fact of which, they said, the present King was well
aware; and they had also drawn attention to lack of control on the
borders and overseas. It was over the King's reaction to these complaints that the Lower House ran into difficulties in this session with
its Speaker.

The Speaker first chosen by the Commons in 1413 was William
Stourton, a lawyer who held the rank of apprentice-at-law, had been
retained as legal counsel by the administration of the Duchy of
Lancaster from 1401 to 1405, and had sat in half of Henry IV's
parliaments.[1] Now (as in 1410) member for Dorset, he had just been
confirmed by Henry V in the office of J.P. in Wiltshire, Somerset,
and Cornwall. He had been connected with the King before his
accession: in the administration of the estates of the Duchy of
Cornwall, in which he was 'the Prince's Chief Steward in the West
and South' certainly between October 1404 and June 1408 (probably

[1] For references and a more detailed survey of Stourton's career, see my paper,
'William Stourton of Stourton', *Proceedings of the Dorset Natural History and
Archaeological Society*, vol. lxxxii (1960), pp. 155–66. For other aspects of Stourton's
career, see the Appendix.

for longer) at an annual fee of 40 marks.[1] It is quite likely that Stourton had also been employed by Henry in the Principality of Wales. He was a friend of Sir Walter Hungerford, now M.P. for Wiltshire, whom the King had recently appointed Chief Steward of the Duchy of Lancaster south of Trent. He was also well known to Sir William Hankford, the newly promoted Chief Justice of the King's Bench, whom he was serving as a feoffee-to-uses and had already named as an executor of his own will. In this document (drawn in July 1410) Stourton had left a bequest of some value to his 'revered lord and father', Archbishop Arundel: if this was a token of friendship with the primate, Stourton's election as Speaker had perhaps exposed the Commons' wish not to lean too far towards either of the parties whose attempts to monopolize control of the royal authority had made so very uneasy the last five years of the previous reign. But to return to the Commons' dispute with Stourton.

When the King demanded that the Commons' oral complaints of lack of governance should be put into writing, Stourton had agreed. Three days later (on 25 May), however, the Commons sent a deputation to protest that their consent had not been obtained. Another week passed, and on 3 June they announced that Stourton was ill and unable to continue. John Doreward, shire-knight for Essex, had led the deputation which had made the Commons' original protest, and it was he whom the Commons now presented as their new Speaker. So it was that the Commons' second choice for the Speakership in Henry IV's first parliament, became second-choice Speaker in the first parliament of Henry V also.

Like Stourton, the new Speaker belonged to an older generation.[2] A member of Henry IV's council during the first half of his reign, since his dismissal in 1406 Doreward had virtually lost contact with high-level politics:[3] in 1413 it was nine years since his last election to parliament, and he was no longer even a J.P. in his own county of Essex.[4] The election of a tried man of affairs who yet was free from

---

[1] Duchy of Cornwall, Assession Roll, P.R.O., E 306/2/7; Duchy of Cornwall, Ministers' Accounts, P.R.O., S.C. 6/813/23, mem. 5v. I owe these references to the kindness of Dr R. W. Dunning.

[2] For earlier references to Doreward, see pp. 137-9.

[3] On 2 June 1407 Doreward was still owed by the Exchequer 200 marks (two years' salary) for his services as royal councillor, being then compelled to release payment of this sum for a free licence to found his chantry at Stanway (a hard bargain) (CPR, 1405-8, 330).

[4] It is conceivable (though inherently unlikely) that Doreward represented Essex in the parliament of 1410, for which the Essex returns are lost. Otherwise

recent political embroilments perhaps confirms the impression that the Commons in Henry V's first parliament were imbued with a spirit of appeasement and compromise between the old and the new régimes.

Once Henry V had inserted men whose personal loyalty he fully trusted into the key positions of the central administration of the Crown, he showed himself ready to let bygones be bygones. This policy 'paid off', not least in re-uniting the royal family. But difficulties were soon to arise in another direction. The Lollards, perhaps disappointed of their hopes of the new reign, were upset by the support which Henry gave to Archbishop Arundel's prosecution and condemnation of his own former friend, Sir John Oldcastle, one of the most active of their sect; and, when Oldcastle escaped from the Tower and plotted rebellion, many Lollards, especially craftsmen and tradesfolk in the Midlands, took up arms to support him, converging on London (where their co-religionists were also numerous) in January 1414. The rising was crushed by Henry with characteristic vigour and sharpness, but Oldcastle himself eluded capture and continued to give trouble. The northern Midlands had for some time been restless and unruly, but it may well have been the wind of Lollard commotion there which had already moved the King on 1 December 1413 to summon his second parliament to meet at the end of January in Leicester, 'the heretics' metropolis' (McFarlane); there can hardly be any doubt at all that it was the threat of actual insurrection which caused him to order, on Christmas Eve, a postponement of the meeting until 30 April 1414.

The Leicester parliament got off to a prompt start in a hall newbuilt for the purpose near the church of the Greyfriars. After listen-

---

the only parliament of Henry IV in which he had sat since 1399 had been that of January 1404. He had been left out of the commission of the peace for Essex in December 1411. After briefly acting as makeshift Speaker in 1413, Doreward was re-elected to parliament when it was summoned to meet at Leicester in April 1414. This was his last parliamentary appearance. Meanwhile, in November 1413, he had been made a J.P. in Essex again, continuing to be re-appointed until his death seven years later. In 1415 he was one of the feoffees of Humphrey, Duke of Gloucester. A year or so later he was involved in a dispute with Bishop Beaufort, then Chancellor, over a piece of woodland near Lexden (Essex) where the bishop, as his brother the Earl of Somerset's executor and royal grantee of the FitzWalter wardship, contested Doreward's claims. Some time before his death Doreward lent to Henry V £100, for the repayment of only half of which his widow was glad to compound with the Exchequer in 1426. Doreward had died on 12 November 1420 and been buried at Bocking.

ing to the advice of Bishop Beaufort, the Chancellor, not to under-
estimate the danger of Lollardy to the fabric of Church and State
alike, nor to overlook the part played by the King in frustrating it,
and also to his announcement—not so edifying but more pleasurable
—that the King was not asking for any direct taxation, the Commons
withdrew to their 'assigned house' in the conventual infirmary. Here
they showed both loyalty and good sense by electing as their
Speaker one to whom the King was very friendly disposed: Sir
Walter Hungerford, knight of the shire for Wiltshire.[1]

Sir Walter was the only surviving son of that one of John of
Gaunt's most trusted servants who had been Speaker in Edward
III's last parliament (Sir Thomas Hungerford). Sir Thomas had
already died and Walter himself had only just about come of age
when, in the summer of 1399, Gaunt's heir, Henry of Bolingbroke,
returned from exile to recover the Duchy of Lancaster. Walter joined
the rebellion whose easy outcome was Henry's seizure of the crown,
and he was one of the large batch of esquires whom the new King
himself dubbed knights on the eve of his coronation. Since then
much of his life had been spent in wearing the royal livery, not a
leisurely, nor indeed an unprofitable occupation in the 'unquiet
time' of Henry IV. A trained soldier, Sir Walter was also an accomplished courtier of cultivated, perhaps even scholarly, tastes. He was
certainly literate. Henry IV appointed Hungerford to be his younger
daughter Philippa's chamberlain, in which capacity he accompanied
her to Sweden in 1406 for her marriage to Eric of Pomerania (King
of Denmark, Sweden and Norway). But it was left for Henry V
properly to appreciate and make best use of Sir Walter's administrative and diplomatic qualities. When, within three weeks of his
accession, Henry made an almost clean sweep in the higher administrative offices of the Duchy of Lancaster, Hungerford's promotion
to be Chief Steward of the duchy estates south of Trent and in
Wales (the position vacated by his father just twenty years before)
was one of the resulting new appointments; and Sir Walter continued to hold the office for nearly a quarter of a century. He was
also sheriff of Somerset and Dorset when Speaker in 1414, the
irregularity of his election to parliament for Wiltshire passing, not
surprisingly, unnoticed.

Perhaps mainly because the Commons had no need to debate any

[1] For references and a detailed treatment of Hungerford's career, see my paper
'Three Wiltshire Speakers', *Wiltshire Archaeological and Natural History Magazine*
pp. 301–41. For Hungerford's later career, see the Appendix.

taxation save tunnage and poundage (which they now extended for
three years, so bringing it into line with the wool-subsidy), the
session was generally even-tempered and lasted for little more than
four weeks. No difficulty was experienced in passing the statute
which 'placed the responsibility for hunting out and destroying
Lollardy upon the shoulders of every royal and municipal officer'
(McFarlane), or the statute which converted a breach of a truce or
safe-conduct into high treason and provided for the appointment of
conservators of truces in the ports, or that which tightened up the
conduct of criminal proceedings against riot; and the Act, passed
at the Commons' request, confiscating for the Crown the lands of
the non-conventual alien priories, was unlikely to displease any but
the die-hard defenders of ecclesiastical privilege. Parliament also
approved what the King did to demonstrate his amicable relations
with his own family and other members of the higher nobility: by
creating his brother John, Duke of Bedford, and his youngest
brother, Humphrey, Duke of Gloucester; by confirming the earlier
promotions of the Duke of Clarence and the Earl of Dorset; by
giving to Richard of Conisborough (brother-in-law of the Earl of
March) the title of Earl of Cambridge; and by declaring Richard's
elder brother, the Duke of York, loyal to the House of Lancaster.
A request made by the Earl of Salisbury to be restored to the lands
forfeited by his father in 1401 was, however, referred to the next
parliament. In this connexion, it is worth noting that one of the
errors alleged against that judgement of Henry IV's second parliament was that it had been made by the Lords Temporal alone, instead of by the King and Lords both Spiritual and Temporal, and,
moreover, without being requested or agreed by the Commons,
*queux de droit serront peticioners ou assentours de ceo qe serra ordeine pur
Ley en Parlement.* It is to Salisbury, not the Commons, that we owe
this lesson in constitutional propriety. In other words, this is an
ex parte statement and has no necessary validity. Which is not to say,
however, that the Commons disagreed with the principle. In fact,
when, during the Leicester session, they protested that their consent
was needed for all official amendments to such of their petitions as
resulted in statutes, the reason they gave was that *the Comune of youre
lond, the whiche that is, and ever hath be, a membre of youre Parlement, ben
as well Assentirs as Peticioners.* It has been shown that this complaint
arose out of the official treatment of common petitions presented in
the previous parliament, and, despite the thesis (and even phraseology)
used in the Earl of Salisbury's claim, there is no reason to believe

that this objection of the Commons was not of their own independent contrivance. The King's reply was seemingly to deny them what they claimed, and the Commons had to make do with it.

There is nothing to indicate what was Hungerford's own part as Speaker in all this. There can, however, be little question that his conduct was satisfactory to his royal master. Certainly, his services underwent, as a result, no devaluation. Within seven weeks of the end of the Leicester parliament Hungerford was off on a royal embassy to treat with the Emperor Sigismund at Coblenz and (after a brief return home to report) spent the winter acting as one of Henry V's agents at the General Council of the Church recently begun at Constance. During the six years between July 1415 and July 1421 he occupied the office of Steward of the King's Household, and from 1417 at the latest until the end of the reign was a member of Henry's Council, spending most of this time in France with the King himself. His being chosen by Henry as an executor of his will and a guardian of his infant son (Henry of Windsor) was to assure him an important place in the next reign. No more need here be said of his later career than that he returned to the scene of his Speakership in 1426, being then summoned for the first time as a peer of parliament along with another member of Henry VI's Council and one of his predecessors in the Chair, Lord Tiptoft.

When parliament next came together, at Westminster on 19 November 1414, it appears that a decision to undertake the recovery of what Henry V regarded as his rights in France, by war if necessary, had already been made in principle. It remained for the government to test the feeling of the estates and, when they were won over, to continue to negotiate, if only until such time as military preparations were complete. Bishop Beaufort, the Chancellor, opening the parliament with a sermon on the text, *Dum tempus habemus, operemur bonum*, took pains to impress upon it that peace at home was a happy augury for success abroad; he was also able to suggest, in support, that an expansion of the patrimony of the Prince would result in greater financial advantages to his country in the future than losses by taxation in the present. By electing the Chancellor's cousin, Thomas Chaucer, for his fourth term as Speaker,[1] the Commons may perhaps have conveyed their general sympathy with the official line.

[1] Since his last Speakership in 1411, Chaucer had been M.P. for Oxfordshire in Henry V's first parliament in 1413. To it he had secured the return (as burgess for both Taunton and Wallingford) of Lewis John, a London vintner with

There can be no doubt that Thomas Chaucer was acceptable to the government. The accession of Henry V had seen his instant re-appointment to all his royal offices, including the Chief Butlership. At this time Chaucer was also very close to his cousin, Bishop Beaufort, the Chancellor. This is attested by the fact that when, in September 1413, Beaufort sealed the patent giving Chaucer his new appointment to the keepership of the royal forests of Woolmer and Aliceholt (Hampshire), he did so at the nearby manor of Worldham where, this being one of Chaucer's own estates, he was presumably his cousin's guest.[1] That Chaucer was in Henry V's trust is confirmed not only by his being selected (in November 1413) as sheriff of Hampshire (an office he was still holding when elected for Oxford-shire to the autumn parliament of 1414), but also, and much more convincingly, by his inclusion in a very important diplomatic mis-sion that was sent to Ypres in June 1414. One aim of this embassy was to negotiate an alliance with the Count of Holland. Its much more important object, however, was to continue, with the Duke of Burgundy himself, negotiations for an alliance (begun by the duke's envoys at the recent parliament in Leicester) on the basis of an offer of marriage between Henry V and one of Burgundy's daughters. It was less than a month after his return from this mission[2] that Chaucer was elected Speaker in the November parliament. Regarding his contacts with the King, it may further be noticed that Chaucer's son-in-law, Sir John Philip, whose body was to be brought home for burial from Harfleur less than a year later, was one of the King's personal comrades: Philip's brass in Kidderminster church records how *Henricus quintus dilexerat hunc ut amicus*.[3] The success attending the Commons' preferment of Chaucer's own private petitions in this 1414 parliament, has already been noticed.[4] No doubt his work as Speaker deserved it. For after a very short session of even less than three weeks, the Commons confirmed their approval of the govern-ment's policy by granting two whole tenths and fifteenths, making

---

whom he had contracted as Chief Butler for considerable amounts of wine for Henry IV's Household, and for whose recent appointment as Master of the Mints in the Tower and at Calais he had stood surety (*CCR, 1413–19*, 66). In November 1414, as Chief Butler, Chaucer was still owed some £523 by Henry IV's executors, for wines purveyed during the late reign (*Rot. Parl.*, iv. 35).

[1] *CPR, 1413–16*, 102.

[2] J. H. Wylie, *The Reign of Henry V*, i. 414; *DKR*, xliv. 554; Exchequer Issue Roll, P.R.O., E 403/617, mem. 6.

[3] H. A. Napier, op. cit., 33.   [4] See above, p. 90.

the first payable as early as Candlemas (2 February) 1415. That the second was not to be collected until a year later suggests, however, that the recommendation (by both Lords and Commons) that every effort should be made to reach a peaceful settlement with the French —a policy of negotiation before resort to war—was quite seriously meant. (It was not unprecedented, although unusual, for two such subsidies to be granted for collection in one year.)

The issue of the writs for the next parliament, which were dated 12 August 1415, was the first important act of the Duke of Bedford in his capacity as *Custos Anglie*. On the previous day, Henry V had sailed from Portsmouth at the head of the great fleet collected to carry his army to the Seine. The parliament was to meet at Westminster on 21 October, by which time, the King was probably hoping, he would be in a position to supply it with news of signal military success. This looked hardly likely when, at Michaelmas, the opening of parliament was postponed for a fortnight, perhaps in accordance with instructions from the royal base at Harfleur: admittedly, the siege of this key-port itself had been successfully ended a full week before this change of parliamentary plan, but the losses of English effectives (mainly from dysentery) had been heavy, reducing the army by almost a third. A week before parliament met on 4 November, however, the great news of the astounding victory won at Agincourt (on 25 October) had come through. 'As the King gave all honour to Almighty God, so must all honour be given to the King': this was the gist of Bedford's announcement communicated at the opening of parliament by Chancellor Beaufort, who himself went on to preach from the now highly suitable text, *Sicut et ipse fecit nobis, ita et nos ei faciamus*. Eight or nine days later,[1] this shortest parliament on record since the reign of Edward III was dissolved. Apart from the ratification (at the Commons' request) of the judgements against the conspirators of the Southampton plot, there was little to record of the business of the session save the grants of taxation. But these were important: in their gratitude to the King, the Commons allowed the still outstanding tenth and fifteenth (voted the year before) to be levied in mid-December (instead of at Candlemas 1416), and another such subsidy was made due in less than a year's time (at Martinmas 1416); the wool-subsidy and tunnage and poundage were given to the King for life, a grant for

---

[1] *Chronicon Adae de Usk* (ed. E. M. Thompson, p. 127) says that parliament was dissolved on St Brice's Day (13/14 November). The parliamentary grant, usually announced on the last day, was dated 12 November.

which there was no precedent except the short-lived concession extorted by Richard II in 1398, and even that had not included tunnage and poundage. The Commons' sole reservations were that Henry should not dispose of it by grants for life or term of years, and that his successors should not be entitled to regard it as a precedent. Not from long before 1398, certainly never since then, had the Commons proved so suggestible.

Perhaps no Speaker ever had a more comfortable passage through a session than Sir Richard Redmayne, the knight of the shire for Yorkshire who, aged about sixty, held office in this parliament of 1415.[1] The head of the family of Redmayne of Levens (Westmorland), Sir Richard, by his marriage with the elder daughter of Lord Aldbrough[2] enjoyed possession of considerable estates in the West Riding of Yorkshire, especially at Harewood in Wharfedale, where he was the near neighbour of Henry IV's Chief Justice, William Gascoigne. Born about the time of the battle of Poitiers, Redmayne's early manhood, during the first half of Richard II's reign, had been mainly spent in royal service on the Scottish March, where his father, one of Edward III's professional captains, was a march-warden and also keeper of Roxburgh castle. By 1388 Sir Richard had been accepted as a royal retainer and was granted annuities eventually together worth nearly 100 marks.[3] He went with Richard II on both his Irish expeditions (1394-5 and 1399), during the second being master of the King's horses, notwithstanding his appointment as sheriff in Cumberland. Perhaps mainly because of his connexions

[1] For references and further details of Redmayne's career, see my paper, 'Two Medieval Westmorland Speakers', *Transactions of the Cumberland and Westmorland Antiquarian and Archaeological Society*, New Series, vol. lxii (1962), pp. 113–44.

[2] This marriage was contracted some time between September 1393 and July 1399. Sir Richard Redmayne's wife's father was William Lord Aldbrough who died in 1388, leaving a son, William, who died without issue in 1391. The latter's coheirs were his two sisters, Elizabeth, the widow of Sir Brian Stapleton who later married Redmayne, and Sybil, the wife of Sir William Ryther. Redmayne's marriage brought him possession of a moiety of the Aldbrough estates which were fortunately quite unencumbered by rights of dower. His own estates round Levens were insignificant by comparison, and he found more scope for his energies in Yorkshire. Before 1415 he had been M.P. for Yorkshire in 1406 (when he was one of the auditors of accounts demanded by the Commons) and in the second parliament of 1414.

[3] In 1386 Sir Richard had been connected in a military capacity with Richard II's friend, Robert de Vere, and in 1390 similarly with Henry Percy (Hotspur). He was confirmed as a royal retainer in 1390 and served Richard II as sheriff of Cumberland in 1393-4, 1396-7, and 1398-9.

with his step-brother, Lord Greystoke, and Henry Hotspur, both of
whom in his absence had given great support to the rebellion of Henry
of Bolingbroke, Redmayne lost nothing by the revolution of 1399.
In fact, Henry IV very soon (31 October 1399) confirmed him in all
his royal fees, and when these later on fell into arrears compensated
him with royal wardships. Redmayne was sheriff of Cumberland
again in 1401–2; he was sheriff of Yorkshire in 1403–4[1] and escheator
there in 1404–5.[2] These last two appointments in the most disaffected
of the English shires suggest that his loyalty to the Lancastrian
dynasty was regarded as beyond dispute: he did in fact help suppress
the local revolts led by the Percies and others in these years and later,
serving with the royal militia and on judicial commissions set up to
punish rebels. It was probably in these circumstances that Redmayne
first became well known to the young John of Lancaster, Henry
IV's third son, later Duke of Bedford. Certainly, his diplomatic
work on the Scottish border in 1409–10 (when Prince John was at his
headquarters in Berwick as Warden of the East March) brought them
into close contact. This link (especially remarkable in view of Redmayne's Speakership in a parliament under Bedford's presidency)
was strengthened by the grant to Bedford of the barony of Kendal,
of which Redmayne was a tenant at Levens. And the attachment
clearly grew stronger: it must further be noted that when, before
returning to France in July 1417, Henry V re-appointed Bedford to
act as his Lieutenant in England, Redmayne acted as a member of
the duke's council; that when, on 4 October 1417, Bedford was received into the confraternity of the abbey of St Albans, so, as one
of the duke's retinue, was Redmayne himself; that on the same day
(according to the *Liber Niger* of the abbey) the duke requested the

[1] In his capacity as sheriff of Yorkshire, Redmayne in June 1404 conducted,
from York to Pontefract, William Serle, a former body-servant of Richard II
who had just been seized on the Border and brought south by the Earl of
Northumberland (when the earl came to Pontefract to meet Henry IV and surrender his castles). Serle, who in 1399 had escaped to France and then returned
to Scotland, had helped foster the notion that Richard II was still alive, which
had given the Percies help in raising rebellion in 1403 and always caused the
government some embarrassment. Serle was now executed at Pontefract.

[2] After the suppression of the Yorkshire rising of 1405, Redmayne is known
to have accompanied Henry IV on the expedition to recover Berwick from the
Earl of Northumberland's forces and to get possession of certain other Percy
strongholds. It was on 9 August that the King gave him, rent-free, the custody
of his stepson's manor of Carlton, first granted him two years before at an
annual farm of £70; the gift was, moreover, soon back-dated to Michaelmas
1404.

monks to pray for Redmayne's stepson, Sir Brian Stapleton (then very recently killed in Normandy), as one who was *multum sibi dilectus*; and (for good measure) that before Bedford's death in 1435 Redmayne's grandson and heir had become the duke's master-forester of Kendal. Clearly *persona grata* with Bedford, Redmayne enjoyed the King's own confidence, too. At his accession Henry V had apparently curtailed Redmayne's royal fees somewhat; but he used his services in local commissions, for example, as a J.P. in Westmorland and the West Riding. Moreover, on 1 December 1415, a week after his triumphant return to Westminster from France and, of course, following Redmayne's successful Speakership, the King made him sheriff of Yorkshire again.[1] It may be added that, although Redmayne himself had been too old to join Henry V's army, his son (Richard) and stepson (Stapleton) had done so and been in the thick of it at Agincourt.[2]

Between the autumn of 1415 and the summer of 1417, when he again invaded France, Henry V's policies at home and abroad were being made to serve his intention to remain what Agincourt had made him: 'the arbiter of European politics' (Stubbs). To state this more prosaically, he prepared the diplomatic encirclement of France in anticipation of a renewal of the war which should be irresistible and conclusive in its effects. The year 1416 was particularly notable for Henry's achievements in the diplomatic field, most significantly at the 'summit-conference' in England with the Emperor Sigismund: the latter, in his anxiety to promote the success of the General Council at Constance, was won over to accept in the Treaty of Canterbury (August 1416) an offensive and defensive alliance; and he and Henry had a further meeting (in October) at Calais, where they were joined by Duke John of Burgundy.

During this time two parliaments were held, both in 1416. In the first, which met on 16 March, the Commons' Speaker was Sir Walter Beauchamp of Bromham (Wilts.), sitting for the only time in his career (so far as is known) as a knight of the shire.[3] The elder son

---

[1] Since being sheriff of Yorkshire in 1403–4, Redmayne had been sheriff of Cumberland in 1411–12.

[2] Redmayne was again M.P. for Yorkshire in 1420 and 1421 (the last parliament of Henry V's reign). All his royal annuities were confirmed to him at the beginning of Henry VI's reign. Aged about seventy, he died on 22 May 1426 and was buried with his wife in the Blackfriars at York.

[3] For references and a more detailed treatment of Beauchamp's life, see my paper, 'Three Wiltshire Speakers', *Wiltshire Archaeological and Natural History Magazine*, vol. lvi, pp. 342–58. For Beauchamp's later career, see the Appendix.

of the head of the family of Beauchamp of Powick (a cadet branch of
the family of which the Earl of Warwick represented the senior line),
Sir Walter, through a fortunate marriage, enjoyed possession of all
the considerable estates in the Vale of Pewsey and elsewhere in
Wiltshire belonging to the families of De la Roche and De la Mare.
(Half he held *jure uxoris*, half by royal grant of wardship.) He had
joined the royal Household in the rank of esquire at the very beginning of the reign of Henry IV, by whom he was well rewarded for his
continuous support, including military service, especially by the
grant of an annuity of £40 (for life) out of the royal revenues from
Gloucestershire, by a grant of the custody of two Duchy of Lancaster
manors and of the royal forest of Braden in Wiltshire (worth another
£40 a year), and also by appointments to the shrievalty of Wiltshire
in 1403 and 1407. It would appear that Walter's royal annuity was
not renewed by Henry V in 1413. But Walter's father, Sir William,
was confirmed by Henry in possession of the office of constable of
Gloucester castle (originally granted him in 1392); and the resumption of the French war gave Walter himself a chance to make a fresh
start in the royal service. He took full advantage of the opportunity:
he served in the expedition of 1415 with a personal retinue of three
men-at-arms and twelve archers and was knighted in the course of
the campaign. Immediately on his return home (25 November 1415),
as a 'King's knight' he was granted the custody of the lordship of
Somerford Keynes (then in royal wardship following the death of
the Duke of York at Agincourt), this estate being leased to him rent-
free, provided its income did not exceed £20 a year. It was at this
juncture that he was elected to parliament for Wiltshire and became
Speaker.

Beauchamp's first session as Speaker lasted for just over three
weeks (from 16 March to 8 April 1416). During it the Commons
advanced the payment of the tenth and fifteenth voted in the previous parliament by five months (from Martinmas to Whitsuntide
1416). Following a break for Easter, parliament met again on 4
May, a week after the Emperor Sigismund's landing in England.
When it was dissolved is not known; but the second and final
session is unlikely to have been long, if only because the King was so
busy with diplomacy. One of the important topics discussed during
the parliament was the payment of military wages, a matter which was
soon quite satisfactorily dealt with from the Speaker's own point of
view: on 6 June the Exchequer paid him £286 odd (on the account
of the Treasurer for the War), this being most of what was his due

for service in the 1415 campaign. The best, however, was yet to come. Joining Henry V's second expeditionary force in 1417 and taking part in the systematic conquest of Normandy, Sir Walter was appointed to be the first English *bailli* of Rouen, the duchy capital, as soon as it surrendered in January 1419. Then, in less than two years (probably in July 1420), he became Treasurer of the King's Household (and *ex officio* Treasurer for the War). In October 1421 he relinquished this key position in the whole organization of royal military finance, only to become Queen Katherine's first Steward of Household and Chief Steward of those Duchy of Lancaster estates comprised in her dower. Henry V had already (in June 1421) appointed him as one of the special 'working' executors of his will.

The writs of summons for the second parliament of 1416 were dated at Sandwich on 3 September, immediately before Henry V crossed to Calais to continue his negotiations with Sigismund and the Duke of Burgundy. The King returned home just in time for the opening of parliament on 19 October, and the session ended with parliament's dissolution a month later (on 18 November). The Chancellor, having first reviewed the objects of Henry's previous meetings with parliament, had demanded its help in fulfilling the King's rightful purpose in France which (in view of the stubbornness of the enemy) could now only be brought about by a continuance of the war. Formal ratification of the Anglo-Imperial treaty of Canterbury was obtained. The King renewed the general pardon of two years before; he also undertook (following a *grevouse compleinte* from the Commons) to alleviate the effects of the Statute of Truces so far as relations with Scotsmen were involved. But the chief business of the session was the grant of two tenths and fifteenths, three-quarters of which were made due so soon as Candlemas 1417 and the remainder at Martinmas following. Although the Commons showed their concern at the increased pressure of direct taxation by stipulating that no fresh tax should be demanded before the present grant had been collected, and that recourse should not be had to the recent practice of advancing the time of payment originally agreed for a subsidy, this double subsidy was in itself a lavish concession: it meant, in fact, that in four years (Martinmas 1413–17) no less than six tenths and fifteenths would have been levied (not very far short of what had been granted during the whole of the previous reign).[1]

The Speaker who presumably had helped with contriving the

[1] Of tenths and fifteenths, eight in all had been granted to Henry IV.

Commons' present vote was Roger Flore of Oakham, who was representing Rutland in his fifth successive parliament.[1] Flore had married into money made in the export-trade in wool,[2] but his own career was that of a lawyer with a special aptitude for administering big collections of estates. This was an employment which brought him into contact with a fair number of magnates, chief among whom, and even from the time of Richard II, had been Edward, the late Duke of York, who eventually (in 1415) had made him one of his feoffees-to-uses and an overseer of his will.[3] Locally, in Rutland, Flore had served the Crown as escheator in 1405–6, as sheriff in 1406–7 and 1412–13, and as escheator in 1414–15 (this time in Northants as well).[4] Such appointments were of course nothing out of the way for a man of Flore's capacity. Already, even before he was Speaker, his abilities had caught the King's notice, and Henry had included him among the trustees of the property with which he had endowed his newly founded Bridgettine nunnery at Syon. It was less than a fortnight after the close of his first experience of the Speakership that, on 1 December 1416, Flore followed the late Sir Roger Leche of Chatsworth as Chief Steward of the estates of the Duchy of Lancaster north of Trent.[5] And this office automatically gave him entry into the Duchy Council as well as involving him in membership of the commissions of the peace in the eleven counties of his bailiwick, to which were soon added (by separate appointment in February 1417) Cheshire and the palatinate of Lancashire. Retaining his chief stewardship until his death in 1427 (except in

[1] For references and a fuller account of Flore's career, see my article, 'Roger Flore of Oakham', *Transactions of the Leicestershire Archaeological and Historical Society*, vol. xxxiii (1957), pp. 36–44. Flore had already been M.P. for Rutland in 1397 (Jan.), 1399, 1402, 1404 (Oct.), 1414 (twice), 1415 and 1416 (March).

[2] Flore had married Katherine, the daughter and heir of William Dalby of Exton (a Calais stapler who died in 1404). In 1394 he himself had been a partner in an export of wool lost in transit from Lynn to Calais. He was his father-in-law's principal executor.

[3] On 20 October 1399 Edward of Norwich granted to Flore for life the keeping of his park at Flitteris in the royal forest of Leighfield and the custody of the warren of his lordship of Oakham.

[4] Flore acted as a J.P. in Rutland from November 1397 to the end of Richard II's reign and again from January 1406 until his death. He frequently served Henry IV on other local commissions, for example, collecting subsidies and raising loans.

[5] R. Somerville, *History of the Duchy of Lancaster*, i. 420. Flore's annual fee as duchy chief steward was £40, and he enjoyed an allowance of 5s. for every day spent in administering the office.

M

Lancashire and Cheshire, where he was superseded in 1425), Roger Flore remained a member of the higher administrative staff of the Duchy of Lancaster throughout the period covered by his later Speakerships.

If it was intended to observe the condition attached to the financial grant of November 1416, there was little point in summoning parliament again much before November 1417. It did in fact meet on 16 November 1417. Henry V had already left England on his second expedition into France, and so parliament assembled under the Duke of Bedford who once more had been left behind as *Custos Anglie*. Flore was again elected Speaker. In the meantime, on 21 July, a few days before setting sail from Southampton, the King had drawn up fresh arrangements for the future disposal of those parcels of the Duchy of Lancaster already (in 1415) entrusted to a body of feoffees for the fulfilment of his will. The new proposals included the nomination of a group of twelve, from among whom the existing feoffees were to choose fresh colleagues in the event of death reducing their own number. Speaker Flore, most likely because he was a high-ranking official of the duchy, was one of these new reserve-feoffees.

When parliament met, Henry V's campaign had even then been so successful as to give him control of central Normandy, and his government at home had little trouble in securing a generous grant. At the end of a month's session, the Commons once more conceded a double-subsidy, one tenth and fifteenth to be levied at Candlemas 1418, the other a year later, again on condition that these terms were not 'abbreviated'. Also, the Commons successfully requested that parliamentary authority should be used to strengthen the safeguards for the repayment of a loan of £14,000 contributed by Bishop Beaufort who, having resigned the Chancellorship on the day of the King's departure for France, was now at Constance, busy negotiating his own promotion to the Cardinalate with the new Pope, Martin V. Whether Flore played much of a part in the transaction of Beaufort's guarantee is not known. But it was certainly the Speaker who, on the last day of the session (17 December), conveyed the Commons' suggestion that Lord Charlton of Powys should be recommended to the King for his diligence in capturing the Lollard leader, Sir John Oldcastle. This was three days after the latter had been adjudged in parliament as a traitor to both God and the King and executed.

No firmer testimony of Roger Flore's efficiency as Speaker in

1416 and 1417 could be required than the fact of his election to that office for the third time running. This came about when, after an interval of nearly two years, the Duke of Bedford again met parliament on 16 October 1419. The war in France was still going well: Rouen had fallen at the beginning of the year; no later than the summer Paris itself was being directly threatened. With the murder of Duke John of Burgundy by friends of the Dauphin at Montereau in September, the way lay open to the formation of an Anglo-Burgundian coalition which would make a victorious settlement almost inevitable. (Negotiations for the alliance were actually proceeding during the parliamentary session.) In the meantime, it was necessary perhaps even to intensify the war-effort, running the risk of financial over-strain. And the main point of the speech with which the Chancellor (Bishop Langley of Durham) opened parliament was to emphasize the King's justification. Hostilities had been forced on him by the French failure to respond to his diplomatic approaches: *Necessitas causat bellum, et non Voluntas*; hence the Chancellor's theme, *Bonum facientes, non deficiamus*. That parliament certainly felt uneasy over the effects of the war on the English economy is clear from its concern with the export of coin. Anxiety on this score moved it to require that revenue from taxation should be spent on army-stores in England and also on the purchase of wool, which, if exported directly for sale in Normandy, would provide funds for the payment of the troops there. In considering the possible political effect of war-costs, parliament's evident reluctance in 1419 to repeat the big votes of supply made in 1416 and 1417 must be taken into account: a whole tenth and fifteenth was voted as usual for Candlemas (1420), but what was granted for Martinmas following was no more than a third part of such a subsidy.

It was not long before this decline in parliamentary generosity was made more significant still. For, although by the Treaty of Troyes of May 1420 Charles VI of France was compelled to accept Henry V as his son-in-law and as Regent and Heir of his Kingdom, when parliament met the Duke of Gloucester on 2 December following (the day after Henry entered Paris in triumph), it made no financial grant at all. As the Chancellor's opening speech itself referred to the *fiblesce et poverte des gents du . . . Roialme* and to the scarcity of money, perhaps no grant was asked for. But if this were so, it could hardly be because none was needed. A more fitting opportunity to make fresh demands, it may have been felt, would be provided when the King himself came home; and this he was bound to do soon.

Certainly, the Commons were by now rather touchy over Henry's long absence and themselves petitioned for him to return, bringing his Queen. This was not, of course, in order to make it easy for themselves to succumb to his claims on their generosity. Rather, his very success had given rise to some anxiety: now that he was recognized as Heir of France, they wished to be assured of the superiority of the English to the French Crown (along the lines of Edward III's undertaking of 1340). And, having been told that their petitions could not be engrossed before receiving the King's personal assent, even if he were overseas, they asked that, both now and in the future, their petitions should be either answered during parliament or disregarded altogether (a petition which was itself referred to the King). Short though this parliament presumably was—it can scarcely have lasted for much longer than a fortnight—there seems not to have been so cordial an atmosphere as in earlier meetings during the reign.

The Commons' Speaker in this 1420 parliament had only been chosen after an election so closely contested as to require a count of votes.[1] The result of this division was to show the Commons' preference for Roger Hunt of Chawton, knight of the shire for Bedfordshire, over John Russell, an apprentice-at-law who had been engaged as legal counsel by the administration of the Duchy of Lancaster, year by year, ever since 1403. Of the two nominees, Hunt had the longer parliamentary experience—he had represented either Bedfordshire or Huntingdonshire in all Henry V's previous parliaments for which the electoral returns of these counties are known, certainly in six out of the eight which had met since 1413 (including the last two).[2] He also was a lawyer,[3] but of greater distinction and with better political connexions than Russell. From August 1408 until the end of 1409 Hunt had occupied the post of King's Attorney-General and eventually (in 1438) was to become a Baron of the Exchequer. He may well have owed his legal appointment of 1408 to the influence of Sir John Tiptoft (the Speaker of 1406), who at that

[1] See above, p. 63.

[2] During a long parliamentary career, Hunt was M.P. for Huntingdonshire in 1407, 1413, 1414 (April), 1417, 1419, 1421 (May), 1422, 1423, 1425, 1426, 1427, 1429, 1431, 1432, and 1433, and for Bedfordshire in 1414 (November), 1416 (March), and 1420 (that is, in certainly every parliament between 1417 and 1433, save that of December 1421, the last of Henry V's reign).

[3] He was probably the Hunt who figures in the list of surnames of members of Lincoln's Inn admitted before, and still surviving in, 1420 (*The Admission Book of Lincoln's Inn*, p. 2).

time was Treasurer of England.[1] There is surely no disputing the closeness of Hunt's connexion with this important Lancastrian administrator who, not very long before Hunt was Speaker, had been Treasurer-General of Normandy and was still Seneschal of Aquitaine. In fact, since 1415, when Tiptoft had first assumed office as governor of the English territories in south-west France, Hunt had acted as Tiptoft's financial agent in England, many large sums paid by the Exchequer having gone through his hands.[2] Tiptoft was actually in Guienne when Hunt was Speaker in 1420, and other men of importance with whom Hunt had relations were then with the King in northern France, for example, Sir Walter Hungerford, on whose behalf Hunt had acted as deputy-steward in the Duchy of Lancaster estates south of Trent in 1415–16.[3] Otherwise, in the middle years of his career, Hunt would appear to have had no special contacts of his own with the royal administration.[4] This was far from being the case with Thomas Chaucer, his successor in the Speakership in the next parliament, at which Henry V himself was present in the spring of 1421.

After a continuous absence of nearly three and a half years, Henry V had returned to England on 1 February 1421. One reason for his homecoming was to secure formal ratification, by parliament, of the Treaty of Troyes; another was to have his Queen crowned; but his chief motive was to stir up fresh interest in the war against Dauphinist France. Henry had much to do, and clearly it would take time. It was not until 26 February, two days after the Queen's coronation,

[1] CPR, 1405–8, 459; E. Foss, The Judges of England, iv. 138; Privy Seal warrants for issue, P.R.O., E 404/24/437. The annulment of the patent of his predecessor in the office of Attorney-General recalled that Hunt had been promised it at the instance of Archbishop Arundel (then Chancellor), Bishop Beaufort, and others.

[2] For example, on 18 May 1415 Hunt conveyed to Plymouth the £1,883 6s. 8d. supplied by the Exchequer to Tiptoft as Seneschal of Aquitaine. When Tiptoft was sent on an embassy to the Emperor Sigismund in April 1417, £60, an advance towards the costs of his journey, were paid through Hunt's hands. In July 1419 £300 were similarly paid as part of Tiptoft's wages as Seneschal, and in Easter term 1420 the Exchequer made Tiptoft an assignment for £80 and a payment in cash of some £2,541, both by Roger Hunt's hands. In February 1422 Hunt stood surety when Tiptoft was granted the wardship of the heir of Sir Thomas de la Pole, brother of the Earl of Suffolk.

[3] Robert Somerville, op. cit., i. 430.

[4] Hunt served on many local royal commissions, including commissions of array and for raising loans. He was made a J.P. for Huntingdonshire in April 1416 and for Bedfordshire in February 1422. At this later date he was of the quorum in both counties.

that he summoned parliament to meet some nine weeks later (on 2 May). This long interval Henry occupied in a far-ranging progress through much of his kingdom (from which he did not allow even the news of the defeat and death of his brother Clarence at Baugé to deflect him), paying his respects at important local shrines, but also encouraging military recruitment and extorting war-loans as he went. This last authoritarian exercise, Henry was determined should enable him to meet parliament not needing to demand any subsidy after all. And so it was, thanks mainly, however, to a single loan of 26,500 marks (£17,666 13s. 4d.) from Bishop Beaufort, who was still owed over £8,300 from previous advances. By this last huge loan Beaufort was virtually compounding for two grave offences: his acceptance, without the King's leave, of a cardinalate and papal legateship in December 1417, and his disobedience of a royal order to appear at the treaty-making and the King's marriage at Troyes in May 1420. Henry V was now ready to let bygones be bygones, but in 1419 he had been so suspicious of Beaufort's ecclesiastical ambitions as to send the bishop's own cousin and retainer, Thomas Chaucer, to spy on his conduct and discover his plans. This Chaucer did, reporting to the King direct, at first by secret correspondence, but later, in the spring of 1420, in person.[1] It is a tribute to Chaucer's intelligence that he had been able to discharge so successfully this task of acting as royal watch-dog without losing Beaufort's confidence. He had, in fact, done his best to conciliate the King.

Thomas Chaucer's behaviour in this difficult episode, of course, did no more than confirm Henry V's reliance on his character and abilities. After his Speakership in the autumn of 1414 when war had been decided upon, Chaucer continued to hold his Household office of Chief Butler, receiving in July 1416 assignments at the Exchequer and on the customs to meet the sum of over £2,800 due to him for the wines he had provided for the expedition which Henry V had taken to France in 1415. Chaucer himself had contracted to join the royal army of that year with a retinue of 11 men-at-arms and 36 archers.[2] His retinue, having served at the siege of Harfleur (where two of the men-at-arms died), also fought at Agincourt. But Chaucer himself had fallen ill before even the

[1] For a discussion of the quarrel between Henry V and Bishop Beaufort and of Chaucer's difficult part in it, see K. B. McFarlane, 'Henry V, Bishop Beaufort and the Red Hat, 1417–1421', *EHR*, lx (1945), pp. 316–48.

[2] M. B. Ruud, *Thomas Chaucer* (Minneapolis, 1926), pp. 24–5, 104.

expedition sailed from Portsmouth and so took no part in it.[1] He did, however, go overseas with the King in the summer of 1417, and his preoccupation with diplomatic work[2] between then and his return to England early in 1419 was apparently such as to require his temporary resignation of the Chief Butlership (in November 1418). Crossing the Channel again in the spring of 1420, in order to report to the King on Bishop Beaufort's *intents*, he had been once more employed in diplomacy, this time on the embassy to Britanny whose object was to negotiate the acceptance of the Treaty of Troyes, first with the Lieutenant and the prelates and barons of the duchy, and then with the duke himself.[3] Chaucer's knowledge of the Treaty of Troyes, which the parliament of May 1421 was going to be asked to ratify, was probably one factor moving the Commons to elect him as their Speaker on this occasion.[4] Very likely another was their awareness of his

---

[1] Chaucer's son-in-law, Sir John Philip, one of the feoffees in the Duchy of Lancaster estates set aside to help the fulfilment of Henry V's will, died ten days after the fall of Harfleur.

[2] After the surrender of Caen early in September 1417, Henry V was prepared to negotiate if only to confuse the French; and on 1 October, and again in mid-December, Chaucer was one of an embassy instructed to treat for peace (T. D. Hardy, *Rotuli Normanniae*, 167, 169, 205).

[3] *DKR*, xli. 776; xliv. 620; xlii. 375, 379.

[4] Chaucer certainly had friends in the Lower House, including John Golafre (M.P. Berkshire) and another of his own feoffees-to-uses, William Bord, M.P. for Taunton (where Chaucer's occasional influence on elections has already been noted). Perhaps even by this time Chaucer's only daughter Alice had married her second husband, Thomas Montagu, Earl of Salisbury, for whose restoration to his father's dignity the Commons successfully petitioned in this parliament. Under Henry VI Chaucer again represented Oxfordshire in the parliaments of 1422, 1426, 1427-8, 1429-30, and 1431. (It was by parliamentary authority that on 5 December 1422 his appointment for life as Chief Butler was renewed.) In these years he considerably increased his royal grants, especially of wardships, including in 1431 the wardship of his wife's great-niece, Eleanor, daughter of the Lord Moleyns who was killed during the siege of Orleans, where Chaucer's son-in-law (the Earl of Salisbury) had also met his death (in 1428). Meanwhile, the parliament of 1423-4 saw Chaucer appointed to the King's Council where, although he retained a place until his death, his attendances seem to have become very spasmodic (*Rot. Parl.*, iv. 201; *PPC*, iii. 155, 157, 163, 169, 266; iv. 263). He accompanied the Duke of Bedford and Cardinal Beaufort to Calais in March 1427. By the time of his last election to parliament (in 1431) his only daughter (Alice) had re-married, her third husband being William de la Pole, Earl of Suffolk. The latter, in June 1434, when Steward of the King's Household, was associated with Chaucer in his offices of constable of Wallingford castle and steward of the honours of Wallingford and St Valery and the four and a half hundreds of Chiltern, by a grant in survivorship. Chaucer died five months later, on 18 November 1434, and was buried at Ewelme (Napier, op. cit., 44).

previous experience of this office, which he was now being called upon to hold for the fifth time. Unquestionably, he was altogether acceptable to both the King and the greatest of his creditors, the Bishop of Winchester, whose estrangement he had himself done something to end.

Not the least important of the items of business during the session was to regularize, in advance, decisions of the Council giving security for the repayment of all loans financing Henry V's next expedition. But the need for parliamentary confirmation of the royal letters patent embodying Beaufort's security for *his* loans was made the subject of a special petition on the Commons' part. The terms in which the Commons recommended it, especially their reminder that the bishop's loans would not only very materially assist the further prosecution of the war but also be *pur l'aise de vostre povre Communalte d'Engleterre*, suggest that it was no more than the financial aspect of the deal between Henry V and Beaufort which attracted their interest and approval. (Perhaps the Speaker alone among the Commons realized all that lay behind it.) Certainly, what this and other loans had done was to free the Commons (as in the last parliament) from bother over taxation. And because the Commons were seemingly too apathetic to raise constitutional difficulties over forced loans, nothing untoward happened to disturb what proved to be the last of Henry V's parliaments which he himself attended.

On 10 June 1421 the King left England for the last time, once more entrusting the country to the Duke of Bedford. On the day of his departure he sealed his final testament, in which, now knowing that his Queen was pregnant, he most probably made arrangements for a 'regency' in England in the event of his death during the minority of the expected child. On 6 December, at Windsor, Queen Katherine gave birth to a son, fruit of the union of Troyes, the first prince to be born to the House of Lancaster since its acquisition of the Crown: indeed, the first royal heir-apparent to be born to a reigning sovereign for nearly a century. When this event took place, the second parliament of the year was completing its first week of session, having met on 1 December. It is possible that the opening of parliament had been timed roughly to coincide with Queen Katherine's *accouchement*, so that the realm, through its representatives, might learn and, in them, share the joy. Be this as it may,[1]

[1] In the whole of its previous history, parliament had not been summoned to meet so close to Christmas as now, save in 1332, 1403 (a parliament finally put off until the New Year), and 1420. This last and so neighbourly a precedent weakens the suggestion to some extent.

there were obviously other than sentimental reasons for a meeting of parliament, and we scarcely need doubt that Henry V himself had left instructions that it should assemble before the year-end; it is even likely that the writs of summons were actually issued on 20 October on orders from the King, and partly at least in accordance with his appreciation of the situation in France.

Since his return overseas, Henry's military efforts had made it quite clear to the French of both parties that the English defeat at Baugé on Easter Eve had been no more than a temporary reverse. His army had ranged as far south as Orleans; then, on 6 October, he had invested Meaux, the strongest Dauphinist centre within reach of Paris. But an increase in funds from England was needed, and in a quantity which only parliament could supply. The main item of business in the parliament of December 1421, during a session which can hardly have lasted for more than three weeks, was therefore the Commons' financial grant. This seems to have been made only with some reluctance, or at least with no great enthusiasm: it did not exceed a single tenth and fifteenth; payment of even this modest vote was to be spread over a year, one moiety being made leviable at Candlemas 1422, the other at Martinmas following; moreover, the Commons were so anxious over the state of the currency as to make it a condition of the grant that, if payment of the tax was made in gold by weight, a discount of 15 per cent should be allowed.

During this short parliament the office of Commons' Speaker fell to the lot of an Essex lawyer, Richard Baynard of Messing who, though he was now about fifty years old, had previously sat in parliament only twice (in 1406 and 1414).[1] He had been closely connected with the important Essex family of the FitzWalters, which perhaps had disposed Henry IV to make him the first escheator of his reign in Essex and Hertfordshire (1399-1400). Baynard had also had friendly relations with his stepfather, John Hende, a London alderman and one of the foremost of Henry IV's and Henry V's financial backers in the City, a connexion which was probably responsible for Baynard's brief tenure of the office of controller of the customs at Ipswich in 1407-8.[2] Despite all this, Baynard had had a somewhat colourless career: although recently he had served in Essex on royal commissions for raising war-loans (to which he himself had modestly contributed) and had been called upon to witness the demise of the manor of Weathersfield (Essex) by the

[1] For further details relating to Baynard, see the Appendix.
[2] CPR, 1405-8, 297, 373.

surviving feoffees of the deceased widow of Thomas of Woodstock to the King's feoffees of the Duchy of Lancaster (following a settlement of the shares of the Bohun inheritance during the first parliament of 1421),[1] Baynard held no office under the Crown at the time of his Speakership. (He was not even a J.P. in his own county.) That within two months of the conclusion of the parliament, he was restored to the Essex bench and was then made one of its *quorum*, may be taken to suggest that his behaviour as Speaker had won him some esteem in official quarters. But he never again occupied the Chair, although elected to three of Henry VI's parliaments before his death in 1434. The parliament in which he attained the Speakership proved to be the last of Henry V's reign. Within nine months of its dissolution the King was dead.

[1] *CCR, 1419–22*, 202.

CHAPTER 8

Under Henry VI, to 1445

THE calamity of Henry V's early demise befell at Bois de Vin-
cennes near Paris on 31 August 1422. Henry had made provision
for the government of England if his successor were under age,
declaring that his younger surviving brother, Gloucester, should take
charge, while the elder, Bedford, acted as regent in Normandy and
also (failing the Duke of Burgundy) elsewhere in France. The late
King had further stipulated that the guardianship of the person of
the infant Henry of Windsor should be committed to a small group
of his own trusted friends—the Duke of Exeter, the Bishop of Winchester, the Earl of Warwick, and Sir Walter Hungerford (the former
Speaker and lately Steward of the Household). But evidently it was
now felt that all arrangements for the government of England
should be decided by parliament. And so, on Michaelmas Day, the
Council summoned parliament to meet forty days later. During
this interval, in accordance with the Treaty of Troyes, the infant
Henry VI had succeeded to the throne of France on the death of his
grandfather, Charles VI. On 5 November a representative and well-
attended meeting of peers sanctioned Gloucester's commission to
open, hold and dissolve parliament, in agreement with the Council.
Two days later Henry V's body was entombed in Westminster
Abbey. Two days later still, on 9 November, parliament began.[1]

This time the Commons' choice of a Speaker fell again on Roger
Flore, the Oakham lawyer and civil servant[2] who had held the office
three times running in the years 1416–19, since when he had sat in
none of the three intervening parliaments. During those years Flore
had served on royal war-loan commissions in his own county and on
one occasion, in the spring of 1421, in Northamptonshire as well.
Much private business had continued to come his way, and he was
in greater demand than ever as a feoffee-to-uses. Since 1419 he had

---

[1] For a review of the business of this first parliament of Henry VI, see my
book, *The Commons in the Parliament of 1422*, Chapter VI. For a discussion of the
problem of the regency, see my article, 'The Office and Dignity of Protector of
England, with special reference to its Origins', *E.H.R.*, lxviii (1953), pp.
193–233.

[2] See the paper referred to in note 1, p. 167.

acted as one of the attorneys of Richard Beauchamp who was killed at the siege of Meaux in March 1422 (very shortly after Henry V had created him Earl of Worcester). More recently Flore had evidently been involved in some business in which the Earl of Worcester's cousin, Richard Beauchamp, Earl of Warwick, had an interest, hence a present (of £2) given him by Warwick in 1420-1 for his good offices (*amicitia*). In 1422 Flore sat for Rutland as usual, this time along with his son-in-law, Sir Henry Pleasington. He was still Chief Steward of the Duchy of Lancaster estates north of Trent, having been re-appointed on 1 October (separately for Lancashire and Cheshire on 10 October).[1] In this capacity he was soon to be working, especially on behalf of Henry V's duchy feoffees, in Lancashire. Flore's continued tenure of the duchy stewardship was particularly significant in relation to his Speakership, because an important part of the business of Henry VI's first parliament was to approve what was necessary to fulfil Henry V's will—the liquidation of his own debts and the satisfaction of the still unpaid creditors of Henry IV, tasks which partly depended upon the duchy enfeoffments. Not surprisingly, there were others in the Lower House besides Flore who had an interest in all arrangements affecting the duchy estates. Among them were two of Henry V's executors and feoffees, John Wodehouse (Chancellor of the Duchy) and John Leventhorpe (the Receiver- and Attorney-General). They also included one of the Duchy's legal counsellors, Robert Darcy, who, as receiver of the Essex estates of Henry V's late grandmother, the Dowager Countess of Hereford, was still deeply involved (as was Leventhorpe) in completing the 1421 agreements for the partition of the Bohun inheritance between the two coheirs, Henry V and his cousin, the Countess of Stafford, and in arranging for the incorporation of the royal purparty in the *heritage de Lancastre*.

There were, of course, matters of much greater significance than these, with which the parliament of 1422 was called upon to deal, but in which Speaker Flore is not likely to have had any greater personal interest than the bulk of his fellow-members. Certainly, he himself did not head the deputation sent to ask the Lords for the names of those who were now to be appointed as Chancellor, Treasurer, and Keeper of the Privy Seal. This request was answered at the beginning of the second week of the session, when a deputation of seven lords let it be known that those in office at the end of the previous reign had been re-appointed. (The parliament-roll, however, makes

[1] R. Somerville, op. cit., i. 419.

no mention of any announcement to the Lower House of the changes made before the dissolution when, although Bishop Langley of Durham remained Chancellor, William Kynwolmarsh was superseded as Treasurer by John Stafford, the latter's place as Keeper of the Privy Seal being taken by William Alnwick.) The Commons as a body are likely to have been much more closely interested in the most important single matter requiring parliament's decision: the question, how the royal authority was to be exercised during what was bound to be, unless the child-king died, a long minority.

Since the Duke of Gloucester, the younger of the King's two uncles, aimed to be regent in accordance with the terms of Henry V's will, and the Lords were determined that control should rest either with themselves or, when no parliament or 'great council' was in session, with a council of their own choosing, the settlement of that problem was bound to be very difficult. Harking back to the precedent of Richard II's accession when no regency had been established, objecting to Henry V's settlement by his will on the ground that it had been contrived without parliamentary sanction, and exploiting an awareness of the invidious position to which Bedford, the elder of the King's uncles and his heir-presumptive, might be reduced if Gloucester were given all the authority he demanded, the Lords were able to impose their will. Admittedly, Gloucester was to be allowed the distinctive title and office of Protector and Chief Councillor, together with the exercise of certain modest rights of official and ecclesiastical patronage. That concession, however, was not only limited in substance but, so far as Gloucester himself was concerned, was limited still further by being made dependent upon the absence of Bedford, who was to be Protector instead whenever he came to England. All of this was chiefly a matter for the Lords to settle. None the less, and probably early in the dispute, the Commons had expressed a wish to be informed who should have *the governance of this Reme undre our souverain lord* [the King] *bi his high auctorite*. And it was this petition which afforded Gloucester an opportunity to object that, unless he were given some such title as Governor, the Commons would be left without a proper answer. There is, however, no evidence to suggest that the Lower House itself was dissatisfied at the treatment accorded its petition: it did, in fact, assent to what was finally (on 5 December) agreed regarding the status of the King's uncles.

The Commons were also consulted when, after the names of the new councillors had been formally declared at their request, the Council submitted a list of the conditions upon which it would take office. This document was carried to the Commons by a delegation from the Lords who wished to know their mind (*lour entent*), a procedure which was not merely formal, as the Commons' amendment of one of the articles of the document makes clear. The Commons did not, however, do what they had been able to do in 1406; then they had exacted the conditions under which the Council was to operate (admittedly, only until the next parliament); the conditions under which Henry VI's Council was to work were being laid down by that Council itself and had been already agreed by the Lords before being inspected by the Commons. That the Lords were evidently able to carry the Commons with them may have been partly due to the inclusion in this new Council of three of their former Speakers: Tiptoft (1406), Hungerford (1414), and Beauchamp (1416). But these were the only commoners in a body predominantly aristocratic in composition. Perhaps the Commons were chiefly impressed by the general unity among the Lords. But that they did not follow an independent line of their own was most probably because, by not being asked to vote direct taxation, they were without that practical bargaining power which royal financial needs usually gave them. In fact, all they granted in 1422 was a renewal of the wool-subsidy and the subsidy of tunnage and poundage, made necessary by the expiry of Henry V's grant for life; and of these two subsidies, the former was now lowered in rates, and the latter restricted to aliens; neither was voted beyond 9 November 1424. The presentation of this grant on 18 December 1422, the day of the dissolution, was Speaker Flore's last act as a parliamentarian. His experience of parliament, extending through a quarter of a century and a dozen meetings, now came to an end: he was not to sit in any of the four parliaments that met before his death in the autumn of 1427.[1]

The second parliament of the new reign met on 20 October 1423, in accordance with writs issued on the anniversary of the King's accession (1 September). The political atmosphere in which it came together was anything but tranquil. Admittedly, the existing Council was to be re-appointed during the parliament with only minor changes, but the terms on which it now consented to act show that

---

[1] Flore was appointed, however, as one of the parliamentary proxies of the abbot of Croyland in 1425 and 1426. He was buried in the parish church at Oakham, where his modest house in the High Street still stands. He had remained Chief Steward of the Duchy of Lancaster estates north of Trent until his death, except in Lancashire and Cheshire where he relinquished office on 9 July 1425.

it had already experienced difficulties in its conduct of affairs. This was even the case over foreign policy. The Duke of Gloucester's ambition to exploit his marriage with Jacqueline of Hainault, the 'half-divorced wife' of the Duke of Brabant, was seriously jeopardizing the Anglo-Burgundian alliance, despite the fact that the Duke of Bedford, by marrying Burgundy's sister, was simultaneously doing his best to strengthen it. Fortunately, the northern sky gave a brighter prospect: on 21 November, the Commons were able to send a deputation to the Lords thanking them for the Chancellor's statement on the progress of negotiations with Scotland, and early in 1424 these resulted in the liberation of James I of Scotland (captive since 1406) and his marriage with the niece of the Duke of Exeter and Bishop Beaufort, the nuptials being celebrated in Southwark by the bishop himself.

The financial outlook, however, was far from encouraging. All hopes of a prompt fulfilment of the wills of Henry IV and Henry V, which involved the payment of their debts, including all wages and other costs incurred in the French war and still outstanding at Henry V's death, were already disappointed; and much of the two sessions of this parliament (20 October–17 December 1423 and 14 January–28 February 1424) was taken up by both Lords and Commons in sanctioning the demands made by the executors of Henry IV and Henry V, and in answering the petitions of some of the most important of their creditors. Henry of Windsor himself (although not yet two years old) was brought into parliament for the first time half-way through the autumn session (on 17 November), but enthusiasm did not reach to a vote of any direct tax. Nor did the prolongation of parliament beyond Christmas, partly decided so that the members of the Lower House might inform their neighbours at home of the Crown's great necessity, affect their resistance. All the financial help the Commons would give the Council, after sessions totalling fifteen weeks, was a two years' extension of the subsidies on wool plus tunnage and poundage on aliens (until November 1426). They supported a complaint from Italian exporters that the grant of the wool-subsidy in the previous parliament had been faultily engrossed, with the result that they had been overcharged by ten shillings a sack. Now, however, despite the fact that the Council had been prepared to allow this complaint, the Commons confirmed the higher rate, so regularizing the error alleged. Otherwise, the terms of their grant were no more generous to the government than before.

The Speaker during this parliament of 1423–4 was he who had failed in the contested election of 1420: John Russell, an apprentice-at-law who was now sitting for Herefordshire in his seventh successive parliament.[1] Save that he did not rise so high in royal service, he was similar in type to his predecessor, Roger Flore: a busy lawyer whom public employment did not prevent from using his professional abilities on behalf of a large and wealthy clientele. From 1403 to 1421, year by year, Russell had been retained as legal counsel to the Duchy of Lancaster.[2] Under Henry V especially, he had served the duchy administration in a variety of other ways: he sometimes acted on its judicial enquiries; occasionally as a financial agent, as in 1417 when the King sent him into Wales to treat with duchy tenants for a subsidy to assist the second military expedition to France (a mission which resulted in Russell's collection of some £1,500);[3] and also, at least by the end of the reign, as chief steward of the duchy estates in Gloucestershire.[4] Russell retained this local office at Henry VI's accession and was probably still holding it when Speaker. He had been a J.P. in Herefordshire continuously since 1407, a J.P. in Gloucestershire also in Henry V's earliest years, the royal escheator in Herefordshire in 1410–11, 1415–16, and 1419–20, and sheriff in 1417–18. Regarding his relations with the nobility, special notice must be given to his connexion with Edward, Duke of York (as feoffee and, along with Speaker Flore, as overseer of his will);[5] with Joan, widow of William Lord Beauchamp of Abergavenny (on whose behalf he had been involved in 1417–19 in an important settlement of the reversion of lands held by Lord Burnell)[6]; with John Lord Haryngton of Aldingham (as an executor);[7] and with James Lord Berkeley (for whom he was acting in 1422 as chief steward of his 'borough' of Wotton).[8] This last connexion is of particular interest: young Berkeley, heir to the barony on his uncle's death in 1417, had seriously quarrelled over the family estates with the Earl of Warwick, husband of the heir-general, and had only

---

[1] Russell was M.P. for Herefordshire in 1414 (April), 1417, 1419, 1420, 1421 (May and December), 1422, 1423, 1426, 1429, 1431, 1432, and 1433.

[2] R. Somerville, op. cit., i. 453.

[3] Ibid., 184.   [4] DKR, xliii. 271.

[5] CPR, 1413–15, 350; CCR, 1413–19, 294; 1429–35, 134, 214, 260; A. Gibbons, Early Lincoln Wills, 146.

[6] CPR, 1416–22, 302, 305–6; CCR, 1419–22, 86–90; S. Shaw, History of Staffordshire, ii. 245; VCH, Bucks., iv. 415.

[7] C. E. H. Chadwyck Healey, History of West Somerset, 256.

[8] R. Somerville, op. cit., i. 453.

secured the property with the help of the Duke of Gloucester (for whom a reversionary interest in a substantial part of it had been fabricated as an inducement to intervene). It is just possible that Gloucester's political interest was being indirectly consulted by the Commons when they elected Russell as their Speaker. Russell was well known, however, especially through his connexion with the Duchy of Lancaster, to men who were politically not in sympathy with the Protector.

The fourteen months which elapsed between Henry VI's second and third parliaments were a time of increasing political tension within the government itself. They also saw a rise of discontent among the mercantile community. Especially was this the case in London, where there was strong hostility to alien merchants, particularly the Flemings. Taking advantage of these grievances and his own personal popularity in the City, the Duke of Gloucester decided to exploit his wife's territorial claims in the Low Countries and led an expedition into Hainault and Brabant in November 1424. The enterprise not only proved futile in itself, but provoked the active, military intervention of the Duke of Burgundy, so endangering the Anglo-Burgundian alliance and devaluing Bedford's hard-won victory over a large Dauphinist army at Verneuil in August. At home in England, where Bishop Beaufort had been made Chancellor for the third time (in July 1424), the Council's distrust of the Protector was now intensified. So much so that, when, in February 1425, resistance in London to the Chancellor's policy of favouring the Flemings and other foreign merchants threatened to become violent, the Council took the opportunity to reinforce the Tower garrison and to put Sir Richard Wydeville, a chamberlain of the Duke of Bedford, in charge of the fortress. This interference in what Gloucester regarded as strictly his own sphere of authority as Protector, on his return to England in April 1425 accentuated the tension between him and the Chancellor. So doubtless did the fact that for the first time in the reign Gloucester was not allowed any commission to act in parliament as the King's lieutenant when the session began on 30 April. Instead, the three-year-old King was himself brought in to witness the opening of parliament.

The Commons' Speaker in this parliament was Sir Thomas Waweton of Great Staughton, knight of the shire for Bedfordshire, who was probably in his early fifties. He was not of the type of lawyer-administrator which continuously since 1416 had occupied the Chair. He had, however, a long parliamentary experience reaching

N

back to 1397 and, although he had twice been sheriff (of Beds. and
Bucks.), in 1415–16 and 1422–3, which meant that he had been
ineligible to sit in the three parliaments which met in those years,
he had been a member of the Lower House no less than six times
since the beginning of Henry V's reign.[1] The Commons probably
now chose him as Speaker partly because of the influential connexions he enjoyed, partly with a view to some of the business they
were likely to entertain in the course of the session.

It is not known for how long Waweton had been a retainer of
Edmund, Earl of March, the last direct representative of the Mortimer claim to the crown, who had been sent out of the way to
govern Ireland early in 1424. But at the time of the earl's death there,
as recently as January 1425, Waweton had been in receipt of the very
handsome fee of 40 marks a year drawn from the Mortimer manor of
Ryhall (Rutland), an estate which, as a result of a successful petition
for livery of dower presented in this parliament, soon passed into
the possession of the widow of the earl, Anne, a sister of the Earl of
Stafford.[2] The reversion of the manor was vested in Joyce, Earl
Edmund's only surviving sister and a cousin of the Earl of Huntingdon (whom the Dowager Countess of March was soon to marry).
The Lady Joyce herself was married to that important Lancastrian
administrator and member of the royal Council, Sir John Tiptoft (the
Speaker of 1406). Tiptoft and Waweton were cousins (the sons of
half-brothers) and, since Tiptoft had used Waweton's good offices as
a feoffee in his Cambridgeshire estates,[3] well known to each other
and friendly. This connexion may well have been strengthened by
Waweton's ties with Tiptoft's brother-in-law, the late Earl of March,
and is likely to have become firmer still because of Tiptoft's interest
(through his wife) in the Mortimer estates. There is no doubt of this
interest of Tiptoft's: on 24 February 1425, five weeks after Mortimer's death, he had managed to secure from his fellow-councillors
appointment as chief steward of all the Mortimer castles and lands in
Wales and the Marches for as long as they remained under Crown
control, during the minority of the heir, the thirteen-year-old Duke
of York. In the course of his Speakership, Waweton was evidently

[1] Waweton was M.P. for Huntingdonshire in 1397 (Jan. and Sept.), 1401,
1402, 1414 (Nov.), 1420, and 1422, and for Bedfordshire in 1413, 1414 (April),
1419, 1425, and 1432. For more particulars regarding Waweton, see the
Appendix.

[2] *Rot. Parl.*, v. 399b; *CCR, 1422–9*, 222; *VCH, Rutland*, ii. 270.

[3] *CCR, 1422–9*, 70–1; *Feudal Aids*, i. 178.

drawn even closer to the centre of political action when, on 25 May, the wardship of the Mortimer estates was granted to the Protector, Gloucester, himself.

Waweton was also personally connected in some way with the primate, Archbishop Chichele. The precise nature of the relationship cannot be determined. But it can hardly have been any casual interest which prompted Waweton to attend upon the archbishop when, on 28 August 1425 (less than seven weeks after the dissolution of parliament), Chichele declared in the parish-church of his birthplace (at Higham Ferrers, Northants.) his establishment of a college of priests there, Waweton being one of the witnesses of the deed granting the site of the college in free alms.[1] If Speaker Waweton (on the basis of this slender evidence) could be regarded as closely connected with Chichele, it might make it less difficult to understand how, in the course of the parliament of 1425, Gloucester fared so well, or at least how the duke's political opponent, Henry Beaufort, the Chancellor, fared so ill. For Chichele, fearing a threat to his metropolitan authority from the ecclesiastical ambitions of his powerful suffragan of Winchester, was very liable to oppose him or at any rate assist those who opposed him for other reasons. But this is probably grossly to overrate the influence, on affairs and events, of both Primate and Speaker.

The parliament of 1425 sat from 30 April until 14 July, excluding a short break of less than a week for Whitsuntide. It was early in the session that there came to a head the long dispute between the Earl of Warwick and John Mowbray, the Earl Marshal, who claimed precedency in the Upper House. Since Mowbray was a friend of the Protector at this time—he had been with him in his recent excursion to the Netherlands—the settlement of the suit in his favour, by restoration to his father's title of Duke of Norfolk (which the Commons asked the Lords to induce him to accept), can probably be interpreted as an indirect victory for Gloucester's party. There are other and clearer signs, however, that the parliament went well for this interest: not only was a lenient view taken of Gloucester's quarrel with Burgundy, but finally both Houses approved a government loan of 20,000 marks (payable by instalments over the next four years) to help Gloucester meet the debts he had incurred in pursuit of his own private foreign policy. And while Gloucester was borrowing, his enemy Beaufort was still lending: on 6 June the Chancellor received letters patent giving him security for repayment of a

[1] *CPR, 1422-9*, 473-4.

loan of no less than £11,000. The irony of the situation can hardly
have been lost on Beaufort. But he certainly needed to buy support,
if only to offset the unpopularity of the government's mercantile
policy for which he was being held mainly responsible.

The Commons themselves were full of objections on behalf of
English merchants. They complained that rebates of subsidy on wool
lost in transit were being disallowed, although these had been provided for by special stipulations in the subsidy-grants of both 1422
and 1423. There was also *moche altercacyon*, a London chronicler tells
us, *bytwyne the lordys and the comyns for tonage and poundage*. When the
Commons now, for the first time in the reign, granted tunnage and
poundage as a charge on English merchants, they did so for little
more than a year, and so we may take it that the official demand
itself was disputed. But it is also pretty certain that there was some
contention over the conditions attached to even this limited grant
and to the three years' extension of the wool-subsidy and tunnage
and poundage payable by alien merchants (from 1426 to 1429): the
chief of these conditions subjected all foreign merchants to very
stringent 'hosting' arrangements. This was clearly an attack on the
Chancellor's partiality towards foreign traders, and Beaufort did
nothing to improve his standing with the English mercantile community by immediately breaking the requirement, as a result of
which, the London writer says, *there was moche hevynesse and trowbylle
in this londe*. Apart from the subsidies on trade, parliament yet again
made no financial grant.

It is doubtful whether Speaker Waweton derived much satisfaction from its sessions, unless it was on account of the Commons'
successful support for the petition of the Countess of March and for
a series of petitions on behalf of her future husband, the Earl of
Huntingdon, a prisoner-of-war in France since the battle of Baugé,
whose liberation the earl's stepfather, Sir John Cornwall, was doing
all he could to bring about. Waweton was not even re-elected to the
next parliament and did not, in the event, sit again for nearly seven
years.

Unfortunately, the 'heaviness and trouble' that followed the parliament of 1425 did not arise solely from disagreements between the
Chancellor and the Londoners in the field of foreign trade. The
mutual suspicion and nervousness felt by both Protector and Chancellor resulted in an *émeute* at London Bridge on 30 October between
what was virtually Beaufort's own private army of retainers, gathered
in Southwark and reinforced by contingents of Lancashire and

Cheshire archers, and Gloucester's supporters in the City. The Chancellor's fears were such that he wrote to Bedford, complaining of the threat to the public peace afforded by Gloucester's actions and requesting his return from France. For a short time Gloucester dominated the Council, taking the young Henry of Windsor into his custody and organizing yet another, if only small, expeditionary force to assist his wife in Hainault. But Bedford's homecoming shortly before Christmas, automatically (under the constitutional settlement of 1422) made him Protector and also deprived Gloucester of his headship of the Council. Refusing to be reconciled with Beaufort, Duke Humphrey even declined to attend Council meetings. And so matters still stood when parliament met on 18 February 1426.

On his way from the Channel coast to London, Bedford had been met and evidently won over by the Chancellor. They had agreed with the Council when and where parliament should meet, and, on 7 January, Beaufort had issued the writs of summons. That parliament was not to meet at Westminster, for the first time for nearly twelve years, was in itself a rebuke for the Londoners, which Bedford soon deliberately emphasized by the cool way in which he received a deputation of welcome from the City. London could not be trusted to remain calm or passive where Gloucester's interest, especially in his quarrel with Beaufort, was concerned. The decision to meet at Leicester can hardly have been taken because it was here that parliament had last met (in 1414) away from the normal seat of government. The choice of Leicester had more than that to recommend it. Negatively, it was far distant from London. Positively, being itself the centre of one of the old Lancastrian honours, its choice was perhaps partly determined by a desire to evoke a sense of dynastic solidarity. But it should also be remembered that Leicester had once been a place where 'every second man you met was a Lollard', the tainted centre of a region where heresy had a firm hold. And that the Lollard sect was still thought capable of giving trouble is clear from the reference which Beaufort made, in his sermon opening the parliament, to the need for observing God's law and protecting God's flock *contra perfidorum Hereticorum et Lollardorum invasionem*. Most importantly of all, Leicester was quite close to a number of great Duchy of Lancaster lordships in Derbyshire and Staffordshire, including some immediately controlled by Henry V's feoffees (of whom Beaufort was the chief), and also quite near to the numerous Staffordshire estates of the young Earl of Stafford, who had married Beaufort's niece (Anne Neville) and was probably disposed at least to sympathize with the Chancellor in this crisis which it was the first concern of the parliament to resolve or appease.

Efforts to settle the quarrel between Duke Humphrey and Beaufort were, of course, being made before parliament met, when the Court was moving northwards through the Midlands. At St Albans on 29 January 1426 Bedford and the Council decided to send to Gloucester a small deputation, headed by Archbishop Chichele and the Earl of Stafford. Its purpose was to inform Gloucester that the Council would be at Northampton on 13 February to discuss the agenda of parliament; to ask him to attend this meeting, even if Beaufort was present, promising safety for both him and his household, and offering an impartial enquiry of the causes of the quarrel (to which, the envoys were to say, Beaufort was entitled both as a peer and as Chancellor); but to insist that, if the dispute had not been settled when parliament met, it would be his duty to attend as soon as it met and for as long as it lasted: all this, in view of the need for harmony among the lords, upon which depended the successful despatch of parliament's business. With his case not at all helped by the complete failure of the expedition very recently sent to Hainault, Gloucester perhaps preferred to meet his peers in the parliament. He also doubtless expected some support from the Lower House. However this may be, Humphrey evidently refused to be reconciled with his uncle in advance of the meeting at Leicester.

This failure to end the deadlock obviously affected the conduct of the business of the session. Parliament had got off to a very bad start. There was great tension and serious danger of open violence: even though the members were told not to carry weapons, they armed themselves with bludgeons, so that the parliament was given the sobriquet, *the parliament of battes*. Admittedly, it was on the appointed day, 18 February, that Beaufort as Chancellor opened the session in the great hall of the castle in Henry VI's presence, Bedford being then commissioned to act for the King. But it was not until 7 March, and only after a deputation from the Commons had importuned the Lords to reconcile their dissensions, that Gloucester and Beaufort even agreed to accept arbitration by a committee of peers; and yet another five days went by before (on 12 March) Archbishop Chichele announced the committee's decision before King, Lords, and Commons together, and the two antagonists shook hands. Evidently, even the business of the Commons had been badly held up: not before the eleventh day of the session were they able, or was opportunity given them, to present their Speaker.

Their choice by then had fallen on Sir Richard Vernon who, only
five days before parliament met and less than a month after ceasing
to occupy the shrievalty of Nottinghamshire and Derbyshire, had
been elected to represent the latter shire.[1] Now about thirty-six years
old, Vernon was an important landowner in the north Midlands,
with estates in Derbyshire, Staffordshire (where he had been sheriff
in 1415–17[2] and knight of the shire in 1419), Shropshire, and
Cheshire. At Haddon in the Derbyshire Peak and also at Harlaston
and Wichnor in Staffordshire, he was a tenant of the Duchy of Lancaster honour of Tutbury. His connexion with the duchy had long
been very close. In 1401, when only ten years, he had become the
ward of his near neighbour, Roger Leche of Chatsworth,[3] who, then
an esquire of Henry IV's Household and in the second half of his
reign Steward of the Household of the Prince of Wales, became on
the latter's accession Chief Steward of the Duchy of Lancaster north
of Trent and also Chamberlain of the Duchy. Vernon himself, on
3 March 1424, being then a knight of the royal Household, had been
appointed steward and master-forester of the duchy lordship of the
High Peak, and constable of the castle of the honour. He was still
holding the stewardship and constableship at the time of his Speakership, and in fact continued to do so until 1444.[4] It is quite possible
that Vernon favoured the Chancellor's side in the great cause at
Leicester for other reasons than his association with the Duchy of
Lancaster: when, in 1410, the widow of his great-uncle, Sir Fulk de
Pembridge (whose heir he was), collegiated the church at Tong
(Salop), she included among those for whose good estate the warden
and his fellow-priests were to make prayer, Thomas Beaufort, the
bishop's brother, later created Duke of Exeter, with whom her late
husband seems to have been quite intimately connected; then, in
1414, after the patronage of the church had been made over to
Richard Vernon, and a royal licence had allowed the nearby alien
priory of Lapley (Staffs.) to be annexed to the church, the name of

[1] For a more detailed study of Vernon's career, see my article, 'Sir Richard
Vernon of Haddon, Speaker in the Parliament of Leicester, 1426', *Derbyshire
Archaeological Journal*, vol. lxxxii (1962), pp. 43–53. Vernon had been M.P. for
Staffordshire in 1419 and for Derbyshire in 1422. He sat for Derbyshire again
in 1433.

[2] In 1427–8 Vernon was once more sheriff of Staffordshire. Here he had been
a J.P. from 1417 to 1422 and was so again from 1430 to 1432. Except between
1432 and 1437, he was a J.P. in Derbyshire from 1423 until his death in 1451.

[3] *DKR*, xxxvi. 499.

[4] R. Somerville, op. cit., i. 551–2.

Bishop Beaufort himself was added to the bede-roll.[1] This, however, is the only direct evidence for Vernon's connexion with the Beauforts, and, obviously, it long antedates his Speakership. The evidence for his close attachment to Humphrey, Earl of Stafford, although for the most part of later date than 1426, is much more conclusive: Sir Richard was the earl's tenant in his manor of Pitchcott (Bucks.),[2] by 1430 was one of his feoffees-to-uses in certain of the Stafford lordships in Kent,[3] and later (in 1445) almost certainly owed his appointment as Treasurer of Calais to the same Humphrey Stafford, who (by this time Duke of Buckingham) was Captain of Calais and Lieutenant of the March of Calais.[4] Related to the Beauforts by marriage, the Earl of Stafford was one of the committee of peers chosen at Leicester to arbitrate between Gloucester and the Chancellor: his importance can only have increased the respect accorded his client, the Speaker.

The accommodation reached between Gloucester and his uncle of Winchester on 12 March was followed on the next day by the latter's resignation of the Great Seal, it being understood that the bishop would soon be going on pilgrimage. At the same time Bishop John Stafford of Bath and Wells gave up the office of Treasurer. There is no shortage of evidence to prove John Stafford's friendship with Duke Humphrey, and no doubt his resignation was something of a *quid pro quo*. Bishop Kemp of London, who had acted as Duke

---

[1] Dugdale, *Monasticon*, vol. vi, part 3, p. 1402 et seq.; *CPR, 1408–13*, 280. Whether Vernon kept up this Beaufort connexion with any degree of intimacy is not known. But that Gloucester disapproved of him may be assumed from the fact that when, in 1432, the duke temporarily seized control of the government, Vernon was dropped from the office of J.P. in both Derbyshire and Staffordshire.

[2] *VCH, Bucks.*, iv. 90.   [3] *CCR, 1429–35*, 357.

[4] *DKR*, xlviii. 365. Vernon gave up his Calais office in May 1451, soon after the Duke of Buckingham resigned his captaincy of the town to the Duke of Somerset. The Stafford connexion was not the only aristocratic tie Vernon enjoyed. He was evidently well known to another Staffordshire magnate, James Lord Audley, for whom he was appointed to deputize as a royal justice in south Wales in 1431 (*CPR, 1429–36*, 116). In 1439, the Duke of Norfolk made him steward of his Derbyshire estates, and, sometime before 1448, this connexion brought him a three years' occupation of the office of steward in the Court of Chivalry (*HMC Report, Rutland MSS.*, iv. 29; F. Devon, *Issues of the Exchequer*, 463). In June 1450, while still Treasurer of Calais, Vernon was given for life a number of associated Crown appointments in south Wales: the offices of sheriff of Pembrokeshire, constable of the castles of Pembroke and Tenby, master-forester of Coydrath, and steward of certain royal lordships in the same area. He died, however, in 1451 and was buried at Tong (Shropshire), where he is represented in his effigy as wearing the Lancastrian collar of esses (SS).

Humphrey's representative at the council summoned to meet in Paris in September 1425 to arbitrate between him and the Duke of Burgundy, now took charge of the Chancery, and Walter Lord Hungerford (Speaker in 1414) became Treasurer of the Exchequer.

There was no time to do much more before Easter, but before Bedford prorogued the parliament on 20 March, there had been trouble in the Commons over finance. The Commons were agreeable to the Council being authorized to raise Crown-loans up to £40,000 before midsummer 1427, but at least some of them—the parliament-roll says that there were *diverse oppiniones*—objected to the lack of respect paid to the conditions attached in the previous parliament to the grant of tunnage and poundage. Bedford, however, although only after seeking legal advice, refused to meet the complaint, insisting that the subsidy must be paid, ill-kept conditions or no. By this the Commons would seem to have been made more uneasy still. Certainly, the terms of the grant which Speaker Vernon announced at the end of the second session (29 April–1 June) suggest that the Lower House remained in some disquiet on this point: tunnage and poundage on alien merchants the Commons renewed for the same two years as they did the wool-subsidy (November 1429–31), but tunnage and poundage payable by English merchants were renewed for only one year (November 1426–7). Moreover, in one of their petitions the Commons harked back to the stipulation, attached to all previous grants of the wool-subsidy during this reign, regarding drawback for wool lost in transit; they now said that they had preferred a petition about this in the last parliament, *the whiche petition was not answered to noon affecte after the contenue of the same*. But all that the Council would even now promise was to expedite the use of its discretionary powers in the matter of allowances. This question of taxation apart, the second parliamentary session at Leicester was not particularly noteworthy, unless account is taken of the great ceremony held on Whitsunday, when Bedford knighted the four-year-old King who then himself dubbed thirty-six others, including the young Duke of York.

Notwithstanding the Commons' complaints, the Leicester parliament had been successful in producing at least some appearance of political unity. And as long as Bedford, in confident alliance with the Council, controlled the royal administration, this new-found equilibrium was maintained. But in March 1427 Bedford returned to France. Bishop Beaufort went with him, at Calais on Lady Day received from the duke's hands the red hat conferred by Martin V (in May 1426), and then left to undertake a crusade against the Hussites in the capacity of papal legate. In France, Bedford was soon made to realize that military reinforcements were an imperative need; and yet, in England, Gloucester, now automatically restored to the Protectorate by his brother's departure, was beginning to think of once again providing military support for his wife. Although Jacqueline still retained a hold on a few Dutch towns, her cause was well-nigh lost. None the less, the Council was actually so tolerant towards Gloucester (or chivalrous to his wife) as to give some financial support for Gloucester's forces. But this was only on the understanding that these were used simply as town-garrisons, and that no offensive action was taken without parliament's approval; and the Council, perhaps moved by Bedford's strong protest against this new anti-Burgundian move, soon stiffened in its attitude towards the Protector. When parliament next met, their relations, no longer cordial, did not improve.

The autumn parliament of 1427 came together on 13 October and was opened in the King's presence by the Chancellor, John Kemp (now promoted to the see of York). That Gloucester could still count on a considerable volume of support among the Commons is suggested by their election as Speaker of John Tyrell of East Horndon (Essex).[1] For if Tyrell was at this time any lord's man, he was Gloucester's: he and his son William had served in the duke's retinue in the French expedition of 1415; certainly in 1416, and perhaps even still, he was steward of Gloucester's estates in Essex; in 1418 he was one of the mortgagees in a number of the duke's manors in Suffolk, Essex, Worcestershire, and Pembrokeshire and some estates in reversion in the Isle of Wight. In 1420, on behalf of Gloucester (then *Custos Anglie*) Tyrell had been involved in the shady transaction between the duke and Lord Berkeley by which the latter secured seisin of the Berkeley inheritance as heir-male in opposition to the heir-general, the Countess of Warwick, and her husband, Richard Beauchamp. It was doubtless by Gloucester's influence that, as recently as 13 February 1427, Tyrell was made steward of the honours of Clare (Suffolk) and Thaxted (Essex) until the majority of the Duke of York, nephew and heir of the late Earl of March (the bulk of whose lands had been granted to Gloucester to hold in ward-

[1] For references and more information about John Tyrell, see my book, *The Commons in the Parliament of 1422*, pp. 226–9. Tyrell had been M.P. for Essex in 1411, 1413, 1416 (March), 1417, 1419, 1421 (May), 1422, and 1425, and was to be so again in 1429–30, 1431, 1433 and 1437.

ship), and that, soon after 1 April following, along with the great canonist, Dr William Lyndwood, Tyrell went on an embassy to Holland in connexion with the affairs of the Duchess of Gloucester. To say all this is not to say that Tyrell was solely dependent on Gloucester for the position of influence he enjoyed. He was most likely the largest non-baronial proprietor in his own county of Essex. Here and in Hertfordshire (the other part of a joint-bailiwick) he had been sheriff in 1413–14 and 1422–3. Essex he had represented in no fewer than eight parliaments since 1411. In this parliament of 1427, he was now sitting for Hertfordshire for the first and (as it proved) the only time in his career, his brother Edward (then royal escheator in Essex and Hertfordshire) being one of the shire-knights for Essex. John's own election to this parliament was irregular, because when it took place he was sheriff of Norfolk and Suffolk (his term of office lasting from December 1426 to November 1427) and the election of sheriffs was prohibited. He was well connected locally, being a feoffee-to-uses of Lord FitzWalter (a friend of Gloucester's) and of Richard Baynard, the lawyer who had been Speaker in the last of Henry V's parliaments and who now led the Commons' deputation to the Upper House to announce Tyrell's election as Speaker. Tyrell was always, in fact, in great demand as a trustee of estates. Among his own feoffees were included at this time the Earl of Stafford, John Hotoft (Treasurer of the King's Household), and John Fray (a Baron of the Exchequer). Tyrell had also been connected, if in a more casual way, with other members of the Council, for example, Lord Tiptoft, Lord Cromwell, and Lord Scrope, for each of whom, at one time or another, he had stood surety when they were granted important royal wardships or custodies-at-farm. So far as is known, Tyrell's connexion with the Court at this time arose only indirectly out of his close connexion with the Protector. But, very early in the reign, he had married (as his second wife) the widow of a former Keeper of the Great Wardrobe of the Household (John Spenser). It was as a result of this marriage that Tyrell was involved in long negotiations with the Council over the repayment of debts owed by Henry V's executors to his wife as her former husband's executrix: although these debts had amounted to no less than £2,700, not until December 1424 had arrangements been made for the payment of a mere quarter of what was due, spread over as long a period as five years, failing which Tyrell was once more to approach the Council and the late King's executors.

So far as can be seen, no movement of great political significance

disturbed the meetings of the first session of this parliament of
1427–8 in which Tyrell first acted as Speaker. At the beginning of
the session, it is true, Gloucester urged the inadequacy of his powers
as Protector, but did not then bring his complaint to a head. After
eight weeks, the session ended on 8 December, when the duke
adjourned parliament to 27 January 1428. Despite all his perversity,
there is no doubt that Gloucester was still very influential politically:
for evidence of this we need hardly look further than the appointment of John Tyrell himself on 10 December 1427, only two days
after the close of his first session in the Speakership, to the office of
Chief Steward of those estates of the Duchy of Lancaster north of
Trent (excluding Lancashire and Cheshire) that were not enfeoffed
to assist the administration of Henry V's will. (This office, in which
he succeeded the former Speaker, the late Roger Flore of Oakham, Tyrell was to hold until not long before his death in 1437.)[1]
Gloucester would have been well advised to work within the frame-
work of the constitutional settlement of 1422, strengthening his
authority by taking every opportunity to assist his friends, in such a
way as this, into positions of administrative responsibility. What he
now determined instead, however, was to launch a frontal attack on
conciliar authority as exercised over the past five years.

The resulting conflict of views inevitably made the second session
of the 1427–8 parliament extremely disturbed. Gloucester, in fact,
could hardly have chosen a worse time to assert himself. There was
trouble in the ecclesiastical sphere over Pope Martin V's demand for
the repeal of the anti-papal Statutes of Provisors and Praemunire,
which had resulted in the spring of 1427 in the suspension of the
Archbishop of Canterbury, Henry Chichele. Now, in January 1428,
Chichele begged the Commons to promote the repeal of the offend-
ing statutes. All that they would do, however, was to protest against
the misrepresentation in the Curia from which the primate had
suffered, and to demand that, by embassy or letter, Chichele be
exculpated so that any process in the Curia could be quashed. There
was trouble for Gloucester personally in the attitude of the Londoners to his wife's cause in the Netherlands. Now tired of both
Jacqueline and her interests, the duke was probably inclined to welcome Martin V's invalidation of his marriage in January 1428 as
something of a relief. But support for Jacqueline in the City and the
general anti-papal feelings of the moment combined to embarrass
him further. It was in such a situation that, on 3 March, he com-

[1] R. Somerville, op. cit., i. 420.

mitted himself to a statement in the Upper House that he would withdraw from parliament until such time as the Lords had redefined (and, presumably, extended) his authority as Protector, and that, although discussion of business might go on in his absence, it must not be concluded. The Lords, in their answer, had no hesitation in reminding Humphrey that he and Bedford had accepted the limitations placed on the Protector's authority in 1422, that he must continue to accept them, and that, summoned to parliament, it was his duty to attend. In making such a declaration, the Lords made no appeal to the Commons, but undoubtedly they were strengthened by their awareness of the popular disgust felt at Gloucester's desertion of Jacqueline and abandonment of her interests. That such feelings were at least strong in London, there is no question. It was about this time that women from the City Stocks Market protested in parliament itself against the duke's attitude towards his wife and his adulterous connexion with Eleanor Cobham, and on 8 March even the Mayor and Aldermen themselves came to parliament to insist that Jacqueline should be rescued. Gloucester's reputation in the Lower House itself obviously followed this downward trend. For, although on 25 March, the last day of the session, Speaker Tyrell included the duke among the lords recommended by the Commons, their grant of tunnage and poundage from native merchants for a further year and of a curious tax on parishes and knights' fees was accompanied by a demand that, *in singuler comforte of the saide Commens and of all thoos that they been comyn fore*, measures should be taken for the safety of the Lady of Gloucester *that liveth in so greet dolour and hevynesse*.[1] The presentation of this condition tied to the money-bill can have given the Speaker, in view of his close connexion with the duke, little cause for any personal satisfaction.

Gloucester's own disappointment with the outcome of the parliament of 1427-8 must have been increased by the Council's subsequent recall of the Earl of Warwick from France to follow the late Duke of Exeter (Thomas Beaufort) as the King's moral tutor (*magister Regis*). Humphrey's marriage with Eleanor Cobham further smeared his reputation and reduced his prestige. And when, in August 1428, he attempted to do his duty as Protector by intervening up in Bedfordshire in a local squabble between two of his fellow-members of the Council, the Duke of Norfolk and the Earl of Huntingdon, the former, who had shown active sympathy with Gloucester's foreign policy in the winter of 1424-5 and was certainly no

[1] *Rot. Parl.*, iv. 318.

friend of Warwick's, now even declined to meet him. It was only the return of Cardinal Beaufort, the toughest of Gloucester's opponents, later in the summer of 1428, or rather the circumstances in which Beaufort came home, which gave the duke an opportunity to regain influence.

In view of the prevalent anti-papal feeling, following Martin V's recent attack on the Statute of Provisors and his needless severity towards Archbishop Chichele, this was hardly the best of times for the Cardinal to seek substantial English help in men and money for a fresh papal crusade in Bohemia and, more particularly, to initiate his legateship in England. The uneasiness felt by the royal Council as a whole concerning the outcome of Beaufort's appointment meant that for once its views coincided with Gloucester's own; and when the Cardinal published his legatine commission in November 1428, it was with the full approval of the Council that the Protector protested against its being exercised without Crown authority. Further, when Beaufort visited the northern border in February and March 1429 (an outing undertaken to improve Anglo-Scottish relations as well as to negotiate Scottish support for his crusade), advantage was taken of his absence to raise the question of his right, now that he was a cardinal, to continue to hold his see of Winchester. This matter was shelved. But the conflict between the main purpose of his legateship—the recruitment of a crusading army—and the pressing need for a fresh military effort in France soon proved too direct to be passed over. At first prepared to allow the Cardinal half (but no more) of the force he required, in July the Council was forced by the military crisis in France to insist that his recruits should be diverted to relieve the Duke of Bedford near Paris. Beaufort complied.

The deterioration of the military and political situation across the Channel just could not be ignored. In May 1429 Joan of Arc had relieved Orleans (under siege since October 1428); in June, a force under Lord Talbot had suffered a sharp defeat at Patay; on 17 July Charles VII was crowned at Rheims. Only a week or so later did Beaufort and his contingents enter Paris. Not before the end of October did he return to England, having done his best to keep Philip of Burgundy true to the English alliance by arranging his appointment as Regent of all English-held France, save Normandy where Bedford continued in control. In England, in the meantime, there was an awakening consciousness of having done too little, and that too late. There is some evidence even of panic. Parliament had

been summoned to meet on 13 October by writs issued on 12 July;
three weeks later, on 3 August, fresh writs went out requiring it
to meet on 22 September, three weeks earlier than was originally
intended.

The office of Speaker now fell upon William Allington, Esquire,
who, though well turned fifty, was sitting, as knight of the shire for
Cambridgeshire, for only the third time.[1] Although he had secured
the marriage of two of his sons with the coheiresses to the very
seemly possessions of the Argentine family in Hertfordshire, Norfolk,
Suffolk, and Buckinghamshire, his own territorial assets at Horseheath and Bottisham (Cambs.) and in Hertfordshire were only very
modest. His career, however, had not been without some elements of
distinction. As a young man in his twenties, that is, by 1395, he was
closely attached to John Holland, half-brother of Richard II and
son-in-law of John of Gaunt; and it was this connexion which, on
8 February 1398, secured him the post of Treasurer of Calais (where
John Holland, now Duke of Exeter, was in nominal command as
Captain). Before the end of Richard's reign, Allington was also an
esquire in the royal retinue. Despite this connexion and Holland's
fatal treason in January 1400, Allington had little trouble in adjust-
ing himself to the effects of the revolution of 1399, and he was soon
assured of Henry IV's acceptance. Not only was he allowed to remain a member of the royal Household, but in July 1403 became
Treasurer of the Exchequer of Ireland, with a salary of five shillings
a day when officially occupied. This appointment was a direct result
of his taking service with Thomas of Lancaster, Henry IV's second
and favourite son, who had been made Lieutenant of Ireland in 1401,
and in fact Allington only discharged his official duties in person on
those rare occasions when Thomas of Lancaster himself visited
Ireland, in 1403 and 1408.[2] Allington's connexion with Thomas,

[1] For references and a fuller discussion of Allington's career, see my article,
'William Allington of Horseheath, Speaker in the Parliament of 1429–30', *Proceedings of the Cambridge Antiquarian Society*, lii (1959), pp. 30–42. The precise
date of Allington's appointment as Treasurer of Calais in 1398 was found after
the writing of this article (in Belvoir Castle Archives, Royal grants, no. 475). So
was the fact that Allington had previously been M.P. for Cambs., in 1410 and
1416 (Oct.). This information (derived from P.R.O., E13/126, mem. 9 and
E13/133, mem. 9v.) I owe to the vigilance of Dr R. W. Dunning.

[2] Allington probably retained his office as Treasurer of Ireland until June
1413, when Henry V appointed a different Treasurer as well as a new Lieutenant
of Ireland. Allington was certainly still Treasurer in February 1411 when
Thomas of Lancaster gave him a letter of general acquittance of all actions
relating to his accounts (Belvoir Castle Archives, Royal grants, no. 472).

who was created Duke of Clarence in 1412, remained constant and close: having become one of Thomas's feoffees in the Crown lands granted him in Holderness, he was made one of the executors of the duke's will in July 1417. This was when Clarence accompanied his brother, Henry V, on the second invasion of France. But Allington himself stayed on in England, where shortly afterwards he became a member of the Council which assisted the Duke of Bedford in the government of the country during the King's absence. In July 1418 Allington crossed to Normandy. Evidently, his services were required for diplomatic and administrative rather than military employment: in May 1419, not long after the fall of Rouen, he was put in charge of the finances of the Norman duchy with the title of Treasurer- and Receiver-General, his authority being extended in January 1420—to keep pace with fresh acquisitions of territory— over the whole of the *pays conquis*.[1] How satisfactory were his operations may be gauged from the fact that not only was he retained in office after Clarence was killed at Baugé (March 1421), but was also immediately made custodian of the castle and town of Caen, his own financial headquarters. Moreover, he continued to discharge these offices until Henry V's death in August 1422.[2] Allington then returned to England, and this proved to be the end of his direct interest in the English administration in France.

It was only now, indeed, that the full, serious effect of Clarence's death on Allington's own career became really evident. For with the accession of the infant Henry VI Clarence would certainly have become, as heir-presumptive to the throne, either Protector in England or Regent in France: so far as Allington was concerned, the great prizes were no longer in prospect. But he continued to be busy as one of his dead lord's feoffees and executors, was sheriff of Cambridgeshire and Huntingdonshire in the first year of the new reign (having previously held this joint-bailiwick as sheriff in 1414-15 and as escheator in 1415-16), and in January 1424 was again made a

---

[1] Before this appointment Allington had been given some houses at Harfleur, and in December 1419, after a visit to England which ended with his return to France in the retinue of the Duchess of Clarence, he was granted an annual royal pension of £100. He also got possession of lordships at Ivelle-sur-Seine and elsewhere in the *vicomté* of Pont Audemer (given him by the Duke of Clarence), a house at Honfleur, and property at Warranville in the *vicomté* of Caen.

[2] In July 1420 Allington was made one of a commission appointed to reconsider the English truce with Brittany, and early in 1421 was acting as a conservator of the truce.

member of the royal Council.[1] It is reasonable to suppose that he may have owed this last appointment to the influence of Bishop Beaufort and perhaps Lord Cromwell, both of whom were his co-feoffees in the Clarence estates and members of the King's Council. (The bishop was also the natural protector of the Dowager Duchess of Clarence's sons by her earlier marriage with his brother, John Beaufort; and Lord Cromwell was using Allington's services as one of his feoffees-to-uses in his property at Tattershall and elsewhere in Lincolnshire.) Allington was also friendly with the son of his own first patron: John Holland, Earl of Huntingdon, a cousin of the Duchess of Clarence, who had fought with Clarence at Baugé and been taken prisoner. Allington had, in fact, subscribed as much as 200 marks towards the earl's ransom. He was still a member of the King's Council as late as March 1427 and, although he probably came off it soon after this, he clearly continued to enjoy the confidence of his fellow-councillors: at least he was appointed sheriff of Cambridgeshire and Huntingdonshire once more in November 1427, serving for the usual annual term until November 1428. It was under his successor in the shrievalty, his friend Sir Walter de la Pole,[2] that he was elected for Cambridgeshire to the parliament in which he served as Speaker. In the situation confronting parliament, Allington's former headship of the financial administration of the English conquest in France and his recent membership of the royal Council were probably his most important qualifications for the Speakership.[3]

The first session of this parliament lasted from 22 September until

---

[1] Allington's fee as a member of the King's Council was the normal one for an esquire: £40 a year (minus 4s. for each day of absence). There is a record of his attendance at council meetings in February and July 1424, February 1425, July 1426, and March 1427.

[2] For an account of Sir Walter de la Pole, who had himself been one of the Duke of Clarence's retinue in Henry IV's reign, see my book, *The Commons in the Parliament of 1422*, pp. 172–5.

[3] A J.P. in Cambridgeshire from 1401 to 1407 and from 1417 to 1420, Allington was again re-appointed in 1433, then retaining office until 1439. But after his Speakership he seems to have made little impact even locally. In 1430, 1431, and 1434, however, he helped raise royal loans in Cambridgeshire and Huntingdonshire and in 1436 was a local commissioner of array, but otherwise was seemingly of little account. It was his son William who was M.P. for Cambridgeshire in 1433, 1437, and 1439–40, escheator there and in Huntingdonshire in 1436–7, and sheriff in 1437–8 and 1450–1. The Speaker died on 19 October 1446, being buried at Horseheath where his 'brass' described him as once Treasurer of Ireland and Treasurer of Normandy. It was his grandson who was Speaker in 1472–5 and 1478.

o

20 December 1429, the second from 14 January to 23 February 1430. Their outcome was of considerable importance, immediate and long-term. To help counterbalance the effect of the disquieting turn of events in France, especially the coronation of Charles VII, it was thought advisable that the nearly eight-year-old Henry of Windsor should also be crowned as King of France. But first he must needs be crowned in England. And so he was, on 6 November 1429, in the middle of the first session of the parliament. It was as a direct consequence of the coronation that on 15 November Gloucester resigned the office of Protector. Duke Humphrey retained his title of Chief Councillor, but the end of his Protectorship was likely, at first at any rate, to enhance the power of the Council, in which the actual exercise of the royal authority continued to be vested. Another attack on Cardinal Beaufort, for which Gloucester must be held responsible, not surprisingly misfired. This was when, near the end of the first session (on 18 December), the peers resolved that Beaufort, although a cardinal and legate of the Roman See, should not merely be admitted to membership of the King's Council, but even be urged to attend its meetings (except when Anglo-papal issues were on hand). And the Commons endorsed the Lords' view of Beaufort's position: in making their grant of a second tenth and fifteenth on 20 December (payable at Christmas 1430), in addition to the one already granted on 12 December (and payable on 14 January 1430), they prefaced it with a special recommendation of the Cardinal of England. It was the least they could do: Beaufort's sacrifice of his Bohemian crusade had lost him much credit at the Roman Curia; and his loans to the Crown, which amounted in the last year alone to nearly £24,000, were also costing him dearly. Knowing something of Allington's own history, we may suspect that as Speaker he had had some share in this testimonial from the Lower House. In making their second grant of direct taxation, the Commons described themselves to the King as *trustyng fully . . . thorogh suche comfort as we have conceived be* [by] *our Lordes . . . that we shall have knowelech of gode and sadde governance in every partie of this your seid Roialme, or* [before] *ye dissolve this your present Parlement.* Despite, in view of the government's need of supplies, the strength of their position, the Commons themselves, however, imposed no new administrative requirements. They could well afford, of course, to be generous with funds, for their double-subsidy was the first grant of direct taxation of the regular sort to be made in parliament for eight years. Tunnage and poundage were merely renewed until the next parliament. In the second session,

however, the wool-subsidy was continued until November 1433, and the time of collection of the second tenth and fifteenth was advanced by more than a month (from Christmas to 18 November 1430). By what the Commons probably regarded as an all-out effort to save the situation in France, now quite seriously endangered, Henry of Windsor was enabled to leave England on St George's Day 1430, for his crowning in his mother's country, with a company fit to answer the requirements of protocol and even to some extent to meet the more urgent demands of the military situation.

A brief notice may be given to the statutory definition, made during this parliament in answer to one of the Commons' petitions, of the qualification for voting in shire-elections. Speaker Allington himself must have been well aware of the recent disputed election in Huntingdonshire which (with other disputed elections in Buckinghamshire and Cumberland) doubtless contributed to the proposal. It had been his friend and successor as sheriff, De la Pole, who had been prevailed upon to hold a second election for the county at Huntingdon, because the first had been interfered with by intruders from Bedfordshire. The Commons' petition resulted in a statute which limited the electorate of every county to its 40s. freeholders. Since this qualification was to be in force for the next four centuries, it is that statute which, from the point of view of the constitutional historian, makes chiefly memorable the parliament in which Allington was Speaker.

Early in 1430 the French continued to attract military success, even in the lower valley of the Seine. It was, in fact, on the day after the dissolution of the 1429–30 parliament (24 February) that the forces of Charles VII took Château Gaillard. None the less, soon after the seizure of Joan of Arc three months later, it became safe for Henry VI to move overland from Calais to Rouen, where he made a state entry on 29 July. Nearly another year and a half, however, were to elapse before he could be crowned in Paris. England, in the meantime, had been governed by Gloucester (acting as *Custos*) along with those members of the Council who had not accompanied the King to France. The rest of the year 1430 passed off calmly enough. So did the only parliament which met during Henry VI's absence abroad, even though Cardinal Beaufort came home to attend it.

Summoned in good time (on 27 November), parliament met on 12 January 1431. Gloucester, content for once to bide his time, had now recovered some measure of authority. This is more than hinted by the way parliament was opened. Whether or not the Chancellor,

Archbishop Kemp of York, was ill (as the parliament-roll asserts), the duty of declaring the causes of summons fell to Dr William Lyndwood, now Secondary in the office of the Privy Seal. It was Lyndwood who had been engaged in 1427 as diplomatic envoy to Holland about the affairs of the then Duchess of Gloucester, Jacqueline of Hainault. His fellow-envoy, it will be recalled, had been John Tyrell, one of Gloucester's most trusted agents, who soon afterwards became Speaker in the parliament of 1427–8 and, in the course of his Speakership, Chief Steward of the Duchy of Lancaster north of Trent. Re-elected for Essex in 1429 and now once again returned, it was Tyrell whom, for a second time, the Commons chose to be their Speaker in 1431. Since 1427 he had continued to occupy his duchy appointment. Recently, in May 1430, he had contributed to Crown-loans raised in Essex and Hertfordshire by a royal commission to which he himself belonged.

The country in general was well aware of the financial burden imposed by such activities. Indeed, when hinting that a reasonable peace with France, Spain, and Scotland would be welcome, both Lords and Commons made no bones about saying so. None the less, on 20 March 1431, after a ten weeks' session, Tyrell was empowered to announce a series of parliamentary grants: a tax of £1 per knight's fee (alternatively, on every £20 worth of annual income from land), to be raised at midsummer; a tenth and fifteenth, leviable in November; a further third of such a subsidy, due at Easter 1432; and, of the subsidies on trade, a two years' extension of tunnage and poundage (until Martinmas 1432), together with a year's extension of the wool-subsidy which guaranteed its collection until Martinmas 1434. Even taking into account that the land-tax proved unworkable and had to be rescinded in the next parliament, the total vote was not ungenerous.

Certainly, John Tyrell lost no credit by his Speakership. By the end of the session, it had been decided that both he and Dr Lyndwood should join Henry VI in France as members of his Council.[1] Perhaps it was already intended that Tyrell should also be appointed as Treasurer of the King's Household and to the co-ordinate office

[1] On 16 March 1431, just before the end of his Speakership, Tyrell was paid by the Exchequer a *regardum* of £100 as a member-elect of the King's Council in France for the next half-year, and on the same day and on 21 April he received, respectively, £40 and £108 odd as advances on wages of war for himself and his retinue (Privy Seal warrants for issue, P.R.O., E 404/47/195). An additional advance of £100 was made to him on the day of parliament's dissolution.

of Treasurer for War instead of John Hotoft of Knebworth, who had acted in this dual capacity ever since 1423. Tyrell was formally appointed on 25 May 1431, Hotoft's salary of 100 marks a year (charged on the fee-farm of Lincoln) being transferred to him in September following. He continued to hold this chief financial office of the Household until April 1437.[1] Meanwhile, neither his departure for France nor his new appointment was allowed to affect his tenure of office as Chief Steward of the Duchy of Lancaster estates north of Trent; in fact, on 23 April 1431 he had actually been re-appointed with the right to have a deputy, a privilege of which he availed himself before he left for France.[2] It was during the summer of 1431, very likely when he assumed office as Treasurer of the Household, that Tyrell was made a knight.

Tyrell's lord, Duke Humphrey, busied himself in the spring of 1431 in crushing a mild outbreak of Lollard unrest in the Midlands, but otherwise the year passed without major incident. At least this was so until, in November, Gloucester once again raised the question of Cardinal Beaufort's right to continue as Bishop of Winchester. If this move was made partly to mask the duke's plans for the future, the Council was left in little doubt of the self-regarding nature of his policy, for he also demanded a permanent increase of his own personal salary. Consideration of the ecclesiastical problem was deferred until the King's return; the financial proposal, however, was accepted, even despite the combined attempt of the Chancellor and the Treasurer to defeat it. And, as soon as Henry VI came home, Gloucester turned the tables on these and others of his critics among the officials on the Council by contriving their dismissal: on 25 February 1432, only four days after the King returned to Westminster, Archbishop Kemp was superseded as Chancellor by Bishop Stafford; on the following day, Lord Hungerford gave place at the Exchequer to Lord Scrope (another of Gloucester's allies); and then, on 1 March, Lord Cromwell was followed as Chamberlain by Sir William Philip (whose sister-in-law was stepmother to the Duchess of Gloucester), and Lord Tiptoft gave up the Stewardship of the Household to Sir Robert Babthorpe.

On the day of Kemp's dismissal, parliament was summoned to

---

[1] Exchequer, Accounts Various, P.R.O., E 101/408/9; 408/13. For Hotoft, who now became King's Chamberlain of the Exchequer, see my *Commons in the Parliament of 1422*, p. 191.

[2] R. Somerville, op. cit., i. 420. Tyrell's deputy duchy-steward was John Pury, M.P. for Kent in 1433 and for Dover in 1435.

meet eleven weeks later. During the interval, the political atmosphere quite clearly became more heavily charged. Cardinal Beaufort, on hearing that he was threatened with impeachment for treason, wound up his diplomatic exchanges with the Duke of Burgundy in Flanders and returned home to face the attack in person. Not merely that, but no more than five days before parliament was due to meet, the Duke of Norfolk, the Earls of Suffolk, Huntingdon, Stafford, Northumberland and Salisbury, together with Lord Cromwell, were specially ordered by letters under the Privy Seal to bring only their normal retinues to the parliament. That these writs were identical need not of course be taken to imply that the recipients were thought to be of one mind, much less that they were all opposed to Gloucester. Quite certainly, they were neither. But the writs did at least indicate the government's nervousness.

The parliamentary session opened, as arranged, on 12 May 1432. On the next day Gloucester gave out to the Lords that it would be well to reassure the Lower House of their unity and of his own intention as Chief Councillor to fall in with majority decisions. This was done on the third day when the Commons came to present their Speaker. The election to the office of John Russell, knight of the shire for Herefordshire, throws little light on the temper of the Lower House at this stage. It may well be that the Commons chose Russell chiefly for his lawyerly qualities and were not forgetful that he had already been Speaker (in 1423–4).[1] This is not, of course, to say that they were uninfluenced by other considerations. In 1426 Russell had been involved as a feoffee in a settlement of estates arranged in anticipation of the marriage of the Earl of Huntingdon with Anne, sister of the Earl of Stafford and Dowager Countess of March, a settlement which was still not completed as late as the end of 1430.[2] In 1432, along with Cardinal Beaufort, Bishop Langley of Durham, and Lord Hungerford, Russell was still acting as a feoffee of the late Duke of York (Edward of Norwich). And it was during this parliament of 1432 that Richard, Duke of York (now newly come of age but not yet a member of the Lords), successfully petitioned that parliament should formally approve livery of seisin of all the entailed estates to which he was entitled as nephew and heir of

[1] Since being Speaker in 1423, Russell had sat for Herefordshire in the parliaments of 1426, 1429–30 and 1431. After 1432, he was to sit only once again, in 1433. He had served as a commissioner for raising Crown-loans in Herefordshire in 1426, 1428, 1430, and 1431, and, of course, as a J.P.

[2] *CCR, 1422–9*, 274; *CPR, 1429–36*, 4, 114; *Rot. Parl.*, iv. 384.

both Edward of Norwich and Edmund Mortimer, Earl of March, a request which was granted on condition that within five years the duke paid 1,000 marks to the Crown and nearly £1,000 to the Duke of Gloucester, who had the wardship of the bulk of the Mortimer lands.[1] Conceivably, Russell's position as a feoffee in part of York's inheritance had had something to do with his election, although York's affairs were by no means the most important business of the session.

The parliament of 1432, which lasted nearly nine weeks (from 12 May to 17 July), represented in all a qualified success for the Duke of Gloucester. Admittedly, when Beaufort demanded that, if he were to be impeached for treason, his accuser should stand forward, it was none other than Gloucester himself who, on behalf of the Council, attested the Cardinal's loyalty; and, at the Commons' request, Beaufort eventually secured an exemption from the penalties of the Acts of Provisors and Praemunire. On the other hand, the Cardinal's additional complaint against the seizure of royal jewels given him in pledge was not satisfied until 3 July, and only then on condition that he deposited an additional £6,000 for them, made a further loan of yet another £6,000, allowed the repayment of earlier loans amounting to 13,000 marks to be postponed, and undertook to be governed by the Council in his future relations with the Papacy. The effect of all this was to leave the Cardinal somewhat stranded and even isolated. Meanwhile, on 16 June, Lord Cromwell had been misguided enough to challenge his dismissal from the Chamberlainship as contrary to the Council ordinances of 1429: his request for an enquiry was shrugged off by Gloucester with the bland statement that the dismissal had been decided by him and the Council. This was no answer at all, but Cromwell had to accept it. Gloucester, in other words, was left secure. But that the confidence felt by the Commons in a government

---

[1] *Rot. Parl.*, iv. 380, 389–90, 392, 406; *CCR, 1429–35*, 134. The royal Council favourably answered a petition, submitted in the parliament of 1433 by the Duke of York, in which he asked that the Exchequer should be permitted to make allowance for payments he had made at Henry V's requirement, amounting to all of the 10,000 marks at which his fine had been assessed, except for about £800 (of which he now asked to be released). Immediately before the parliament of 1433, the duke had undertaken to apply £100 to the building of his uncle Edward's college at Fotheringhay, to content his executors within two years and, after John Russell and Edward's other feoffees had given him seisin of the estates they held in trust, to grant certain annuities specified by Edward's will, including one to Russell himself (*Rot. Parl.*, iv. 465; *CCR, 1429–35*, 214, 260, 264).

under Gloucester's control was by no means complete is suggested by their financial grant. The reason they gave for requesting an annulment of the subsidy on knights' fees and landed-income voted in 1431—that it was too complicated—was valid enough. But all that Speaker Russell was able to announce on the last day of the session to take its place was a grant of a mere half of a tenth and fifteenth, itself payable in moieties (the first not until November following, the second even a year later still), plus an extension of the wool-subsidy for a year (November 1434–5) and tunnage and poundage for two (November 1432–4). The Commons are not likely to have been suited by the Council's rejection of the 6d. extra charge on poundage, by which they had meant to discriminate against alien merchants. So far as can be seen, Russell himself got nothing out of his Speakership: his appointment (in November following) as the next royal escheator in Herefordshire could scarcely be counted any reward.[1]

Between now and the next parliament it was the situation in France which gave rise to most disquiet. The English forces were, at best, no more than holding their own. Duke Philip of Burgundy was still out of step with his English allies. Nor were his personal relations with Bedford improved when his sister, Bedford's wife, died in the autumn of 1432, especially since the English duke not only hastily married again but chose for his bride, without Burgundy's agreement, Jacquetta of Luxembourg, the daughter of one of Burgundy's own great vassals. In these circumstances the French understandably were stiffening in their attitude towards English moves in the direction of a diplomatic settlement; in April and May 1433 they even declined to send envoys to a conference at Calais, where Bedford, Gloucester, Beaufort, and the English Chancellor, Bishop Stafford, had all gathered to receive them. It was on 24 May, the day after Gloucester and the Chancellor arrived back in England, that parliament was summoned to meet some six weeks later, on 8 July. Both Bedford and the Cardinal returned home in time for the session, Bedford after an absence of over six years. General discontent was now growing in the country on account of the war, or rather because of its costliness and indecisive character. Even Bed-

[1] In 1434 Russell served on a few royal commissions in Herefordshire which automatically came his way as M.P. Then and in 1436 he was also a commissioner for raising Crown-loans. He himself advanced 40 marks in 1435 and was asked for 100 marks in 1436. He died in the spring of 1437, the writ of *Diem clausit extremum* to the royal escheator in Herefordshire being issued by Chancery on 20 June.

ford's own military reputation was being questioned, so that, unless he was able to reassert his personal influence, no adequate offer of support by parliament was likely to materialize.

On the first day of the parliament, after listening to a sermon from the Chancellor on the need for harmony among the lords, justice from knights and other *mediocres*, and obedience from lesser men, the Commons went off to elect the Speaker. Their choice fell on the lawyer, Roger Hunt, who had been Speaker in 1420. Since then he had sat for Huntingdonshire in every parliament except the last of Henry V's reign. But it can hardly have been just because he was a seasoned parliamentarian that the Commons elected him on this occasion. There is no doubt of Hunt's abilities as a lawyer: as long ago as in 1408–9 he had been the King's Attorney-General in the courts; and five years after his present occupation of the Chair he was to become Second Baron of the Exchequer (at the instance of Cardinal Beaufort) and remain in office for certainly the next ten years (1438–48), perhaps until his death.[1] But he was well known as the adviser and agent of more than one great magnate who had been politically active both before and since the time of Henry VI's accession. When acting in the parliament of 1425 as leading counsel for John Mowbray, the Earl Marshal, in his suit for precedence of the Earl of Warwick (solved by Mowbray's recognition as Duke of Norfolk), Hunt described himself as having *of long tyme beon of counseill with his seid Lord Erl Mareschall*.[2] How far back this Mowbray connexion went is not known, but it continued to be close: Hunt's involvement in riots at Huntingdon in 1426 and 1427, for which he was indicted in 1429 before the Earl of Huntingdon and other of his own fellow-J.P.s in the county, was possibly the result of his supporting the Duke of Norfolk in his quarrel with the earl;[3] certainly,

[1] *CPR, 1436–41*, 219; Exchequer, K.R., Accounts Various, Account-books of the Keeper of the Great Wardrobe, P.R.O., E 101/409/2–18. Although not himself Speaker at Leicester in February 1426, Hunt had headed the deputation from the Commons which at the beginning of the session asked the Lords to compose the quarrel between Gloucester and Henry Beaufort. The Lords' answer was a written undertaking to act impartially (*Rot. Parl.*, iv. 296).

[2] *Rot. Parl.*, iv. 267–75.

[3] Further to the charges of rioting in 1426–7, Hunt, according to an indictment made before Lord Grey of Ruthin and other J.P.s at Bedford on 3 October 1429, had recently aided and abetted a murder at Eton (Beds.), and when (on a writ of *certis de causis*) the case was brought into the King's Bench on 12 November he went bail for the two men accused of the murder. A year later (in November 1430), these indictments were quashed in the King's Bench as insufficient at law (Coram Rege Roll, P.R.O., K.B. 27/674, Rex roll, mem. 154).

in May 1429 Hunt was appointed by Norfolk as one of his executors and attorneys-general, and two years later he was acting as the duke's feoffee.[1] But when the parliament of 1433 met, Norfolk had been dead for the best part of a year, so that the most important single political influence to which Hunt was then exposed is likely to have been Lord Tiptoft's.

For a long time Hunt and Tiptoft had been even intimately associated. When, under Henry V, Tiptoft was Seneschal of Aquitaine and Treasurer-General of Normandy, Hunt had regularly acted as his liaison with the Exchequer,[2] and in 1433 Hunt had been one of Tiptoft's feoffees-to-uses for over a quarter of a century. As recently as May 1431, when Tiptoft made an enfeoffment of certain of his manors in Cambridgeshire and Middlesex, Hunt was one of the trustees who figured in the settlement.[3] It was within only a few weeks of this transaction that Hunt took an oath in Chancery that 16 tuns of Gascon wine, seized by the collectors of tunnage and poundage at London and Bristol, had been imported by Tiptoft for domestic consumption, so that the wine could be released as duty-free; and it was but a few days later still that when, on 5 July 1431, Lord Tiptoft obtained a royal grant of the wardship of some of the estates of the late Chief Justice Hankford, Hunt was one of his sureties at the Exchequer. It had probably been by Tiptoft's influence that, in February 1433 (by which time Tiptoft was once more attending meetings of the Council), Hunt himself leased from the Exchequer the manor of Kersey (Suffolk), an estate recently held in dower by the widow of the Earl of March, of whose coheirs Tiptoft's wife was one.[4] Tiptoft was no friend of Humphrey of Gloucester who in 1432 had dismissed him from the Stewardship of the royal Household. And Hunt's election as Speaker in 1433 may perhaps be taken to suggest that the Lower House was now not very likely to provide much support for the policies of Gloucester and his friends.

On 13 July, only two days after Hunt's election, the Duke of Bedford protested in the presence of both Lords and Commons against complaints that he had been negligent in the conduct of the war in France. Bedford's challenge was enough to silence criticism, the Chancellor making haste to reply that this was the first that the King or any member of his Council had heard of such *profana verba*

---

[1] F. Blomefield, *Topographical History of Norfolk*, i. 236; *Chichele Register*, ed. E. F. Jacob, ii. 474.

[2] See above, p. 171.   [3] *HMC Report, Rutland MSS.*, iv. 86.

[4] *CCR, 1429–35*, 89; *CFR, 1430–7*, 43, 143; *CPR, 1429–36*, 59.

et scandalosa, and that Bedford's loyalty was not in question. The
first session lasted until 13 August, parliament being then adjourned
for two months. Already, however, important changes had taken
place in the administration: William de la Pole, Earl of Suffolk, who
had recently married the daughter of Thomas Chaucer, Cardinal
Beaufort's cousin and friend, was now Steward of the King's Household, and on 11 August Lord Cromwell had superseded Lord Scrope
as Treasurer of the Exchequer. The formal reasons given for the
adjournment were that there was plague in London, that the Commons wanted fuller information about riots and cases of maintenance, and that the peers must be allowed some part of the autumn for
sport. There can, however, be no doubt that what was chiefly needed
was time for the new Treasurer to overhaul and survey the accounts
and prepare a financial statement.

How depressing this statement was bound to be had already been
made clear on the last day of the first session. Then, in order to supply
the Household during the recess, parliament authorized Cromwell to
raise £2,000 by cutting down on all but the most recent Exchequer
assignments of revenue. Hardly·had the second session begun before,
on 18 October, the Treasurer made an interim report, showing that
the Crown debts stood at £168,000, and that the next two years'
income was already assigned to royal creditors. To make a simple
calculation of our own: unless the situation improved, the King's
indebtedness in another two years' time would stand (if we accept
Mr J. L. Kirby's estimate of the average annual expenditure as
£57,000) at some £282,000. The financial outlook was very gloomy.
And to make it gloomier still, Cromwell emphasized the current fall
in the yield from taxation. What he demanded was an inspection of
financial records by the Lords, a valid appropriation of income to the
Household, and a promise of support from the Council, at least to
the extent of being ready to consult him before making grants from
the revenue. These conditions were approved, the Lords undertook
to work upon the Commons, and the Treasurer himself presented a
statement in the Lower House. The situation was not beyond recall:
a grant of four extra subsidies, if backed up with votes by the Con-
vocations of Canterbury and York, would more than have accounted
for the existing arrears. But parliament had so far not granted much
more than this during the whole of the reign, and although it was
now prepared to mortgage future revenue further than it was already
bespoken—by allowing the Council to take up loans to the value of
100,000 marks (in theory)—the financial grant which Speaker Hunt

was able to declare at the end of the session (in the last week before Christmas) was not even a full single subsidy, but a tenth and fifteenth clipped of £4,000 (i.e. reduced by over 10 per cent); the payment of this tax, moreover, was to be by no fewer than four instalments spread over as long a period as the next two years.[1] Tunnage and poundage were renewed for two years (November 1434–6). Admittedly, woollen cloth exported by denizens was now made chargeable to poundage for a year. But the main increases in taxation on trade were made by the Lower House to fall upon foreign merchants (in so far as their diminishing interest in *direct* intercourse with England would permit).[2]

That the Commons' grant was likely to be quite inadequate to energizing a great military drive in France might have been already predicted nearly a month before the end of the parliament. For on 24 November Speaker Hunt had put forward a recommendation from the Commons that Bedford should stay in England. Their grounds were that, valuable though they knew his work in France to be, his stabilizing influence as head of the Council was needed at home.[3] (The Commons had been specially exercised during the

[1] This is the first occasion on which the tenth and fifteenth were subjected to a general reduction by a large sum in round figures.

[2] A double charge of 6s. per tun on sweet wines imported by aliens was granted for three years (Nov. 1434–7), and over the same period foreign exports of wool were subjected to a subsidy of 4 instead of 2½ marks per sack (a rise of 60 per cent).

[3] *Rot. Parl.*, iv. 423. On 5 November, during this second session, Hunt had been appointed sheriff of Cambridgeshire and Huntingdonshire. He did not desire the office and several times petitioned to be excused through a deputation of 36 of his fellow-members, headed by Sir John Tyrell, the Treasurer of the Household, then M.P. for Essex. The Chancellor and others of the Council, however, stated that Roger's losses would be compensated, and he held the office, in fact, for two whole years together (until Nov. 1435). His costs amounted to £200, but it was not until February 1443 that he was granted an Exchequer assignment to that amount on the proceeds of tunnage and poundage in the port of London (*CPR, 1441–6*, 150; P.R.O., *Lists and Indexes*, ix (List of Sheriffs), 13). This was even despite his appointment at the Exchequer as Second Baron which he had held since 5 November 1438. In this office Hunt was very active in Huntingdonshire, Bedfordshire and Buckinghamshire as a commissioner for raising Crown-loans in the 1440's. Even otherwise, it seems to have taken much of his time. In July 1441, however, he accompanied Dr Lyndwood, then Keeper of the Privy Seal, and the great London mercer, William Estfeld, on a partly diplomatic, partly commercial, embassy to the Netherlands (*DKR*, xlviii. 349). Hunt was still one of the four Exchequer Barons in 1448. The date of his death is not precisely known, but he was certainly no longer alive in July 1456 (*CCR, 1454–61*, 146).

session over the prevalence of violence and law-breaking, cases of maintenance in particular, and members of both Lords and Commons alike had taken oaths not to interfere with the course of justice.) The Lords also agreed that Bedford should remain, and for the time being he accepted. On 18 December, three days before the dissolution, approval was given to his terms, which left no doubt of his intention to exert a real control over government. And so he stayed, but not for long. After withstanding, in a Great Council in April and May 1434, another attack on his past conduct in France, this time patently the work of his brother Gloucester, Bedford went overseas again in July in a mood of disappointment at his failure to stir the country to more sincere and greater efforts for the war.

Although it was the suppression of a number of peasant risings in Normandy itself that engaged the Regent's attention on his return to France, English arms enjoyed some success during 1434. This was especially so in Maine and Picardy. In the following year, however, all went amiss. And when, after not meeting for nearly two years, parliament once more came together at Westminster, on 10 October 1435, it was in extremely depressing circumstances for the country at large.

When parliament had been summoned on 5 July, the great congress from which it was hoped that a comprehensive Anglo-French peace-settlement would emerge, was about to assemble at Arras. When parliament met, that conference had failed, the Duke of Bedford was dead, and the Anglo-Burgundian alliance had fallen apart. Even with Burgundian support, the English forces in France had for some time been losing ground. Without that support, for the English to demand from the French a recognition of even the *status quo*, much more to insist on the validity of the settlement of Troyes, amounted to an inability to face realities. Actually to extend the war, unsuccessful in France, against Burgundy, was madness itself. And yet, when news reached England that Duke Philip had acquired territories on the Somme (until then nominally loyal to Henry VI) as part of the price of reconciliation with Charles VII, all the anti-Flemish feeling, long pent-up in the interests of the Anglo-Burgundian alliance, was suddenly let loose. The speech opening parliament, in which the Chancellor gave an incomplete and misleading impression of the Arras conference, especially of Burgundy's actions before and since, was calculated to inflame the sense of outrage still further. The defection of Burgundy was not to be borne. And so, how to prepare not only for a renewal of the war in France, but also for hostilities in this new direction, became the main business of the Lords and Commons.

Left by his brother's death heir-presumptive to the throne, and with his former anti-Burgundian policy seemingly justified, Humphrey of Gloucester now rose in public esteem. On 1 November, three weeks after the session began, he was appointed to follow Bedford as Lieutenant of Calais with an extended authority over Picardy, Artois and Flanders: a direct challenge to Burgundy. An indenture embodying Gloucester's conditions of service in the Marches of Calais and Picardy had already been accepted by the Lords, with the sole amendment that it should hold for nine instead of twelve years (as from July 1436). Some diplomatic effort was also made to establish an anti-Burgundian alliance in Germany and the Low Countries. The Commons successfully applied for a seven years' suspension of the Statute of Truces, with the clear intention of encouraging English privateers to embarrass Flemish trade; and it was probably during the session that the decision was taken to send a fresh expeditionary force to France under the Duke of York as Lieutenant-General. With government credit recently (in May 1434) so low that the raising of £50,000 by loans (to finance the expedition then proposed by Gloucester) had been derided as impossible, parliament's willingness to authorize the Council to raise twice that amount between now and the next parliament gives some idea of its excitement. Judging from the grants made after a ten weeks' session and only two days before Christmas (a late date which in itself suggests reluctance on the Commons' part to meet the government's requirements in full), the Commons' warlike enthusiasm had somewhat abated, at least so far as its financial implications were concerned. They voted a graduated income-tax, payable a fortnight after Easter 1436, on freehold-lands and offices worth £5 a year and upwards (the whole of which yielded in fact no more than about £9,000, most of it being contributed by the lords and other well-to-do landowners). But, this apart, all that the Lower House was prepared to do was to repeat the meagre grant of two years before: a single tenth and fifteenth, again subject to a cut of £4,000 and payable as before in four instalments spread over two years, plus a confirmation of the subsidies on trade until Martinmas 1437 (including, however, a reduction of ½ mark per sack on alien exports of wool).

Modest though these grants were, it was perhaps to encourage the Speaker in their final negotiation (or possibly just after they had been agreed) that, a week before the end of the session, the Exchequer paid him a personal reward of £13 13s. 4d. To the parliamentary historian, it is this monetary allowance to John Bowes, expressly for his services as Speaker, which makes him chiefly memorable, being the first instance on record of such a payment. Because, otherwise, apart from his actual election to the Chair in 1435 and his two years' tenure of the Recordership of London later on (1440–2), the career of this Nottinghamshire lawyer was somewhat colourless and untypical of a Speaker of this period.[1] This is not to say that Bowes had no local standing or was unknown to the central government: his lands at Costock and Rempstone (Notts.) were extremely modest, but he had already sat twice as knight of the shire (in 1429 and 1432); he had been a J.P. of the *quorum* in Nottinghamshire since 1422, the royal escheator for Nottinghamshire and Derbyshire in 1428–9, and a J.P. in Leicestershire in 1431–2. Moreover, although there is no sure evidence that he enjoyed the benefit of a close connexion with any of the important members of the King's Council at this time, it is very probable that he was at least known to Lord Cromwell, the Treasurer, who was far from wanting influence in Nottinghamshire: the two men had been associated (in the summer of 1434) as members of a royal commission set up to detect cases of concealment of the feudal and judicial rights of the Crown in the county. It is possible, too, that Bowes was well acquainted with Lord Tiptoft: the latter enjoyed the wardship of the estates of the late Lord Roos of Belvoir, and Roos had made Bowes one of his feoffees in April 1430. (This was shortly before Lord Roos crossed to France, where soon afterwards, only two days after taking charge of the administration of Paris, he accidentally lost his life by drowning.) This interest in the Roos estates could also have brought Bowes into touch with Edmund Beaufort, a nephew of the Cardinal, who married Lord Roos's widow. There is firmer evidence that Bowes was connected with John Lord Beaumont, who had been summoned to parliament since 1432: in 1427–8 Bowes had been one of a small syndicate which acquired an Exchequer lease of Beaumont's mother's and grandmother's dower-estates (mostly in Leicestershire and Lincolnshire),

[1] For references and more details of Bowes's career, see my article, 'John Bowes of Costock, Speaker in the Parliament of 1435', *Transactions of the Thoroton Society of Nottinghamshire*, vol. lx (1956), pp. 8–19. Bowes was again M.P. for Nottinghamshire in 1439–40 and for London in 1442. He was Recorder of London from 13 July 1440 to 14 July 1442, when the City gave him an annual pension of 20 marks. His last appointment as J.P. in Nottinghamshire fell in July 1444, less than a month before his death.

an arrangement for which Lord Beaumont's father-in-law, Sir William Philip, K.G., stood surety. It is worth noting that Sir William, promoted King's Chamberlain by the Duke of Gloucester in 1432, was still in office when John Bowes was Speaker. Perhaps it would not be going too far to think of Bowes as at least indirectly connected with Gloucester. The suggestion receives some slight confirmation from other quarters: from no later than 1425 Bowes had been a feoffee in certain manors (in Nottinghamshire, Leicestershire, and Lincolnshire) belonging to Sir Thomas Chaworth, father-in-law of Lord Scrope of Masham who was certainly a friend of Duke Humphrey; besides, Bowes was both a near neighbour and the friend of a former chamberlain of the Duke of Bedford, Sir Thomas Rempstone, who in 1437 was to become Lieutenant of Calais, an office not likely to have come his way without Gloucester's backing. But Bowes's aristocratic connexions are for the most part elusive and, even where demonstrable, somewhat casual. Perhaps it was mainly respect for him as a lawyer which had moved the Commons to elect him Speaker in 1435.

What was done during the parliament of 1435 had the eventual effect of 'boosting' the English war-effort across the Channel during 1436. But at first the French retained their advantage. In January they took Harfleur and wrested the Caux peninsula from English control. In April the English were put out of Paris. Measures for the defence of Calais against Burgundian attack were, however, taken in time, and Duke Philip's investment of the town failed after three weeks. Gloucester, the new Lieutenant here, did not himself arrive soon enough to see Burgundy depart and, after a short punitive raid into nearby Flanders, returned to England. Meanwhile, the Duke of York (now aged twenty-four) had taken up his command in Normandy as Lieutenant-General and Governor and achieved some success in the Pays de Caux.

When parliament next met on 21 January 1437 at Westminster (not Cambridge, as had been originally intended), the political tide was evidently still running strongly in Gloucester's favour. And it continued to do so throughout the nine weeks' session which ended on Wednesday in Holy Week (27 March). Parliament finally agreed on a tenth and fifteenth (subject to the now usual rebate of £4,000), one half to be paid in November following, the other a year later; and it also guaranteed the subsidies on trade for as much as three years (November 1437–40). The Commons' appropriations, being all exclusively for the upkeep of Calais, were largely so much support for

Gloucester, its Lieutenant: following his complaint before the King and Lords (on 25 February) that his Calais retinue was suffering from desertions on account of arrears of pay, it was decided that the whole of a loan of 2,000 marks from Henry V's feoffees in the Duchy of Lancaster should go to meet the wages and victualling of the garrisons of Calais and the March; and when Gloucester further petitioned the Commons to appropriate 20s. per sack of the wool-subsidy for their payment and to authorize the Treasurer to meet any deficit, this also was granted by both Houses, the appropriation being formally incorporated in the subsidy-bill.

That the Commons would be so amenable to Gloucester's influence might almost have been presumed from their election to the Speakership of Sir John Tyrell, Speaker in 1427-8 and 1431, Chief Steward of the Duchy of Lancaster north of Trent since 1427, and Treasurer of the King's Household since 1431, who throughout his political career had been one of Gloucester's retainers. For some time Tyrell had also had relations with the Duke of York, which originally were perhaps a by-product of Gloucester's enjoyment of the wardship of the bulk of the Mortimer lands during York's minority: as early as 1427 Tyrell had obtained a royal grant of the stewardship of the Mortimer lordships of Clare and Thaxted until York came of age;[1] in the parliament of 1433 he had been appointed as one of the overseers of the administration of the effects of the late Earl of March,[2] whose nephew and heir the duke was; early in 1436 he had been involved as a feoffee in a mortgage of Mortimer estates arranged by York before he crossed to Normandy;[3] and now, in 1437, he was even acting as the duke's Receiver-General in England.[4] Not only, therefore, did Tyrell, as Treasurer of the King's Household and *ex officio* Treasurer for War, fill the rôle of royal paymaster of York's forces overseas, but he was also the duke's own principal financial officer at home, responsible for the collection of his private income. That Tyrell could now be attached simultaneously to both Gloucester and York seems to presuppose some understanding or community of interest between the two magnates who were, by natural inclination, leaders of the party strongly in favour of an active prosecution of the war in France. His election as Speaker possibly suggests that the

---

[1] CPR, 1422-9, 353, 395, 401.
[2] Rot. Parl., iv. 470.
[3] CPR, 1429-36, 514.
[4] B.M., Egerton Roll 8781. (I owe this important reference to Mr K. B. McFarlane.)

P

Commons recognized the alliance and approved of the policy of the two men.

Both these suppositions receive some confirmation from the fact that, when Tyrell became ill during the parliament and, on 19 March, had to be replaced as Speaker,[1] the Commons' choice this time fell on William Burley, who acted for the rest of the session (a mere nine days, as it happened).[2] An apprentice-at-law with a long and almost continuous parliamentary experience—during the past twenty years he had sat for Shropshire in all but three parliaments, including each of the last six—Burley was well qualified on these grounds alone. His ability and usefulness as a practising lawyer are well attested by his employment over the years by this and that member of the peerage holding estates within reach of his own place at Broncroft in Corvedale (between the Clee Hills and Wenlock Edge): as feoffee and executor to Thomas, Earl of Arundel (Treasurer of England from Henry V's accession until his death soon after being invalided home from Harfleur in 1415); as feoffee to Hugh Lord Burnell (who died in 1420); as feoffee to John Lord Talbot (later Earl of Shrewsbury); as steward of the castle and lordship of Oswestry for the Earl of Arundel who died on active service in France in 1435, when Burley was confirmed in the office by letters-patent under the Great Seal. Burley had long been well known in government circles: he had been a J.P. of the *quorum* in Shropshire since 1416, royal escheator in the county in 1416–17, sheriff in 1425–6, escheator once more in 1432–3 and yet again in 1435–6, having been appointed for this third term of office as escheator when attending the parliament of 1435. During that session, along with a number of other lawyers, mostly M.P.s like himself, he had been specially engaged to further the royal business in the parliament, and had been paid (by the Exchequer) special rewards, amounting to £6 6s. 8d., for helping to 'engross' the parliamentary grant. But what is particularly important about Burley, from the point of view of the politics of the parliament in which for a short time he first acted as Speaker, is the fact that ever since February 1428 he had been serving as the Duke of Gloucester's

---

[1] Tyrell almost immediately afterwards resigned his office of Treasurer of the Household and the Chief Stewardship of the Duchy of Lancaster (the former to Sir John Popham on 17 April, the latter to the Earl of Suffolk on 23 April). He died during the summer (before 1 September 1437) and was buried in the church of the London Austin Friars.

[2] For references and a fuller account of Burley's life, see my paper, 'William Burley of Broncroft, Speaker for the Commons in 1437 and 1445–6', *Transactions of the Shropshire Archaeological Society*, vol. lvi (1960), pp. 263–72.

deputy (and by Gloucester's own appointment) in the office of Justice of Chester and North Wales. It may safely be presumed that in 1437 Burley was also connected with the Duke of York: his place in Corvedale was no more than an hour's ride from Ludlow, one of the great Yorkist power-points, and although the first positive evidence of this connexion is not available until 1442, when Burley was steward of the Duke of York's lordship of Montgomery and a member of his council with an annual fee of 20 marks, his tenure of these offices and the amount of his fee together suggest some length of service; certainly later on, Burley became even prominent as a Yorkist retainer and partisan.

Both Tyrell's and Burley's connexions with Gloucester and York suggest some sort of liaison between the two dukes. But if this was the case, there can be little doubt that in 1437 Gloucester was the more influential partner. Not that York should be underrated. No member of the House of Lancaster was likely to forget that, as both heir-general and (after Henry VI) heir-male of Edward III, York's claim to the throne by mere pedigree was superior to its own, which meant that his conduct would always be liable to scrutiny. But his territorial power, now that he was in full command of it, alone made him a force to be reckoned with and worth an effort to keep him contented. That this was so is illustrated not only by his appointment to France in 1436, but also by what happened within a week or two of the end of the parliament of 1437 itself: the Council's refusal (on 7 April) to fall in with York's demand to be recalled from Normandy until his successor had relieved him in person, was quickly followed (on 17 April) by the appointment of one of his firmest retainers and a member of his council, Sir John Popham, to succeed ex-Speaker Tyrell, his Receiver-General, as Treasurer of the King's Household, *alias* Treasurer for War.

Precisely a year and a half went by after the dissolution of the 1437 parliament before, on 26 September 1439, the next parliamentary writs of summons were issued. Meanwhile, the military situation in France had continued on the whole to favour the French. During 1438 they had demonstrated their self-assurance by invading Gascony, without easing up in the north. In the summer of 1439 they had taken Meaux, the last stronghold remaining to the English east of Paris. Although prepared to negotiate, they were not as keen to do so as was the English government or, for that matter, the Duke of Burgundy. In fact, Cardinal Beaufort was now hoping to come to terms and, if possible, renew the alliance with Burgundy, partly to safeguard the economic interests of England in Flanders and Brabant, partly to reduce English military commitments: it would at least be worth trying to secure Burgundian mediation between England and France. A meeting at Calais in January 1439 between English and Burgundian embassies, led respectively by Beaufort and his niece, the Duchess of Burgundy, was followed by another at Oye (between Calais and Gravelines) in July and August, when representatives from Charles VII also attended. This second conference, whose main task was to arrange a peace-settlement between England and France, utterly failed in this respect: although the English were ready to bargain on the basis of 'a sliding-scale of concessions to be offered in turn' (Radford), the French demand that Henry VI should renounce the French crown and agree to do homage for whatever lands he retained in France, was actually referred to the King and Council in England, only to be turned down. This rejection was mainly a result of pressure from Gloucester. It was his last major intervention in the conduct of English foreign policy, and it virtually sealed the fate of the English dominion in France: in seeking to salvage too much, the English were eventually to lose all. Gloucester, however, was unable to prevent the Cardinal from concluding a three years' truce with Burgundy, which would at least ensure the safety of Calais as well as facilitate the defence of Normandy.

This *rapprochement* with Burgundy, Gloucester's old enemy, is clear evidence of the growing strength of Beaufort's political position in England. He and his friends had now begun to control the royal government and administration, and also to canalize royal patronage and the disposal of offices so as best to suit their own interests. They were being allowed to do so by a combination of factors: Henry VI's own feckless generosity; the occupation of offices about his person and in the Household by men who supported the Cardinal or wished him well; the pliability of those lords of the Council disposed to be favourable; and an attitude of indifference, and failure to attend its meetings, among those inclined to be unsympathetic. Only in time of parliament, when important lords from outside the Court party came in, and when, occasionally, the Commons were ready to challenge or disapprove some aspect of government policy, was disturbance at all likely.

When parliament met at Westminster on 12 November 1439, the Commons immediately chose as their Speaker an apprentice-at-law from Northamptonshire who was now coming to the front as an administrative expert in the royal service: William Tresham of

Sywell.[1] Tresham's family had not long been settled in Northamptonshire. But by the time of his first Speakership his own influence there was very soundly based: from 1424 he had been one of the *quorum* of the commission of the peace and, having first represented the shire in parliament in 1423, he had been elected since 1427 to as many as five out of the last seven parliaments.[2] He acted as feoffee-to-uses and executor to a number of the lords and gentry of the shire and region, and his son married a daughter of William Lord Zouche of Harringworth. In so far as Tresham's administrative ability was at all exploited by the Crown during Henry V's reign, it would appear to have been mainly by the Exchequer.[3] This was still to some extent the case in the 1430's: in June 1434 he was paid £1 at the Exchequer as a special reward for work on financial records ordered by the Treasurer (Lord Cromwell), and in December 1435 was given nearly £10 for services on the King's behalf in the current parliament, including a share in the engrossment of the subsidy-bills. In the spring of the year in which he first became Speaker, he was engaged in a royal commission of enquiry into the value of Crown lands in Northamptonshire, especially those held in dower by the recently deceased Queen Joan, Henry IV's widow; and from the revenues of some of these (the manors of King's Cliffe and Brigstock) Tresham soon secured substantial annuities for himself. He frequently served on local commissions in Northamptonshire, including those for raising Crown-loans. How closely Tresham was connected with Cardinal Beaufort it is hard to say, but certainly the prelate and the lawyer were known to each other, and a continuing connexion is very probable: when, early in 1432, the Cardinal had been threatened in his absence by proceedings under a writ of *praemunire*, Tresham was one of the two lawyers engaged to act for him as attorneys-general pending his return; and Tresham's appointment in 1437 (jointly with Richard Wydeville, a former chamberlain to the Duke of Bedford and now father-in-law to Bedford's widow, Jacquetta of Luxembourg) as steward to Henry V's feoffees in the Duchy of Lancaster estates in Northamptonshire, Huntingdonshire,

[1] For references and a more ample treatment of Tresham's career, see my biography, 'William Tresham of Sywell', *Northamptonshire Past and Present*, vol. ii, no. 4, pp. 189–203.

[2] Tresham had been M.P. in 1423, 1427–8, 1429–30, 1432, 1433, and 1435.

[3] In March 1415 Tresham was appointed by the Treasurer as an auditor of all the accounts of royal officials in south Wales, and in April as paymaster for ships commandeered between Thames and Severn to take part in Henry V's invasion of Normandy.

Bedfordshire, and Buckinghamshire, could hardly have been made without the approval of the Cardinal, who was chief among the three feoffees still surviving (the others being Archbishop Chichele and Lord Hungerford). When first he acted as Speaker, in 1439, Tresham was also one of the lawyers retained as counsel by those administering for Henry VI the parts of the Duchy of Lancaster not put in trust by Henry V.

It was possibly Tresham's links with the agencies controlling the duchy which made it advisable for the Commons to elect him Speaker in 1439. Certainly, duchy revenues came up for consideration during the parliament when the deplorable state of the finances of Henry VI's Household was being discussed: after *great murmour and clamour* against the Household's failure to pay its way and its abuse of purveyance, the Commons not only appropriated a quarter of a tenth and fifteenth to Household funds, but also secured a diversion of five years' income (Michaelmas 1439–44) from the unenfeoffed portions of the Duchy of Lancaster as well as from the Duchy of Cornwall to the satisfaction of Household debts, together with a reluctant and guarded promise from the Cardinal and his co-feoffees to put their surplus revenues at the disposal of the Treasurer of the Household. These arrangements, which in fact did no more than regularize and extend an already existing appropriation of duchy revenues to 'state purposes', were approved by the Commons in the second session of this parliament.[1]

The first session had lasted until 21 December 1439, when parliament was adjourned to Reading. Here, from 14 January 1440, it continued to meet for about a month. This second session evidently proved a very uneasy one. When Archbishop Kemp, the leading upholder of Beaufort's diplomatic policy, was permitted both to become a cardinal and to retain his see of York, the Duke of Gloucester openly showed his resentment, even going so far as to urge the dismissal of both cardinals from the Council, on the pretext that it had fallen under their complete control. This grumbling was all to no purpose. The Commons, however, opposed the government over its policy of commercial appeasement towards Flanders and the Hanseatic League, resisted pressure from the Court, and only granted supplies—a subsidy and a half (minus £6,000) spread over two years, and an extension of the wool-duties and tunnage and poundage for three years—on condition that a poll-tax should be levied during this period on foreign merchants, whose operations were still further cramped by new 'hosting' regulations.

[1] R. Somerville, op. cit., i. 204–5.

No halt was called during 1440 to the search for peace with France. In the autumn the Duke of Orleans, who had then been captive in England for a quarter of a century, was liberated. This was done in the hope that he would assist Anglo-French negotiations or, alternatively, foment more trouble for Charles VII among the French princes than had already been caused by the recent war of the Praguerie. The liberation of Orleans was an even major defeat for the Duke of Gloucester, who had openly obstructed it and finally disclaimed all personal responsibility. In the meantime, the war continued with the English on the defensive, their re-occupation of Harfleur failing to balance the French gains in Upper Normandy. There was certainly little in the situation to encourage the Duke of York who once again, in July 1440, was appointed Lieutenant-General of France and Normandy (in succession to Cardinal Beaufort's nephew, John, Earl of Somerset); and in fact nearly a year passed before York took up his command (in June 1441).

Despite, or rather because of, the ascendancy of the Beaufort faction, the English political scene remained in a troubled state. Indeed, York's appointment in France may well have been designed to divide him from his political ally, Gloucester, one of whose charges against Cardinal Beaufort in 1440 had referred to the *estrangement* of York (and other lords) from the King's confidence. What little was left of Gloucester's reputation was lost when his duchess (Eleanor) was charged in the summer of 1441 with encompassing the King's death by magic. Duke Humphrey's inability to prevent her trial, condemnation, disgrace, and imprisonment for life shows how discredited he was; and, although he continued to attend meetings of the Council, his influence on its proceedings was now negligible. Nothing stood in the way of Beaufort and his party. None the less, their policy, partly because of the methods by which they pursued it, still failed to command popular support. It was not until January 1442 that parliament once more came together.

Not since 1419 had there been an instance of a Speaker being re-elected: now, in 1442, Tresham was again chosen by the Commons. That he was still personally acceptable to the Court, there is no question. Within three months or so after his previous Speakership, he had been given for life a royal annuity of £40 from the Crown lands at King's Cliffe in Northamptonshire (on 15 May 1440) and a year later (on 27 May 1441) a share in an annuity of £20 from the royal demesne estate at Brigstock (also in Northamptonshire), with the prospect of the whole of it on the death of the existing annuitant (a serving-woman of the late Queen Joan). Meanwhile, in September 1440, Tresham had been made one of Henry VI's feoffees in all the estates of the alien priories then in royal control. By September 1441, if not before, he was in annual receipt of a royal livery of cloth as one of the esquires of the Household. Between then and the opening of parliament early in 1442 he had received a royal charter granting him rights of free warren in his own demesnes and the lands he held in reversion in his own county of Northamptonshire. Here, and in Huntingdonshire, Bedfordshire, and Buckinghamshire, he was still steward to the Duchy of Lancaster feoffees, and he was also, as before, one of the legal advisers to the duchy council.

It is just as well to remember these Household and Duchy connexions of Tresham's. For it was probably he who, as Speaker in the two months' session of this parliament (25 January to 27 March 1442), was responsible for piloting the bill for the amalgamation of the duchy property held by Henry V's feoffees with the duchy estates held by the King, the earlier appropriation of duchy revenues to the support of the royal Household being now not only confirmed but extended for an additional three years (i.e. until 1447). This parliament of 1442 regularized, too, certain recent Exchequer assignments to Household funds from the Southampton customs and went on to charge the same source of revenue with a further annual sum of 5,000 marks for the next three years. By way of criticism, the Commons put in a request for the appointment of a committee of the Lords to reform the ordinances of the Household, drawing special attention once more (as at Reading) to the problem of purveyance. They were also disgruntled with the treatment of their petitions. Furthermore, they showed their dissatisfaction with the government's mercantile policy in a demand that English merchants should be treated in areas controlled by the Hanseatic League as its members were treated in England, and by complaining about evasion of the Calais Staple. When the Commons petitioned that in future *dames de graunde estate* charged with treason or felony should be given the same trial as lay peers would be entitled to, they were doubtless criticizing the procedure used against the Duchess of Gloucester. Their votes of taxation—a single tenth and fifteenth (minus £4,000) spread over nearly two years, the grants on trade extended for no longer than two years, the tax on aliens continued for no less—were subject to careful appropriations, especially for the safe-keeping of the sea: all of this suggests a lack of confidence and some distrust. With government credit sunk so low, it was legally important that the

Commons should authorize the Council to negotiate Crown-loans; but to envisage the possibility of these loans amounting to the sum actually mentioned—£200,000—between then and the next parliament, was quite absurd, unless the Commons anticipated an inordinately long interval before parliament reassembled. Nearly three years passed, in fact, before it did so. In the meantime, on 3 July 1442, not very long after his second Speakership and perhaps partly in recognition of his work in the office, Tresham was to be given a promise (in the shape of a patent granting him the reversion at the next vacancy) of the offices of Chancellor of the Duchy and Chancellor of the County Palatine of Lancaster, on the understanding that when this appointment materialized it should be Tresham's for life. As it happened, he had to wait nearly seven years before taking possession.

These years were characterized in England by a growing disrespect for the royal authority. This took shape in sporadic eruptions of serious disorder in every quarter of the realm, culminating in 1441 in riots in the West Country between the men of the Earl of Devon and Sir William (later Lord) Bonville over their rival claims to the stewardship of the royal Duchy of Cornwall, and in 1443 in disturbances in the north between the men of Archbishop Kemp and of the Earl of Northumberland. Overseas, nothing would go right. In northern France the Duke of York was hardly able to hold his ground. He seemed at times, in fact, to be content to do no more. On the other hand, he did not hide his resentment when, to meet a full-scale French attack on Gascony, the Cardinal's nephew, John, Earl of Somerset, was given a crudely co-ordinate command in March 1443. This appointment, 'engendered of nepotism and party feeling' (Ramsay), resulted in a well-supported expedition which none the less ended in fiasco: never having even reached the south-western duchy, Somerset came home to die in the spring of 1444, his brother Edmund succeeding to the earldom. Negotiation for a peace, or else a foreign marriage for Henry of Windsor which might provide the basis for a dynastic settlement with his uncle of France, was a more urgent necessity than ever.

With an eye to their own political future, the Beaufort faction determined to have the contriving of this marriage. And so it was. In February 1444 Suffolk was put at the head of an embassy to work for the retention of Normandy and Guienne in full sovereignty in return for a renunciation of the French crown and Henry's marriage with Margaret of Anjou, a niece of the French queen. Having secured a personal indemnity for all he might have to do, Suffolk lost no time and within little more than two months was busy negotiating at Tours. The English peace-terms were quite unacceptable, and no more than a truce for two years could be got. But a royal betrothal was soon arranged. On his return to England Suffolk was rewarded with the title of marquess (in September 1444) and soon re-crossed to France with a great retinue (nearly 500 strong) to bring back the King's bride. A marriage by proxy was celebrated at Nancy early in March 1445, and then, by way of Paris and Rouen, Margaret and her retinue came to the Channel coast, crossed from Honfleur, and landed in England on 9 April. A fortnight later, on St George's Day, she and Henry were married by no more distinguished a prelate than William Aiscough, Bishop of Salisbury, in no more distinguished a place than the house of Premonstratensian canons at Titchfield in Hampshire.

CHAPTER 9

Under Henry VI, from 1445

EVIDENTLY buoyed up by the limited diplomatic success represented by the negotiation of the royal marriage, the government had decided by 13 January 1445 that now was a favourable time to meet parliament once again. And when Margaret of Anjou arrived in England, parliament had in fact already concluded one session of nearly three weeks. Opened on 25 February with a sermon preached by the Chancellor, John Stafford (Archbishop of Canterbury since 1443), on the somewhat optimistic text, *Justicia et Pax osculate sunt*, parliament had been adjourned on 15 March with orders to reassemble on 29 April. Short though this first session was, it had none the less already produced a financial grant of sorts. The Commons' Speaker, William Burley the lawyer, was authorized to declare a vote of a half tenth and fifteenth (minus the usual rebate of £2,000), payable at Martinmas following, two years, that is, after the collection of the final moiety of the 1442 subsidy. But nothing had been done about renewing the subsidy on aliens which had already expired in November 1444, or about tunnage and poundage which was due to expire on 1 April next ensuing, or about the wool-subsidy which would give out in the following autumn. What little had been granted hardly suggests a quickening of the national pulse.

The choice of William Burley as Speaker[1] confirms this seeming evidence for a non-committal attitude on the part of the Lower House. He was quite the most experienced of the knights of the shire, having sat for Shropshire in every parliament since 1427, and already he had briefly acted as Speaker in 1437. Since then his governmental and aristocratic connexions had become certainly neither fewer nor less influential. In December 1437, when he was instructed to serve on a commission to secure the aids due to the Crown on the death of the King's mother (Queen Katherine) from her lordships in North Wales and the March, it was probably in his capacity as the Duke of Gloucester's Deputy-Justice in Cheshire and North Wales. And when Gloucester was superseded as Justice by the Earl of Suffolk in February 1440, the latter immediately appointed Burley as one of *his* deputies. It was perhaps knowledge gained in the

[1] See p. 216, n. 2.

administration of this office which enabled Burley in December 1441 to go before the King's Council and allege that William Troutbeck (the recently dismissed Chancellor of the County Palatine of Lancaster and Chamberlain of Chester) had embezzled the profits from the lands of a lesser tenant-in-chief in Cheshire, Shropshire, and Herefordshire, and to win the promise of a reward of £100 if the information proved correct. But Burley's services to the royal administration had been sometimes more important than this. Occasionally they had been employed even in parliament: on the very day after his appointment by Suffolk as Deputy-Justice of Chester and North Wales, he received (at the Lower Exchequer) £5 as a special reward for his 'labour and diligence . . . in expediting certain matters touching the King's profit' in the recent parliament at Reading (of which he himself was a member); and it may well have been partly in recognition of similar services that on the last day of the next parliament (1442) he was given for life a royal annuity of £40 (over half of it charged on the fee-farm of Shrewsbury, the rest on three royal manors in Staffordshire). In the year following his Speakership, he was also to receive a royal livery of cloth from the Great Wardrobe, almost certainly as a lawyer retained by the Crown. Burley's appointment by Suffolk in 1440 as Deputy-Justice in Cheshire and North Wales does not necessarily mean that his association with Gloucester then came to an end. Indeed, in August following, he was included with the duke in a commission of oyer and terminer in south Wales, where Gloucester was now Chief Justice. Moreover, he had come to enjoy the confidence of the Duke of York, certainly not later than Michaelmas 1442; by that time he was acting as the duke's steward in his lordship of Montgomery and as a member of his council with a fee of 20 marks a year. This connexion with York is only likely to have been strengthened by Burley's relations with another great Marcher lord, John Talbot, Earl of Shrewsbury; he had long been one of Talbot's feoffees-to-uses, and in 1443 was a witness to an important settlement of his manors at Whitchurch (Salop). Talbot was York's right-hand man in his conduct of the defence of Normandy. Burley was thus connected with the leading members of both 'the peace-party' and 'the war-party' (although with some more closely than others) when the Commons made him their Speaker in 1445.

It must of course be admitted that all the magnates to whom Speaker Burley was demonstrably attached, were taking care to appear to approve of the French marriage. York had used Margaret of Anjou with great courtesy on her passage through Normandy; Shrewsbury had assisted at her homecoming; Gloucester had welcomed her to London. No untoward incident had disturbed her coronation on 30 May, during the second session of the parliament. Moreover, on 4 June, when Suffolk repeated an earlier statement of his conduct as ambassador for the marriage, Burley conveyed to the marquess the congratulations of the Commons. It must also be noted that when the Speaker asked the Upper House to commend Suffolk to the King and secure the enactment of his *declaration, laboures, and demenyng*, Gloucester was among the particular lords who seconded the petition. Perhaps the war-party and the Commons, too, had been mollified by Suffolk's suggestion that the truce he had negotiated could be put to good use if opportunity were taken to strengthen our castles in France.

On the day after thus paying tribute to Suffolk, parliament was adjourned to 20 October. No additional financial grant had been made during the second session. Perhaps the Commons could be prevailed upon to vote one in the autumn, especially if the discussions with a French embassy (due to appear in London in mid-July) turned out to be unproductive. If, on the other hand, this embassy offered acceptable terms of peace, and the need for another financial grant ceased to be so urgent, it would be convenient for parliament to be still in session and able, without loss of time, to confirm the diplomatic agreement (as required by the Treaty of Troyes). In the event, no more than a seven months' continuation of the truce resulted from the summer talks. And yet the autumn session of parliament failed to produce a fresh financial grant. This was the case, even though the Duke of York crossed the Channel to attend parliament (in order to bring home to it the need for more support) and Adam Moleyns, the Keeper of the Privy Seal, did not succeed in postponing hostilities (by extending the truce to 1 April 1447) until after parliament had been adjourned (on 15 December) for yet another session. This fourth session—and never before had a parliament run to four sessions—lasted from 24 January to 9 April 1446. Only then would the Commons agree to vote another grant, and not a generous one at that. Admittedly, the subsidies on Staple exports and tunnage and poundage, of which all the previous grants had now expired, were back-dated and made payable for over four years (until Martinmas 1449); and, regarding direct taxation, Speaker Burley was able to announce a vote of one and a half tenths and fifteenths. But this last subsidy was not only to be levied in three instalments payable

at yearly intervals (at Martinmas 1446, 1447, and 1448): it was also to
be subjected to a rebate half as much again as had become usual
during the past decade, so that the whole grant was cut by £9,000
(about 16 per cent).

During the last session of the parliament, the Commons had
accommodated the King in a variety of ways. They had confirmed a
series of patents in which he had made enfeoffments of certain Duchy
of Lancaster estates to fulfil his last testament. They had endorsed
another series of patents embodying the endowment of his colleges
at Eton and Cambridge, and had ratified an allocation of estates and
money-grants for the Queen's dower which together were worth
10,000 marks a year. Moreover, on the day of the dissolution
(9 April), after the whole parliament had listened to the Chancellor
declare that the King was intending, on his own responsibility, to
meet Charles VII in France in October, it agreed to waive the requirement of the Treaty of Troyes that before such a step could be taken
the assent of the three estates of both England and France was
necessary. Parliament could hardly have been so complaisant, had
it known that already (just before Christmas 1445) Henry VI had
privately undertaken to surrender Maine, to the Queen's father and
uncle acting on behalf of Charles VII, by the end of April. Kept in
ignorance of this deception, parliament seems to have closed in a
state of harmony.

So far as is known, Burley got nothing for his pains during its four
sessions, which together amounted to half a year's service. At least,
he secured no direct grant from the Crown. The borough of Shrewsbury, however, recognized his 'labour in parliament about the business of the town',[1] arranging for a London draper to provide him
with a gift of cloth worth £4. When, after a break of nearly two
years, parliament next assembled, Burley was not even available to be
Speaker: it may be that he had stood down (perhaps because the
meeting was to be in Suffolk) or had failed to be re-elected. Whatever
the reason—and others are conceivable—it was the first time in
twenty years that he had missed a parliament.[2]

[1] This business of the town is set out in a long petition from the borough to
the Commons asking them to seek parliamentary authority for a constitution
which had been on trial for some time. Burley was probably already standing
counsel to the burgesses; certainly he was their legal adviser at the end of his life
(with an annual fee of eleven shillings).

[2] Burley was again M.P. for Shropshire in the parliaments of 1449–50, 1450–1,
and 1455–6. By 1450 he had thrown in his lot entirely with the Duke of York
and was generally recognized to be one of his closest and most influential

The intention that Henry VI should go to France in 1446, to pursue negotiations in person, did not come to anything. Nor as yet had the King's engagement to surrender Maine. But such an undertaking had been made: if it became publicly known, how much more if it were honoured, trouble would be in store. This was especially likely if it was the Duke of Gloucester (still the royal heir-presumptive) who led the inevitable protest. It did in fact prove necessary, or was thought advisable, to silence him. It was evidently decided to impeach him. And, once this decision was taken, parliament was summoned, first (by writs of 14 December) to meet on 10 February 1447 at Cambridge, and then (by fresh writs issued on 20 January) to meet instead at Bury St Edmunds, 'a place where Suffolk was strong and where Gloucester would be far away from his friends the Londoners' (Stubbs). The parliament had already been in session for over a week when Duke Humphrey appeared with a modest retinue at his back, only to be immediately arrested. Now in his fifty-seventh year, he died, probably of a stroke or from shock, five days later. The corpse, laid out publicly for inspection for a single day, was then taken to St Albans for burial. (Some six or seven weeks later Humphrey's great rival, Henry Beaufort, passed away at Winchester.) Meanwhile, in the parliament itself, although the Council and Exchequer were empowered to raise loans up to £100,000, no demand for taxation was made. The Commons themselves promoted bills on behalf of the Queen and the royal colleges newly founded at Eton and Cambridge. By parliamentary authority, Gloucester's widow was excluded from any right to dower or jointure. But otherwise there was little official business transacted. And so the parliament ended on 3 March, after a session of barely three weeks.

The member whom the Commons chose to be their Speaker at Bury St Edmunds was the lawyer, William Tresham, who had sat for Northamptonshire in all but two of the parliaments of the last twenty years and had already been Speaker in 1439-40 and 1442.[1]

---

supporters. In November 1455, during his last parliament, he three times headed a deputation from the Commons to the Lords urging (in the end with success) the appointment of York as Protector (*Rot. Parl.*, v. 284-6). He died on 10 August 1458, leaving a widow and two daughters, one of whom (Jane) was married to Thomas Littleton of Teddesley (Staffs.), who became a Justice of the Common Bench in 1466 and is notable in the history of English law as the author of *Tenures*, which Coke described as 'the ornament of the Common Law'.

[1] See p. 219, n. 1. Although not re-elected Speaker in 1445, Tresham had sat as usual for Northamptonshire. It is worth noting that at this time he was in

Tresham's prospects of the Chancellorship of the Duchy of Lancaster, promised him in 1442, had not yet matured. But since November 1443 he had been one of a large committee of thirty-one feoffees entrusted by Henry VI with those Duchy of Lancaster estates (worth nearly £3,400 a year) which had been set aside to guarantee the completion of his will; and on 10 December 1447 he was to be appointed by the King as chancellor to this group of feoffees, with custody of a special seal and at an annual fee of £40. Between-whiles, in February 1445, Tresham had surrendered his royal annuity of £40 charged on the manor of King's Cliffe, but only so that this grant could be converted into one in survivorship for the joint benefit of him and his son Thomas. (The latter, who was M.P. for Buckinghamshire at Bury St Edmunds, had by now become a member of the royal Household as an Esquire of the Hall and Chamber.) Since March 1446 father and son together had also shared another grant in survivorship, again worth £40 a year, chargeable to the revenue in the hands of the Receiver-General of the Duchy of Lancaster (as from Michaelmas 1445). Only a week before the parliament of 1447 met, William Tresham had been given a special reward at the Exchequer for diligent labour undertaken for the King's profit (its nature not specified). In the light of this various evidence, there can be no doubt that his election as Speaker had been entirely acceptable to the Court.

For William de la Pole, the parliament at Bury had marked the zenith of his dominance. His elimination of Humphrey of Gloucester was itself a success which proved, politically, too costly. For Gloucester soon came to be regarded as a martyr, especially by those who supported Richard of York. Also, York himself was given fresh cause for personal discontent by being passed over for the post of Lieutenant-General in France in favour of Edmund Beaufort; and his appointment for ten years as Lieutenant of Ireland (in July 1447), generally regarded as tantamount to banishment, was hardly calculated to soften his resentment.

The situation in France, too, gave no real sign of improvement. Although English diplomacy during 1447 won from the French an extension of the state of truce until January 1449, this was only achieved at the cost of releasing Maine. The surrender of Le Mans itself, however, had to be compelled by force of French arms (in

---

receipt of an annuity of £10 granted him by William Lord Lovell and charged on the revenues of the lordship of Titchmarsh (Lancashire County Record Office, Earl of Derby's muniments, DDK/1746/13).

March 1448); and Edmund Beaufort's military appointment, being clearly intended to result in an eventual resumption of active hostilities, allowed the French to entertain further doubt of the honesty of English professions of a desire to make peace. Recently promoted Duke of Somerset, Beaufort crossed to Normandy in May 1448. Neither side created any serious disturbance of the truce. But clearly, when once it had expired, it would be only a question of time before Charles VII went on with the re-conquest, all the stronger for the long suspension of the war. It was not, however, until 2 January 1449, the day after the truce had run out, that Henry VI again summoned parliament to find means to continue the struggle. Before parliament was dissolved, in mid-July, the French had already launched a heavy assault on Normandy.

When parliament met at Westminster on 12 February 1449, De la Pole, who had been made Duke of Suffolk in the previous summer, took the seat appropriate to his new rank for the first time. But, now that the peace policy had been tarnished by the surrender of Maine and in any case was evidently failing of its main purpose, he could command no firm support. This was true in even the Lower House, despite the strong representation enjoyed there by the royal Household and the election of John Say, knight of the shire for Cambridgeshire, as the Commons' Speaker.[1]

It perhaps says much for the initial solidarity of the Household element among the Commons that Say was elected at all. For not only was he an intimate member of the royal circle, but had been actively associated with the diplomacy of 'the peace-party'. Of Say's closeness to both Henry VI and Suffolk, there can be no question: in 1444 he had been a member of the embassy sent under Suffolk to treat for a peace and the King's marriage; and in a lampoon that was to be written soon after the duke's murder in 1450 he is included among the traitors of his 'progeny', being made to contribute to the blasphemous 'office' for the dead minister the words, *Manus tue fecerunt me*. John Say first appears as a member of the royal Household in 1443 as one of the *valetti camere domini Regis*. Between then and 1449 his importance as one of the King's own personal entourage had clearly grown: before the end of 1447 he was being described in royal grants as a gentleman-usher of the Chamber, figuring in the Household accounts as one of the *scutiferi aule et camere domini Regis*;

[1] For references and a more detailed account of John Say's life, see my paper, 'Sir John Say of Broxbourne', *East Hertfordshire Archaeological Society Transactions*, vol. xiv, part 1 (1959), pp. 20–41.

by the time he became Speaker his official designation was Esquire of the Body. In the meantime, his royal annuities had been multiplying: by a patent of October 1444, he was granted £10 a year for life from the receipts from the aulnage of cloth in Norfolk; a few months later, he became entitled to nearly as much again (6d. a day) from the royal revenues in Staffordshire; and in November 1446, he got £32 10s. a year, for the lives of himself and his wife, from the Norfolk aulnage, in exchange for the £10 annuity of 1444. In addition to these pensions, on the very day of his first election to parliament (in 1447 as M.P. for Cambridge), he had been paid £20 by the Exchequer as a special reward from the King and, during the short session at Bury St Edmunds itself, he had been given not only the wardship and marriage of his wife's daughter by her first marriage,[1] but also a grant for life of the manor of Lawford near the Stour estuary in north Essex. A year later (in February 1448) Henry VI made him a present of a cup of silver-gilt out of the stock in the jewel-house. Offices in the royal gift had also been coming his way: his grant for life of the post of Coroner of the Marshalsea of the Household in October 1444 was only to mature at its next vacancy, but the grant for life of the Keepership of the Privy Palace at Westminster, which he received in March 1445, was immediately available. No doubt profitable in some way while they lasted were his appointments in successive years (1446–7, 1447–8) as royal escheator, first in Cambridgeshire and Huntingdonshire and then in the adjacent joint-bailiwick of Norfolk and Suffolk. Actually during the parliament of 1449, and when John Say was Speaker, Henry VI made him one of the re-constituted committee of feoffees in those Duchy of Lancaster estates set aside for the administration of the royal will, and another of the new patentees was John's brother William, formerly a theologian of New College, Oxford, and now Dean of the Chapel Royal. (The official bill establishing the new trust was approved by this parliament.) How intimately at this time John Say was attached to Henry VI's person as an officer of the Chamber, is made clear by the fact that even during the parliament, indeed only three days after

[1] Say's first marriage was to Elizabeth, a daughter of Lawrence Cheyne of Fen Ditton (Cambs.) and the widow of Sir Frederick Tilney of Ashwellthorpe (Norfolk). Say's stepdaughter and ward, Elizabeth Tilney, married Humphrey Bourchier, a nephew of Henry Viscount Bourchier (later Earl of Essex) and of Thomas Bourchier, Bishop of Ely (1443–54) and Archbishop of Canterbury (1454–86). In the year after Humphrey's death (at the battle of Barnet in 1471) she married Thomas Howard, who was created Earl of Surrey in 1483 when his father, John, was made Duke of Norfolk.

his formal recognition as Speaker, he was in attendance on the King when no more serious business was on hand than granting a pardon to a Glastonbury monk who, without a royal licence, had purchased a papal bull of migration.

Whether or not the Household element among the Commons itself failed to give firm support to the régime—and certainly the gentlemen and yeomen of the Household and the clergy of the Chapel Royal did not scruple to exploit the government's embarrassment by petitioning for payment of large arrears of salary out of the feudal revenues of the Crown—the Lower House as a whole made heavy weather of what was its main duty from the royal point of view. Admittedly, the grant of tunnage and poundage, due to expire early in April 1449, was renewed for an unusually long period of five years.[1] But this meant no actual increase of revenue; and, although parliament was made to listen to a report sent from France by the Duke of Somerset and designed to shock it into a sense of its financial responsibilities, all the direct taxation it voted during a first session lasting seven weeks was a mere moiety of a tenth and fifteenth (minus £3,000), this half-subsidy being itself divided into two, one part being made payable no earlier than November following, the other not until a year later still (in November 1450). Even in its second session, 7–30 May, again at Westminster, parliament got no further than approving an anticipation of the yield from taxation by authorizing royal loans up to a total of £100,000; and it is much more likely to have been the government's wish to overcome parliament's reluctance to enhance the earlier vote than any fear of plague (the reason formally alleged) which prompted it to order an adjournment to Winchester. Here parliament sat for a month, from 16 June until dissolved on 16 July. During this third and final session, the Commons were moved to vote another half-subsidy (again curtailed by £3,000). The grant was once more made payable in two instalments, and although the first of these instalments would have the effect of doubling what was due in November following, the collection of the second was deferred until as late as November 1451. In fact, what the complete grant amounted to was no more than about £30,000, the whole of which would not be levied until almost two and a half years had passed. To this the Commons merely added an annual poll-tax, for four years, imposed on aliens in general but to the special disadvantage of Italian and Hanseatic merchants, a single

[1] This grant is prospectively significant in its length, anticipating the grant for the King's life in 1453.

poll-tax on unbeneficed priests (subsequently voted down by the prelates), and a continuance of the wool-subsidy (until April 1454) to bring it into line with tunnage and poundage. In view of the dire military threat to Normandy, all the grants taken together were a niggardly provision: so much so that, since the wool-subsidy was largely earmarked by the Commons for the defence of Calais alone, it would seem that the mercantile interest in the Lower House was more anxious for the safety of the Staple than disturbed by the prospect of the utter loss of Normandy. (And yet the importance of Calais was declining on the admission of the staplers themselves; hence their protest against the infringement of their privileges by royal licences to avoid the town, from which the Queen and Suffolk were the principal beneficiaries.) Somerset's plea from France—that parliament should consider *the grete, inestimable, and well nygh infinite cost and effusion bothe of Good* [wealth] *and Blood, that this land hath borne and suffered for that land sake*—had virtually gone unanswered.

None of parliament's continued failure to face reality, or rather, perhaps we should say, nothing in parliament's appraisal of the growing hopelessness of the military situation in Normandy, affected Speaker Say's own credit at Court. Not only had he been granted for life an additional royal annuity of 50 marks on the eve of the first adjournment of parliament, but less than a week before the third session began at Winchester (10 June), he was given the reversion of the combined offices of Chancellor of the Duchy and Chancellor of the County Palatine of Lancaster on the decease or resignation of the then Chancellor, William Tresham; whenever he came into possession, Say was to hold for life, with fees of 100 marks a year and the right to appoint deputies. He was not to have long to wait, in the event. In the meantime, in December 1449 he was made sheriff of Norfolk and Suffolk, and held office for the customary annual term.[1]

---

[1] Say came well out of the Resumption Act passed by Parliament at Leicester in June 1450, being penalized only to the extent of having to surrender an annuity of £9 2s. 6d. and his office of Keeper of the Privy Palace at Westminster: he was allowed by the King to retain grants together worth over £65 a year. He was also lucky to evade the rebels from Kent who immediately afterwards entered London under Jack Cade: they indicted him of treason at the Guildhall. Doubtless he had made himself scarce, because he escaped the fate of his kinsman, the ex-Treasurer, Lord Saye, whom the rebels put to death. In December 1450 Say's grant of the reversion of the office of Coroner of the Marshalsea of the Household (made in 1444) was waived. But he remained an esquire of the Household; and in 1452 the keepership of the privy palace at Westminster was restored to him, and he continued to occupy it, very probably until his death.

All through the summer of 1449 affairs in France were going from bad to worse. The English sack of Fougères in Brittany in March had given Charles VII a pretext for formally declaring war. It was not until the end of July that he did so. But already his armies were on the move and exacting reprisals. One Norman town after another fell into their hands, a remorseless process which resulted in the surrender of Rouen itself on 4 November and the fall of Harfleur on Christmas Day. Somerset had retired to Caen, which still held out, as also did Cherbourg and the garrisons of the Côtentin. Meanwhile, only ten weeks had gone by between the dissolution of the first parliament of the year and the issue of writs (on 23 September) summoning Lords and Commons to meet again on 6 November. By this time, that Rouen was ready to capitulate must have been public news on this side of the Channel. The foreign policy of the government was not only bankrupt, but seen to be bankrupt. Feeling ran high. Parliament strongly reacted to the general emotion.

The Duke of York was now the natural leader of any opposition to the discredited party of the Court likely to result in political action. After his appointment as the King's Lieutenant in Ireland in 1447, he had managed not to leave England for a year and a half. But he had gone in the end and, when the second parliament of 1449 met, he was still in Ireland. He was, in fact, to stay there until the late summer of the following year. In November 1449, however, there were some among the Commons by whom York was evidently not forgotten. For as soon as parliament met at the Blackfriars in London, the Lower House chose one of his retainers as their Speaker: Sir John Popham of Charford, knight of the shire for Hampshire.[1]

Popham's previous parliamentary experience was slight (and also distant in time)—he had sat for Hampshire only once before (in 1439-40)—but his military, administrative, and diplomatic career had been long, frequently strenuous, and not without distinction. That he was a knight-banneret and in 1447 had been nominated (although not successfully) for election to the Order of the Garter (to fill the vacancy created by the death of Humphrey of Gloucester) bespeaks his reputation as a professional soldier. In this second parliament of

[1] For references and a more lengthy account of Popham's career, see my article, 'Sir John Popham, knight-banneret, of Charford', *Proceedings of the Hampshire Field Club*, vol. xxi, part 1, pp. 38-52. I owe a fresh piece of detail to Dr J. M. W. Bean. This is of a grant in tail male to Sir John Popham, dated at Paris on 3 May 1429, of a house *en la vieille Rue du Temple* in Paris. The house was called *l'ostel de Thorigny* and presumably had belonged to Popham's predecessor in the seigneurie of Torigny-sur-Vire (Archives Nationales, Register JJ 174, no. 291).

1449 he alone of the Commons was a veteran of Henry V's first French campaign of 1415. For his prowess at Agincourt, where he served in the retinue of Edward of Norwich, Duke of York, Popham had been given a very generous royal annuity of 100 marks. Later on, in 1417, Henry V made him *bailli* of Caen and, in 1421, captain of Bayeux, and also gave him the castles and seigneuries of Torigny-sur-Vire and Planquery, in addition to houses at Caen and Bayeux, all in tail male. In 1418 Popham had followed his father as constable of Southampton castle. He seems not to have stayed on in France after Henry V's death, but certainly he returned in 1425 to serve under the Regent, Bedford, as captain of St Suzanne in Maine: it was probably then that he was given the office of Chancellor of Maine and Anjou, those very provinces which, now in 1449, Suffolk was suspected of having released in the course of his efforts to salvage Normandy and Guienne from the French re-conquest. Between 1425 and 1435 Popham spent much of his time in France, attached to Bedford's staff as one of his chamberlains (so William of Worcester informs us). Just before and also after Bedford's death, Popham's knowledge of the situation in France caused him to be included in a number of important diplomatic missions: as a member of the embassy to the Congress of Arras in 1435, of a mission to France in 1438 (when he also acted as an inspector of garrisons),[1] and of the large party which attended the important conference with the Burgundians and the French at St Omer in 1439. It was perhaps partly because he was spending so much time abroad that in April 1439 he was replaced in the post of Treasurer of the King's Households which he had then been occupying for exactly two years. This appointment, which carried with it the office of Treasurer for War, had come Popham's way in April 1437 most probably because the Lancastrian government was needing to give Richard, Duke of York, some assurance that he would be repaid the large debts he had incurred as the King's Lieutenant-General in France in 1436-7. There is certainly no question of the close connexion between Popham and the duke either at that time or later. Already in 1433, shortly before his coming of age, York had allowed Popham to retain an annuity of 20 marks, first granted by his uncle and pre-

---

[1] After conferring with the Earl of Warwick and his council at Rouen, Popham's business was to visit Brittany to see the duke and to treat for peace there with the Bastard of Orleans and other representatives of the Duke of Orleans (still a prisoner in England) and also with an embassy from Charles VII. He was absent from England for seven months.

decessor in the title, Edward of Norwich; then, in 1436-7, Popham had served with the duke in his council of war in Normandy; and when, in 1440, York was about to resume his military command in France, one of the conditions of his acceptance was that Popham should again be a member of his council. It was to serve in this capacity that Popham crossed the Channel in the winter of 1441 for the last time.[1] Meanwhile, in 1438, he had been allowed to draw his old royal annuity of 100 marks from the fee-farm payable by the duke to the Exchequer for the custody of the castle and cantred of Builth. It is also worth noting that Popham was the duke's tenant in the two manors he held in the Isle of Wight. Since his final return from France early in 1442, Popham had served the Crown on nothing more spectacular than local commissions, some of which, however, had been commissions to muster some important drafts for France, including the Duke of Somerset's expedition in 1443.

That in November 1449 the Commons in the first instance chose Popham as their Speaker suggests their concern for the situation in France, and possibly the growth of some feeling in favour of Popham's lord, Richard Plantagenet. To say all this is not necessarily to throw any doubt on Popham's loyalty to the Lancastrian dynasty as such. But his own personal history, the loss of his estates in Normandy, and the difficulties he had experienced in recovering what was due to him from Henry VI's Exchequer are hardly likely to have made him a potential tool in the hands of the Court party. Having assisted in the winning of much of what was now all but lost, he represented something of a reproach to the royal administration, and his appearance at the head of the Commons can only have discomfited the Court. He himself might have found his election as Speaker embarrassing, or at least uncongenial. However this may be, when, on the grounds of old age (he was about sixty years old) and wounds and infirmities received in the service of the King and his father, Popham asked to be exonerated, his request was granted: a peculiar and indeed unique proceeding in the history of the medieval Speakers.[2]

[1] Popham left England on 1 December 1441, taking with him £5,000 for the payment of York's forces; he returned at the end of February 1442.

[2] Popham did not again sit in parliament. But he continued to serve on occasional local royal commissions and lived for another thirteen years. He was not able to secure a complete exemption from the Resumption Act of 1455, the royal annuity of 100 marks which he had held since 1417 being cut down to 40 marks. (It was by this time being paid by the Duke of York out of revenues accounted for by his receiver for Dorset and Somerset.) Popham survived until

Faced with electing a substitute for Popham, the Commons immediately chose William Tresham, who had sat for Northamptonshire in each of the preceding five parliaments and been Speaker in three of them: hardly a distinguished member of the Lower House, but a capable lawyer, a tried administrator, an experienced parliamentarian, well known to many men of influence, and evidently acceptable to the tottering régime. It is true that he was already the Duke of York's feoffee in the manor of Hambleton (a former Mortimer estate in Rutland) and, when murdered in the following summer, was going to a rendezvous with the duke following the latter's unauthorized return from Ireland. It is also worth bearing in mind that it was York who had most to gain by the elimination of the Duke of Suffolk, in whose impeachment during this parliament of 1449–50 Tresham was to act as the Commons' mouthpiece. None the less, it was as recently as February 1449 that Tresham had been allowed to take up the office of Chancellor of the Duchy of Lancaster (of which he had been granted the reversion nearly seven years before), the culmination of a career which, moreover, had developed during the years when Suffolk had been *priviest of the King's counsel* and had occupied an influential place (as Chief Steward of the Duchy) in the duchy council. During his last Speakership, at Bury St Edmunds, Tresham had been ready enough to play Suffolk's game. It will not do, therefore, simply to write him off as an out-and-out Yorkist partisan any more than as a quondam devotee of Suffolk's who had turned coat. It would certainly be going beyond the evidence to suggest that, as Speaker, Tresham engineered the downfall of Suffolk. At the same time there is no question that he had ties with some of Suffolk's enemies, including York and also Lord Cromwell of Tattershall (who worked behind the scenes to promote Suffolk's impeachment).[1] If Tresham played in this parliament a leading rôle in developments which almost amounted to a 'court-revolution', it was because, as the Commons' Speaker, he had no option but to play the part which they assigned him. (In any case, it

---

14 April 1463, when Maurice Berkley, an Esquire of the Body to Edward IV, was one of his executors. He was buried in the London Charterhouse, in one of the two chapels which he himself had already endowed.

[1] When, in December 1443, Tresham became a feoffee in all the Bedfordshire manors of the late Lord Fanhope, it was apparently on behalf of Ralph Lord Cromwell, who claimed a right of purchase against Fanhope's stepson, the Duke of Exeter. For Lord Cromwell's interest in Suffolk's impeachment, see p. 50, n. 1.

is well to bear in mind that the Commons' temper in this crisis was much more hostile to Suffolk than friendly to York.) That all this was realized by the government, and that what Tresham had to do as Speaker was not held to his discredit or detriment at Court, is suggested by his retention of the Chancellorship of the Duchy of Lancaster until his death (which followed Suffolk's by as much as five months) and also by his continuing among the esquires of the royal Household, with whom, moreover, he was exempted from the Resumption Act of this parliament of 1449–50. Perhaps there were men at Court not reluctant to see Suffolk made a scapegoat.

Even before this parliament met, at least one of the King's ministers had lost confidence, and the administration soon seemed moribund. The Treasurer, Bishop Lumley of Carlisle (an old protégé of the late Cardinal Beaufort and friend of the Duke of Suffolk),[1] resigned in the autumn. On 9 December (a week before the end of the first session) he was followed by the Keeper of the Privy Seal, Bishop Moleyns of Chichester (who was murdered at Portsmouth during the Christmas recess by military reserves waiting for transports to Normandy). Archbishop Stafford, Chancellor since 1432, gave place on 31 January 1450 (early in the second parliamentary session) to Archbishop Kemp of York, a faithful Lancastrian but no friend of Suffolk's. Already, during the first session, Suffolk himself had been charged by Lord Cromwell with instigating one of his affinity to murder him in Westminster Hall; and when, on the very first day of the second session (22 January), the duke sought to clear his name of insinuations of treachery, this provoked an attack from the Commons which soon developed into an impeachment for treason and other offences. The case dragged on, and it was not until 17 March that the duke was banished, even then on the King's mere authority. Just under a fortnight later parliament was adjourned (on 30 March). When Suffolk, on his way to the continent, was murdered at sea on 2 May, it was in the fourth day of its third session, up in the Midlands at Leicester, far away from the turbulence of the capital and, incidentally, only a day's ride from the Speaker's own home at Sywell in Northamptonshire.

During the first and second sessions the Commons had been withstanding all royal demands for a grant of taxation: even rumours that parliament would not be dissolved until it made a vote had failed to

---

[1] For Lumley's politics, see R. L. Storey, 'Marmaduke Lumley, bishop of Carlisle, 1430–1450', *Transactions of the Cumberland and Westmorland Antiquarian and Archaeological Society*, N.S., vol. lv, pp. 112–31.

affect their resistance. At Leicester, too, the Commons refused a subsidy of the ordinary kind, declaring that, since the country was so poverty-stricken, *we canne, may, ne darr not, in eny wyse charge youre people with such usuell charges as afore this tyme to yowe have be graunted in yowre Parlementes.* And when in the end Tresham was able to announce a grant, this was nothing more substantial than a graduated tax of 6*d.* in the £ on incomes from land worth less than £20 a year, 1*s.* in the £ on incomes of more than £20, 2*s.* in the £ on incomes of over £200; besides, it was all made conditional upon the appointment of four special treasurers (a device not used since 1404), the acceptance of an appropriation to the Household of some £11,000 a year for seven years, together with an Act of Resumption of all royal grants since the King's accession. Because—according to statements made earlier in the Parliament—the royal debt stood at £372,000, Household expenditure at £24,000 per annum, and the King's own annual income at no more than £5,000, none of these provisions did more than scratch the surface of the problem; and, in any case, the Commons' expectations of the resumption proved ill-founded. The government never intended that it should be a complete resumption, and the administrative action taken was both dilatory and half-hearted.[1] The men of the Household saw to it that they at any rate emerged virtually unscathed: by provisos of exemption, they managed to retain of their grants twice as much as they agreed to resign. Speaker Tresham certainly came out of this business with no very serious discomfiture to himself. Out of royal annuities amounting to not less than £100 a year, he merely surrendered one worth £20. He did not live long to enjoy his luck, being murdered on 23 September 1450 when going to meet the Duke of York on his way up to London after returning from Ireland.[2]

The military situation in France was now almost hopeless. The last army of English reinforcements had been disposed of in a pitched battle at Formigny in mid-April 1450. Another three months, and all Normandy was back in French hands, the Duke of Somerset having retired to Calais even before the end of June. But what had caused

[1] B. P. Wolffe, 'Acts of Resumption in the Lancastrian Parliaments, 1399–1456', *EHR*, lxxiii (1958), pp. 598–603.

[2] It looks as though the responsibility for Tresham's murder and the wounding of his son Thomas should be laid at the door of Edmund Lord Grey of Ruthin, a prominent member of the Lancastrian party until his desertion to the Yorkists at the battle of Northampton in 1460. Some local trouble may have been the motive for the crime, and the men who did it perhaps thought that Tresham's meeting with York would justify or extenuate the outrage.

the hasty break-up of the Leicester parliament early in that month was the news of rebellion in southern England. A revolt in Kent under Jack Cade was quickly followed by outbreaks in Essex, Surrey, Sussex, and Wiltshire. These risings were soon put down, and Cade was killed, but not before the men of Kent had forced their way to London, where they put to death the ex-Treasurer, Lord Saye and Sele. The rebels had required the punishment of the late Duke of Suffolk's *false progeny and affinity*. They had also shown an unmistakable hostility towards the Queen: William Aiscough, Bishop of Salisbury, who had performed the royal marriage-service, was murdered down in Wiltshire; the safety of Margaret's chancellor, Bishop Bothe of Lichfield, and of her confessor, Bishop Lyhert of Norwich, had been threatened. The insurgents, too, had demanded a new government of 'true' barons and the recall of Richard of York from Ireland, presumably to lead such an administration. Whether or not York himself was privy to the risings and sympathetic to their aims, at least some of his closest friends were. Certainly, the duke's later reactions did nothing to allay suspicion. In August, on his own initiative, he returned from Ireland and, after being denounced as a traitor, gathered forces on the Welsh border. Marching to Westminster in September, he forced his way through to an audience of the King, of whom he demanded reform and changes in the royal Council. He then awaited parliament's meeting in November.[1] Meanwhile, the Duke of Somerset had been called home from Calais and, more provocatively still, made Constable of England.

The political history of the next four and a half years is largely one of the attempts of York and his sympathizers to make head against the alliance between Somerset (Suffolk's successor in the job of propping up the Lancastrian dynasty) and Queen Margaret. The contest was all the more bitter because, inevitably, so long as the royal marriage continued unfruitful, the royal succession was left problematic and attracted attention as a political issue. York (the heir-general and, after Henry VI, heir-male of Edward III) and Somerset (the prospective heir-male of John of Gaunt) were contenders for the claim to be considered heir-presumptive to Henry VI. In any case, the Lancastrian administration was dangerously discredited. For York to be given control of government would be hazardous in the extreme for many members of the Court party. If Somerset were preferred, York's position would be similarly imperilled, despite some backing from among the nobility.

[1] Parliament had already been summoned by writs issued on 5 September.

During the autumn of 1450 York and his friends busied themselves in 'labouring' the elections to parliament in the shires where they had influence. And, when parliament met on 6 November, it was soon made clear that the duke enjoyed the support of at least a fair number among the Commons. This much may be inferred from the fact that, over a week before even York and his nephew, the Duke of Norfolk, came with their great retinues to Westminster, Sir William Oldhall was elected by the Lower House as its Speaker. Oldhall was York's chamberlain.[1]

It was Oldhall's first experience of election even as a knight of the shire. He was sitting for Hertfordshire. Here he held a small but compact collection of manors in and near Hunsdon (where he had already embarked upon a building programme which, even though it was to fail of completion, cost him not far short of £5,000). Some of this property had come to him from the Duke of York by either sale or lease for life. Oldhall's other lands, including his patrimony, were mainly in Norfolk, where his father (Edmund) had been in great demand as an estate-agent, continuously holding the office of receiver of the Duchy of Lancaster lands in the county under John of Gaunt, Henry IV and Henry V.

William Oldhall had consistently followed a career of arms in the French war and become one of the great professional soldiers of the time. And he and many of his fellow-survivors of the military *débâcle* across the Channel were now disappointed, sour, and unforgiving men; even in 1450 they were ready for mischief; soon they would be eager to bring down the dynasty which had failed itself, and them too. Oldhall had been with Henry V's forces in Normandy from 1416 onwards as a regular member of the retinue of Thomas Beaufort, Duke of Exeter, paying only occasional visits to England (mainly because of litigation on his own account). After Henry V's

[1] For references and a fuller discussion of Oldhall's career, see my paper, 'Sir William Oldhall, Speaker in the Parliament of 1450-1', *Nottingham Medieval Studies*, vol. v, pp. 87-112. C. E. Johnston, 'Sir William Oldhall', *EHR*, xxv (1910), should also be consulted. Since publishing the paper in *Nottingham Medieval Studies*, I have been informed by Dr J. M. W. Bean that in the year 1448-9 Oldhall was steward of the Duke of York's lordships of Thaxted and Clare (where he was also constable of the castle). His fees of office were 50 marks a year. More than half as much again (£51) came Oldhall's way in the form of an annuity, once charged on the ducal lordships in Gloucestershire, now (in 1448-9) payable by the duke's receiver in the counties of Norfolk, Suffolk, Huntingdon, Cambridge, Essex, Middlesex, Surrey, and Sussex (P.R.O., Ministers' Accounts, 1113/10). For some facts relating to Oldhall's later career, see the Appendix.

death, unlike so many of his captains, he remained on active service across the Channel, successively under the Duke of Exeter, the Earl of Salisbury (with whom he won his spurs at the battle of Cravant in 1423), and the Regent, Bedford (with whom he fought at Verneuil in 1424). Oldhall's promotion can hardly have been hindered by his relationship (as brother-in-law) with Robert Lord Willoughby of Eresby, K.G. (himself brother-in-law to the Earl of Salisbury). But his own ability is clearly borne out by his occupation of the office of Seneschal of Normandy in 1425, and by the captaincies of castles and towns which he soon came to hold in the *pays conquis* (at Monsoer, St Laurence de Moitiers, Argentan, and Essey). In October 1428 he was also the recipient, by a grant in tail, of lands in the Norman *bailliages* of Rouen, Caen, and Evreux valued at 200 *livres parisiens*.[1] His energy and prowess, and also his closeness to Bedford as a member of his staff, are amply attested, not least by the Regent's recommendation in 1429 that he should be made a Knight of the Garter (in which report are detailed some of Oldhall's exploits). After Bedford's death in 1435, by which time Oldhall was a knight-banneret, he served the great Regent's successors in the French command, first with the Duke of York in 1436–7, next with the Earl of Warwick in 1437–9, and then again with York in 1441–5, in the weary task of holding on to what was left of the English conquest. In 1441 Sir William's personal retinue numbered 42 lances and 146 archers, and he was by then a member, perhaps even the foremost member, of York's chief council at Rouen. Already he was one of the duke's feoffees-to-uses in England and soon (almost certainly by 1444) was his chamberlain. Oldhall's experience of affairs in northern France by this time was so extensive that Henry VI wrote to York under his signet requesting that he should be spared for a visit to England, so that he could advise him and the Council *in such things as shalbe occurrent and touche our Reaume of France and Duchie of Normandie, as he that of reason shuld have mooste perfite knowlege in the same, considering his longe abode with you there, and of your Counseil*.

When York himself came home in 1445, Oldhall remained his chamberlain and a member of his council. In 1447 he was the first of the duke's three nominees for the late Duke of Gloucester's stall in the Garter chapel at Windsor (to which Alphonso V of Portugal was elected), and early in 1449 he crossed with York to Ireland. Although he probably had a hand in encouraging Cade's rebellion (as the

[1] I am grateful to Dr J. M. W. Bean for this particular information. He found it in the French Archives Nationales, Register JJ 174, no. 230.

Lancastrians later asserted), he was certainly with York when, or immediately after, the latter returned from Ireland and landed in north Wales, in the summer of 1450. The duke, in fact, when a little later he forced his way into Henry VI's presence at Westminster, complained that the groom of the Chamber who had been instructed to arrest him at his landing and put him in Conway castle, had also been told *to strike off the head of Sir William Oldhall*.

There is no shadow of doubt that Oldhall participated in the duke's *coup* of September 1450. When, over a year and a half later, in Easter term 1452, following the failure of York's insurrection at Dartford, the pendulum had so swung in favour of the Court party that legal proceedings could be taken in the King's Bench against some of York's supporters for their actions in 1450, a jury was to present that at Westminster on 27 September 1450 Sir William Oldhall of Hunsdon, *pro magnificencia et exaltacione dicti Willelmi*, had plotted the death of the King or, failing that, to bring about 'discord between the King and the lords and between the lords and the men who had assembled to rise in war against the King'. Oldhall was unquestionably preeminent in the Duke of York's counsels at that time. In a letter of 6 October 1450, in which Justice Yelverton's secretary wrote to John Paston that York had applied to the King by bill to have a number of his opponents arrested without option of bail, it was stated that at Westminster on the previous day, Oldhall had had an affable talk with the King which had lasted *more thanne to* [two] *houres*. And the letter went on to say that Henry had there and then asked Oldhall to speak to York and get his support for John Penycok (one of the Esquires of the Body who had been denounced by the Kentish rebels in the previous June): the duke's tenantry would need to be persuaded to allow Penycok's bailiffs to collect rents from those of his lands which lay among the duke's own lordships. Oldhall put the King off by saying that York's tenants would disobey any instructions of that sort. He also gave the King to know that the mood of the *western men* was such that, when Lord Hoo, the ex-Chancellor of France, had met the duke at St Albans, he (Oldhall) had been compelled to intervene to protect him from their hands, risking his life to do so.

Lord Hoo was not alone among the Lancastrian courtiers to seek Oldhall's good offices in this crisis in their affairs. Others included the two East Anglians, Sir Thomas Tuddenham (one of the late Duke of Suffolk's close adherents who had recently been dismissed from the Keepership of the Great Wardrobe but was still clinging to his office of Chief Steward of the Duchy of Lancaster north of Trent) and John Heydon (the lawyer who shared with Tuddenham the office of duchy steward in Norfolk, Suffolk, and Cambridgeshire). Both these men were working at this time through the Yorkist lawyers, William Burley (Speaker in 1445) and Thomas Young of Bristol, to have Oldhall's *good lordshep*: and they were prepared (according to the letter of Justice Yelverton's clerk of 6 October) to *profyr more thanne to* [two] *thowsand pownde* to secure it. It was in just this situation that John Paston, then personally embroiled with Tuddenham and Heydon in Norfolk, was advised by letter to wait upon the Duke of York when he moved from Walsingham to Norwich, to *cherse* [cherish] *and wirchep well Sir William Oldhalle*, and to *spende sum what of your good now, and gette yow lordshep and frendshep ther, quia ibi pendet tota lex et prophetae.* Thomas Lord Scales, who had assisted the government against Cade in London in the previous June and was a fairly sound loyalist, had evidently already realized where he too could best make headway: the letter written by Yelverton's secretary on 6 October stated that Scales and Oldhall *arne made frendys*. Sir Thomas Tuddenham seemingly had no such luck: some time in November 1450 Justice Yelverton himself wrote to a correspondent saying that Tuddenham was alleged to have told *the falsest tales* of Oldhall and the writer; not surprisingly, Yelverton gave it as his opinion that *it wer ful necessarye and profitable to the Kyng and to his pepil for to have othir officers in his duche* [of Lancaster].

The first session of the parliament which met on 6 November 1450 ran until a week short of Christmas (18 December), the second from 20 January 1451 to 19 April, and the third and final session from 5 May following into the last week of the month. It is probable that only when York and his kinsmen, Norfolk and Warwick, came up to town, on 18 November 1450, did parliament seriously get down to political business, and that to the four remaining weeks of this first session should be attributed the initiation of the more exciting proposals and measures of the parliament. These were the bill of attainder against the late Duke of Suffolk, which Henry VI refused; a similarly unsuccessful attack on the duke's widow, who was a cousin of the Duke of Somerset; the bill for the removal from the verge of the Household of a number of courtiers, chief among whom was the Duke of Somerset, on account of their alleged misbehaviour with the King, a bill whose sting Henry himself removed by excluding Somerset and the other peers named, together with any who were his own personal attendants; and the bill for another Act of

Resumption, submitted on the ground that the Act of the previous spring had *not been effectually had*. The last of these bills not only asked for a reduction of the endowment of the King's colleges at Eton and Cambridge, but also required that the recipients of future royal grants should incur forfeiture of even their own lands, unless the grants were approved by a committee comprising the Chancellor, the Treasurer, the Keeper of the Privy Seal, and six other lords of the Council. This first session also saw a *great division* between York and Somerset: on 1 December an attempt was made to arrest Somerset and, although he escaped, his London house was ransacked. (So, on the following day, were the houses in the City belonging to Lord Hoo and Sir Thomas Tuddenham.) In the spoiling of Somerset's property at the London Blackfriars, Speaker Oldhall himself took a hand. Moreover, in Easter term 1452, he was to be indicted in the King's Bench of having urged men from Kent and others on that day (1 December) to kill the lords and magnates so that, in the great hall of the King's pleas (Westminster Hall), the courts of the King's Bench, Chancery, Common Bench, and Exchequer there openly sitting, they committed their treasons and felonies 'to the final destruction of these courts and of the laws and customs of the land, appearing in manner of war and shouting, "Justice, justice" '.[1]

Something of a revulsion of feeling in favour of the Court seems to have occurred during, if not even before, the Christmas recess. In answer to a petition of the Commons, Cade had been attainted of treason. It was the Duke of York himself who, on 14 December, received a commission to try the rebels of the previous summer in Kent and Sussex. But the Duke of Somerset was appointed as Captain of Calais, a key post. This apart, it is clear that Somerset now recovered some influence: in February 1451 his friend, Abbot Bowlers of Gloucester, who, until lately a member of the royal Council, had been imprisoned by the Duke of York at Ludlow, and whose removal from the Household had so recently been demanded by the Commons, was preferred to the vacant see of Hereford (a diocese in York's own main territorial sphere of influence). When, during the third session of the parliament, Thomas Young, the lawyer-burgess for Bristol, moved in the Lower House (as William Worcester tells us) for the recognition of Richard of York as heir to the throne (a proposal perhaps more particularly directed against Somerset than the King), parliament was immediately brought to a close. Perhaps at this stage the move was a last and reckless

[1] Coram Rege Rolls, P.R.O., K.B. 27/777, Rex roll, mem. 7.

throw by the Yorkists. Certainly, Young was committed to the Tower.

The parliament of 1450–1 clearly had settled little that was to York's advantage. But neither had the government regained much ground. It could hardly be said that political stability had been achieved. So far as finance was concerned, a Resumption Act had been passed which 'restored a considerable measure of control over the endowed revenues of the Crown to the Exchequer' and permitted a settlement of income on the royal Household.[1] The Chancellor, when opening parliament, had urged the need for taxation, especially to meet the situation in Aquitaine. No subsidies, however, were granted, if we exclude parliament's confirmation of the graduated tax on income from land voted at Leicester in the spring of 1450. (In November 1450, when parliament met, it had been stated that this tax was still unpaid, because of *lak of diligence* on the part of commissioners and sheriffs and *lak of entendaunce* of those chargeable.)

Precisely how Oldhall acted as Speaker to further the Yorkist interest during the parliament of 1450–1, is not known. But if he derived any personal advantage as a result of his services, this was soon lost. In fact, in the next two years all went wrong for both him and the master he served. Even by the end of 1451 Oldhall had been driven to enter the sanctuary of St Martin the Great in London, where he was to remain, except for brief intervals, until after the Yorkist victory in the first battle of St Albans in 1455. And in the parliament following the one in which he acted as Speaker—the Reading parliament of 1453—the Commons successfully attainted him for treason, so that all his estates were forfeited and went for a time into the possession of the King's half-brother, Jasper, recently created Earl of Pembroke.

The year 1451 saw the French overrun Gascony. At home there was considerable disorder and disturbance, especially in the West Country. Open hostility between York and Somerset was temporarily suspended, the King doing his best to keep up a pretence of peace between them. Early in 1452, however, York was back where he had been at the time of his return from Ireland in 1450, solemnly insisting on his loyalty but prepared to use armed force to impose his views upon the King. On 1 March 1452 the duke and his private army were at Dartford, threatening the capital; but he was outwitted into disbanding his men, and instead of the Duke of Somerset being arrested

[1] B. P. Wolffe, op. cit., *EHR*, vol. lxxiii, pp. 604–8.

R

to stand trial (as York demanded), it was York who found himself
a prisoner. The Council, however, let him go after certain under-
takings exchanged between the parties. It was probably as part of the
price which the Somerset group paid for this pacification with York
that John Tiptoft, Earl of Worcester, the son of the Speaker of 1406
and a friend of York's, succeeded Lord Beauchamp as Treasurer of
the Exchequer on 15 April 1452. None the less, Somerset and the
Court party were undoubtedly left with the upper hand for the time
being, witness the translation (in July) of Cardinal Kemp, the Lord
Chancellor, from York to Canterbury, and the translation, from
Lichfield to York, of William Bothe, the Queen's Chancellor, whose
removal from Court had been demanded by the Commons in the last
parliament. Partly in an effort to win popular support, the government despatched an expedition to the Bordelais under the old Earl
of Shrewsbury as Lieutenant of Aquitaine. It was in the spirit of
optimism to which Talbot's deceptively quick success gave rise that
Henry VI, on 20 January 1453, summoned parliament to meet at
Reading on 6 March.

The choice of a place where parliament would at least be free of
the influence of York's partisans among the Londoners, suggests
that the government was still none too happy on his account. But so
strong did the Household element among the Commons turn out to
be (17 per cent of the House as against 6 per cent in 1450) that it is
hard to escape the conclusion that Court influence was brought to
bear upon the elections for the shires and boroughs and met with an
abnormal degree of success. Certainly, the parliament of 1453–4 was
distinctly more friendly towards the administration than any for
some time past.

That the Commons were so predisposed may reasonably be
deduced from their election of Thomas Thorpe[1] to the Speakership.
Thorpe had sat along with Speaker Tresham in the parliament of
1449–50 for Northamptonshire (where he had estates in the Nene
valley).[2] In 1450 he had been returned for Ludgershall.[3] Now, in
1453, whilst his son Roger sat for Truro, and his servant, Thomas

---

[1] For references and a detailed account of Thorpe's career, see my article,
'Thomas Thorpe, Speaker in the Reading Parliament of 1453', *Nottingham
Medieval Studies*, vol. vii (1963), pp. 79–105.

[2] Thorpe held the manors of Barnwell All Saints and Lilford.

[3] At Ludgershall Thorpe replaced an earlier nominee, the son of William
Yelverton (JKB) who was pushed in for Old Sarum instead (J. C. Wedgwood,
History of Parliament 1439–1509, Register, pp. 172–3).

Cross, for Heytesbury, he himself was knight of the shire for Essex (where, at Great Ilford, he usually lived when not at his London house in Aldersgate Ward).[1] Thorpe was a professional civil servant, an Exchequer official of considerable administrative experience, deeply involved in current politics.[2] It was on or about 20 July 1437 that he was first appointed as one of the summoners of the Exchequer, and, at a salary of £4 a year, he was still occupying this office in 1441.[3] Even then he seems to have been connected with the Beaufort family; there is at least no doubt that he was associated with Master John Somerset, a kinsman of the Beauforts who was then physician to the King, Chancellor of the Exchequer, and Keeper of the Exchange and Master of the Mint in the Tower;[4] and it was perhaps due to John Somerset's influence that Thorpe was appointed as joint-Controller of the Mint in September 1442 at 40 marks a year (an office for which he was to be solely responsible for two years before he resigned it in May 1450).[5] His promotion in April 1444 to be Treasurer's Remembrancer, again at an annual fee of 40 marks, his re-appointment to this office for life in September following, and the grant of January 1446 by which he received an additional fee of 50 marks a year, plus a Christmas livery of a cap, gown and tabard of the kind worn by a Baron of the Exchequer (the whole of this grant being back-dated nearly four years), Thorpe may well have

[1] In Essex, apart from the manor of Clayhall at Great Ilford, Thorpe possessed property at Barking, Chigwell, and Stanford Rivers. His messuage in London, in the parish of St John Zachary, was called 'The Walnut Tree'.

[2] It was almost certainly as a member of the staff of the Exchequer that, along with another Exchequer clerk, Thorpe stood surety in April 1438 for a small group of London tradesmen, grantees of a royal lease of a small collection of estates in Buckinghamshire (CFR, 1437–45, 33). He himself soon acquired a lease or two at the Exchequer along with minor local offices in the Treasurer's gift: the office of troner and weigher at Berwick-on-Tweed (Feb.–Oct. 1440) and also at Newcastle upon Tyne (May 1440–Oct. 1442), together with a share in the right to farm the aulnage of cloth in Herts. (1439–46). I owe the approximate date of Thorpe's appointment as one of the summoners of the Exchequer to Mr C. A. F. Meekings of the Public Record Office who kindly sent me word of it.

[3] P.R.O., E 403/743.

[4] In December 1441 and October 1442 John Somerset's half-yearly fee as Chancellor of the Exchequer (20 marks) was paid him at the Lower Exchequer by hand of Thomas Thorpe; and in May 1443 the two officials shared a grant of the wardship of a tenant of the see of Canterbury, the temporalities of which were under royal control because of the death of Archbishop Chichele (Issue Rolls, E 403/743, 747; CFR, 1437–45, 262).

[5] CPR, 1441–6, 125, 193.

owed (at least in part) to Lord Sudeley who was then Treasurer.[1]
The Exchequer came under fire with Sudeley's successors: as we have
seen, Bishop Lumley resigned in September 1449, and Lord Saye was
murdered in Cheapside during Cade's rising in July 1450. The rebels
evidently detested Thorpe too.[2] But he came through that crisis
unscathed; and, although his colleague, the Chancellor of the Exchequer, John Somerset, was amongst those whose removal from
Court was demanded by the Commons in the parliament of 1450–1,
Thorpe himself did not figure in the list. He held on to his post as
Remembrancer under the new Treasurer, Lord Beauchamp of
Powick, seemingly without difficulty.[3] But when the Earl of Wor-
cester, one of York's friends, was made Treasurer in April 1452, it
was not long before Thorpe ran into trouble: in Trinity term the new
Treasurer ordered an enquiry into defects in the records of his
Remembrancer, and in Michaelmas term Thorpe was removed.[4] The
Beaufort interest, to which Thorpe was closely attached, was none
the less too powerful for the Treasurer, even in his own department.
And not only did Thorpe secure a royal patent on 22 November 1452
promising him the Chancellorship of the Exchequer for life when
Master John Somerset died, but a week later there was issued a
Privy Seal warrant authorizing the Exchequer to pay him £200 (by
the King's especial grace and *considering the good and aggreable service
done . . . and also the greet costes, charges, troubles and vexacions that he
hath hadde and suffred for us*). Moreover, he was soon able to defy the

[1] *CPR, 1441–6*, 363, 396; *CCR, 1441–7*, 336; P.R.O., E 101/409/13, 18;
410/4, 7; E 403/751, 753, 759. Having recently surrendered his office at the
Tower Mint, Thorpe was exempted from the Resumption Act of 1450 except
for a single annuity of £10 enjoyed since 1442 (*Rot. Parl.*, v. 199).

[2] A popular dirge for the late Duke of Suffolk associated Thorpe with William
Cantlowe, a London mercer and alderman who assisted the government with
loans: 'Arys up, Thorp and Cantelowe, and stond ye togeder And syng *Dies
illa, dies ire*' (*Three Fifteenth Century Chronicles*, ed. Jas Gairdner (Camden Society,
1880), p. 103). In August 1450 at Rochester Thorpe was indicted before a royal
commission sent down to satisfy the Kentish rebels.

[3] On 8 April 1451 Thorpe in his capacity as Remembrancer was paid £10 as a
special reward, mainly for great diligence shown during the previous Michaelmas term in proving an undervaluation of the estates of the late Duke of
Suffolk and for some extra work involved in dealing with the Resumption Act
of 1450, probably with the new bill in mind (P.R.O., E 403/781). Nearly a year
later, in February 1452, he was able to secure (for 340 marks) a royal grant of
the wardship of the two daughters and coheirs of John Helion, an Essex landowner (*CFR, 1445–54*, 259, 263), which a year later he sold to Sir Thomas
Tyrell.

[4] P.R.O., E 403/791; 796, mem. 10.

Treasurer, eject his competitor for the Remembrancer's office (Richard Ford, formerly Clerk of the Pipe), and re-occupy the place. Once reinstated, Thorpe offered to resign, but only provided he was given the office of Third Baron of the Exchequer. This was contrived: the then Third Baron, William Fallan, resigned when given a yearly pension of 40 marks by Ford, who again became Remembrancer, and Thorpe took Fallan's place.[1] Certainly by 26 April 1453 Thorpe was Third Baron. It may perhaps be presumed that he began the Easter term in that office.[2] But whether this promotion had already taken effect when parliament met at Reading on 6 March remains a matter of doubt.

The atmosphere in the Lower House at Reading cannot have been other than congenial to its Speaker. One of the Commons' earliest demands in this opening session was that their petition of 1450—that the Duke of Somerset and his supporters be banished from Court—should be *put in oblivion*, and they now also petitioned for a resumption of all royal grants made to those who, a year ago, had been out with the Duke of York at Dartford. Besides, within the short space of the three weeks from 6 to 28 March (Wednesday in Holy Week), when parliament was adjourned for Easter, the Commons voted a tenth and fifteenth. This tax was made payable in two annual instalments and subject to the now usual deduction of £6,000. But it was the first grant of its kind to be made since 1449. More significant still, the Commons now made a grant to the King, for life, of the wool-subsidy from 3 April 1454 (and at higher than the existing rates) together with similarly extended grants of tunnage, poundage, and the poll-tax on aliens.[3] To all of this was added a grant of 20,000 archers for six months' service when required. During the second parliamentary session, held at Westminster between 25 April and 2 July, this particularly novel imposition was scaled down and then suspended for two years. But this was only done on condition that the Commons made a special grant for the war in Guienne, and in fact they now voted another half tenth and fifteenth.[4] Payment of this additional grant, although again to be made in two instalments, was to be intercalated between the two payments of the earlier subsidy,

[1] *CPR, 1452–61*, 43; Privy Seal warrants for issue, P.R.O., E 404/69/74; *Rot. Parl.*, v. 342 (no. 25).

[2] P.R.O., E 404/69/134; *CPR, 1452–61*, 64.

[3] The wool-subsidy rate was increased from 33s. 4d. to 43s. 4d. per sack for denizens, from 53s. 4d. to 100s. for aliens.

[4] *Rot. Parl.*, v. 233a.

and for this generosity Henry VI himself thanked the Commons *ore suo proprio*, assuring them of his goodwill. That the parliament was still strongly biased towards the Court is also indicated by the passage of a bill (first presented in the Lords) securing to the Duke of Somerset a future appropriation of all the customs-revenues of Sandwich together with a grant of a noble (6*s*. 8*d*.) on every sack of wool shipped elsewhere. This was to ensure payment of the £21,648 due to him as Captain of Calais, although his predecessor in office (the Duke of Buckingham) was first to be contented of £19,000. It was the Commons themselves who petitioned for the attainder of Sir William Oldhall, the Yorkist Speaker of the previous parliament of 1450–1.

That Speaker Thorpe had so far put his directive skill to good use in the Lower House may reasonably be conjectured from the personal advantages he was able to extract during this phase of Lancastrian ascendancy. In the course of the second parliamentary session itself, he and his son were able to recover their grant in survivorship of the office of porter of the castle of Newcastle-on-Tyne (worth 2*s*. a day) which they had had to surrender under the Resumption Act of 1450.[1] Much more convincing evidence of the administration's sense of Thorpe's value was provided nine days after the close of the session when, on 11 July, the King, 'for certain causes and considerations moving him', ordered the Exchequer to pay the Speaker £200, for which he received an assignment on 24 July.[2] (It is worth noting that this was done by the hands of Thomas Bourne, then M.P. for Steyning, who on the same day was the recipient of Exchequer payments on behalf of the Duke of Somerset himself.) By this time, Thorpe was a member of the royal Council and was active as such, as well as in his capacity of Baron of the Exchequer, during the late summer and early autumn.[3]

While parliament was in recess during the summer of 1453, there occurred an event, the political consequences of which were liable to be serious. Henry VI, seemingly in July, went out of his mind, and for a year and a half was so deranged as to be quite incapable of discharging any royal function. Even the birth of a son and heir on

[1] *CPR, 1452–61*, 64, 81.
[2] Privy Seal warrants for issue, P.R.O., E 404/69/179; Issue roll, E 403/793, mem. 8.
[3] *PPC*, vi. 143–4, 152, 154, 156–7, 331. In August and September 1453 Thorpe was appointed to commissions relating to the royal revenue in North Wales. In October he joined with the Treasurer, the Under-Treasurer, and others in making a loan to the Exchequer of 2,000 marks (E 403/796, mem. 15).

13 October (the day of St Edward, after whom the child was called) was not an unmixed blessing: not only were ugly rumours soon afoot on the score of his paternity, but the Queen herself now began to intervene actively in politics as 'the resolute and implacable defender of her son's rights' (McFarlane) when it became clear that Henry's illness necessitated a regency of sorts. The difficult problem so raised was still unsolved when parliament came together once more, at Reading on 12 November, only to be immediately adjourned (to 11 February 1454). By now the situation was clearly moving York's way: before the end of November, his enemy, Somerset, was imprisoned in the Tower, pending an enquiry into his conduct of affairs at home and also overseas, where, following the disaster at Chastillon, the whole of Guienne had fallen into French hands with the loss of Bordeaux on 19 October 1453.

What now befell Speaker Thorpe may perhaps be regarded as a repercussion of Somerset's disgrace. In the middle of November 1453 Thorpe was still in office as a Baron of the Exchequer.[1] Before the end of the month he had either sought refuge in the sanctuary of St Martin the Great or else had this step in mind.[2] None the less, when parliament reassembled in February 1454, Thorpe was in prison. From the explanation offered by the Duke of York's counsel to the Lords when the Speaker's imprisonment involved an immediate discussion of the Commons' privilege of freedom from arrest,[3] it is evident that sometime during the previous year (presumably during the second session of the parliament at Westminster) Thorpe had gone to the London inn of the Bishop of Durham (Robert Neville) and there impounded certain (unspecified) possessions of the Duke of York. According to a petition submitted by Thorpe's son Roger over thirty years later (in Henry VII's first parliament of 1485), these goods and chattels were *harness and apparatus of war* and were seized by Thorpe on the King's order.[4] A conflation of the two accounts indicates that York, prompted by one Thomas Colt (who was *nigh of councell with the said duke* and M.P. for Warwick in 1453-4), began an action for trespass against Thorpe in the Exchequer, where, as one of its officials, he was entitled to be tried; that Thorpe, having *had diverse daies to emparle atte his requeste and desire*, pleaded not

[1] E 403/796, mem. 12.
[2] CCR, *1447-54*, 484 (a grant on 25 November 1453 of all Thorpe's goods and chattels to the Dean of St Martin's, Master Laurence Bothe, the Queen's chancellor, and others).
[3] *Rot. Parl.*, v. 239.   [4] Ibid., vi. 294.

guilty; that a Middlesex jury found for the duke (*by speciall labour and untrue means* on Colt's part, as Thorpe's son alleged in 1485), the duke's damages being assessed at £1,000, and his costs at £10; and that Thorpe was committed to the Fleet pending payment. This action probably came on after 19 January 1454 when, in a letter from London, it was stated that *Thorpe of th'escheker articuleth fast ayenst the duke of York, but what his articles ben it is yit unknowen*. If this assertion is correct, Thorpe cannot have been very long imprisoned when parliament reassembled at Reading on 11 February 1454.

At Reading the members did no more than listen to an announcement from the Treasurer (the Earl of Worcester) that in three days' time the session would begin after all at Westminster. The problem of who should act as regent during the King's illness was still outstanding. Queen Margaret regarded herself as entitled to act. But York won the first round of the contest when, on the eve of the session, he secured the right to open parliament and conduct its proceedings. Not surprisingly, since Thorpe was still the Commons' accredited Speaker, the session began on 14 February with a petition from the Lower House requesting his liberation as a matter of privilege. The judges declined to advise, on the ground that any dispute over parliamentary privilege was for the Lords to determine. Chief Justice Fortescue, however, while admitting that there could be no general *supersedeas* when parliament was sitting, gave his opinion that it was usual for any person under arrest who was *a membre of this high court of Parliament* to be free to attend, provided that he had not been arrested for treason, felony, surety of the peace, or in pursuance of a judgement in parliament. But York's counsel had urged upon the Lords that Thorpe had committed his trespass since the beginning of the parliament, that the duke's whole action had been both begun and terminated in time of parliamentary vacation, and that, if Thorpe were released on privilege before paying damages and costs, the duke would be deprived of legal remedy. And so they demanded that Thorpe should be kept in custody until he had fulfilled the award of the Court of Exchequer. Notwithstanding the privilege and the fact that Thorpe was Speaker, the Lords ruled that he should remain in prison, and that the Commons should elect another Speaker.[1] An explanation was made to the Lower House by one of the royal serjeants-at-law in the presence of Bishop Bourchier of Ely and other lords, and, on the third day of the session (16 February), a new Speaker was elected.

[1] For Thorpe's later career, see the Appendix.

The Commons' choice now fell upon Sir Thomas Charlton, knight of the shire for Middlesex, a member of a formerly London family now long rusticated at South Mimms and Edmonton but still holding property in the City. Previously elected for Middlesex in 1442 and 1447, Charlton had seldom served on royal commissions in the county and had only become a J.P. there in 1449. But from certainly no later than 1441 he had been one of the Esquires of the King's Hall and Chamber and, having been knighted in 1452, was still on the establishment of the Household when elected Speaker.[1] The Abbot of St Albans tells us in his register that Charlton, whom he likens to the fox (*cautus, callidus et subtilis*), got himself made Speaker in order to secure the Commons' support for his claim to the manor of Burston (Herts.) which the abbey was disputing.[2] But it is possible that what most weighed with the Commons was that Charlton's career and connexions would give his election the appearance of a political compromise. He was a member of the royal Household. His wife's folk, the Vernons of Haddon (Derbyshire), were loyal Lancastrians, one of her brothers (William) being treasurer of Calais, and another (John) sheriff of Pembrokeshire.[3] At the same time, Charlton's own kinsmen on his father's side, the Frowykes (among whom his uncle, Henry Frowyke, was now senior Alderman of London and Mayor of the Staple at Westminster, and his cousin, Henry Frowyke junior, was his fellow-M.P. for Middlesex),[4] were closely connected with the City, where Yorkist sympathy was very

---

[1] Charlton appears in the account-books of the Controller of the Household as receiving an annual allowance of £2 for winter and summer robes in the years Michaelmas 1441-2, 1443-4, 1446-7, 1447-8, 1450-1, and 1451-2 (P.R.O., E 101/409/9, 11, 16; 410/1, 6, 9). Subsequently, in 1455, the Abbot of St Albans could still describe Charlton as *miles quidam de familia domini Regis*.

[2] *Registrum Abbatiae Johannis Whethamstede*, ed. H. T. Riley (R.S.), vol. i, p. 136; *Johannis de Whethamstede Chronicon* (in *Duo Rerum Anglicarum Scriptores Veteres*), ed. Thos. Hearne (Oxford, 1732), vol. ii, p. 534.

The Charltons were seemingly tenants of the abbey in the manor of Burston. Sir Thomas's father and mother alienated the manor to John Fray, Chief Baron of the Exchequer, by a fine levied in 1436, and Fray had granted it to the abbey in 1438. Speaker Charlton repudiated the sale of 1436 and so impugned the conveyance of 1438. The abbot's account informs us that it was by a letter from Lord Cromwell that he first heard of Charlton's 'labour' in 1454 and was enabled to frustrate his plan.

[3] Probably early in 1442, Charlton married Benedicta, daughter of Sir Richard Vernon, the Speaker in the Leicester parliament of 1426 who died in 1451. (For the marriage settlement, see *CCR, 1441-7*, 42-4.)

[4] For the connexions between the families of Charlton and Frowyke, see my book, *The Commons in the Parliament of 1422*, 164, 181-2.

powerful; and he himself, on his mother's side, was second cousin to Alice (Montagu), wife of Richard Neville, Earl of Salisbury, brother-in-law of the Duke of York and now the chief of his supporters among the peerage.[1] In view of the Abbot of St Albans' statement that in 1455 Charlton regarded his kinship with the Countess of Salisbury as having an important bearing upon their dispute over Burston,[2] and because Charlton was one of the earl's feoffees in the manor of Shenley Hall (Herts.),[3] it may well be that this particular one was the most significant of Charlton's connexions at the time of his election to the Speakership.

This session of the parliament, which proved to be its last, ran from 14 February to 17 April 1454. There was much to excite the members, and political feeling ran high. On 15 March, with the agreement of the Lords, the infant Edward of Lancaster was created Prince of Wales and Earl of Chester, which was tantamount to his being publicly recognized as royal heir-apparent. But the death (a week later) of Cardinal Kemp, the Chancellor, strengthened York's position, and this was made all the stronger still when a deputation of lords, sent to Windsor to interview the King about the vacancy in the Primacy and the Chancellorship, returned on 25 March with the news that Henry had shown no sign of understanding their purpose. The question of the regency could no longer be shelved, and York got his way two days later when the Lords nominated him Protector, the Act formally embodying his appointment being passed on 3 April, the day after the appointment of the Earl of Salisbury as the new Chancellor. The Commons' lack of enthusiasm for these arrangements is suggested by the fact that they did not see fit to go back on their refusal, made earlier in the session (on 19 March), to add to the financial grants made at Reading in the previous year. Having then voted the customs and subsidies for the

---

[1] F. C. Cass, *History of South Mimms*, 81. The Speaker's mother, Elizabeth (née Fraunceys), was first cousin to Thomas Montagu, Earl of Salisbury (ob. 1428), whose daughter and heir, Alice, married Richard Neville, Earl of Salisbury. Elizabeth had died as recently as 1451.

[2] *Registrum Abbatiae*, op. cit., vol. i, 202.

[3] *CPR, 1485-94*, 399; *VCH, Herts.*, ii. 266. In February 1458 Charlton was one of the feoffees who settled this estate on the earl's third son John and his wife (a niece of the Earl of Worcester). It was this youngest of Salisbury's sons who in 1453 had quarrelled with Lord Egremont, the younger son of the Earl of Northumberland, so intensifying the feud between Nevilles and Percies which constantly reacted on their attitude to the main political conflict of the period.

King's lifetime as well as a grant of one and a half tenths and fifteenths, they evidently felt that they had already done enough. This being so, the financial business of the session in which Sir Thomas Charlton was Speaker was for the most part restricted to authorizing royal loans borrowed on the security of taxation and to arranging appropriations for the upkeep of the Household, the defence of Calais, and the safe-keeping of the seas. There is no record that Charlton received any douceur for his pains.[1]

The Duke of York virtually controlled the royal administration until after Henry of Windsor had come to his senses about Christmas 1454. The King's recovery brought York's uneasy Protectorate to an end early in February 1455. It also made possible the liberation of the Duke of Somerset. And so soon was Somerset's rehabilitation complete that on 6 March he replaced York in the command of Calais. The main direction of government now changed hands: on 7 March the Earl of Salisbury was dismissed from the Chancellorship, the Great Seal being entrusted to Archbishop Bourchier, the new primate and a moderate man; and on 15 March the Earl of Wiltshire, a firm royalist, took the place of the Earl of Worcester as head of the Exchequer. When Richard of York had had time to react to the new situation, he and his allies, chief among whom were the Earl of Salisbury and his son, the Earl of Warwick, collected their forces in the north and together marched towards London. From Royston and Ware, respectively on 20 and 21 May, the rebel lords wrote first to the Chancellor and then to the King, protesting their abiding loyalty, complaining that their enemies incited the King to mistrust them, and requesting an audience. Neither the manifesto forwarded by Archbishop Bourchier to the King at Kilburn, nor the copy of it which, sent to the King direct, reached the Court at Watford, was allowed to come to Henry's personal notice. Even their purport was suppressed by the Duke of Somerset, Thomas Thorpe (the ex-Speaker who was still a Baron, and now also Chancellor, of the Exchequer), and William Joseph (the King's Secretary), once they had read the letters, or so the Yorkist leaders later alleged in parliament. This embezzlement of their missives, the King's ignorance of their intentions, and also the resistance offered by Somerset, Thorpe, and Joseph at St Albans on 22 May to their final offer to make a personal explanation to the King, were later represented by York and his friends as their excuse for fighting the first battle of St Albans. This engagement resulted in the killing of the

[1] For Charlton's later years, see the Appendix.

Duke of Somerset, the Earl of Northumberland, the Earl of Stafford (son of the Duke of Buckingham), and Lord Clifford. It also involved the capture of the King himself, whom the rebel lords now led back to London. Ex-Speaker Thorpe—rumour had it, and doubtless on this occasion rumour did not lie—had fled the field with the new Treasurer, the Earl of Wiltshire, and others who *left her harneys behynde hem cowardly*. No more than a week later, Wiltshire was superseded at the Exchequer by Henry Viscount Bourchier, brother of the Chancellor and brother-in-law of both the Duke of York and his friend, the Duke of Norfolk. Already, on 26 May, parliament had been summoned. Henceforward, the two main factions did no more than 'preserve certain constitutional formalities without being at all guided by constitutional principles' (Stubbs). And so, on 9 July, parliament met at Westminster to register the new situation.

The changes in the administration that followed close upon the Yorkist success at St Albans hardly warrant us in assuming without question that York and his allies were now so securely in control of the royal authority as to be able to dominate the parliament. The brothers, Thomas and Henry Bourchier, Chancellor and Treasurer respectively, held something of a middle position between the two chief contending parties: their brother John, now for the first time summoned to parliament (as Lord Berners), had been on the King's side at St Albans, and so had their half-brother, Humphrey, Duke of Buckingham. More important than these indications is the fact that the parliamentary peers in general were to show, in their reluctance to accept York as Protector in the following November, that they were not at all enamoured of the duke's ascendancy. Indeed, although during the first session of the parliament (9–31 July 1455) an Act was passed transferring responsibility for *the male journey* of St Albans from the Yorkist leaders to the King's own friends, it was reported that *to the . . . bill mony a man groged full sore nowe it is passed*, and the first session also saw a fresh oath of allegiance taken to Henry VI. Simply to regard the parliament of 1455–6 as a partisan assembly operating smoothly in the Yorkist interest requires a considerable faith in some large assumptions. Regarding the Commons, although the Yorkists had worked hard where possible to secure an amenable Lower House, the elections seem to have resulted in a far from disproportionate unbalance between their supporters and its loyalist elements. The Commons' election of Sir John Wenlock of Someries (Beds.) as their Speaker does something to confirm this

impression.[1] Four years later Wenlock was to be condemned in the
Coventry parliament (1459) for high treason in supporting the
Yorkists in the field, and afterwards he so energetically assisted
Edward IV's accession as to be quickly rewarded with a peerage.
But what evidence is available relating to Wenlock's political posi-
tion in 1455 suggests that, far from having thrown in his lot with the
Yorkists, he was still entirely loyal to Henry VI. Moreover, he was
still, so far as we know, a member of his Household. This is how his
career had hitherto developed.

Sir John Wenlock's family had once belonged to Much Wenlock
in Shropshire, and he himself still had property there.[2] By the end of
Edward III's reign their chief landed interests had come to be mainly
in and around Luton, and Sir John had considerably added to these
Bedfordshire estates by marriage and purchase.[3] He had been M.P.
for Bedfordshire five times since 1433 (the last previous occasion
being in 1449),[4] escheator there and in Buckinghamshire in 1438-9,
and sheriff in the same two counties in 1444-5. He had been a leading
member of the affinity of Lord Fanhope of Ampthill, getting involved
during the late 'thirties in this magnate's local quarrels with Lord
Grey of Ruthin, and Lord Fanhope appointed him as one of his
executors in 1443. In the meantime, Wenlock had joined the royal
Household.[5] He took this step no later than June 1441, when for the
first time he played a part in those tedious and always unsatisfactory

[1] For references and a fuller treatment of Wenlock's life, see my paper, 'John
Lord Wenlock of Someries', *The Publications of the Bedfordshire Historical Record
Society*, vol. xxxviii (1958), pp. 12-48.

[2] It was with the support of Lord Wenlock (as he then was) that, in 1468, the
incorporation of Much Wenlock as a free borough, with representation in
parliament, was secured by royal charter.

[3] Sir John Wenlock's father (John) had married a Bedfordshire heiress,
Margaret, sister of John Briton, and Sir John himself about 1441 married Elizabeth, the widow of Christopher Preston and a daughter and coheir of Sir John
Drayton. Sometime in the last ten years of his life he married, for his second
wife, Agnes, a daughter of John Danvers of Cokethorpe (Oxon.), the widow of
Sir John Fray, Chief Baron of the Exchequer (1436-48) who died in 1461.
Agnes, who was a sister of William Danvers (J.K.B., 1488-1504) and half-sister
to Robert Danvers (J.C.B., 1450-67), being left a widow by Lord Wenlock's
death in 1471, married as her third husband Sir John Say of Broxbourne,
Speaker in 1449-50, 1463-5, and 1467-8. Some of the lands Wenlock purchased
had belonged to Sir John Cornwall, Lord Fanhope.

[4] Wenlock was M.P. for Bedfordshire in 1433, 1437, 1439-40, 1447, 1449,
and 1455-6.

[5] As one of the *scutiferi aule et camere Regis*, figuring as such in the still extant
account-books of the Controller of the Household from 1441 onwards.

negotiations in France which had achieved the union of Henry VI and Margaret of Anjou in 1445 but little else. During those four years Wenlock spent in fact more than half his time abroad: he was a member of Suffolk's embassy which arranged the royal marriage in 1444 and of the party which brought the young Queen to England in April 1445.

These latest enterprises paid rich personal dividends: Wenlock soon won Margaret's regard and had secured appointment to the select little group of the ushers of her chamber even before her coronation (30 May 1445). His official stipend was only 1s. 6d. a day (plus 6d. extra for his yeoman). But he was now in a fair way to make handsome profits from royal patronage. As a by-product of the Queen's enjoyment of the wardship of the estates of the late Duke of Warwick (Henry Beauchamp), in June 1446 he received the constableship of Cardiff castle and the offices of steward and master-forester in the Beauchamp lordships of Glamorgan and Morgannok, which he almost certainly held until the death of the heiress in January 1449.[1] A year before then he was already filling none other than the post of Queen's Chamberlain, with an annual fee of £40; and it was in this capacity that on 15 April 1448 he laid the first stone of the chapel of the Queen's College in the University of Cambridge of which his mistress was patron. Royal grants continued to come his way and, though he made a large loan to the Crown of over £1,000 in December 1449, this was very probably only as an executor of Lord Fanhope's will. Like most of those with direct influence at Court, he secured exemption from the Resumption Act passed at Leicester in June 1450.

Despite the hostility of the rebels under Cade towards the Queen and her friends, Wenlock himself seems not to have aroused their special resentment. Nor did he come in for any particular notice when, during the parliament of 1450-1, the Commons demanded the expulsion of certain members of the Household. None the less, his closeness to the Queen is not in question: it was as her Chamberlain and at her request that in April 1452 he received a royal pardon for having promoted riots at Henley-on-Thames in the previous autumn

---

[1] In May 1446 Wenlock and another usher of the Queen's chamber (Edmund Hampden) were given the reversion of the office of Treasurer of Ireland, but this grant only materialized in December 1461. Another grant which came to nothing under Henry VI was that by which in July 1448 Wenlock was given the reversion of the office of constable of the castle of Bamborough (Northumberland). By no means all of his concessions were so disappointing as these.

(when he and his brother-in-law, an Oxfordshire lawyer, had gathered quite an army of men to obstruct an assize of novel disseisin, in which their opponents were the feoffees of the young Duke of Suffolk and his mother, the Dowager Alice). At Michaelmas 1453 Wenlock was taking his fee as the Queen's Chamberlain at the hands of her Receiver-General and was still in office in January 1454. By July following this was no longer the case.[1] It is unfortunate that we do not know precisely when, much less why, Sir John was superseded. But not only was he on the King's side at St Albans in May 1455, but fought for him there, being carried out of the engagement in a cart, *sore hurt*.

Of course, Wenlock's former association with the Queen is itself hardly likely to have recommended him to the Commons of 1455, unless, perhaps, he had been dismissed from office as her Chamberlain because of some quarrel between them (an assumption which has no evidence to support it). What prompted the Commons, or their steadier elements, to look to him as their Speaker is more likely to have been his connexion with one, and possibly with more than one, of the Bourchiers, whose policy was apparently to prevent either of the main parties from going to extremes: only five days after this parliament ended in March 1456, Wenlock and John Bourchier, Lord Berners, younger brother of the Chancellor and the Treasurer, were the chief recipients of a royal licence to found a gild, in the parish church at Staines, in whose chantry mass was to be celebrated for the good estate of King Henry and Queen Margaret. That, at the time of his Speakership, Wenlock was not yet a convert to Yorkist pretensions is perhaps also suggested by the fact that when, immediately after the beginning of the second session of the parliament on 12 November 1455, it was given out that the King had suffered a mental relapse and the Commons persistently pressed the Lords to recognize York as Protector once again, they evidently preferred to do so through a member of York's own council, the Shropshire lawyer, William Burley (Speaker in 1445), rather than through Wenlock, their accredited Speaker. It is possible that Wenlock, by no means as yet a Yorkist, had none the less himself come to favour a policy of accommodation and compromise, one such as Margaret of Anjou saw no reason to follow, and especially in her son's interest, every reason to obstruct.

The second session of the parliament lasted from 12 November

---

[1] *Catalogue of the Manuscripts of St George's Chapel, Windsor*, ed. J. N. Dalton, pp. 200, 345.

to 13 December 1455. In view of the King's alleged mental lapse and the disturbed state of the country (especially in the south-west where again there was armed conflict between the Earl of Devon and Lord Bonville), the Lords gave in to the pressure from the Lower House and approved York's appointment as Protector, his authority being formally recognized in a commission under the Great Seal on 19 November. Not long after Christmas Henry VI was deemed to have recovered from his breakdown, and York's Protectorate formally ended on 25 February 1456. Parliament, which had continued its sessions on 14 January, sat on until 12 March when it was brought to a close, the chief contending parties being left by the dissolution in a state of uneasy equilibrium. The Commons had made no money-grant, and perhaps were never asked for one. Wenlock's individual part as Speaker in their proceedings lies beyond recovery. But, since sometime in the course of the next two years he became a member of the King's Council,[1] he could scarcely have done his reputation any harm. Certainly during the parliament itself he had done what he could for himself. The terms by which he was to be repaid his large government loan of over £1,000 out of the customs-revenues of Southampton were excluded by the Commons themselves from the Resumption Act of this parliament, and that allowance was confirmed when, in the last session, two Acts were passed guaranteeing repayment to the merchants of the Staple at Calais of their advances of cash for the defence of the town. Not that these provisos did him much good in practice: three years later the debt was still as before. It was not long afterwards that Wenlock transferred his support to the Yorkists.

For three and a half years following the parliament of 1455–6 the state of tension and unsettlement between the Yorkist and Lancastrian parties continued. Archbishop Bourchier retained the Great Seal, and so did his brother the Treasurership, but only until October 1456. Queen Margaret, who was now the leading spirit of the Court faction, had gained such ground since the beginning of the year that she could secure the dismissal of the Bourchiers: the signal perhaps for the 'mediating policy', which they and their half-brother, Buckingham, represented, to be abandoned in favour of a policy of open and determined opposition to the Duke of York. There were those, even at Court, who had genuine misgivings about this tougher Lancastrian policy, for not all who shared this uneasiness

---

[1] For remarks on Wenlock's career after his Speakership, see the Appendix.

were Yorkists; a policy of accommodation was, for one thing, nearest the King's own mind. Efforts were made now and then to reconcile the parties, for example, in the 'love-day' on 25 March 1458, when the chief antagonists went in procession together to St Paul's, in an attempt to suggest that the feuds set going or enflamed by the first battle of St Albans were at an end. But such a policy of appeasement was only spasmodic and in any case had alternated with inept provocation.

By 1459 the prolonged political crisis was working towards an explosion. Not since early in 1456 had parliament met, so that emotions had been denied any outlet by the usual constitutional channel. Both parties spent the year preparing for a 'show-down'. The open breach came in the early autumn, when the Earl of Salisbury led a large Yorkist force down from Middleham (in Wensleydale) and across the northern Midlands so as to join up with York and Warwick at Ludlow; intercepted by the Lancastrian levies under Lord Audley at Bloreheath (Staffs.) on 23 September, Salisbury won the day and got through to the March. The Yorkists' intention was probably to compel an audience with the King as they had done over four years before at St Albans. But the plan misfired: a royal army, centred at Coleshill, moved westwards against the numerically inferior Yorkist forces, and on 12 October at Ludford, in front of Ludlow, after no more than a skirmish, the Yorkist leaders dispersed. York himself fled to Ireland, his eldest son Edward and the Nevilles to Calais. Three days before the Rout of Ludford, perhaps in an effort to sow doubt among their opponents, or to anticipate a demand, the Lancastrian administration had already issued writs summoning parliament to meet in six weeks' time (on 20 November) at Coventry, a favourite resort of the royal family during these difficult years and frequently the scene of meetings of the Lancastrian Council.

It seems fairly clear that attempts were made to pack the Coventry parliament in the royalist interest. In some cases only writs of Privy Seal had been sent to the sheriffs; and the normal method of election was not always followed. The surviving parliamentary returns are far from complete. Even so, it is safe to assume that most members of the Lower House were either in sympathy with the King or prudent enough to dissemble any feelings of friendship towards his enemies. Certainly, the Speaker chosen by the Commons, one of Henry VI's own intimate retinue, cannot have been other than acceptable to the King: Thomas Tresham of Sywell and Rushton in

s

Northamptonshire,[1] the son and heir of the former Speaker, William Tresham, who had been murdered in 1450.

In its earlier stages, Thomas Tresham's career at Court had clearly been shaped and assisted by his father, who had risen to be Chancellor of the Duchy of Lancaster. It was doubtless William Tresham who arranged Thomas's marriage with Margaret, sister of William Lord Zouche of Harringworth (and widow of Edmund Lenthall).[2] From 1443 father and son shared the stewardship of all the Duchy of Lancaster estates in Northamptonshire, Huntingdonshire, Bedfordshire, and Buckinghamshire (apart from the lands of the honour of Leicester), Thomas administering the office by himself after his father's death until replaced by Lord Hastings at Edward IV's accession. The two Treshams had also shared grants in survivorship of certain royal annuities (one of £40 made payable in 1445 from the manor of King's Cliffe, another of equal value granted in 1446 and charged on the revenues of the Receiver-General of the Duchy of Lancaster). Thomas had grown up from boyhood in Henry VI's service at Court and by 1446 was one of the *scutiferi aule et camere Regis*, continuing as such until promoted to be an usher of the Chamber sometime before 1455. That he had been going with his father to meet the Duke of York in September 1450—he was wounded in the ambush in which William was killed—clearly was never held against him, and during the 'fifties his influence at Court grew steadily. Thomas followed his father as Chancellor for the feoffees of the Duchy of Lancaster estates set aside to assure fulfilment of the King's will.[3] In January 1454, during Henry VI's first bout of insanity, he joined with the King's secretary, an esquire of the body, and another usher of the Chamber, in drawing up a petition to parliament asking for a proper garrison to be established under their control at Windsor for the protection of the King and the infant Edward of Lancaster.[4] Nothing came of the bill, but Tresham was clearly no friend of York's. There can be little doubt that he was with the royal forces at the battle of St Albans in May 1455, for although he did not figure among those on whom (in the July parliament) the Yorkist lords fastened the blame for the battle, he was listed in a

---

[1] For references and a fuller discussion of Thomas Tresham's career, see my article, 'Sir Thomas Tresham, Knight', *Northamptonshire Past and Present*, vol. ii, no. 6 (1959), pp. 313–23.

[2] It was her niece, another Margaret de la Zouche, who was wife to William Catesby, Speaker in Richard III's only parliament.

[3] R. Somerville, op. cit., i. 211 (n. 4), 586.   [4] *Paston Letters*, ii. 296.

brief contemporary account among *the solecytouriz and causerys* [solicitors and causers] *of the feld takyng at Seynt Albonys.*[1]

Not a great deal is known of Thomas Tresham during the next two or three years. But he was sheriff of Cambridgeshire and Huntingdonshire in 1457–8 (an office he had held once before, in 1451–2) and in the following year (1458–9) was sheriff of Surrey and Sussex. In the autumn of 1459 the electoral returns to the Coventry parliament were made in his name for the county and boroughs of Surrey, but in Sussex only for the boroughs (because the county court here did not meet between the receipt of the writs and the beginning of the parliament). In the course of his career Thomas had already sat in four parliaments: for Buckinghamshire in 1447, for Huntingdonshire in the two parliaments of 1449,[2] and for Northamptonshire in 1453–4. Although the returns of 1459 have survived for none of these counties, it was probably Northamptonshire which elected him. Whichever it was, his being elected to parliament when sheriff was unstatutory and even against the tenour of the writs. It is not known for sure whether at this time Tresham was Controller of the King's Household, a post he was certainly holding when taken prisoner at the battle of Towton in March 1461; but, since the last discovered reference to his predecessor (Sir Richard Haryngton) falls no later than 1455, it is not improbable that Tresham was holding that office when Speaker.

What with irregular and rigged elections and the prestige recently won by them in the field, the Lancastrians had it all their own way in the meeting at Coventry. A single session of a month's duration (20 November–20 December) sufficed to register their superiority: parliament passed an Act of Attainder against the Yorkist leaders and their chief active supporters (including the two former Speakers, Oldhall and Wenlock); it agreed on a resumption of all royal grants enjoyed by those who had been up in arms against Henry VI at St Albans, Bloreheath and Ludford; moreover, the peers imposed upon themselves a fresh oath of allegiance to the King and undertook to guarantee the right of Prince Edward to inherit the throne. In the course of the session, the committee of feoffees for the King's will was remodelled, Speaker Tresham himself being now included (as his father once had been). There is no doubt that at Coventry he had

[1] Ibid., iii. 29.
[2] When elected to the two parliaments which met in 1449, Thomas Tresham was royal escheator in Northamptonshire and Rutland (serving from November 1448 to December 1449).

handled the Commons successfully: it was expressly for his great efforts (*grandes labores*) in the parliament as well as on account of some losses in the royal service that, at Northampton on 5 February 1460, he was given an annuity of £40 from lands and rents at Stamford and Grantham forfeited by the Duke of York.[1] Already, on the day after the parliamentary dissolution, Tresham had been put on a commission of array in Northamptonshire, part of a general plan to resist any Yorkist risings, and he continued to be busy in the work of penalizing the attainted rebels and suppressing their adherents, until it was all brought to an end by the troubles of the summer of 1460.[2]

Understandably, the Lancastrian government had not ceased to be apprehensive of the dangers of a revival of the rebel cause. With York himself dominating Ireland, and with his eldest son, the Earl of March, and the Earls of Salisbury and Warwick able to recuperate at Calais, there was ample cause for discomfort at Court. In fact, on 26 June 1460 the Earl of March and the Nevilles re-crossed the Channel. Landing at Sandwich, they soon found that Archbishop Bourchier was their friend. Moving up through Kent, where they had an ecstatic welcome, within a week they were entering London. On 10 July, the young Earl Edward and Warwick heavily defeated a disheartened Lancastrian army at Northampton. Here they captured the King, whom, virtually as a prisoner, they paraded in London on 16 July. Nine days later, Warwick's brother, George Neville, Bishop of Exeter, became Chancellor, and on 30 July writs went out summoning parliament to Westminster for 7 October. The royal Council now became largely Yorkist in composition, and, even before parliament met, the Yorkist lords were declared loyal.

The Commons' Speaker in this (in all but name) Yorkist parlia-

---

[1] See above, p. 111.

[2] In the next parliament (the one summoned after the Yorkist victory at Northampton in July 1460) Tresham was excluded from the committee of feoffees. He was also dropped from the commission of the peace for Northants upon which he had sat continuously since 1452. He was not with the Lancastrian army which defeated the Duke of York's forces at Wakefield on 30 December 1460 (when York was killed), but soon afterwards he joined Queen Margaret's army in the north-east, came south, and fought in the second battle of St Albans on 17 February 1461, when he was knighted by the young Prince Edward. Edward IV excluded him from his offer of a general pardon and put a price of £100 on his head. Now Controller of Henry VI's Household, he was taken prisoner at the battle of Towton. In the first of Edward's parliaments Tresham was attainted and sentenced to forfeiture of all his estates, most of which went to one of the ushers of the King's Chamber.

ment was a somewhat obscure and seemingly colourless lawyer, John Green of Widdington and Gosfield (Essex), who had only once before sat in parliament—in 1455–6. About ten years before he became Speaker, Green had married Edith, the daughter and heir of Thomas Rolf, serjeant-at-law, and widow of John Helion, Esquire, of Gosfield.[1] This marriage brought him possession of a number of estates, mainly in Essex, among them the manor of Hawkwoods in Sible Hedingham where his wife was the tenant of Henry Viscount Bourchier. Green himself already had connexions with the Bourchier family: by 1446 he had been associated with the viscount, the viscount's brother Thomas, then Bishop of Ely, and their half-brother, the Duke of Buckingham, as a feoffee (in the manor of Newhall) for Richard Alred (ex-Receiver-General of the Duchy of Lancaster), an interest which he still retained at the time of his Speakership.[2] And with time this link with the Bourchiers had become stronger: at the end of the 1455–6 parliament, when Viscount Bourchier was Treasurer of the Exchequer, Green was associated with the viscount's son Henry (among others) in a royal grant of the wardship of a Somersetshire heiress (Genevieve Hill of Spaxton), for which the patentees later paid £220 at the Exchequer;[3] and it was doubtless with the younger Henry Bourchier's approval that, in November 1460 (when the viscount was again Treasurer), Speaker Green (as he then was) superseded him in an Exchequer lease of the Duchy of Cornwall manor of Newport and the hamlet of Birchanger (Essex);[4] besides, under Edward IV, Green was a co-feoffee of other members of the Bourchier family in a number of Essex estates.[5] Even before his marriage (from 1448) Green was a J.P. in Essex, becoming a member of the *quorum* in 1453. In the meantime, in 1452, he had shared, with his brother William, a royal grant of the wardship of Bumpstead Helion (Essex), during the minority of his step-daughters who were the coheirs. In the following year they were deprived of this wardship in favour of Thomas Thorpe,[6] then Baron of the Exchequer and Speaker, but it would be hazardous, merely in the light of this *contretemps* and of John Green's election to the parliament which followed the Yorkist victory at St Albans in May

---

[1] *CPR, 1446–52*, 427.

[2] *Catalogue of Ancient Deeds*, iv. A 6996, A 7909, A 11888–9; v. A 13113, A 13118.

[3] *CPR, 1452–61*, 285.

[4] *CFR, 1454–61*, 288; *1461–71*, 14, 134, 152, 202.

[5] *CCR, 1461–8*, 66; *1468–76*, 12.

[6] *CFR, 1445–54*, 253; *CPR, 1452–61*, 144.

1455, to think of him as being, then, in any way hostile to the Court party. Not only were his friends the Bourchiers still politically uncommitted, but he himself continued to serve as a J.P. of the *quorum* in Essex. Moreover, it was in 1455 that he actually began to be employed as legal counsel by the Duchy of Lancaster (a capacity in which he was to serve quite continuously until 1466).[1] Besides, his brother William was a 'servant' of the King's Chamber. In the very eventful autumn of 1459 both brothers remained at least outwardly loyal: at the end of the Coventry parliament John was appointed a commissioner of array in Essex to resist any Yorkist risings, and in January 1460, for good service against the rebel lords, William was given the office of bailiff of the lordship of Ware (recently forfeited by the Earl of Salisbury). As late as 15 March John Green received a commission, addressed to him alone, to requisition horses for the Queen's use.[2] Two younger sons of Viscount Bourchier (John and Edward) had been among the Yorkist notables attainted in the Coventry parliament, but the viscount himself and his brother the archbishop had both attended and were among the lords who took the special oath of allegiance to Henry VI. In the early summer of 1460, however, these senior members of the family finally threw in their lot with the Yorkists. The viscount fought with them at Northampton and, on their return to London, was made Treasurer once again. It was perhaps only at the same time that John Green changed front.

The first session of what proved to be the last parliament of Henry VI's reign proper lasted from 7 October to 1 December 1460, and the second from 28 January to 3 February 1461. The most important item of business confronting parliament was the question of the claim to the royal title made by Richard of York on 10 October. A full fortnight passed before this claim was directly answered, but Henry VI then agreed to disinherit his son and allow to York and his heirs the reversion of the Crown. With this compromise York had to be content. The earlier session also saw the annulment, by the Commons' petition, of all the acts of the previous parliament, including its attainders. This general repeal, of course, allowed the appointment of a new committee of feoffees of those Duchy of Lancaster estates set aside for the administration of Henry VI's will, to replace the one created at Coventry. The new committee showed marked changes from the old: most important among the new set were the Yorkist Earls of Salisbury and Warwick and Viscount Bourchier;

---

[1] R. Somerville, op. cit., i. 454.   [2] *CPR, 1452-61*, 558, 585, 579.

its less influential members included Speaker Green.[1] So far as is known, Green played no part in the events which led to the establishment of the Yorkist dynasty in actual possession of the Crown early in the following year. But presumably his services as Speaker in 1460-1, his continued connexion with the Bourchiers, his kinship with Sir Thomas Montgomery of Faulkbourne (Essex), a knight of the Body and Carver to Edward IV who had married Green's step-daughter (Philippa Helion), his activity as legal counsel to the Duchy of Lancaster after its annexation to the Crown, all helped to ensure his retention of the modest position he had quietly built up for himself in the last decade of Lancastrian rule.[2]

Once more Protector, Richard of York had prorogued parliament on 1 December 1460. The duke had then moved northwards, ostensibly to restore the peace, in fact to put a stop to Lancastrian attacks on his own supporters and their property up in Yorkshire. Trapped by a Lancastrian army at Wakefield at Christmas, he fell in the fight there on 30 December, Salisbury, his brother-in-law, being beheaded at Pontefract on the following day. As soon as news of this Lancastrian success got through to the Queen in Scotland, she and her son came south, and at St Albans on 17 February 1461 her army defeated Warwick's forces and recovered possession of the person of Henry VI. The Lancastrians' mistake in failing to attack London allowed Edward, York's heir, and Warwick to enter the City, and here, on 4 March, Edward declared himself King. Losing no time, he followed after the Lancastrian army, which had now withdrawn towards the north, to bring it to battle. After a skirmish at Ferry-bridge (at the crossing of the Aire), on Palm Sunday (29 March) was fought the battle of Towton (just south of the crossing of the Wharfe at Tadcaster), and here the only Lancastrian army then in the field was enveloped in utter disaster. Henry VI and his Queen fled further northwards, eventually into Scotland, with a mere handful of Lancastrian survivors.

Most of the Speakers of the last decade had been caught up in this rapidly changing pattern of events. Thomas Thorpe, Speaker in 1453, was done to death on the day of the second battle of St Albans. (Escaping from his London prison and presumably making an effort to re-establish contact with the Queen, he had been caught by a mob of Londoners in Harringay Park.) Sir Thomas Charlton, Thorpe's successor as Speaker in 1454, was with Warwick at St

[1] *Rot. Parl.*, v. 387.
[2] For Green's career under Edward IV, see the Appendix.

Albans; here he was taken prisoner, only to be soon set free, probably after the battle of Towton. Sir John Wenlock, Speaker in 1455–6, commanded the Yorkist rear-guard at Ferrybridge and also fought at Towton. Thomas Tresham, Speaker at Coventry in 1459, was with the Lancastrian forces in their success at St Albans, where he was among those dubbed knights by the young Prince Edward; and, having subsequently had a price of £100 put on his head by Edward IV, he was taken prisoner at Towton Field. Sir William Oldhall, Speaker in 1450–1 and Richard of York's former Chamberlain, after being implicated in the troubles of 1459 and attainted at Coventry, had died in his bed a few weeks before his master. It is unlikely that Speaker Green was in any of these military engagements.

CHAPTER 10

Under the Yorkists

EDWARD IV's first parliament was summoned on 23 May 1461 to meet on 6 July. It was possible for the coronation to take place on 28 June, but writs had already gone out on 13 June postponing the meeting of parliament to 4 November. There had been a Scottish attack on Carlisle, and in any case the state of England as a whole was still very disordered. Edward, however, used the summer profitably in armed progresses to the south and west; and, when he met his first parliament, only Harlech, of all the fortresses in the kingdom, still held out for the ex-King. No immediate danger threatened, and in parliament all went well. Its main agenda was to recognize Edward's right to the throne as entirely valid by pedigree, to stigmatize the Lancastrian régime as usurpative, to annul the recent compromise under which Henry VI had been entitled to wear the crown for life, to attaint the Lancastrians who had fought against the Yorkist claim, and to confirm the reversal of the attainders enacted at Coventry two years before. All this was done, and the session closed on 21 December. This was virtually the end of the parliament. For, although it met again on 6 May 1462, the King and many of the Yorkist lords were absent, and Archbishop Bourchier instantly dissolved it.

That the Commons had played their part to the King's complete satisfaction was evidently to some extent attributable to their Speaker, Sir James Strangeways.[1] For three weeks after the dissolution Edward ordered 200 marks to be given him as a present, expressly for his 'diligence' as Speaker. Strangeways' personal fidelity to the Yorkist cause stood in no doubt. It had long been prepared for by his earlier career. His family, which had its roots in Manchester, had been of no significance until the beginning of the century, when one and another of its members began to acquire positions of some administrative importance in the service of the Crown (mainly in Wales and Ireland). Sir James's father was the first, however, really to escape the ruck: a lawyer, he became a

[1] For references and a fuller account of Strangeways' life, see my article, 'Sir James Strangeways of West Harlsey and Whorlton', *The Yorkshire Archaeological Journal*, vol. xxxix (1958), pp. 455–82.

puisne judge in the Court of Common Pleas in 1426 and held this office until his death in 1442, acting in the meantime as Justice of North Wales; he was also senior justice in the courts of the Durham palatinate during the episcopate of his friend, Thomas Langley, whose feudal tenant he became in the manor belonging to the Durham see at West Harlsey in north Yorkshire.[1] Such property (including West Harlsey) as Justice Strangeways passed on to Sir James as his heir only supplemented the more extensive and far richer estates which the latter had already held from 1431, ever since his marriage into the long-established baronial family of Darcy. The Speaker's wife, Elizabeth, was one of the two daughters of Philip Darcy who shared between them the inheritance of their grand-father, John Lord Darcy, who had died in 1411. Some of these Darcy lands were in Northumberland, Nottinghamshire, Derby-shire, Leicestershire, and eastern Ireland; but their main concentra-tion was in the North Riding of Yorkshire, between Northallerton and the mouth of the Tees, and included Whorlton castle (the old home of the Menilles). The Speaker's marriage into the Darcy family can only have added considerably to whatever respect he com-manded as the son of a royal judge. His wife's family, especially through its long-lived women-folk, was well and advantageously connected: Lady Strangeways' grandmother, Lord Darcy's widow, had married Sir Thomas Swynford, half-brother to Cardinal Beaufort, the Duke of Exeter, and the Countess of Westmorland; her mother, who was a daughter of Henry Lord FitzHugh of Ravensworth, by two later marriages had other children, among them Sir Richard Tunstall, one of Henry VI's carvers and a Lancastrian die-hard under Edward IV, and Margaret de Bromflete, whose husband was the savage Lancastrian partisan, John Lord Clifford ('the Butcher').[2]

Sir James Strangeways' own chief personal association was with the head of the younger branch of the great Neville family, Richard, Earl of Salisbury, with whom his father had long been connected. In the royal records alone, there is no shortage of evidence from 1440

[1] Justice Strangeways was one of Cardinal Langley's executors.

[2] The grandmother of the Speaker's wife survived until June 1454, the Speaker's mother-in-law (then Baroness Vessy) until September 1457. Only after their death did Sir James and his wife come into a half-share of the dower estates of these ladies, the other part of the Darcy inheritance having already been divided between the Speaker's wife and her sister in 1431. Lands apart, this included the patronage of the priory of Austin canons at Guisborough, one of the very richest of the Yorkshire monasteries.

onwards[1] proving the strength of this attachment, which culminated in Salisbury appointing Sir James Strangeways as one of his executors in May 1459. The Speaker was also well known to other members of the Neville family: as feoffee-to-uses, he served the earl's brother George (Lord Latimer) and the earl's son and heir, Richard, Earl of Warwick; his own eldest son, Richard, married the daughter of Salisbury's next younger brother, William, whom Edward IV raised to the Earldom of Kent in 1461 for his services at Towton.[2] It appears unlikely that Strangeways was conspicuously involved with the Nevilles in the Yorkist revolt of 1455.[3] At least he continued to be employed[4] by the Lancastrian government in a variety of commissions, as a J.P. in the North Riding, occasionally in the East Riding, too, and also, even frequently, as an envoy to help negotiate renewals of the truce with Scotland and to deal with its infractions.

Although made one of Salisbury's executors in May 1459, Strangeways' absence from the list of those attainted at Coventry in November following makes it clear that he had not in the meantime accompanied the earl on the march from Wensleydale to Ludlow

[1] On 29 November 1440 the future Speaker was one of a group of the Earl of Salisbury's clientele granted by Henry VI almost all the lands and rents which at the time of her death (a fortnight before) had belonged to the earl's mother, the Countess of Westmorland. The grantees were to hold to Salisbury's use. The most important part of this property was the Neville estates in Yorkshire, centred on Middleham and Sheriff Hutton, which the countess had held (by right of jointure) since 1425. In 1454 Strangeways was one of Salisbury's feoffees in the lordship of Mold and Moldsdale (Flintshire) and in the following year in the nearby lordship of Hawarden.

[2] One of the Speaker's daughters (Elizabeth) married a kinsman of the Nevilles, Marmaduke Clervaulx, a great-great-grandson of John Lord Neville of Raby.

[3] Strangeways attended the parliamentary election for Yorkshire on 23 June 1455, a month after the battle of St Albans. It looks as if he had kept out of the Yorkist 'show-down' and stayed up in the north. (He would probably have gone on with Salisbury to London, had he been among his retinue at St Albans.)

[4] It was very likely as a retainer of Salisbury's that Strangeways was appointed by the King's Council in August 1450 to be a member of the committee charged to act as receivers and treasurers of the proceeds of the graduated income-tax recently voted by parliament (at Leicester) and of loans to the Crown, all of which they were to spend on the wages of retinues engaged in defence. The link with Salisbury probably also accounts for the suggestion, made in the last session of the parliament of 1453-4, that Strangeways should act as a contact with the merchants of the Calais Staple, from whom the Duke of York required guarantees for controlling the Dover Straits before he would undertake the military administration of Calais. (The Earl of Salisbury was Chancellor at the time of this proposal.)

which resulted first in the victory at Bloreheath and then in the Rout of Ludford, when the earl and his son Warwick had to seek safety across the Channel. In fact, as late as March 1460 Strangeways was confirmed by the Lancastrian administration in his commission of the peace in the North Riding.[1] He was removed, however, on the very eve of the invasion from Calais, led by the Earls of March, Salisbury and Warwick, which culminated in their capture of London and the victory at Northampton. Strangeways had twice been sheriff of Yorkshire (in 1445–6 and 1452–3), but only once knight of the shire (in 1449). Now, to the virtually Yorkist parliament of October 1460, he was returned for Yorkshire, along with his sister's husband, Sir Thomas Montford. He had just been reappointed a J.P. in the North Riding and also associated with Richard of York and his Neville supporters in a commission to arrest and imprison their opponents in south Yorkshire, including some of the gentry of the area and a number of artisans at York who (to use the technical language of the patent) had uttered falsehoods and promoted discord among the magnates, so contravening the Statute of *Scandalum Magnatum*. A week after the end of this parliament, again as a royal commissioner, Strangeways went north with York and Salisbury to suppress the Lancastrian lords, and so was in the thick of it at Wakefield when York was killed and Salisbury led off to execution at Pontefract. There was in fact a rumour current in the south that Strangeways himself was either killed or captured. Captured he may well have been. Assuming this and that he did not escape, he must have been set free after the destruction of the Lancastrian army at Towton: when Edward IV was at York on 10 May 1461 Strangeways was made a J.P. in the West Riding and, together with his eldest son, in the North Riding too. Sir James was put on the commission to deal with Dr John Morton, the ex-Chancellor of the Duchy of Cornwall, who had recently been arrested and charged at York with treasonable offences; he was also included (along with his son and Sir John Conyers, his brother-in-law) in a commission to imprison Lancastrian rebels in the North Riding. It was Warwick who headed the commission.

With Salisbury dead, it is possible that Strangeways had already attached himself more closely to the Kingmaker. The latter, in 1463,

---

[1] On 25 July 1459 Strangeways was appointed to treat for a further truce with Scotland, but he was not, even then, included among those members of the commission authorized to deal with the Scots *de certis secretis materiis*. Nor was he appointed to the next embassy (at the end of October 1459).

was to make him one of his feoffees (for the payment of his debts and to administer his will) and, in 1465, appoint him his deputy-steward in the Duchy of Lancaster lordship of Pickering.

Although no electoral returns from Yorkshire in 1461 have survived, there can be no doubt that it was for this county that Strangeways was re-elected to Edward IV's first parliament. In it, as Speaker, he was to do both the new King and himself much good service.[1] His royal reward of 200 marks has already been noticed. But during the parliament itself he had already taken advantage of his office to get the backing of the Commons for a petition for the recovery of certain of his late wife's[2] family's Irish estates which had been recently forfeited by their local lessee: Strangeways was able to plead that the reason why he and his brother-in-law (Sir John Conyers) had not themselves safeguarded their rights was that they had been *dryven to such streitnesse for the feith, trouth, and service that they had born and doon to his Highnes and to the noble Prynce his Fader, and to other true Lordes of his blode.*[3]

For over three years after Edward IV's seizure of the throne, the north of England remained unpacified. Indeed, for the greater part of this time, the Lancastrians, assisted by their Scottish allies, managed to occupy the most important of the Northumbrian castles. None the less, the Earl of Warwick's foreign diplomacy slowly suffocated all Lancastrian hopes of recovery: Burgundy was kept friendly to Edward IV; Louis XI of France was made to waver in his inclination to help his Lancastrian cousins; the pro-Lancastrian party in Scotland cooled off. In August 1463 Queen Margaret had to abandon Scotland for a refuge first in Flanders and then in France. Earlier in this year in which Margaret took so significant a step, Edward IV had already met his second parliament.

First summoning parliament to meet at York in February 1463, then at Leicester a month later, Edward finally called it to Westminster for 29 April. At the same time he cancelled all previous elections on the ground that in many shires they had been held irregularly. Whether this was really the case, or whether the first elected members themselves had been found by the government to be unsatisfactory in some way, we cannot say. But the King had no reason to be dissatisfied with what this parliament did for him when

[1] See above, pp. 80–1, 93.
[2] Sir James's first wife, Elizabeth Darcy, had died sometime between June 1459 and the beginning of this parliament of 1461.
[3] *Rot. Parl.*, v. 485.

once it met; and in fact he withheld its dissolution for nearly two years, although during this time over a twelvemonth went by without a proper session being held. In the first session, which lasted from 29 April until 17 June 1463, the Commons were prevailed upon to grant an 'aid' of £37,000 for defence. Admittedly, on the single day of the next session (4 November 1463) they asked not only that £6,000 of this amount should be remitted (a reversion to later Lancastrian practice), but also that the levy of half of the now truncated grant should be postponed. None the less, the tax was still left payable within a year. Parliament was then immediately adjourned to meet in February 1464, at York. Here, in the king's absence, it was subjected to three further successive postponements (in February, May, and November) and so came to hold its last, but only second normal, session at Westminster between 21 January and 28 March 1465. This final meeting saw the passage of an Act of Attainder against recent rebels, and parliament also now adopted an Act of Resumption which did not, however, apply to grants of Lancastrian forfeitures and contained many other exemptions. Most important of all, it was now that the Commons granted the wool-subsidy and tunnage and poundage to Edward IV for life, as they had previously done to Richard II in 1398, to Henry V in 1415, and to Henry VI in 1453. Their Speaker in this long drawn-out and often prorogued parliament was John Say, knight of the shire for Hertfordshire, who is unique among the Speakers of this period in serving in both Lancastrian and Yorkist parliaments.[1]

When last he had been Speaker, in 1449, Say was an Esquire of the Body to Henry VI. In September 1450 (when ex-Speaker Tresham was murdered) he became Chancellor of the Duchy of Lancaster and also of the County Palatine and, although his banishment from Court was shortly afterwards demanded by the Commons, had no difficulty in continuing to retain this combination of offices. In April 1454 he joined the King's Council.[2] Still an Esquire of the Body, he was with Henry VI at Kilburn on 21 May 1455, the eve of the first battle of St Albans, when he presented the King with the letter sent by the Yorkist rebel leaders *via* Archbishop Bourchier, the Chancel-

---

[1] See above, pp. 231-4. For references and further details of Say's career, since his previous Speakership and under Edward IV, see my article, 'Sir John Say of Broxbourne', *East Herts. Archaeological Society Transactions*, vol. xiv, part 1, pp. 25-41.

[2] At the time of his appointment as a royal councillor, he was sitting as M.P. for Herts. in the parliament of 1453-4.

lor. It is quite possible that on this occasion Say was acting as a
messenger from Bourchier, with whose family he was already connected (through the marriage of his stepdaughter and ward to the
archbishop's nephew).

It was through his relationship with the Bourchiers that Say
profited rather than lost by the Yorkist success at St Albans. It was
only a week after the battle that the Chancellor's elder brother,
Henry Viscount Bourchier (brother-in-law to the Duke of York),
was made Treasurer; and probably immediately, certainly before 15
July following, John Say became his Clerk in the Exchequer (*alias*
Under-Treasurer), an office which he held until the autumn of 1456
when the viscount was replaced by the Earl of Shrewsbury. (It is
worth noting here and now that Say owed each of his several
occupations of the Under-Treasurership of the Exchequer—in
1455-6, 1460-4, and 1475-8—to this attachment to Henry Bourchier.)
Meanwhile, he had still retained his Duchy of Lancaster offices.
Indeed, it cannot be doubted that in the last unquiet years of Lancastrian rule Say and his family remained in favour at Court: in 1457
he and his son Thomas were together granted (in survivorship) the
office of Coroner of the Marshalsea of the Household (of which
John had had the reversion since 1444); in the same year his brother
William, Dean of the King's Chapel, was preferred to the Deanship
of St Paul's; in 1458 John himself was still active as a member of
the royal Council; and in December 1459 he profited from the suppression of the recent Yorkist rebellion to the extent of being granted
for life the stewardship of certain lordships in Hertfordshire and
Essex forfeited by the Duke of York and the Earl of Salisbury.[1]
None the less, in August 1460, by which time (after the battle of
Northampton) the Yorkists were dominating the Council, Say was
still a member of it. It is clear that he did not intend to play the part
of a Lancastrian die-hard and was prepared, if need be, to follow the
Bourchiers into the Yorkist fold. The primate had welcomed the
Yorkist magnates back from Calais. The viscount had fought with
them at Northampton and shortly afterwards been made Treasurer
once again. Very likely there and then, Say was re-appointed as

[1] In view of this grant and John Say's undisturbed occupation of the Chancellorship of the Duchy of Lancaster, it is difficult to account for the exclusion
of him and his brother William from the committee of feoffees in the duchy
estates set aside for the fulfilment of Henry VI's will, when this committee
underwent a considerable reshaping by an act of the Coventry parliament. The
next parliament (of October 1460) saw them both re-established by a new
settlement.

Under-Treasurer; certainly by February 1461 he was back in office
at the Exchequer. Both he and the viscount were re-appointed at
Edward IV's accession.

John Say's conversion to the Yorkist cause was now complete,
and he found no difficulty in submitting to the new compulsions and
living down his Lancastrian past. He continued as Under-Treasurer
under Henry Bourchier (now created Earl of Essex) until April
1462, under the Earl of Worcester until June 1463, and then under
Lord Grey of Ruthin, remaining in office until Easter 1464. In the
meantime, from the beginning of his reign, Edward IV had retained
him as a member of his Council, and on 5 June 1461 he re-appointed
him for life as Chancellor of the Duchy of Lancaster and on 16 June
as Chancellor of the County Palatine as well; Say was still a royal
councillor in 1468 and kept his Duchy offices uninterruptedly for the
first ten years of Edward's reign (until June 1471). That John Say
had early won the King's own personal confidence is made clear by
the terms of a letter written to him from Bristol on 9 September 1461,
possibly by the Earl of Essex: the writer informed him that the King
*maketh grete bostes of you for the truest and the feithfullest man that any
christen Prince may have, of the whiche I am right glad and joyeux that ye
have soo borne you.*

Certainly, the royal rewards John Say continued to receive were
worth coming by. In fact, less than three weeks after the sending of
this Bristol letter, he was paid 100 marks at the Lower Exchequer as a
special recompense for working out of term as Under-Treasurer on
the collection of a clerical tenth; in May 1462 he got another 50
marks for 'overtime'; a year later (in the course of the first session of
the parliament in which he acted as Speaker) he was granted 200
marks as a special reward for working in the Exchequer on different
occasions *in tempore curie* and in vacation, and for pushing ahead with
searches and scrutinies on the Treasurer's behalf; and only six weeks
later, a few days after the parliamentary session, he was given an
Exchequer assignment of £200 for all his solicitude since the beginning of the reign, as Under-Treasurer and more recently as Speaker.[1]
Say sometimes made considerable loans to the Crown (amounting
to about £500 in the first two years of the reign). But, as Under-
Treasurer, he seems to have had little trouble in getting quick re-

---

[1] On 23 March 1463, hardly a month before the parliament in which he was to
act as Speaker, John Say had also been paid £4 for men and horses hired in the
previous December to help him take Exchequer supplies of cash to Durham
during Edward IV's northern campaign.

payment. And, without mention of pickings on the side, official salaries and royal bonuses were coming in all the time. It is not known that Say received any further financial recognition of his diligence in the Speaker's office. In 1463 and throughout 1464, however, he was in regular receipt of his fee of £40 a year as a royal councillor, and in November 1464 the Exchequer was authorized to pay the fee annually as long as he remained a councillor. At Easter 1464 (during the long interval between the two proper sessions of the parliament in which he was Speaker) Say was replaced as Under-Treasurer by an auditor of long-standing in the department (Hugh Fenn). But, obviously, no adverse political meaning should be read into this supersession: when, three days before the coronation of Elizabeth Wydeville (on the Whitsunday following the dissolution of the 1463–5 parliament), the King created nearly fifty Knights of the Bath, John Say was among the few officials singled out for this honour; and, on 16 August next, he was re-appointed Chancellor of the Duchy and in the County Palatine of Lancaster, with a readjustment of his fees of office presumably resulting from his new rank. Only a month or so before this, his old master, Henry of Windsor, on the run in the north since the great Lancastrian defeat at Hexham (May 1464), had been arrested near Clitheroe (Lancs.), brought to London, and lodged in the Tower.

By this time Say was so risen in influence as to have become a member of a large number of committees of feoffees-to-uses, some of them created by members of the nobility with considerable interest at the Yorkist Court. These included Lord Dinham and even Edward IV's eldest sister, Anne, wife of the attainted Lancastrian peer, Henry Holland, Duke of Exeter, whose daughter in 1466 was to marry Thomas Grey, the Queen's son by her first marriage.[1] It is possible that Say was personally known to Queen Elizabeth herself. Certainly, he had long known her parents, Richard Wydeville and Jacquetta (of Luxembourg), Dowager Duchess of Bedford, who as far back as 1449, during Say's first Speakership, had ordered their receiver in Cambridgeshire to pay him an annual rent of 10 marks. Whether this connexion had been kept up in the meantime is doubtful. For the Wydevilles had been ardent Lancastrians until, with Edward's recognition of his secret marriage to their daughter, they

---

[1] In 1467 Say was also a feoffee of John Young, a brother of Thomas Young (Justice of the Common Bench) and then Mayor of London. In 1468 he was one of the trustees of Ralph Lord Sudeley in estates in Derbyshire, Nottinghamshire, and Rutland.

T

fast became even dangerously eminent members of the Yorkist Court, hostile to, and hated by, many of the Yorkist old-guard, especially the great Earl of Warwick. Regarding the Wydevilles, Say's friends, the Bourchiers, were as usual prepared to re-insure against all eventualities: the Earl of Essex's eldest son married one of the Queen's numerous sisters, and his great-nephew, the young Duke of Buckingham, another. It was along with the Queen's father, Earl Rivers (Treasurer since March 1466), that Sir John Say was made a member of the royal embassy appointed in January 1467 to treat with commissaries of Duke Philip of Burgundy for a truce and also *de intercursu mercandisarum*. This mission was all part of Edward IV's scheme for cultivating friendship with Burgundy, which again helped to alienate the Earl of Warwick, who preferred an alliance with Louis XI.

It was in an atmosphere of growing internal disunity and tension that, on 3 June 1467 at Westminster, the King met his third parliament, in which Sir John Say, still Chancellor of the Duchy of Lancaster and a member of the royal Council, was re-elected Speaker. Evidently satisfied with the constitution of the Lower House, Edward broadly used the stratagem adopted in the previous parliament: a short session from 3 June until 1 July was followed by two prorogations (at Reading on 6 November 1467 and 5 May 1468), parliament meeting once again at Westminster for another short session, between 12 May and 7 June 1468, after which it was dissolved. At the very beginning of the first session came a reminder that the breach between the Nevilles and the King was steadily widening: George Neville, now for two years Archbishop of York and Chancellor for the past seven, did not officiate at the opening of parliament; and five days later he was deprived of the Great Seal, giving way to the then Keeper of the Privy Seal, Bishop Stillington of Bath and Wells. In this 1467 meeting, no grant of funds was demanded. In fact, the King took upon himself to inform the Commons that, if he could manage, he intended to live of his own; it was to this end that parliament's chief financial item of business was another Resumption Act, more comprehensive than the last. The session of 1468, however, opened with an announcement that Edward intended to renew the war with France; and in less than four weeks the Commons responded with a grant of two tenths and fifteenths (payable by instalments in two years and minus £12,000, the usual rebate). Friendship with Burgundy was cemented by the marriage of the King's sister Margaret and the young Duke Charles.

An offensive alliance with Brittany was also concluded; but, although a Breton expedition was prepared, nothing came of this pact. The parliamentary grants none the less continued to be collected. Say's reward for his labours as Speaker had meantime been substantial: a Privy Seal warrant had authorized the Exchequer to pay him £200.[1]

Seemingly not until the summer of 1469 did Edward IV realize the full extent of the Nevilles' treachery and the wide range of disaffection of which the Earl of Warwick especially was the centre. Warwick had instigated Lancastrian movements in the autumn and winter of 1468, which, though they failed, could not be laid at his door. But then, in July 1469, when at Calais he had married his daughter Isabel to the Duke of Clarence, the King's next younger brother, and had incited his kinsmen and friends in Yorkshire to revolt, Warwick threw off the mask. He returned to England, determined to bring down the Wydevilles and restore himself to power. Despite the rebel victory at Edgecote (26 July), the execution of the Queen's father, one of her brothers, and the Earls of Pembroke and Devon, and the capture of the King (who was carried off and held for a time in the Neville stronghold at Middleham in Wensleydale), Warwick failed to re-establish himself. His weakness in the country at large is particularly suggested by his cancellation of a parliament (summoned by his instructions on 10 August) a fortnight before it was due to meet at York on 22 September. But Warwick continued to intrigue and, with Clarence, encouraged those further disturbances in Lincolnshire which the King crushed near Stamford on 12 March 1470 in the 'battle' of Lose Coat Field. Hopelessly compromised and unable to rouse sufficient support, Warwick and his son-in-law a month later fled the country and made for Calais. Refused entry by Lord Wenlock, Warwick sought safety in France. At Angers, with Louis XI's enthusiastic support, he entered an unholy alliance with the exiled Lancastrian Queen, offering to effect the restoration of Henry VI in return for the marriage of Prince Edward, the Lancastrian heir, to his second daughter, Anne. Within three months Warwick and Clarence had returned to England, Edward IV had fled to Flanders, and Henry VI was set at liberty. On 6 October the

[1] In the meantime, in July 1467, Say had been granted (for 100 marks, payable in the Exchequer) the wardship and marriage of the heiress of Walter Raleigh, a Devonshire lawyer. When, during the parliamentary session of 1468, a commission of oyer and terminer was set up at the Commons' request to deal with the Keeper of the Exchange and one of the governors of the Tower Mint for overcharging for coining and for devaluing the silver currency, Speaker Say was one of the Commons' nominees included in the commission.

Readeption began. Three days later Warwick's brother, the northern primate, returned to office as Chancellor. On 13 October, St Edward's Day, Henry was re-crowned. Two days afterwards, parliament was summoned to meet on 26 November.

This parliament of the Readeption sat both before and after Christmas 1470. No parliament-roll has survived. But the parliament is known to have declared Edward IV a usurper, reversed the acts of his parliaments, attainted him and his supporters, confirmed the settlement of Angers by entailing the Crown on Henry and his male heirs with remainder to the Duke of Clarence and his, and approved the appointment of Warwick and Clarence as Lieutenants of the realm. It was seemingly intended that Sir Thomas Tresham, Speaker at Coventry in 1459, should lead the Commons once again, and it is very likely that he did. The business of the parliament being what it was, the rôle can only have been congenial.

It is true, as Tresham had been at pains to point out in a petition he preferred when sitting for Northamptonshire in the parliament of 1467–8, that his loyalty to Henry VI had formerly been tempered by discretion. This petition alleged that he had declined to join the Lancastrian army which defeated the Yorkists at Wakefield in December 1460 when Richard of York was killed; that, although he had fought in the second battle of St Albans and at Towton (where he was taken prisoner), this was because, brought up in Henry's service since youth and being then Controller of his Household, he had had no option; and that after Towton he had been at no *journey or felde* against Edward IV, had come to understand his *title roiall*, and had never left England as some hardened Lancastrians had done. But his attempt to secure rehabilitation had proved a slow, disappointing, and finally quite unsuccessful business: although he had been given a general pardon in 1464 and his petition of 1467 for the annulment of his attainder had received Edward's assent, he failed to achieve a complete restitution of his estates and remained heavily encumbered with debt.[1] As a result, he had dabbled in treason and, following disclosures by the Earl of Oxford during imprisonment, had himself been put in the Tower in November 1468. There he was

---

[1] In his petition of 1467 Tresham said that since by the King's leave he had *bargayned* with the grantees of his lands to the extent of 2,000 marks and could therefore raise no further loans, he was so heavily in debt that he could not even marry off his son and heir. He was unable to offer land as surety for repayment of fresh credits. By May 1466 he had evidently recovered the manor of Broughton near Aylesbury (Bucks.), but was then compelled to mortgage it for £400 and in August 1468 had to confirm the conditional release.

kept without a trial, possibly even until Warwick's return in September 1470. That Tresham would support the Lancastrian Readeption can hardly have been in doubt. Having done so,[1] what steps he took to secure reinstatement in his former lands, to which the parliamentary repeal of the attainders of Edward IV's time now gave him a legal right, cannot be described. But whatever they may have been, they were not effectual for long.

In the middle of March 1471 Edward IV landed in the Humber and four weeks later, having already been joined by Clarence, was in London. Here Henry VI once more fell into his hands. At Barnet Field on 14 April he disposed of Warwick. Queen Margaret and her son, landing at Weymouth on the very same day, spent some time in the south-west raising an army. Edward cut it to pieces at Tewkesbury on 4 May. There, most of the leading Lancastrians, among them the Prince and the two former Speakers, Lord Wenlock and Sir Thomas Tresham, were either killed fighting or executed afterwards.[2] Less than three weeks later, when Edward had returned to London, Henry VI himself was done to death in the Tower.

In spite of a bitter quarrel between the King's brothers, Clarence and Gloucester, over the estates of the late Earl of Warwick (whose younger daughter, the widow of Prince Edward of Lancaster, Gloucester had soon married), in the summer of 1472 Edward IV and his Council considered the domestic situation safe enough to allow a meeting of parliament. This was the first Yorkist parliament for over four years. It came together at Westminster on 6 October, and the Commons straightaway chose as their Speaker a Cambridgeshire lawyer whose reputation was to be remarkably enhanced during the two and a half years over which the life of this parliament extended.

He was William Allington of Bottisham,[3] grandson of the man of

---

[1] On 5 November 1470 Tresham was granted by Henry VI for seven years (as from Michaelmas) the custody of the lands of the ancient honours of Peverell, Boulogne, and Haughley in Bucks., Northants., and Leics., together with the castle and honour of Huntingdon, in return for a yearly farm of £6 6s. 8d. payable in the Exchequer.

[2] For an account of Tresham's death, see the Appendix.

[3] For references and a more detailed account of this Speaker's career, see my paper, 'William Allington of Bottisham, Speaker in the Parliaments of 1472–5 and 1478', *Proceedings of the Cambridge Antiquarian Society*, vol. lii (1959), pp. 43–55. Allington's only known previous experience as M.P. had been in the parliament of 1467–8, when he sat for Plympton (Devon) with Thomas FitzWilliam, the lawyer who was to be Speaker in 1489–90.

the same name who had been Speaker when Henry VI was crowned more than forty years before. A younger son of the heiress to the Argentine lands, he had few estates of his own. All the same he was well connected among the gentry of the Fenlands: his elder brother John, formerly a retainer of Richard, Duke of York, had been Edward IV's first sheriff in Cambridgeshire and Huntingdonshire;[1] John Anstey of Stow-cum-Quy,[2] a lawyer and the bailiff of the Bishop of Ely's lordships in those counties, was his brother-in-law, and it was he who was sheriff in 1472 when Allington was returned for Cambridgeshire and their brother-in-law, William Tailard, for Huntingdonshire. Allington himself was connected with the Bishop of Ely, William Grey, who was a friend of Archbishop Bourchier (his predecessor in the diocese) and had been Treasurer of England for a short time in 1469–70.[3] First appointed J.P. in Cambridgeshire in 1457,[4] Allington had continuously been a member of the *quorum* from 1460 and a J.P. in Huntingdonshire as well since 1464, until dropped from both commissions at the Readeption.[5] That he was

[1] John Allington's wife, Mary, a daughter of Lawrence Cheyne of Fen Ditton and Long Stanton (Cambs.), was sister to the first wife of Sir John Say of Broxbourne, for whom John Allington acted as a feoffee.

[2] This John Anstey was M.P. for Cambridgeshire in 1445–6, 1450–1, 1461–2, and 1467–8, sheriff of Cambridgeshire and Huntingdonshire in 1471–2, and escheator in these counties in 1473–4. His tenure of the office of bishop's bailiff dated from 1453.

[3] On 6 May 1462 Allington was one of Bishop Grey's sponsors when the latter took a ten years' lease of the manor of Isleham, an entailed estate which had belonged to the posthumously attainted Lancastrian Earl of Northumberland and was now in the King's hands. It was a nephew of Bishop Grey, Sir Thomas Grey of Crawdon, who was Allington's fellow-M.P. for Cambridgeshire in 1472–5.

[4] When in July 1459 Allington was excluded from the Cambs. commission of the peace he was escheator in Cambs. and Huntingdonshire (acting from November 1458 to November 1459), and it was when the Lancastrians were still in complete control of the administration that, in February 1460, he was re-appointed a J.P. in the borough of Cambridge. At the same time he was no Lancastrian partisan. This is indicated by his appointment to the *quorum* of the county bench on 26 August 1460, shortly after the Yorkists' victory at Northampton had put the government of the country at their disposal. His earliest special royal commissions under Edward IV were entirely non-political. The share he took at Cambridge in 1462 in helping to straighten out business between the Crown and the colleges of Corpus Christi and King's (Henry VI's recent foundation) was plainly legal in character.

[5] As shortly before the Readeption as June 1470 Edmund Grey, Earl of Kent, whose eldest son had married into the family of Edward IV's Queen, made Allington one of his feoffees at Saxthorp (Norfolk).

trusted by Edward IV is made clear by his appointment on 11 May 1471 (a week after Tewkesbury Field) to act as a commissioner of array in both Cambridgeshire and Huntingdonshire, and two months later to enquire into disaffection in Essex, punish rebels, and take over their estates. He was also restored to the commission of the peace for the borough of Cambridge on 4 November 1471, and a week later was appointed controller of the wool-subsidy, tunnage and poundage at Bishop's Lynn, an office which he continued to hold until his death in 1479. He certainly fulfilled the King's confidence in his rôle of Speaker.

On the Feast of Edward the Confessor (13 October), five days after Edward IV had accepted him as Speaker, Allington declared some of the Commons' views in a great speech made in the King's presence in the Upper House. In it he congratulated the Queen upon her demeanour while the King was in exile, during which, in the Westminster sanctuary, she had been delivered of her first son, Edward (an event which, Allington insisted, had afforded *grete joy and suerte to this . . . londe*); he recommended, too, the conduct of the King's brothers, the Queen's brother (Earl Rivers), and Lord Hastings, those who had suffered from the Lancastrian restoration, and Bishop Alcock of Rochester, the acting-Chancellor; he also saw fit to praise Louis de Bruges, Seigneur de la Gruthuyse (who was now to be given the title of Earl of Winchester), for the great kindness which he had shown to the King in the Netherlands.

This Flemish nobleman was acting in England as the special agent of Charles the Bold in the negotiations which were now going forward for an Anglo-Burgundian offensive alliance against France. The Commons were pressed to grant funds for an aggressive war. At the same time they were urged not to let slip an opportunity both to lessen the danger at home from disbanded soldiers and to recover, in such favourable circumstances abroad, the King's ancestral duchies of Normandy and Guienne together with the French Crown. When the first session of this parliament ended on 30 November 1472, the Commons had already made a preliminary grant of the service of 13,000 archers for a year, at a daily rate of 6*d*. a man. Although, for their maintenance, a grant was made of a special tax of a tenth on all property and income, it was voted on condition that all should be repaid if an expedition had not set out by Michaelmas 1474.

During this session, too, parliament had ratified the titles of Prince of Wales and Earl of Chester, which had already (in June

1471) been conferred upon the infant Prince Edward. It had also approved his endowment with the Duchy of Cornwall (as from Michaelmas 1472). Among the provisos inserted in this latter Act was one for the Speaker himself, safeguarding any grant or office held by him in the duchy. Obviously, Allington's interest was already engaged in this important part of the appanage of the royal heir-apparent. And when, shortly after parliament met again after the Christmas recess (on 20 February 1473), a committee of twenty-five Tutors and Councillors was set up to act for the prince and control his estates in Wales, the Duchy of Cornwall, Cheshire, and Flintshire, until he reached the age of fourteen, William Allington was one of them. He was doubtless appointed because already a member of the prince's own council. It was with other members of this council that, only four days later, the Speaker was included in the commission of the peace for each of the English shires bordering upon Wales, it being intended that the young prince should establish a permanent household at Ludlow and continuously represent the royal authority in the Marches. An attempt was even to be made in the early spring to quell disturbances in this region, following a demand (by parliamentary petition) that the King should either go himself or send *grete myght and power*. Meanwhile, the second session of the parliament had witnessed an important financial arrangement with the Calais Staplers and also a grant, in addition to the special income-tax of the first session, of a subsidy of the usual kind (a tenth and fifteenth), payable at midsummer but on the same conditions as before.

When, after sitting for just two months, parliament was again adjourned on 8 April 1473, Allington accompanied Edward IV in his progress through the Midlands and along the Welsh border between May and September.[1] He took an active part in the judicial proceedings held *en route*, at Hereford being ordered by the King himself, in the presence of the jurors, to take the records of their indictments for delivery to the King's Bench, in order to prevent any covert acquittals. In the interim, on 5 July, along with John Sulyard, a Suffolk lawyer (then M.P. for Hindon) and another of the recently created members of the Prince of Wales's council, Allington had been appointed by Anthony Wydeville, Earl Rivers, the Queen's eldest brother and the Prince's Governor, to deputize for him in his

---

[1] On 5 December 1473 Allington was paid £40 in ready money at the Exchequer for his expenses *in attending upon us this somer season laste passed in the counties of Leicester, Notyngham, Derby, Stafford, Salop, Hereford, and the Marches of Wales*.

office of Chief Butler of England in the port of Ipswich. It looks as
though the Speaker was being drawn into the orbit of the Queen's
very influential family.

The third session of the parliament in which Allington continued
to act as Speaker began on 6 October 1473 and lasted for nearly ten
weeks. No progress had been made with the expedition to France,
and its main public business was to pass a Resumption Act and
approve of the treaty with the Hanseatic League recently concluded
at Utrecht. The session was almost over when, on 10 December,
Allington was re-appointed a J.P. in Cambridgeshire, and then, on
the very last day of the session (13 December) he was for the first
time given a commission of the peace in Suffolk, which he retained
until November 1475.

The proceedings of the fourth session of this parliament, which
started on 20 January 1474, were largely vitiated by uncertainty
about Burgundy's attitude to the proposed English attack on France.
And so the session ended in less than a fortnight. The fifth and sixth
sessions were virtually one session of ten weeks (9 May–18 July)
with a week's break for Whitsuntide. At length, after being shown
that the invasion of France would have to be put off for another
year, the Commons made a grant of a tenth and fifteenth (minus
£6,000, as usual), instead of the similar grant made in April 1473
(which had not yet been collected), plus a supplemental subsidy of
£51,147 to meet the full costs of the force of 13,000 archers originally
voted in November 1472, towards which no more than £31,410 had
so far been raised. The tax was to be collected in 1475, half at midsummer, half at Martinmas; and, although the proceeds were still
not to be turned over to the King until he was ready to cross to
France, the date by which he must do so in order to qualify for the
grant was extended to midsummer 1476. The new Chancellor,
Bishop Rotherham of Lincoln, before proroguing parliament, went
out of his way to thank the Commons for their generosity. And well
he might: 'The whole amount voted in the parliament was nearly
equal to four subsidies to be raised in three years; more than Edward
had received in all the previous years of his reign' (Ramsay). So,
supplied with the sinews of war, the King right away (before the end
of July 1474) committed himself with the Duke of Burgundy's
embassy in London to invade France next spring. The Speaker's
reward for his efforts was a promissory note for £100 down, and
another £100 when the parliament ended.

Evidently, being entirely satisfied with the character and attitude of the parliament, Edward IV was reluctant to dissolve it, and on 23 January 1475 it came together again for its seventh session. This, however, proved to be its last. The meetings were naturally much occupied with the problems of the impending campaign in France, the main financial business of the session being to convert the supplemental subsidy of the previous summer into a grant of a whole subsidy of a tenth and fifteenth and three-quarters of another. (Clearly there was a preference for subsidies of the normal kind.) But this done, the parliament broke up for the last time on 14 March 1475. Its financial provisions alone represented a very solid achievement on the Speaker's part. Allington's mere tenure of office for so extended a period was in itself a substantial contribution to the parliament's work: he had served for seven sessions, spread over two and a half years and totalling over three hundred days, and in the longest parliament ever, up to this time.

Nearly three years passed before Edward IV again met parliament. In the meantime, his long-intended invasion of France had begun early in July 1475 and ended, virtually without a blow being struck, at Picquigny (near Amiens) in the last week of August, when Edward agreed with Louis XI to leave France in return for a life-pension of about £10,000 a year and a payment of £15,000 down. Although the King had been badly let down by his Burgundian ally, this treaty was a shabby conclusion from both English and French points of view. Its financial provisions did, however, entail a welcome postscript to the acts of the 1472–5 parliament: the outstanding three-quarters of a subsidy, leviable at Martinmas 1475, were now remitted by the King.

There is little to record of 1476, but in the following year there came to a head all the disquiet that had long been generated by the King's brother George, Duke of Clarence; and Edward IV decided to end it by getting rid of him. In this he certainly had the backing of the Wydevilles and was probably supported by his other brother, Richard of Gloucester. On 20 November 1477 parliament was summoned to give the colour of judicial propriety to what was intended. William Allington, re-elected for Cambridgeshire (whose county-court happened to be the first to meet after the writs went out), was re-elected Speaker when parliament met on 16 January 1478.

Since his previous Speakership, what is known of Allington suggests his continued enjoyment of Edward IV's confidence and his even closer attachment to the Queen and her family. When, in anticipation of the King's absence abroad in 1475, a Great Council of Regency had been set up to exercise the royal authority under the nominal headship of the young Prince of Wales, Allington was appointed to be a member (along with other officials drawn from the prince's own personal council). After Edward IV came back from France, it is possible that Allington joined the royal Council proper. But if so, he still remained a member of the prince's administration. And then, in July 1477, the Queen had nominated him as one of her Justices-in-eyre in those royal forests granted her ten years before. In view of this growth of Allington's influence at Court, it is hardly surprising that in September 1477, following the death of his brother-in-law (John Anstey), Allington succeeded him (by a grant for life) in the office of bailiff of the liberty of the Bishop of Ely's lordships in Cambridgeshire and Huntingdonshire (outside the Isle of Ely).

There can be no doubt of Allington's own attitude towards the main business of the parliament of 1478: the passage of an Act of Attainder against the Duke of Clarence on the ground that he was incorrigibly faithless and threatened the tranquillity of the kingdom. The Commons approved the bill, and on 7 February Clarence was condemned before the High Steward. But then there was a delay, and it was the Commons who demanded execution of the sentence of death, their Speaker going up before the Lords to request that what was to be done should be done. It was, however, secretly and at the Tower that inside a fortnight Clarence was made away with. No taxation was demanded of the Commons, and a short session of six weeks ended with parliament's dissolution on 26 February. Allington's immediate reward was a Privy Seal warrant for £100 payable at the Exchequer. And he had not long to wait before his status as royal councillor was confirmed for life:[1] this was done in the following August, by which time he was also holding office as the Prince of Wales's Chancellor for the Duchy of Cornwall. He died in the following spring.[2]

After the session of 1478, it was almost five years before Edward IV saw fit to summon another parliament. There can be no question

---

[1] When appointed a member of the King's Council for life on 11 August 1478, he was also given, in consideration of his good service before and after 8 July, the income from a third of the manor of Bassingbourne and of the lands of the honour of Richmond, estates which Clarence had held by royal grant.

[2] He died on 16 May 1479, leaving no issue, so that his heir was his elder brother John, now aged sixty. William was buried at Bottisham where he had already made provision for a chantry in which prayers were to be made for Edward IV, Queen Elizabeth, his wife, and himself.

of his mastery in England during this time, although he was too conscious of the value of his popularity to exert control to the point of oppression. In foreign affairs, too, all was well, at least for a time. It was difficult not to take advantage of Scottish disunity under James III, and Anglo-Scottish relations deteriorated. So much so that, in retaliation against raids from across the Border, English armies twice invaded the northern kingdom, in 1481 and 1482; thanks to the Duke of Gloucester, Edinburgh was temporarily invested and Berwick-on-Tweed permanently recovered. The royal schemes regarding France, however, proved nothing like so successful in the end. Following the Peace of Picquigny, Edward's fear of losing his French pension and the stipulation that his eldest daughter should in due course marry the Dauphin had had the effect of stabilizing his relations with Louis XI. It was also a cause of satisfaction that this *entente* appeared to be reconcilable with Edward's friendship for Mary of Burgundy and her husband, Maximilian of Habsburg. But the hopeful prospect of an Anglo-French dynastic alliance had to be abandoned when, after the death of Mary of Burgundy, her daughter Margaret became engaged to the Dauphin, a match which was finally agreed by Louis XI and Maximilian in the Treaty of Arras of 23 December 1482. Moreover, this treaty brought to an end the French pension which Edward IV had enjoyed for the past seven years. Edward was so mortified at being duped by Louis that, almost certainly in order to consider either a reversion to his former policy of open war with France or the adoption of a policy of blackmail by preparation for war, he summoned parliament to meet at Westminster on 20 January 1483. It proved to be his last. Indeed, he was to survive it by only seven weeks.

A single session of no more than thirty days (parliament was dissolved on 18 February) witnessed the passing of a certain amount of legislation, mainly of a social and economic character. There was also transacted some semi-public business of significance, including the approval of a grant of extraordinary rights on the north-western border to the Duke of Gloucester as a reward for his work against the Scots. Arrangements were also made for the King's second son, the Duke of York, to acquire the Mowbray estates, and for the Queen's sons by her first marriage to be provided for out of the lands of the King's late sister, the Duchess of Exeter. The meeting closed with the voting of a tenth and fifteenth (minus the usual deduction of £6,000, but all payable at midsummer following), along with a tax on foreigners.

The Speakership in this last of Edward IV's parliaments fell to the Under-Treasurer of the Exchequer: John Wood, Esquire, who almost certainly was now representing either Sussex or Surrey, having previously sat for Sussex in 1449–50, Surrey in 1460–1, Sussex once more in 1472–5, and Surrey again in 1478.[1] Wood had strong local connexions with both these counties: he had inherited his own family's estates at West Wittering and elsewhere in Sussex, but had made his home at East Molesey, on the Surrey bank of the Thames not far upstream from Kingston. The manor here had come into his possession (along with estates in Hertfordshire, Essex, Northamptonshire and Cambridgeshire) by his marriage in the early 'fifties to Elizabeth, the young widow of Thomas Morstead (surgeon to each in turn of the Lancastrian kings), a daughter and coheir of the late John Michell, a London grocer who had been Lord Mayor in 1424–5 and 1436–7. Sometime after 1464, when this lady died, John Wood married the sister of Sir Thomas Lewkenore of Trotton (Sussex), sheriff of Surrey and Sussex in 1473–4, who was to be made a Knight of the Bath on the eve of Richard III's coronation but attainted for his part in the Duke of Buckingham's revolt in the following autumn.

East Molesey had met Wood's need for a country-seat handy for Westminster, with which he was closely connected for the greater part of his working life. This was mainly as a member of the staff of the Exchequer. A clerk in this department from not later than 1444, he became Under-Treasurer when the Earl of Worcester became Treasurer in Easter term 1452 and followed this friend of the Duke of York out of office just before Easter 1455. (There is no reason to think of Wood himself as already a Yorkist sympathizer.) During his occupation of this office Wood necessarily became involved in certain commercial transactions of the Crown in the City. But these included the sale and export of royal wool out of which he did very well for himself: not only was he licensed to ship wool from Southampton direct to the Mediterranean, but he embezzled (according to a protest made in parliament during the summer of 1455) no less than £3,000 out of the customs due on wool shipped from London elsewhere than to Calais. His financial gain proved to be a political loss: the petition in which this outcry was raised was rejected,[2] but

[1] For references and a fuller treatment of Wood's life, see my article, 'Sir John Wood of Molesey', *The Surrey Archaeological Collections*, vol. lvi (1959), pp. 15–28.
[2] The petition requested that Wood should be required by a proclamation in he City to appear before the King's Bench early in Michaelmas term, that a

Wood was not restored to office as Under-Treasurer. When Viscount Bourchier was followed as Treasurer by the Earl of Shrewsbury in October 1456, it was rumoured in the Exchequer itself that Wood was to be reinstated. If this was ever a serious proposal, it came to nothing. None the less, it is clear that in the few remaining years of Henry VI's reign Wood was regarded as a dependable member of the Court, and certainly from no later than November 1458 until the summer of 1460 he was Keeper of the Great Wardrobe of the Household.

It was evidently the Yorkists who, after their capture of London and victory at Northampton in July 1460 had brought them to power, deprived John Wood of this new post.[1] But, equally, there can be little doubt that he now came to terms with them. For at Christmas 1460, when M.P. for Surrey, he was appointed to the *quorum* of the commission of the peace in this county.[2] And after Edward IV declared himself King, Wood was soon supporting him: in April 1461 it was as a 'King's servitor' that he was granted the minor office of keeper of swans along the whole course of the Thames from Cirencester to Gravesend; in the following year it was as a yeoman of the Chamber that he was frequently employed as a messenger between the King and the Exchequer, where he apparently became one of the two ushers of the Receipt. From 1464 he was a J.P. in both Surrey and Sussex. In the crisis of the Lancastrian Readeption of 1470–1 Wood had at first maintained a rather non-committal attitude. The Lancastrian administration re-appointed him as a J.P. in Surrey and included him in other local commissions there and in Sussex. But as soon as Edward IV had won the battle of Barnet, Wood made a valid contribution to his cause by helping certain Exchequer officials to guarantee Edward's repayment of earlier loans made to him in the City (perhaps to facilitate the extraction of more).

Especially in view of Wood's former and later record as a civil

---

failure to answer to the charge should be met with a penalty equivalent to the amount of his defalcation (£3,000), and that any attempt on his part to bar or delay process by pleading a royal pardon should involve him in a forfeiture of 10,000 marks (*Rot. Parl.*, v. 335–6).

[1] Wood was still in charge of the Great Wardrobe on 22 May 1460, when, in aid of the expenses of this department, he was granted the wardship of the daughter and heir of John Michelgrove, a Crown tenant in Sussex and Kent. By the end of October he was no longer in office.

[2] His younger brother (another John) was also now made escheator in Surrey and Sussex.

servant, it is perhaps surprising that no administrative prize now came his way. Although he sat in both parliaments of the 'seventies and was sheriff of Surrey and Sussex in 1475–6 and of Essex and Hertfordshire in 1478–9, it was not until Michaelmas 1480 that (after no less than a quarter of a century) he returned to his former office of Under-Treasurer. This was to serve under Henry Bourchier, Earl of Essex, who had been head of the Exchequer since 1471. In the following May (1481) Wood also became Bourchier's deputy in the office of Chief Steward of the estates of the Duchy of Lancaster south of Trent for as long as the earl held it. Wood was still holding both this position and the Under-Treasurership of the Exchequer when he was Speaker early in 1483.

It is not known whether he already enjoyed the Duke of Gloucester's confidence. If not, he certainly soon won it: on 17 May 1483, less than six weeks after Edward IV's death, Wood was called upon to fill the Treasurership of the Exchequer as successor to Essex, the latter having died only a few days before the King. Already, as Protector, Gloucester was controlling the royal administration, nominally on behalf of his nephew, Edward V, and, within a week of his usurpation of the throne, he re-appointed Wood as head of the Exchequer. In April 1484 Richard III was also to make him one of two Vice-Admirals and one of five Commissaries-General of the Admiralty, this at a time when invasion in Henry Tudor's interest was continually awaited. Like his predecessor in the Speakership (Allington), Wood did not long enjoy the rewards of promotion, for he died on 20 August 1484.[1] At least he was spared the final debacle of Yorkist rule which transpired, almost to the day, a year later.

Edward IV's premature death on 9 April 1483 had seriously endangered such internal stability as England had latterly acquired under his rule: the precarious unity of the Yorkist Court was dissolved. There was a struggle to have control of the twelve-year-old Edward V between, on the one hand, the Queen and other members of her family, who had had much to do with the upbringing of the young prince, and, on the other hand, Richard of Gloucester, the sole surviving brother of the late King who had appointed him in his

---

[1] Wood died without issue by either of his two wives, so that the entailed estates of his family went to his younger brother (John) who survived him by little more than a year. On 4 October 1485 he, too, died childless. The Speaker's second wife, Margery (born Lewkenore) survived him by over forty years (until 1525). She remarried, her second husband being Thomas Garth, M.P. for Bletchingley in 1491–2.

will to be Protector during his successor's minority. But this conflict was swiftly and sharply concluded: Gloucester took possession of the person of his royal nephew, assumed office as Protector, secured a deferment of the coronation, and contrived that he himself should be offered the Crown, which he then accepted. A fortnight before this (on 13 June) the Protector had executed Lord Hastings (Edward IV's Chamberlain) for doubt of his support for this act of usurpation, and on the very day when Gloucester's plot to depose his nephew matured (25 June) the Earl Rivers, Edward V's uncle and former governor, was done to death without proper trial at Pontefract. Beginning his reign on 26 June, Richard III was crowned only ten days later.

Troubled by rebellion and rumours of foul deeds, including the murder of his nephews, Edward V and Richard of York, the new King's rule never inspired much confidence. Within no more than four months of the usurpation which he had done so much to bring about, the Duke of Buckingham rose in revolt. Although the rebellion failed, Richard III was still busy crushing it when, early in November 1483, his first parliament was almost due to meet. The parliament was therefore put off until after Christmas, and fresh writs went out on 9 December re-summoning it for 23 January 1484.

During what proved to be Richard III's only parliament (and a short session at that) the member of the Commons who acted as Speaker was William Catesby, apprentice-at-law, of Ashby St Legers. Catesby was sitting in parliament possibly for the first time, in all probability for Northamptonshire.[1] Here and in the neighbouring county of Warwickshire he owned upwards of a dozen manors, to which more had recently been added by royal grant out of the forfeitures of the late Duke of Buckingham and his fellow-rebels in the autumn rising of 1483, the total worth of Catesby's local and other territorial gains being estimated at over £250 a year. The magnitude of these concessions perhaps explains why Catesby did not receive the now almost customary gratuity for his services in the parliament. The grants were, moreover, not all that he enjoyed by royal favour, for under Richard III Catesby's advancement had

[1] For references and a more detailed treatment of Catesby's career, see my paper, 'William Catesby, Counsellor to Richard III', *Bulletin of the John Rylands Library*, vol. xlii (1959), pp. 145–74. What county Catesby represented as knight of the shire is not known. The returns for neither Northamptonshire nor Warwickshire have survived. But Northamptonshire is the more likely alternative, if only because here one brother-in-law of Catesby's (Robert Whittlebury) had just been succeeded as sheriff by another (Roger Wake).

already been swift and gone far: too swift and too far, as later events were to show.

Over twenty years earlier, Catesby's father, Sir William, then a Knight of the Body to Henry VI and one of his Carvers, had so supported the Lancastrian cause as to have his lands seized by Edward IV; and in 1470, in spite of receiving a royal pardon in the meantime, Sir William had adhered to the government of the Re-adeption. (He at least accepted the shrievalty of Northamptonshire at its hands.) This family background can hardly have assisted the future Speaker's career. Fortunately, Catesby had married a daughter of the Lord Zouche of Harringworth who died in 1468, and her relatives seem to have done what they could for him: his wife's mother, a close friend of Edward IV's Queen, and her second husband, Lord Scrope of Bolton (a prominent northern Yorkist, whose adherence to Warwick during the Readeption Edward IV found it prudent to overlook), gave their son-in-law lands in Leicestershire; later on, in 1481, Lord Scrope made him steward and surveyor of all the property he himself held *jure uxoris* in Northamptonshire; and shortly afterwards Lord Zouche, Catesby's wife's brother, gave him a similar office for all *his* estates in half-a-dozen shires of the Midlands. Catesby's evident ability as legal adviser, land-agent, executor, and feoffee-to-uses, was now receiving a much more extended recognition, his other patrons including the Duke of Buckingham, Lord Hastings, Lord Lisle (brother to the Queen's first husband), Lord Dudley, and both the widow and heir of Lord Latimer (uncle to the Kingmaker). As a lawyer, Catesby was now in a very fair way of business.

It was at least partly his deception and betrayal of Lord Hastings, the closest and for him the most important of his patrons, which during the crisis of Richard III's usurpation assisted his transformation into a politician of the first rank. The only official employment under the Crown which Catesby had secured by the end of Edward IV's reign was as one of the legal counsel retained by the administration of the Duchy of Lancaster, a post he filled from no earlier than 1481. His appointment for life on 14 May 1483 (a month before Hastings's execution) to the Chancellorship of the Earldom of March, an office in which he was to be under the orders of Gloucester's supporter, the Duke of Buckingham, suggests that the Protector already approved of him. But his advancement was clearly accelerated by the valuable (if despicable) services he performed in helping secure Hastings's removal and, to some extent, by the Lord

u

Chamberlain's removal itself: on 30 June, when Richard III had been reigning four days, Catesby was not only confirmed in his office in the administration of the Earldom of March, but simultaneously was appointed for life as both Chancellor of the Exchequer and Chamberlain of the Receipt, this last office having been held by Hastings at his death.[1] Furthermore, the new King made him an Esquire of the Body and a member of his Council. Compared with such central offices as these, the constableship of Rockingham castle, the master-forestership of Rockingham, the stewardship of the royal manors of Rockingham, Brigstock and Cliffe (Northants.), to all of which Catesby and Viscount Lovell, Richard's Lord Chamberlain, were jointly appointed for the term of Catesby's life (again in succession to Lord Hastings),[2] the stewardship of the Duchy of Lancaster estates in Northamptonshire,[3] and the post of deputy-butler at Bristol, Exeter and Dartmouth (on behalf of Viscount Lovell, who was now Chief Butler as well as Lord Chamberlain), were quite minor acquisitions, although notable as a collection and, of course, profitable as such. Catesby can only have discharged the responsibilities of these various local royal offices indirectly, and the same must be said of his appointment to the commissions of the peace in no less than eight of the midland shires.[4] For he seems to have been even generally in attendance on the King. Very probably this was the case during the suppression of the autumn risings of 1483; it was certainly so after Richard III returned from the south-west to London.[5] Catesby now became one of the foremost members of the

[1] An important semi-public office which Lord Hastings' fall brought into Catesby's possession was that of steward of all the manors and liberties of the abbey of St Albans. Latterly it had been jointly held by Hastings and John Forster, a Hertfordshire lawyer. When Hastings was put to death, Forster was immediately imprisoned in the Tower and (two days later) forced into transferring the stewardship to Catesby. The appointment was soon ratified by Abbot Wallingford and his chapter (on 1 August).

[2] The Rockingham offices were restored early in 1485 to Sir Ralph Hastings, younger brother of Lord Hastings, who had received a pardon from Richard III and was now one of the Knights of the Body. This restitution was made with Catesby's agreement.

[3] Catesby's wife's stepfather, Lord Scrope, was Chamberlain of the Duchy of Lancaster and ex officio nominal head of the duchy council.

[4] Before the end of 1483 Catesby was a J.P. in Northants., Leicestershire, Warwickshire, Worcestershire, Gloucestershire, Oxfordshire, Berkshire, and Hertfordshire.

[5] On 26 November Catesby was present at Westminster when the King restored the Great Seal to the Chancellor (Bishop Russell of Lincoln). Since 19 October, Richard had kept it in his own possession.

royal Council, soon, in the year of his Speakership, to be lampooned in the famous distich:

The catte, the ratte, and Lovell our dogge
Rulyth all Englande under a hogge.

Which meant (as Fabyan was to put it) that 'Catesby, Ratcliffe and the lorde Lovell ruled the lande under the Kynge, which bare the whyte bore for his conysaunce'.[1]

Once met, the parliament in which Catesby was Speaker sat for barely four weeks, coming to an end on 22 February 1484. But a number of its transactions were of great importance at the time. One of the first matters to come up was the ratification of the proceedings by which Richard had obtained the crown, a bill to this effect being approved first by the Lords and then by the Commons. There followed the attainders for treason of those involved in the recent risings. These included the mother of the future Henry VII, Margaret (Beaufort), Countess of Richmond, who was aunt to the Speaker's wife. (Margaret's husband, Lord Stanley, was allowed to retain her estates during his lifetime.) Another Act invalidated the letters-patent by which Edward IV's relict, Elizabeth Wydeville, enjoyed her grants. The King's need of popularity inhibited the expression of any royal desire for direct taxation, and no such vote was volunteered. The Commons, however, in granting to Richard tunnage and poundage and the wool-subsidies for life, for which there were precedents from the reigns of Richard II, Henry V, Henry VI and Edward IV, took a step that was unprecedented at least to the extent of making such a concession in the first parliament and in the first year of a reign. Even Edward IV had been voted such a grant only in his second parliament and after four years of his reign had elapsed. Whether Richard III would now have been able to get along with as few parliaments as his brother had done, there is no knowing. Certainly, he did not again meet parliament in the eighteen months before his life and reign ended at Bosworth Field on 22 August 1485. It was three days after the battle that, having been taken prisoner, the last previous Speaker was executed at Leicester, an exception to Henry Tudor's otherwise remarkable clemency.[2]

---

[1] The author of the couplet, William Collingbourne, was condemned as a traitor before the end of 1484.

[2] For further particulars relating to Catesby, see the Appendix.

CHAPTER II

In the Early Tudor Period

HENRY VII began his reign in what appeared to be a fairly strong position. He had been head of the House of Lancaster since 1471, and the direct male line of Richard Plantagenet was now extinct (except for the ten-year-old son of Clarence). Obviously, Henry did much to limit trouble by marrying Edward IV's eldest surviving child, the Princess Elizabeth, on 18 January 1486. This marriage was what parliament itself, whether spontaneously or otherwise, had requested. For, on 7 November 1485, a week after the King's coronation, the estates had already come together to give his title their formal approval. (And such a title it was that this approval and Henry's marriage could not but mend it!) The chief of Richard III's supporters were attainted. Those of Henry's friends who needed rehabilitation at law secured it. His own attainder, it was agreed by the judges, needed no reversal. Neither, in their view, did the attainder of the Commons' Speaker, Thomas Lovell of Enfield and Halliwell in Shoreditch (Middlesex),[1] who had incurred forfeiture of his estates for supporting Henry's cause in the rising led by the Marquess of Dorset in 1483.[2]

In 1485 Thomas Lovell might have looked forward to a successful career in the common law and reasonably expected to become a serjeant-at-law and end up a judge. He was aged about forty and for over twenty years had been a member of Lincoln's Inn where (having held office as Treasurer and Reader) he was now one of the Governors. The rewards of a place at Court and in the royal executive under the shrewd managing director who wore the crown, exercised a stronger pull. Lovell lacked nothing of political sense, and the way to his preferment lay surely open: already, before the parliament, he had succeeded his predecessor in the Speakership (Catesby) in the office of Chancellor of the Exchequer, having been appointed for life on 12 October 1485;[3] an Esquire of the Body,[4] he had also been made Treasurer of the Chamber and a member of the royal Council.[5]

[1] I am grateful to Mr R. Virgoe for allowing me to see some unpublished notes on Lovell's career.

[2] *Rot. Parl.*, vi. 246. [3] *CPR, 1485–94*, 18. [4] Ibid., 23.

[5] W. C. Richardson, *Tudor Chamber Administration*, 110–12. For some facts regarding Sir Thomas Lovell's later career, see the Appendix.

With Lovell as Speaker, it is hardly surprising that this first Tudor parliament showed itself realistic and competent. And this was particularly the case in matters financial. Not only was there an Act of Resumption, applying to grants of Crown-lands since 1455; the Commons, almost inevitably, did for Henry what less than two years before they had done for Richard III, that is, grant him tunnage and poundage and the wool-subsidies for life. Of particular interest to the Speaker himself was the appropriation of £14,000 a year to Household expenditure, more especially since the King clearly intended to keep inside this limit. For all of this and sundry other minor matters a session of less than five weeks proved enough. The prayer of the Commons, made by Lovell and supported by the Lords, that Henry should marry Elizabeth of York, brought it to a felicitous end on 10 December. Parliament was merely adjourned for Christmas. A second session, which began a week after the royal wedding, ended early in March 1486. It was not specially eventful.

When, after nearly two years, parliament next assembled, Henry's position was more firmly established. There was still disaffection in some parts. But in the previous summer (1487), on the Fosse Way at Stoke near Newark-on-Trent, the King had crushed the rebellion, first raised in Ireland, in support of the pretender, Lambert Simnel. The time was now come to crown the Queen who, over a year before (20 September 1486) and almost as soon after their marriage as was possible, had given him an heir (Arthur). Elizabeth's coronation took place on 25 November 1487, by which time parliament had been sitting for over a fortnight (since 9 November). Otherwise, the main interest of this single session (which lasted for a further three weeks) lies in the measures taken to safeguard public order, including a statute enlarging the discretionary jurisdiction of the Council, and in the first substantial grant of direct taxation of the reign—two whole tenths and fifteenths.

The amount conceded may well have reflected credit on the managerial powers of John Mordaunt, Esquire, of Turvey (Beds.), who, in this second parliament of the reign, succeeded Sir Thomas Lovell as Speaker.[1] At any rate, the government allowed him £100

---

[1] *DNB*, xiii. 852–3; J. C. Wedgwood, *History of Parliament, 1439–1509, Biographies*, pp. 607–8.

Mordaunt had been returned to Henry VII's first parliament. When elected Speaker he was probably sitting for Bedfordshire, from which he was returned in 1495. In the meantime, he had been M.P. for Grantham in 1491–2. It was as a royal serjeant-at-law that he was summoned by individual writ in 1497 and 1504.

for his services in the session. A member of the Middle Temple and since 1483 a J.P. of the *quorum* in Bedfordshire, Mordaunt had fought at the recent battle of Stoke. His legal career was eventually to achieve some distinction, but this came too late for real prosperity: not until 1495 was he called to the degree of serjeant-at-law; and although, after being appointed Chief Justice of Chester before the turn of the century, he became Chancellor of the Duchy of Lancaster for life in June 1504, he died before this year was out.[1] It is worth noting that in his will he recalled as a benefactress the late Countess of Warwick, the Kingmaker's widow and mother of Richard III's Queen (who had died in 1492), if only because it had been during the parliament in which Mordaunt was Speaker that the countess, being then legally restored to the family estates wrested from her in 1474, immediately settled all but one upon the Crown.

When Henry VII's third parliament came together, his chief concern was over relations with France. These were deteriorating. He wished for no break, but could hardly welcome the French intention to stifle the independence of the Breton duchy. On this account he had to prepare for possible war, by alliances abroad (with Maximilian of Austria and Ferdinand of Spain) and also by taxation at home. And so parliament met on 13 January 1489.

The Commons' Speaker for the occasion was Sir Thomas Fitz-William, a lawyer of the Middle Temple (like his predecessor) and Recorder of London from shortly before the accession of Richard III (19 June 1483).[2] The City's regular habit of electing its Recorder to parliament began with FitzWilliam, and he had represented it in Richard III's only parliament (of 1484) and in both of Henry VII's parliaments so far held. His parliamentary experience went much further back than this: a member of a Lincolnshire family with its chief estates at Mablethorpe and Louth, he had sat for the city of Lincoln in 1459 and then again in 1478, having in the interval been burgess for Plympton (Devon) in 1467–8. Now, in 1489, because it had been apparently decided that he should be Speaker and it was the custom for the Speaker to be a knight of the shire, although he

[1] Mordaunt was knighted on 18 February 1503 when the King's second son, Henry, was created Prince of Wales. On 6 April 1504, the year of his death, he was appointed High Steward of the University of Cambridge. His first son, John, who had been a servant of Prince Arthur's, was to be summoned to parliament in 1532 as Baron Mordaunt.

[2] Wedgwood, op. cit., *Biographies*, 336–7. Oftener than not since 1458 FitzWilliam had been a J.P. in the parts of Lindsey in Lincolnshire. He was on the commission of the peace there when Speaker and until his death.

was first of all returned once again for London he was subsequently elected for the county of Lincolnshire.[1] The prominent part which, as Recorder, FitzWilliam had played in the proceedings at the Guild-hall on Midsummer's Day 1483—when the Duke of Buckingham had importuned the citizens to ask Richard of Gloucester to take the crown and, owing to the lack of response, the Recorder had seconded the request—if not forgotten, had at least been forgiven. He had been present at the great civic welcome given to Henry VII at Shore-ditch at his entry into the City after the victory at Bosworth, and at the start of the first parliament of the reign had come forward in the Commons (so the Colchester M.P.s told their fellow-burgesses on their return home) to inform the House how notice of the Speaker's election was customarily given to the Lord Chancellor. Evidently, he had no cause not to feel self-assured. In March 1486 he was granted the manor of Saltfleetby (Lincs.) for life, and Henry knighted him in the same year.

The parliament in which FitzWilliam filled the office of Speaker was to run to three sessions, the first of six weeks, a second of seven weeks in the autumn, and a final session of five weeks which closed at the end of February 1490: it proved to be the longest of all Henry VII's parliaments. The year covered by its meetings was in general one of great difficulty. The country clearly resented the taxes which parliament allowed: not only did they cause a rising in north Yorkshire, but, of the £75,000 which the Commons granted in February 1489 to maintain an army of 10,000 archers, little above a third had been collected twelve months later; and the Commons, to meet the balance, then offered no more than a tenth and fifteenth, and even this they eventually reduced to about £30,000 (the cut being in aid of poor towns). In the meantime, one of Henry's allies, Maximilian, despite English help in the Netherlands, had come to terms with Charles VIII of France; and, for want of any real assist-ance from his other ally, Ferdinand of Spain, the 6,000 English troops sent to resist the French in Brittany had worked to no pur-pose. Besides, although the treaty of Medina del Campo, signed on 27 March 1489, had stipulated a marriage between the Princess Katherine and Henry's son, it represented a policy more advanta-geous to Spain than England, since it virtually committed Henry to

[1] FitzWilliam was not re-elected for London to the next parliament in 1491, although he remained Recorder until replaced by Sir Robert Sheffield shortly before September 1495. He died on 4 March 1497 and was buried at Hagenby priory, Lincolnshire.

continue a war with France at Ferdinand's pleasure. Henry was left in something of a quandary; it was at the same time difficult for him to continue the war and yet dangerous for him to withdraw and make peace. The parliament of 1489–90 had sat in an uneasy time, and it was in an atmosphere of doubt and anxiety that it ended. Its Speaker had earned his reward of office, the usual £100.

In Brittany nothing went Henry's way, but he was bent on continuing the war, alone if need be. Evidently, money raised by 'benevolence' was not enough, and on 17 October 1491 parliament met again. The Commons' choice of Speaker augured especially well for the furtherance of royal demands, for they elected Richard Empson of Easton Neston (near Towcester),[1] then sitting for Northamptonshire where he had been a member of the *quorum* of the commission of the peace since 1475. An apprentice-at-law and sometime Reader at Middle Temple Inn, Empson had already made a name for himself as a judicial expert in the royal administration. Dismissed by Richard III from the office of Attorney-General for the Duchy of Lancaster, to which he had been appointed by Edward IV in 1478, he had been reinstated for life by Henry VII in the first month of his reign (13 September 1485) and was to continue to hold this post until moved up into the Chancellorship of the Duchy in October 1505.[2] More recently, in August 1489, he had been made a justice-in-eyre for such royal forests as were under the control of the Queen, and in 1490, the year before his Speakership, for all other royal forests. His close administrative association with Edmund Dudley was still to come; neither had yet acquired the bad reputation which allowed Henry VIII to sacrifice them as scapegoats for the severity of his father's fiscal policies.[3]

Empson's Speakership seems to have been entirely successful from the standpoint of finance. Certainly, in less than three weeks the Commons conceded two whole tenths and fifteenths (minus £6,000), the first due in April, the second in November, 1492. They even undertook a third subsidy should the King campaign abroad for more than eight months. And so, on 4 November 1491, the first session ended. The very brevity of the time taken to agree upon such a scale of taxation is in itself evidence of the warmth of parliament's sympathy with Henry's policy; and, despite the capitulation of Anne,

---

[1] *DNB*, vi. 782–3; Wedgwood, op. cit., *Biographies*, 300; A. R. Ingpen, *The Middle Temple Bench Book*.

[2] R. Somerville, op. cit., i. 406; 392.

[3] For further details of Empson's career, see the Appendix.

the Breton heiress, and her marriage, only a month later, to Charles VIII of France, Henry's military preparations went on apace throughout the winter. No attempt to go back on the decisions of the first session of the parliament was made in the second (26 January-5 March 1492). In October 1492 Henry crossed the Channel with a large army, besieged Boulogne, and then allowed Charles VIII to buy him off in the Treaty of Étaples (on 3 November): a repetition of the Treaty of Picquigny, and just as diplomatically sensible and financially profitable. None the less such a culmination angered many of Henry's subjects, who now begrudged the expense of helping furnish the campaign or serving on it themselves. Under a stipulation of the treaty itself, parliament was to confirm it. Perhaps hardly surprisingly, it was not until October 1495 that parliament met and could do so.

When the King summoned this parliament, his situation was again not without discomfort. Since 1492 another Yorkist *apparition*, Perkin Warbeck, the son of a townsman of Tournai who claimed to be Richard, Duke of York, and the only surviving son of Edward IV, had been causing Henry some anxiety in Ireland, France and Flanders, and also at home where Warbeck's cause gave a lead to the plots of English Yorkists. As recently as February 1495, William Stanley, the brother of the Earl of Derby and Henry's own Lord Chamberlain, had been executed for taking a treasonable interest in the imposture. More recently still, Warbeck had been fitted out in Flanders with an expeditionary force. Admittedly, his attack on Deal in July was a fiasco and, when he took himself off to Ireland, his siege of Waterford was nothing more fortunate. But Warbeck, though now a fugitive, did not lack friends who could be more of a nuisance than himself. When, on 15 September, Henry summoned parliament to meet a month later (14 October), he must have known that James IV of Scotland, having already honoured the pretender with regal hospitality, was then preparing to cross the border on his behalf. The interval of a bare four weeks between the issue of the summonses and the opening of parliament suggests a sense of urgency in Henry's mind.

This parliament of 1495 lasted for a single session of some ten weeks (from 14 October to 21 December). Again the Commons' Speaker was a lawyer: Robert Drury of Hawstead in Suffolk,[1] knight of the shire for that county as he had been in the previous parliament. Educated in the University of Cambridge and at Lincoln's Inn

[1] *DNB*, vi. 57-8; Wedgwood, op. cit., *Biographies*, 284.

(where, entered in 1473, he had been a Reader in 1487 and a Governor in 1488–9 and 1492–3), Drury had been serving on the *quorum* of the commission of the peace in Suffolk since 1488. It is possible that he was already acting as deputy to the Earl of Oxford in his office of Chief Steward of the Duchy of Lancaster estates south of Trent, a post which Drury was certainly occupying by Michaelmas 1498 and was long to retain, even after the accession of Henry VIII.[1] It was not until Henry VIII's reign that Drury really became eminent: in 1516 he was made a Knight of the Body; ten years later he was a member of the Privy Council, next in precedence after Sir Thomas More. There can be no doubt, however, that he was in favour at Court in 1495: for the Commons' conclusion of their Speaker's election was communicated to the Lords by such friends of the King in the Lower House as Sir Reginald Bray (Knight of the Body, Privy Councillor, and Chancellor of the Duchy of Lancaster), Sir Richard Guildford (Knight of the Body and Controller of the Household), and Richard Empson (Attorney-General of the Duchy and Speaker in the last parliament).[2] Perhaps the most interesting of the acts of this parliament was that which is sometimes described as 'for security under the King *de facto*': it was to prevent any person serving the King under arms from being afterwards attainted of treason, a measure of doubtful validity, but perhaps intended to display the King's readiness to forgive hoary disputes and animosities. Regarding finance, a fresh appropriation of revenues for the Household— amounting to over £13,000 a year—was allowed, and authority was given for a proclamation that those who within three months did not contribute to a 'benevolence' recently granted to the King would be liable to imprisonment. But no regular subsidy was voted. All the same, at the end of the parliament Speaker Drury was given £100 as official stipend.[3]

[1] Drury may well have been deputy-Chief Steward before 1498 when he is first referred to in this capacity in the Duchy records. The previous known holder of this office is James Hobart, who was occupying it in Trinity term 1485. Hobart is not known to have acted later than this, and, moreover, became Attorney-General to the Crown in November 1486. The Earl of Oxford had been made Chief Steward for life on 22 September 1485. After the earl's death on 10 March 1513, Drury continued in the deputyship under his successors and as such attended meetings of the Duchy Council until at least February 1524. By 1526, however, he had been superseded (Somerville, op. cit., i. 431).

[2] *Rot. Parl.*, vi. 458. The procedure followed on this occasion was apparently a little unusual, or else it is more fully recorded than in other parliament-rolls.

[3] Regarding Drury's later career, the following facts may be added to what has been said: he supported the King against the Cornish rebels at Blackheath

In 1496 Henry VII's affairs prospered. In February, Maximilian's son, the Archduke Philip, was prepared to expel all English political exiles from the Netherlands in return for an important commercial treaty, the *Magnus Intercursus*. In September, a Scottish invasion, on behalf of the *soi-disant* Richard IV, was beaten off. At the beginning of October, Ferdinand of Spain concluded a new treaty for the marriage of his daughter Katherine with Henry's heir-apparent, Prince Arthur. Later in the month, a Great Council, attended by a number of merchants and townsmen, undertook that the next parliament would grant £120,000, and a fortnight later (20 November) the writs of summons went out. Admittedly, when Henry immediately tried to anticipate the promised grant by raising loans, the invitations to subscribe were only moderately successful: the response, in fact, fell short by more than half. Parliament, however, in a comparatively short session of eight weeks (between 16 January and 13 March 1497), did what it could to make up the deficit.

Not a great deal is known of the earlier career of the knight of the shire whom the Commons now chose as their Speaker: Thomas Englefield of Englefield (Berks.).[1] But it is at least evident that his reputation as a lawyer was already well established. It was in his own county, at Reading, that in 1489 he first acted as a justice of gaol delivery. But in March 1493 he was appointed to serve in that capacity and as one of the *quorum* for the peace in each of the English shires of the March of Wales, at the same time being also authorized to act as a justice of oyer and terminer in the principality proper. The nominal head of this commission was the six-year-old Prince of Wales, and there can be no doubt that Englefield was appointed to these various judicial offices as one of Prince Arthur's council:[2] he was certainly with the prince at Shrewsbury in the following year (1494), when he and other members of this council for Wales were

---

in June 1497 when he was knighted; in 1509 he attested Henry VIII's renewal of the treaty with Scotland; in 1510 he sat in the first parliament of the new reign for Suffolk (as before); in 1520 as a Knight of the Body he attended the King at the meeting with Francis I at the Field of Cloth of Gold and was also at Henry's subsequent conference with Charles V at Gravelines. He died on 2 March 1536 and was interred at Bury St Edmunds.

[1] Wedgwood, op. cit., *Biographies*, 301. Englefield's wife, Margaret, daughter of Richard Danvers of Prescot (Oxon.), was niece of William Danvers, Justice of Common Pleas at the time of Englefield's Speakership.

[2] Power to appoint the justices of oyer and terminer was granted to the Prince of Wales on 20 March 1493, the date of Englefield's commission (*CPR, 1485-94*, 441).

entertained at the borough's expense.[1] Further evidence of the closeness of this connexion is Englefield's association with the prince and
some of his household staff in a royal commission set up in February
1495 to enquire about the forfeited estates of Sir William Stanley in
North Wales, Flintshire, Cheshire, and Shropshire;[2] and it was to be
the prince's marriage with Katherine of Aragon (on 14 November
1501) that provided the occasion for Englefield's being made a
knight.[3] We may in fact think of his election as Speaker in 1497 as an
easy compliment to the royal heir-apparent. But his Speakership is
sure to have been acceptable to the King: it was Sir Thomas Lovell,
now Treasurer of the Household (Speaker in 1485–6), who headed
the Commons' deputation which took word that the election had
been made.[4]

Stimulated by Cardinal Morton the Chancellor's emphasis on the
continuance of danger from Scotland, which had broken a seven
years' truce before half its time (1494–1501) had run, parliament was
generous enough to vote two tenths and fifteenths for fitting out an
army. The grant did not amount to what had been pledged by the
Great Council in the autumn, and the Commons offered to double it
if necessary. Taxation of this order was a heavy burden, and the
Commons stipulated that it should be rescinded if peace was made,
and that in any event nobody should be liable to the second tax who
did not enjoy an income of 20s. a year from land or hold personal
property worth 10 marks. Even so, discontent was quite inevitable:
the appearance of an army of Cornish rebels at Blackheath in June
following was a direct result of parliament's complacence. But its
financial policy 'paid off' so far as Scotland was concerned. Following the repulse of a Scottish invasion, there was concluded the Treaty
of Ayton (30 September 1497) which led eventually (in 1503) to the
marriage of Henry's daughter Margaret to James IV: a climax
which, whatever the debt to Spanish diplomacy, was a real success
for the English King. The year 1497 also saw Perkin Warbeck's
capture; the year 1499, his execution along with his fellow-prisoner,
the Earl of Warwick (a cousin of the Queen). The first of the Tudors
now occupied a position of respectable strength in Europe, and at
home his dynasty was as secure as could be.

---

[1] C. A. J. Skeel, *The Council in the Marches of Wales* (London, 1904), p. 202.

[2] *CPR, 1494–1509*, 29.

[3] W. A. Shaw, *The Knights of England* (London, 1906), vol. i, p. 146.

[4] *Rot. Parl.*, vi. 510. For further details of Englefield's career, see my remarks
anent the parliament of 1510 when he again acted as Speaker.

Only when strictly necessary had Henry VII summoned parliament, and never twice within a twelvemonth. In one instance over three and a half years had elapsed between meetings (March 1492–October 1495). After the session of 1497 it was not until 25 January 1504 that parliament assembled once more. And this parliament's single session of nine weeks turned out to be the only one in all the second half of Henry's reign. His freedom from dependence on parliament was such that the Act of 1504 authorizing him to repeal attainders at will was in part even formally justified on the ground that he did not intend, *without grete necessarye and urgent causes, of longe tyme to calle and summone a newe Parliament.* Thanks to a considerably enhanced revenue and to its efficient and economical handling, Henry could afford such an abstention. But, although he excused this policy as meant *for the eas of his Subgiects,* he may well have been thinking of his own. For clearly his experience in this last of his parliaments was none of the happiest. According to Roper's *Life of Sir Thomas More,* the King's demand in 1504 for three 'fifteenths' (roughly £90,000)—as a reasonable commutation of an aid for the knighting of his son Arthur (dead these two years past) and another for the marriage of his daughter Margaret—was turned down by the Lower House. And Henry, after agreeing to a petition that he should accept £40,000 in lieu of the aids, saw fit to mollify the Commons by foregoing no less than £10,000 of even this amount. The Speaker in this uneasy session had been none other than Edmund Dudley, one of the most enthusiastic, talented, and resourceful of the royal fiscal agents. M.P. for Lewes in 1491-2, Dudley was now sitting (as he had done in 1495) for Sussex.[1]

Sir Francis Bacon, while not sparing of his strictures on this friend and fellow-extortioner of Richard Empson in his *Life of Henry VII,*[2] condescended to describe him as being 'of a good family'. At least in this, Bacon was right enough. Dudley was a grandson of the Lord Dudley who, having fought for Henry VI at St Albans (1455) and Bloreheath (1459), served Edward IV as Constable of the Tower (1470-83) and acted as Chamberlain to Edward's consort, Elizabeth Wydeville. The Master William Dudley who was Dean of the King's Chapel in 1475 and held the see of Durham from 1476 until his death in 1483, was Edmund Dudley's uncle. The lady who was Edmund's wife at the time of his Speakership was the

[1] *DNB,* vi. 100-2; Wedgwood, op. cit., *Biographies,* 285-6; *Edmund Dudley, The tree of common wealth;* ed. D. M. Brodie (Cambridge, 1948), pp. 1-11.
[2] Op. cit., ed. J. R. Lumby, p. 190.

daughter of Edward Grey, Viscount Lisle (who had died in 1492), and sister to the Viscount Lisle who was made a Knight of the Bath when (during the parliament of 1504) the King's surviving son, Henry, was created Prince of Wales; and she was a cousin of the Marquess of Dorset (half-brother of the late Queen, Elizabeth of York).[1] Elizabeth Grey was Dudley's second wife: his first had been a daughter of Thomas Windsor, usher of the Chamber to Richard III and his constable of Windsor Castle, whose lands had been seized and restored by Henry VII all within a month of the battle of Bosworth.

Dudley had studied at Oxford and then, about 1478, when he was in his middle-'teens, had entered one of the smaller law-schools affiliated to Gray's Inn. He had become a barrister of the Inn. That his ability as a lawyer was worth respect, there can be no question: according to Polydore Vergil, Henry VII was attracted by his legal knowledge even at the time of his accession; from November 1496 until December 1502 Dudley was under-sheriff of London, an officer (chosen by the civic authorities) whose chief function was to advise the sheriffs in the exercise of their jurisdiction; and early in 1503 he was ordered by the Crown to assume the degree and estate of serjeant-at-law, in October following paying 70 marks for an exemption. Although there is no certain evidence from before September 1504 of his being paid as a royal councillor, it is very likely that at the time of his Speakership Dudley was already a member of the Council, of which he was to become President in July 1506. He then came to be entrusted with a prominent share in its judicial work, carried out in Star Chamber and the Court of Requests. As early as 1492, at Boulogne, Henry VII had drawn him into the negotiation of the peace with France. But it was mainly in those branches of the royal administration which demanded a combination of legal finesse with financial acumen that Dudley's powers were to be given their widest scope: in the drafting of indentures and recognisances relating to the duties of officials, the assessment of feudal dues, the regulation of fines payable before forfeited estates were restored or outlawries reversed, in short, in implementing that tough policy which Bacon,

[1] In November 1511, hardly more than a year after Dudley's execution, his widow married Arthur Plantagenet, an illegitimate son of Edward IV. She survived until about 1530. It was her son by Edmund Dudley, John (born in 1502), who was created Viscount Lisle in 1542 (after the death of his stepfather who had enjoyed the title since 1523), Earl of Warwick in 1547, and Duke of Northumberland in 1551, and was executed in 1553 for instigating the usurpation of the crown by his daughter-in-law, Jane Grey.

perhaps with too little impartiality, laid at Empson's and Dudley's doors and, in any case, perhaps too severely castigated: that series of extortionate contrivances by which these two administrators, 'lawyers in science, and privy counsellors in authority, . . . turned law and justice into wormwood and rapine', and for which, virtually, these two former Speakers went to the block in 1510.[1]

Even before his Speakership, Dudley was unpopular in the City. This was partly because of his one-sided interference in the dispute between the Merchant Taylors and the civic authorities from 1503 to 1505, partly because he was frequently at odds with prominent London merchants caught out in frauds against the revenue. He himself did more than dabble in commercial speculation, sometimes on borrowed money, sometimes on capital won in the course of official duty. (Dudley certainly did not lack either lands or other wealth: at his death his estates lay in thirteen counties, and his goods were estimated to be worth more than £5,000.) Detested at large, he was entirely trusted by Henry VII who, eleven days before his death on 21 April 1509, made him one of the executors of his will.[2] Empson was another. And so was Lovell, the Speaker in Henry's first parliament and, since 1492, Treasurer of his Household, an office he was to retain under the new King.

The accession of Henry VIII gave fair promise of a more liberal régime than the persistent tensions of his father's reign had made possible. Not yet eighteen, the King was himself eager to enjoy those pleasures of body and mind proper to a Renaissance prince. The political situation at home and abroad allowed him scope enough: he was the first king for over a century to be free of rival claimants to the throne, and yet, being the only surviving son of his father, all hopes of a continuance of stability rested upon him; he took over a full treasury and a well-trained administration; his marriage with Katherine of Aragon a fortnight before his coronation

---

[1] The actual charge on which Dudley was arraigned before a special commission at the London Guildhall on 16 July 1509, was one of constructive treason: that, when Henry VII was on his death-bed, Dudley summoned his friends to attend him under arms in London as soon as the King died, this being construed as a scheme to attempt the life of Henry VIII. Put into the Tower, he was subjected to a fresh attack in Henry VIII's first parliament, when the introduction of a bill of attainder (which passed the Lower House) drove him to attempt an escape. Pressed by Dudley's enemies, Henry VIII signed the warrant for his execution, which took place on Tower Hill on 17 August 1510. The next parliament reversed the attainder.

[2] N. H. Nicolas, *Testamenta Vetusta*, p. 35.

on 24 June 1509, after a long and uneasy period of betrothal, con-firmed English friendship with Spain. Besides, at least for the time being, it was possible to keep up an understanding with France and Scotland. Between the summoning and the meeting of the first par-liament of the reign, however, a Venetian envoy was writing home that parliament was being called about relations with France. It was even stated in this despatch that there was already some talk of war.

When Henry opened parliament on 21 January 1510, such a meet-ing had not been held for nearly six years. It was now evidently decided to abandon this policy: in the next parliament the Chancellor, Archbishop Warham, was to expatiate on the necessity for even fre-quent meetings; and, in fact, in the first seven years of the reign, parliament was to average a session a year. Henry was also willing to meet complaints and demands for redress of grievance, especially with a view to introducing a more humane system of fiscal adminis-tration. And his first parliament proceeded to define several legal points whose ambiguity had been exploited in the interests of the revenue. It also attainted of treason the two members of Henry VII's Council most closely associated with the recent policy of financial extortion, the former Speakers, Empson and Dudley. Thrust into the Tower on the second day of the reign, both were to be executed, after a long respite, on 17 August 1510.

The Speaker elected by the Commons in January 1510 was another Speaker of the previous reign. This was Sir Thomas Engle-field, who had held office, in 1497, during the last parliament but one. He had then been involved in the administration of Wales and the Marches as a member of Prince Arthur's council, and continued to act regularly in this capacity until Arthur's death in April 1502. That misfortune did nothing to end this particular engagement of Englefield's interests: in June following he was appointed as one of the justices of oyer and terminer and commissioners of array in North and South Wales and in the English border-shires, where he also continued to serve as a J.P. of the *quorum*; and in 1505 he was appointed Justice of Chester, in 1506 a Justice of Assize in North Wales, and in 1508 a Justice of Assize in South Wales.[1] These judi-cial promotions can only have been made with the approval of Henry VII, who before the end of his reign made Englefield a mem-ber of his Council. But almost certainly they brought Englefield into close touch with Prince Henry after his creation as Prince of Wales in 1504. And Henry's accession brought Englefield nearer to the

[1] Wedgwood, op. cit., *Biographies*, 301.

front: he was one of the committee, presided over by the Earl of Surrey (the Treasurer), which was authorized to determine claims to perform ceremonial services at the coronation;[1] and he was re-appointed to the royal Council, of which he continued to be an active member until not long before his death in April 1514.[2] Three weeks after his Speakership he was given a royal annuity of £100 for counsel and attendance about the King's person,[3] in 1512 was one of a committee set up to control the discharge of the King's debts to Henry VII's executors,[4] and in September 1513 was made one of the feoffees of certain royal manors for the fulfilment of the King's will, who were licensed to alienate them to the dean and canons of St George's Chapel, Windsor.[5] Englefield's Speakership in 1510 had been brief, but especially on that account (considering its results) entirely creditable to his reputation.[6]

With Pope Julius II anxious to abandon the League of Cambrai against Venice and, in order to expel the French from north Italy, already scheming to establish a Holy League which England might be ready to join, it is perhaps surprising that no plans for military expenditure were submitted to parliament. But the young King was far from parsimonious, and so a parliamentary subsidy would in any case be welcome. A session of five weeks proved long enough for the Commons to agree in voting tunnage and poundage and the wool-subsidy for the King's lifetime and, in direct taxation, no less generous a grant than two tenths and fifteenths, a grant equal to what had been made during Englefield's first Speakership, only not so hedged around with limitations. Evidently satisfied with what had been achieved, the King dissolved parliament on 23 February 1510.

Almost two years went by before parliament met again. But, once met, it continued in being for over two years and had three sessions, totalling twenty weeks. Its first session began on 4 February 1512.

---

[1] L. and P., *Domestic and Foreign, Henry VIII*, vol. i, part 1, no. 81.
[2] Ibid., no. 313.   [3] Ibid., no. 414 (53).
[4] Ibid., no. 1493.   [5] Ibid., no. 2330 (4).
[6] Sir Thomas Englefield was still a member of the Privy Council when Henry VIII campaigned in France in the summer of 1513. In fact, he and Warham, Surrey, and Lovell appear to have been the only members left behind in England (ibid., no. 2067). But 7 September 1513 is the last date on which Englefield is known to have countersigned a royal warrant, and he died on 3 April 1514. His son and heir, Thomas, later (1526–37) a Justice of the Common Bench, was then twenty-six years old. The former Speaker was buried at Englefield. Owning the manor here, he also died seised of Speenhamland, which he had bought from George Lord Abergavenny.

By then the peaceful foreign policy of the first two and a half years of the reign was already undergoing a complete transformation. In fact, the parliamentary writs of summons were only issued (on 28 November 1511) a fortnight after Henry had joined the papal coalition of the Holy League, along with Ferdinand of Spain (his father-in-law), the Emperor Maximilian, and the Venetians. The object of the alliance was to push the French out of Italy, a decision which Henry had immediately confirmed by undertaking with Spain to make war on Louis XII before the end of April 1512. Parliament was meeting to vote ways and means and also to consider the problems of national defence: to counter not only *the high and insatiable appetite* of the French King, but also *the subtle, untrue, and crafty ymaginacion* of Henry's brother-in-law, James IV of Scotland. Despite the misgivings of Foxe and Warham—the latter, as Chancellor, opened parliament on 4 February with a discourse on the text, *Justitia et Pax osculate sunt*—parliament was ready to support a more positive policy: on 20 February Julius II's bull telling of the injuries inflicted on the Holy See by Louis XII was first opened to the Lords and then the Commons; by the end of the month a bill for the Marquess of Dorset and his expedition to Guienne was set in motion; and on the eve of the prorogation of parliament on 30 March, the Commons, through their Speaker, Sir Robert Sheffield,[1] made a grant of two tenths and fifteenths.

That Sheffield's election had been announced in the Lords by a deputation led by the Controller of the Household (Sir Edward Poynings) would indicate that it was entirely acceptable to the Crown. Sheffield was not a member of the royal Council, as so many of his recent predecessors had been. He was, however, a wealthy lawyer of about fifty years old with some considerable general experience and ability, well connected by family and other ties; and evidently he was at this time in the King's good graces, as he had been in Henry VII's.

Most of the property Sheffield possessed was in the north-east Midlands. His father, a barrister of the Temple who had been retained as counsel to the Duchy of Lancaster under Edward IV and Richard III,[2] had acquired by marriage estates in Lincolnshire, notably the manors at Butterwick (in the Isle of Axholme) and South Coningsby. Chilwell and Babbington in Nottinghamshire had been added by Sir Robert's own marriage, his wife being Elena, a daughter

[1] *DNB*, xviii. 16; Wedgwood, op. cit., *Biographies*, 760.
[2] R. Somerville, op. cit., i. 454.

of Sir John Delves of Doddington (Cheshire) and Uttoxeter (Staffs.) who, when Treasurer of Henry VI's Household, had been killed at the battle of Tewkesbury in 1471.[1] With such estates in prospect for his son and heir, Sheffield was able to marry him to the sister of Thomas Stanley, second Earl of Derby, who (through her mother) was second cousin to Henry VIII.

Sir Robert himself seems, however, to have had much of his own way to make. His first proper royal appointment came only in March 1493, when Henry VII made him steward of all the estates in the Bishop of Durham's liberty of Howdenshire (Yorks.) during a vacancy of the see.[2] But then, in 1495, Sheffield became Recorder of London, an office which he did not relinquish until April 1508, and, in the meantime, he represented the City in each of the last three of Henry VII's parliaments (in 1495, 1497, and 1504). It was as Recorder of London that, along with the mayor and one of the sheriffs, he was knighted by Henry VII on 17 June 1497, when the King entered the City after defeating the Cornish rebels at Blackheath.[3] Royal favour, doubtless helped by his own standing in the region of his estates, then brought him a useful collection of local offices and other perquisites. And in February 1501 he gained a half-share in a 20 years' lease of the custody of the royal castle and gaol of Lincoln[4] and another half-share in the wardship of the lands of the late Andrew Dimmock, another Lincolnshire man who had been Second Baron of the Exchequer at the time of his death.[5] And in February 1508, just before Sheffield ceased to be Recorder of London, Henry VII made him steward for life of the Leicestershire and Nottinghamshire manors of the late Viscount Beaumont.[6] Sir Robert was among the recipients of royal liveries when he attended Henry VII's funeral,[7] and Henry VIII not only retained him as constable, and keeper of the gaol, of Lincoln Castle and as a J.P. in Lindsey,[8] but three months after his accession (on 20 July 1509) appointed him as well to be

---

[1] L. and P., Domestic and Foreign, Henry VIII, vol. i, part 1, no. 438 (3) m. 18; CCR, 1485–1500, no. 482. It was at Butterwick that, according to Leland, Sheffield began to build stately . . . as it apperith by a great Towr of brike.

[2] CPR, 1485–94, 422.

[3] C. L. Kingsford, Chronicles of London, p. 215.

[4] R. Somerville, op. cit., i. 583.

[5] CPR, 1494–1509, 232.

[6] Ibid., 572.

[7] L. and P., op. cit., vol. i, part 1, no. 20 (p. 12).

[8] Ibid., vol. ii, part 1, no. 2537. At the time of his death Sheffield was Custos Rotulorum in the parts of Lindsey.

steward of all the Crown lands in the soke of Kirton-in-Lindsey and at Hull and other places in south Yorkshire, an office which Sheffield kept until his death.[1]

All in all, it is hardly surprising that the Speaker of 1512–14 was well known at Court. Sir Thomas Lovell, who was Treasurer of the Household to both Henry VII and Henry VIII and also had connexions with Nottinghamshire, was evidently even something of a friend: at least Sheffield was to make him the overseer of his will.[2] It is especially worth noting, too, that at the time of Sir Robert's election to the Speakership he was already known to Thomas Wolsey,[3] then the King's Almoner, who was doing all of his best to encourage his sovereign in a policy of continental intervention. In 1517, the year before his death, Sheffield was to insult and quarrel with Wolsey and, as a result, spend some time in the Tower.[4] But in the two years of his Speakership there can hardly have been anything wrong between them. Certainly, Sheffield did what he could in support of the war-effort, and not only as Speaker: when, in May 1512, the Marquess of Dorset was directed to the conquest of Guienne, and various gentlemen contributed soldiers to the expedition, Sir Robert Sheffield's contingent numbered fifty, a figure not exceeded, apparently, by any other commoner.[5]

Without assistance from Ferdinand of Aragon, who simply exploited the English force as a screen against French interference with his conquest of Navarre, Dorset's expedition was a complete fiasco, and his mutinous army came home in October 1512. The King was disgusted but not dismayed. It was imperative to restore his credit abroad: the war with France must continue. And parliament, in its second session (from 4 November to 20 December 1512), backed him up with a grant of another tenth and fifteenth, coupled with a graduated tax on landed income, or movables, or wages, payable in the following summer. The large reward of £200 with which, in January 1513, the Speaker was credited in the *King's Book of Payments* (the account-book of the Treasurer of the Chamber) is

---

[1] *L. and P.*, op. cit., vol. i, part 1, no. 132 (70).

[2] N. H. Nicolas, *Testamenta Vetusta*, pp. 555–6.

[3] A royal grant, to a groom of the ewery, of the office of bailiff in a Gloucestershire hundred—not precisely dated but attributable to the first year of the reign —was jointly certified by Wolsey and Sheffield before being countersigned by the Lord Treasurer and others of the Council (*L. and P.*, op. cit., vol. i, part 1, 448 (8)).

[4] See below, pp. 320–1.

[5] *L. and P.*, op. cit., vol. i, part 1, no. 1176 (3).

sufficient comment on the value put by the King on Sheffield's services in the Lower House during the session.[1]

Although Henry again found himself left in the lurch by his father-in-law of Spain after they had agreed on a joint invasion of France, he himself crossed the Channel with a great army on 30 June 1513. In the course of a short campaign in Artois, he won the battle of the Spurs (13 August) and then took Thérouanne (23 August) and Tournai (25 September). Between times, James IV of Scotland had been killed and his army decimated at Flodden Field on 9 September. English prestige stood higher than since Henry V, and before the King came home he concluded plans with Ferdinand and the Emperor Maximilian for a concerted attack on France in the next year. Meanwhile, on 27 August, five days after James IV had come south across the Tweed, Sir Robert Sheffield had been instructed to adjudicate on all disputes arising in Lincolnshire out of a seizure of the property of Scottish nationals.[2] A week later, on 3 September, the Speaker's brother (and executor-to-be), Sir Thomas Sheffield, Treasurer of the English preceptory of the Order of the Knights of the Hospital of St John, then on his way with a colleague from this country through Germany and northern Italy to the headquarters of his Order at Rhodes, was being given an audience by the Doge of Venice: the two Hospitallers, both of whom had been told earlier in the year to furnish companies for the great royal expedition of the summer, were now acting as ambassadors for Henry VIII. They had been charged to assure the Signory of Henry's friendship, declare his dissatisfaction with their mutual allies of the Holy League, and explain why, in what circumstances, and on what sort of conditions, he might be compelled to come to terms with France. It was not until six weeks later (on 13 October) that a letter of 13 September reached Venice and, with its news of the taking of Thérouanne, the imminent fall of Tournai, and the victory of Flodden, brought the changed picture of events into view.[3]

Preparations for the renewal of the French campaign went ahead during the winter of 1513–14. On 7 November parliament was put off until 20 January 1514. After only a short delay, it met on 23rd, from when it continued in session until its dissolution on 4 March. Sometime before this step was even decided, in consideration of the victories of the previous year a poll-tax of no less than £160,000 was

---

[1] Ibid., vol. ii, part 2, p. 1459.   [2] Ibid., vol. i, part 2, no. 2222 (16).
[3] Ibid., nos. 1836 (3), 2234, 2254, 2263; *Cal. S.P.*, *Venetian*, *1509–19*, nos. 285–6.

conceded, elaborately graduated in its incidence and made payable at midsummer by local commissioners nominated by the Commons themselves. A number of other stipulations, unprecedented in both their character and complexity, were added in an attempt to ensure a full yield: on 18 June the local commissioners for the tax were to deliver one part of their indentures to the Barons of the Exchequer, and a fortnight later another part to a committee consisting of the Lord Treasurer, the Justices of the Benches, the Speaker of the Parliament, one of the knights for every shire, two citizens of London, one M.P. from each of eighteen important towns, and any others of the Lower House who cared to attend; if parliament should continue so long, all matters touching the certificate were to be *ordered and set in further direction by the Commons*; otherwise, the Lord Treasurer's committee was to have parliamentary authority not only to fine the commissioners for any negligence, but also—and of much greater significance—to increase the rate of the tax if its yield failed to reach the total granted, this new assessment to be made within twelve weeks, reported on in twenty-four, and paid up in forty. Even in February 1515, the tax had produced little more than £50,000 (less than a third of what had been granted), and it is not surprising that doubt was expressed whether the committee was entitled to make good so great a deficiency, and that the matter was left over for another parliament to decide. (When the original sum granted was finally raised, its collection was nearly three and a half years overdue.)

None of this, of course, redounded to Speaker Sheffield's discredit: although re-elected to the next parliament, he was not chosen Speaker, but he led the Commons' deputation to announce his successor's election and, in addition to the gratuity he had received after the second session of his Speakership, he was given another £100 on 24 April 1515.[1] This sum he again received at the hands of Sir John Heron, the Treasurer of the King's Chamber (since 1492), whose continuance in office and freedom from accountability in the Exchequer had happened to be secured by a statute passed in the course of Sheffield's Speakership (in 1513).

Since the dissolution of parliament on 4 March 1514, the situation abroad had undergone a seemingly radical change. Henry's plans to renew the French war had collapsed with the defection of his allies, Ferdinand and Maximilian. Duped once again by his father-in-law, Henry made peace with Louis XII in July 1514 on terms which sug-

[1] *L. and P.*, op. cit., vol. ii, part 1, no. 372.

gested that at last he had taken the measure of Ferdinand's deceit: Tournai remained in English hands, the annual English pension under the Treaty of Étaples was stepped up, and on 9 October Henry's sister Mary married the French King. Discussions over the possibility of the brothers-in-law co-operating in an attack on Spain —to push Ferdinand out of his recent acquisitions in Navarre and to prosecute Henry's rights in Castile—portended a new war-budget. In any case, urgent financial reasons why another parliament should not be long deferred, were already present: the hopelessly inadequate revenue collected from the subsidies recently granted.

Summoned on 23 November, the new parliament met on 5 February 1515. For their Speaker the Commons now chose Thomas Neville of Mereworth (Kent),[1] a member of the King's Council. His election was unquestionably very acceptable to the King, who knighted him in the presence of the Lords and Commons at his official presentation: a new precedent, according to the Clerk of the Parliaments. The latter's note on the ceremony in the Lords' Journal[2] refers to Neville as *ex nobili domo et familia procreatus, germanus frater Domini Burgevenney*. Born about 1480, he was the fifth son of George, second Baron Abergavenny. His eldest brother, George, who had come into the title on their father's death in 1492 and been summoned to parliament since 1497, had stood high at Court, certainly since Henry VIII's accession: in December 1512, as the representative of the Beauchamp family, he had been granted by the King the castle and lands of Abergavenny, these and his other estates being settled on himself and the male heirs of his body, his brother Thomas lying next in the entail; in January 1513 he had been appointed Warden of the Cinque Ports and constable of Dover castle; created a Knight of the Garter in April, he was Captain-General of the royal army in France from June to October 1513 and more recently, from May to August 1514, had been acting as Chief Captain of the English forces in the March of Calais. The Speaker's younger brother, Edward, who had been an Esquire of the Body from the beginning of the reign, had also served, as a member of the King's guard, in the army of 1513 and been knighted at the fall of Tournai; a year later, Edward was again in France, this time (in October 1514) in Paris, for the coronation of the King's sister Mary.

Not a great deal is known of Thomas Neville before his Speakership, but his career appears to have been cast in an administrative

[1] *DNB*, xiv. 302.
[2] *Journals of the House of Lords*, vol. i, p. 20.

mould. Before the end of Henry VII's reign he was a royal councillor and, as such, enjoying considerable annual fees amounting to over £86, which Henry VIII at once confirmed.[1] There is no question that he was a member of the Council when elected Speaker: as recently as 15 July 1514 he had been granted an annuity of £100, during good behaviour, 'for his good counsel to be given and attendance about the King's person to be made',[2] and there is a record of his countersigning (as a councillor) a royal grant to the Earl of Derby of his mother's inheritance on 28 November 1514.[3] It was perhaps partly because of this office that, a J.P. in Kent from September 1512, he was also put on the local benches of Middlesex, Surrey and Sussex in the course of 1514. Thomas Neville's influence at Court can hardly have been diminished by his recent marriage to Katherine, the widow of George Lord FitzHugh (ob. January 1513), she being a sister of Thomas Lord Dacre,[4] Warden of the West March towards Scotland since 1486, who had given of his best at Flodden Field.

Few Tudor Speakers can have had a more difficult passage through office than Sir Thomas Neville. External affairs, especially English relations with France, which in the autumn of 1514 had seemed to be entering a more settled state, soon gave rise to fresh anxiety. For on 1 January 1515, over a month before parliament was due to meet, Louis XII died. His successor, Francis I, confirmed Louis' treaty with England on 5 April 1515 (the day on which the first of the two parliamentary sessions of the year ended). But this was only so that Francis should be left free to follow his designs in northern Italy; and after his great victory at Marignano (13 September) he reconquered the Milanese and threatened the papacy. In order to make doubly sure that England would not interfere, Francis did his best to cause trouble across her northern border: he encouraged the Duke of Albany in his bid to wrest the regency of Scotland from James IV's widow, Henry's sister Margaret, who, at the end of September, had to seek refuge in Northumberland. Coming on top of the resentment at Francis' phenomenal success south of the Alps, this nearer development stirred Westminster to thoughts of war. When parliament met for its final session in November 1515, it was given out that it must discuss an expedition against Scotland. The financial situation, however, acted as a damper: war was out of the question, at least on the continent. Here it appeared more economical to offer

[1] L. and P., op. cit., vol. ii, part 1, p. 874.
[2] Ibid., vol. i, part 2, no. 3107 (42).   [3] Ibid., no. 2499 (72).
[4] The Complete Peerage, ed. Vicary Gibbs, vol. iv, pp. 18 et seq.

subsidies and stiffen resistance wherever French ambition was causing anxiety. Obviously, even such a temporizing policy would be
costly; and in the sphere of parliamentary taxation the year 1515 was
sometimes one of frustration, always one of difficulty.

Parliament had been in session for only five days when, on 10
February 1515, a powerful delegation from the Upper House, headed
by the Chancellor, pointed out to the Commons the King's intentions and necessities. It did not fail to draw their notice to the fact
that less than a third of the taxes voted in the previous year had been
collected: of £160,000, nearly £110,000 was still outstanding. When
the first session ended on 5 April, it had been agreed that this outstanding sum should be provided by a new general subsidy of 6d.
in the £, to be assessed before Michaelmas and paid by 21 November.
But it is evident that the financial experts were working in the dark,
because it was also agreed that, if this grant fell short by as much as
£30,000, a second similar subsidy should be levied a year later; if, on
the other hand, a less serious deficit resulted, provision was to be
made by the Speaker and others of the Commons in a meeting in the
Exchequer Chamber with the Chancellor, the Treasurer, and the
judges. In fact, when the autumn session began on 12 November,
the deficit was found to be over £64,000, so that before the dissolution on 22 December the Commons had not only to sanction the
hitherto provisional second subsidy (payable in November 1516) but
also add to it a tenth and fifteenth (payable in November 1517). That
this extra vote was made to follow the traditional form suggests
some general dissatisfaction at the new type of subsidy, and possibly
some concern over the sheer bulk of the current impositions. Much
more probably, however, the merit of a tenth and fifteenth was its
certainty, even though its incidence was inequitable.

As if difficulties over finance were not enough, both sessions of
this 1515 parliament were confused by disputes over ecclesiastical
rights of jurisdiction and other problems affecting the liberty of the
Church. During the first session, parliament was quite convulsed by
the passions aroused in the heresy case of Richard Hunne. This
further inflamed the strong feelings already excited by the more
general question of benefit of clergy. A statute of 1512 had denied
the privilege to murderers and robbers among the clergy in minor
orders, those 'half-breeds of later medieval civilization, laymen
except for their privilege, clergy except for their character' (Pollard).
That statute had been enacted only until the next parliament, and in
the meantime Pope Leo X had formally re-emphasized the freedom

of the clergy from secular jurisdiction. It was now necessary to decide whether the act should lapse or be confirmed. The subsequent dispute over clerical immunity caused serious trouble in both Houses, and during both sessions of the parliament: in the first session, a Commons' bill to renew the act was scotched in the Upper House, where the bishops were against it and the temporal peers divided in opinion; in the second, the quarrel was extended when Convocation cited the Franciscan, Dr Standish, for lecturing in public against both the validity of minor orders and the exemption of the clergy from lay jurisdiction, even when these were sanctioned by papal constitutions. After the judges declared Convocation liable to a *praemunire*, Wolsey made a partial submission on behalf of the clergy. His proposal to refer the matter to Rome was disallowed, but when the Commons persisted with bills regarding both benefit of clergy and heresy, he was able to persuade the King to dissolve parliament.

Difficult though both sessions of the 1515 parliament proved, it is evident that the conduct of the Commons' Speaker himself had been satisfactory to the government. Neville was given a reward of £100 after even the first session (in June 1515),[1] and this may have been repeated after the close of the parliament. He certainly continued to be a member of the Privy Council and, in that capacity, was to be a signatory to the treaty of peace with France (and to the supplementary treaty for a marriage between the Princess Mary and the Dauphin) concluded in October 1518.[2] By this time he was Keeper of the King's Wards.[3] Incidentally, his predecessor in the Speakership, Sir Robert Sheffield, was now nothing like so fortunate. During the first session of the parliament of 1515 Wolsey had made use of him to re-draft the Resumption Act. But it looks as though Sheffield took even a leading part in encouraging the Commons in their anti-clerical policy and so incurred Wolsey's hostility: in July 1517 he was committed to the Tower for his contempt in complaining about the Cardinal to the King and, after being let out, was put back in February 1518. Wolsey now charged him

[1] *L. and P.*, op. cit., vol. ii, part 2, p. 1468.
[2] Ibid., nos. 4469, 4475.
[3] Ibid., no. 4230. Of Neville's later career, it may be noted that he was in the royal entourage at Henry VIII's meeting with Francis I at the Field of Cloth of Gold and at subsequent meetings with the Emperor, Charles V, at Gravelines (in 1520) and in England (in 1522); that by 1532 he was steward of the abbey of Westminster; and that he died on 29 May 1542 and was buried at Mereworth. His first wife, Katherine Dacre, had died in 1527. His second wife was the widow of a wealthy London goldsmith (Robert Amadas).

(maliciously, Sheffield alleged) with the felony of harbouring a murderer. But the real cause of his offence was evidently that he had been 'fast in the cause of the temporalty' in 1515, and had later stated that 'it was unhappy that the lords temporal were at variance at that time, for, had not that been, my lord Cardinal's head should have been as red as his coat was'.[1]

It was as cardinal that Wolsey had assumed the headship of the English Church in the final session of the parliament of 1515. His rise to this ecclesiastical eminence had followed fast upon his achievement of the position of chief adviser to the King. Consecrated Bishop of Lincoln in March 1514, within half a year he had been translated to York; a year later and he was elected to the Sacred College. The red hat itself did not arrive in time for the re-opening of parliament, as Wolsey had desired; but on the first Sunday of the second session (18 November) the ceremony of its conferment was made as impressive as could be. Even so, the Cardinal's earliest experiences as the mainstay of the ecclesiastical interest can only have been distasteful, his intention in 1515 being to make himself responsible for any church reforms and to exclude parliament from all share in them. This partly explains his pursuit of the legateship *a latere* (not acquired until 1518) and also his aversion to parliament. That his replacement of Archbishop Warham as custodian of the Great Seal on the day of the dissolution of the parliament of 1515 (22 December) would entail a reversal of the policy of regular consultation with parliament, could hardly have been unexpected. Not so long ago, Warham had been advising frequent parliaments. With Wolsey as Lord Chancellor, 'on parliament was imposed its longest recess till the days of Charles I' (Pollard), the next longest being none other than that which followed it. In the fourteen years of Wolsey's rule (1515–29), parliament met only once. This was in 1523.

It would hardly be in place to discuss in detail Wolsey's policy as Lord Chancellor and Legate. His control of the Great Seal (to which he clung as though it was almost a personal chattel), together with

---

[1] Ibid., nos. 3487, 3591. Examined before Wolsey on 13 February 1518, Sheffield confessed that he had spoken as reported of the *variance* between the lords temporal and the Cardinal, surrendered his royal pardon (kneeling in the middle of the Council and breaking the seal), and put himself on the King's mercy, asking Wolsey and the other lords to intercede for him. He was liberated on his own and his son's bail (ibid., no. 4616), but died later in the same year (between 8 August and 9 December). He was buried in the church of the London Augustinians. His son and heir, Robert, died in 1531, leaving a son, Edmund, who was created a baron at the accession of Edward VI.

his dominance in the Council, allowed him a complete mastery of the courts of Star Chamber, Requests, and Admiralty. He did not fail to make energetic use of the court of Chancery itself and, especially by promoting its jurisdiction over trusts and uses, finally settled that it should develop as a court of equity. As legate *a latere*, he regulated the whole system of ecclesiastical jurisdiction in each of the provinces of Canterbury and York. His administration in both the temporal and the spiritual sphere was detested. It seemed to be too omni-competent. But since he was extremely efficient in dispensing justice and utterly tireless, and Henry VIII's reliance on his counsel was both unlimited and exclusive, his authority held firm. In domestic administration, Wolsey sought no assistance of parliament. Rather, when, after a break of more than seven years, parliament met in 1523, it was to face the financial consequences of Wolsey's vigorous foreign policy, the aim of which was to achieve for England an international importance that in fact was hardly warranted by her own resources.

Given Henry VIII's self-conscious pride and Wolsey's own ambition to cut a figure in continental diplomacy, English policy abroad was likely to remain positive in conception. Active intervention along the lines of 1512–13 was at first, of course, quite precluded by Francis I's early military and diplomatic successes. In 1516 it was impossible to make headway against him. In 1517 there even began a fresh rapprochement between England and France which culminated in October 1518 in Wolsey's negotiating (in London) a 'universal peace' between Pope Leo X, Maximilian I, and the Kings of England, France, and Spain, their avowed object being to make possible a joint crusade against the Turks. Admittedly, in order to enjoy the prestige of appearing as the conservator of the peace of Christendom, England relinquished Tournai to the French. But the town had been expensive to occupy, and the price of its surrender was no less than 600,000 crowns: moreover, it was agreed that Henry's infant daughter Mary, the heir-presumptive, should eventually marry the Dauphin. Henry and Francis continued to appear to be on good terms until even as late as the summer of 1520, when they met in Picardy on the Field of Cloth of Gold. This magnificent exchange of royal civilities seems, however, to have been no more than a 'portentous deception' (Pollard). The English King was just about to conclude an offensive and defensive alliance against France with his nephew by marriage, the Emperor Charles V, who had recently visited him in England; and this treaty was to be implemented as soon as a state of open enmity was reached between Charles and Francis.

Ever since 1516, when Charles of Habsburg, already master of the Netherlands, followed Ferdinand V in the rule of Castile, Aragon and Naples, and more rapidly since 1519, when he had succeeded Maximilian I in the Habsburg lands and also in the imperial title, tension had been growing between the two princes. Charles intended to retain Spanish Navarre. Francis possessed much of Charles's Burgundian inheritance and was occupying the imperial fief of Milan. Each appeared to threaten the other's security: Charles seemed to encircle France, Francis to jeopardize Charles's lines of communication. Both were anxious for English support as a useful makeweight. Wolsey's aim was to exploit the rivalry. But his freedom of diplomatic manœuvre was really limited, not least by domestic considerations: the English nobility and people were traditionally anti-French in feeling; the English commercial classes, in view of their strong links with Flanders and Charles's control of its wool-market, were imperialist; Queen Katherine, who in her person represented the value of the Spanish alliance, used what influence she had on behalf of her imperial nephew. Charles had his difficulties: Lutheranism portended serious disunity in Germany; the revolt of the Communeros was on his hands in Spain. But for England to war against him at this juncture was unthinkable. And, if for the next two years after 1520 Wolsey contrived to make Charles and Francis continue to bid against each other, this was only to allow England to extract a maximum of concessions from Charles when finally she committed herself to his support in the field. After a war on several fronts during 1521—in Navarre, Flanders and northern Italy—late in the year the Anglo-imperial alliance was confirmed. Wolsey's chagrin when Adrian of Utrecht, Charles's tutor, was preferred to himself for the papacy in January 1522 could hardly count for as much as Francis's seizure of the wares of English merchants at Bordeaux in March following and his suspension of the payment of the annual pensions to England (Wolsey's own included). And Charles, during another personal visit to England between 26 May and 6 July, had no difficulty in securing (by the treaty of Windsor) the promise of an immediate English invasion of France, the hand of the Princess Mary, and an agreement to eradicate heresy. Very shortly afterwards the Earl of Surrey raided the Breton coasts and later in the summer led an army, 15,000 strong, from Calais across the French frontier. This enterprise proved not only futile in itself, but provoked the Scots into some divertive show of hostility, so that in April 1523, Surrey, the leader of the vanguard at Flodden, was sent to retaliate by devastating the valley of the Tweed. Two days after parliament met, he was moving his forces forward from New-castle upon Tyne to Berwick. Three days later still, Lord Dacre invaded on the west.

It was almost entirely because of the financial strain that was being imposed by this busy foreign policy that Wolsey had been driven to assemble parliament. In the previous year he had begun a levy of forced loans worth as much as a property-tax of a tenth on the laity and a fourth on the clergy. But, although this amounted to over £350,000, it fell short, by more than half, of the cost of a single twelvemonth of war. With French influence apparently ruined in Italy, Charles V undertaking to invade southern France from Spain, the Duke of Bourbon (the Constable and most powerful of the peers of France) promising to revolt, and an English expeditionary force ready to move into north-eastern France from Calais under the Duke of Suffolk, there now seemed to be a great opportunity to achieve tangible successes in France, perhaps even to recover the French crown for Henry VIII. But if the Anglo-imperial plans for 1523 were to be realized, a stupendous additional financial effort was still required.

Faced by this situation, Wolsey summoned parliament to meet at the Blackfriars in London on 15 April 1523. And then, vis-à-vis the Commons, he immediately did what he imagined was all for the best by arranging that the Speakership should go to one of their number whom he trusted. Wolsey's nominee for the office was Sir Thomas More,[1] the forty-five-year-old Under-Treasurer of the Exchequer. Having acted for some time as the Cardinal's go-between with the King, More was fully conversant with the details, and alive to the financial consequences, of their continental policy. But given his previous career and abilities, it is hardly likely that the Commons were at all unready to choose him. His reputation, and not only in Court circles, was already established. But reputation for what, and with whom?

Born in 1478, More had been sent to Oxford as a boy by his patron, Cardinal Morton, Henry VII's Lord Chancellor. There he had soon grown into a refined and cultivated student of classical

---

[1] William Roper, *The lyfe of Sir Thomas Moore*, ed. E. V. Hitchcock (Early English Text Society, Orig. Series vol. 197 (1935)); R. W. Chambers, *Thomas More* (London, 1938); *DNB*, xiii. 876–96.

learning, developing an interest which ripened with his friendship for many of the leading English, and some of the continental, exponents of the latest enlightenment. (Among them were Grocyn, Linacre, Colet, Lily, and the great Erasmus of Rotterdam.) His own chief original literary output—the *History of Richard III* and the *Utopia,* both written in his thirties and before (as *hereticis molestus*) he lapsed into theological hack-work—revealed a lively and sensitive mind, critical of contemporary society and opposed to violence whether applied from above or below; the *Utopia* especially, for all its satire and political scepticism, is instinct with moral purpose.[1] Though More was noted among his friends for his love of fun (*festivitas*) and an easy charm (*suavitas*),[2] his own inner life seems always to have been governed by a hankering after spiritual things; and it is quite believable that when, deeply attracted by the ideals of the London Carthusians, he lived with them (*without vowe*) for a few years after attaining his majority (1499–1503), he genuinely hesitated whether to abandon the law for the priesthood as his vocation. However that may be, it was as a lawyer and, by the time of his Speakership, as a lawyer in the service of the Crown that, with all his various attributes and interests, More had come to be best known, certainly to men of affairs in London and the world at large.

There can be little doubt that appreciation of his lawyerly capabilities eased his acceptance by the Commons for the office of Speaker in 1523. It was then nearly thirty years since, himself the son of a London barrister, he had begun his formal legal training as a student in one of the Chancery inns (New Inn). Although in 1501 he became a Reader at Furnival's Inn, his first allegiance then was to Lincoln's Inn. Here, where he had been entered in 1496, he read for the bar, became a Bencher (in 1509), and was Reader twice (in 1511 and 1515) which, as was noticed by Roper (his son-in-law and biographer), was *as often as any Judge of the Lawe doth reade*. Meanwhile, at the age of twenty-five, he had sat for London in Henry VII's last parliament (1504). On this occasion, his opposition to the

[1] For a criticism of More's literary output, see the expert examination to which it is subjected in C. S. Lewis, *English Literature in the Sixteenth Century* (Oxford, 1954), pp. 165–81.

[2] For a remarkable personal description of More by Erasmus in 1519, see *L. and P.,* op. cit., vol. iii, part 1, p. 394. But compare the remarks of Edward Hall on More when appointed Chancellor in 1529: *a manne well learned in the tongues and also in the Common Lawe, whose witte was fyne and full of imaginacions, by reason wherof he was to muche geven to mockyng, whiche was to his gravitie a great blemishe* (*Hall's Chronicle,* p. 761).

demand for a heavy subsidy for the marriage of the King's eldest daughter to James IV of Scotland is alleged to have been so outspoken as to result in his father, then a serjeant-at-law, being imprisoned and fined. He himself thought of leaving the country. In 1508 he did in fact go abroad, visiting the universities of Louvain and Paris, and the welcome he gave Henry VIII's accession strongly suggests personal relief from a cramping fear of royal disfavour. It was only now that More began his official career, although his first appointment was one within the gift of the civic authorities of London, the office of under-sheriff (that is, legal adviser in cases coming under the jurisdiction of the sheriffs), which he held from September 1510 until July 1518. Bringing in about £400 a year, this office was so lucrative that when More abandoned it, he did so presumably only because of increasing absorption in the business of the Crown.

His earliest employment in this field came in 1515. It was then that he went on a mission to Flanders to treat with the Council of Charles of Habsburg and also to try to resolve some commercial disputes between the London merchants and the Hansards; and soon after this (in 1517) Wolsey made use of his services in negotiations with France. In June 1518 More was first paid a royal annuity of £100, and it was in this year that he was made a judge in the Court of Requests. But at the same time he also became much more deeply involved in matters of diplomacy, and on this account was made a member of the Privy Council. Part of his duty was to act as a liaison between Wolsey and the King; and Henry, with whom More was necessarily in frequent personal touch, so frankly enjoyed his company that their relations were friendly, even affable and familiar. In April 1520 More was again a royal envoy to the Low Countries, assisting with the preparations for the Emperor's visit to England which took place in the following month. He himself attested the treaty for the interview between Charles and Henry. He was present at the Field of Cloth of Gold in June, it being there that he was again told to help with negotiations over English disputes with the Hanseatic League. In the summer of 1521 he was again busy with diplomatic work, attending upon Wolsey himself at Calais and Bruges. He was still acting as the Cardinal's go-between with the King, whom, incidentally, earlier in the year, he had been advising about that anti-Lutheran tract, the *Assertio VII Sacramentorum*, which now won for Henry from Leo X the title of *Fidei Defensor*.

More was already Under-Treasurer of the Exchequer. He had

been appointed on 2 May 1521 and shortly afterwards was knighted. The office carried with it an annual salary of £173 6s. 8d. This stipend was handsome enough, especially considering that he still enjoyed his councillor's fee of £100 per annum. But between then and his Speakership, More secured additional sources of income by royal gift: on 8 May 1522 he was granted (in fee simple) the manor of South in the township of Tonbridge (Kent), forfeited for treason in the previous year by the Duke of Buckingham; and on 7 March 1523 he was assigned the wardship and marriage of Giles, son and heir of Sir John Heron, formerly Treasurer of the King's Chamber (1492–1521), who had died in the previous spring.[1] But notwithstanding his being evidently in great favour with the King and Wolsey, More was personally not in sympathy with their policy of war against France. Nor was he afraid to declare himself. He wrote of the war to Wolsey in September 1522: *I pray God if hit be good for his Grace and this realme, that than it may preve so, and ellis in the stede therof, I pray God send his Grace one honorable and profitable peace.*[2] It was of the scheme of foreign conquest itself that More disapproved or was dubious. But his opinion can hardly have been uninfluenced by his awareness of the damaging effects a big campaign was bound to have on the royal finances for which, as Under-Treasurer, he had a special concern.

From Wolsey's point of view, it was now the Commons' business to supply the sinews of war. This proved a far from easy task: after a full fortnight's sessions the members were no nearer a solution, and their temper was rising high: there was extravagant talk of the cost of the army for a campaign in France leading to coining in leather, of Thérouanne having cost the King *more than twenty such ungracious dogholes could be worth*, and of the folly of seeking possessions in France while Scotland was still independent.[3] So that Wolsey himself *condescended* to the Lower House on two days running. At first, there was even some dispute in the House how he should be

---

[1] On 29 September 1525 Giles Heron was married to Cecily, one of More's own daughters; and on the same day her sister Elizabeth married William, son of Sir John Dauncy, Knight of the Body. More's favourite daughter, Margaret, had been married in July 1521 to William Roper, a young lawyer of Lincoln's Inn, the son of John Roper, Clerk of the Pleas in the Court of King's Bench, and grandson of Sir John Fineux, a former Chief Justice of the Court. When More was Chancellor of the Duchy of Lancaster, William Roper became deputy to the Chief Steward for the south parts of the duchy (R. Somerville, op. cit., i. 431).

[2] *L. and P.*, op. cit., vol. iii, part 2, no. 2555.

[3] Ibid., no. 2958.

Y

received, whether only with a few lords (which perhaps would have been according to precedent) or with as great a following as he cared to bring. But More amusingly won the members over to admit Wolsey's whole retinue, on the ground that, since the Cardinal was already known to be angry with the burgesses for gossiping outside about parliament's business, any further careless talk could be blamed on his own entourage. And so Wolsey entered the Commons in some state.

At his first visit (on 29 April) the Lord Chancellor expatiated on the intolerable wrongs done to the King by Francis I. Then, stating that the war was unavoidable, he exhorted the Commons to cover its cost with a subsidy of £800,000, that is, a grant of 4s. in the £ of every man's lands or goods. On the following day, however, despite the Speaker's urgent support for Wolsey's proposal, the Commons complained that the King's recent income from loans and his present demand would together be almost equivalent to a subsidy of a third. Moreover, they sent a deputation to ask Wolsey that, because such taxation was impossible, he should suggest to the King that an easier sum be demanded. The Chancellor's prompt and only answer to this plea was a second visit, this time to overawe and if necessary hector the Commons into compliance. Expressing disbelief in the alleged poverty of the realm, Wolsey repeated his demand for nothing short of the whole grant. The House held its peace, none of the members, not even those he singled out, giving him an answer: *a mervailous, obstinate silens*. Nor was the Cardinal's angry embarrassment allayed by the Speaker's intervention. The tenor of More's reply, however smooth his compliments, was as independent as he knew the Commons themselves had a right to be in such circumstances: attributing the hush to the members' being intimidated by the Cardinal's presence (which evidently they were not!), he went on to assert that for any of them to answer would be inexpedient and also contrary to their ancient liberty of debating in private, excusing himself as unable to respond for want of any instruction. And so, displeased with the Speaker, *that had not in this parliament in all things satisfied his desire* (Roper), and generally much put out, Wolsey retreated.[1]

Yet another fortnight passed before, on 13 May, the Commons agreed to vote supplies. They now undertook to make a grant, payable in each of two years, of a shilling in the £ on lands or goods worth more than £20, 6d. in the £ on those valued at between £2 and £20, and a poll-tax of 4d. on men over sixteen assessed at short

[1] *Hall's Chronicle*, pp. 655–6; William Roper, op. cit., pp. 16–19.

of £2, foreigners paying double. All this was only managed—as an unknown M.P. wrote to the Earl of Surrey—after *the grettiste and soreste hold in the lower Hous for payemente of ijs of the £ that ever was sene, I thinke, in any parliamente,* the matter having been *debated and beatten xv or xvj dayes to gidder,* and not before the knights of the King's Council and others of his servants and gentlemen in the House had been for a long time *spoken with and made to say ye* (in other words, won over into making an efficient majority). Surrey's correspondent, after expressing amazement at the unprecedented amount and some doubts about its collection, informed him that he thought that parliament would soon be dissolved, *nowe that this matier is soo ferre passid.*[1] But Wolsey was still not satisfied, showing his annoyance by telling the Commons, untruthfully, that the Lords had fallen in with the whole of his demand and granted 4s. in the £. And so the Court party among the Commons, led by Sir John Hussey of Sleaford, formerly Henry VII's Controller of Household and now Master of the King's Wards and Chief Butler, did their best to accommodate the Cardinal and step up the amount: Hussey proposed that gentlemen with lands worth over £50 per annum should continue to pay 1s. in the £ for an additional, third year. Some of this class in the House objected. But, when a vote was taken, although only ten or twelve supported the motion, none were against it, and the burgesses abstained, so that by a small minority all the gentlemen were further charged, *for the whiche graunte, Sir Ihon Huse had muche evill will* (Hall).[2] It was presumably straight after this that, on 21 May, parliament was prorogued for three weeks.

During this Whitsuntide recess, the burgesses themselves were believed to be ready to grant an additional shilling in the £. But when parliament had resumed on 10 June, and the landowners moved that their own grant of a shilling in the £ for a third year should be matched by a grant of a shilling in the £ on goods in the next (a fourth year), there was again *muche reasonyng.* Over two weeks went by, and on 27 June the issue was still in doubt, the gentry being in favour of the new additional grant, the burgesses opposed. The House was so much at variance that the latter not only *severed theimselfes from the knightes of the sheres* but also *stifly affirmed that the mocioners of this demande wer enemies to the realme* (Hall). However, Speaker More interceded and got them to come together, so that

[1] *Original Letters,* ed. Henry Ellis (London, 1824), vol. i, p. 220; *The Lords' Journals,* vol. i, pp. lxxvi–xc.
[2] *Hall's Chronicle,* p. 657.

eventually, but even then only *after long perswadyng and privie laboryng of frendes*, the extra grant for a fourth year was agreed. This result seemingly was not achieved much before 6 July when, in a letter to Lord Darcy, Sir John Hussey wrote that *the Parliament goeth forth, and sums of money are granted, as ye know well enough.* Progress was certainly being made, but Hussey could only add—a *cri de cœur*—that *we be yet so busied with common causes in the Parliament, that there is no leisure to solicit our own particular matters.*[1] Common causes, including the passage of some anti-alien acts to placate the Commons, kept the parliament in being for yet another month and more: on 29 July it was adjourned for two days to admit of reassembly, on account of plague in the City, at Westminster. Here on 13 August, after More's presentation of the subsidy-bill and other formalities, this second wearisome session ended and parliament was dissolved. To appreciate the fatigue of the members in general and still more that of the Speaker, it only needs to recall Thomas Cromwell's well-known cynicisms in the letter he wrote to John Creke at Bilbao on 17 August: *I, amongst other, have indured a parliament, which continued by the space of seventeen whole weeks, where we commuted of war, peace, strife, contention, debate, murmur, grudge, riches, poverty, penury, truth, falsehood, justice, equity, deceit, oppression, magnanimity, activity, force, attempraunce, treason, murder, felony . . ., and also how a commonwealth might be edified and also continued within our realm. Howbeit, in conclusion, we have done as our predecessors have been wont to do, that is to say, as well as we might, and left where we began.*[2]

Although Sir Thomas More had evidently desired to preserve, perhaps even to enlarge, the liberties and customs of the Lower House, it would appear that in this parliament he had done as much for the government as was consonant with the basic function of his office. Wolsey none the less was so dissatisfied with his conduct (More's son-in-law Roper tells us) that he wished he had promoted somebody else to be Speaker; he even went so far as to suggest to the King that More should be sent, against his own wish, as ambassador to Spain.[3] And yet the Cardinal was not so uncharitable as to decline to write on More's behalf to secure him the Speaker's usual fees of £100 at the Exchequer and £100 from the King's Chamber.[4] More, of course, was just too valuable a servant to be either alienated or dispensed with. And, not only did he continue to act for

---

[1] *L. and P.*, op. cit., vol. iii, part 2, no. 3164.
[2] Ibid., no. 3249.   [3] Roper, op. cit., p. 19.
[4] *State Papers, Henry VIII*, vol. i, part 1, pp. 124, 127.

Wolsey as his go-between with the King, but before very long received other marks of Wolsey's confidence. In view of the strong local objections to the royal charter (of April 1523) by which Wolsey intended the Chancellor of the University of Oxford and his officials to have an exclusive jurisdiction over all persons enjoying the privileges of the University, More's appointment as High Steward of the University on 10 June 1524 was almost certainly one brought about at Wolsey's instance. Towards the end of the following year he was also made High Steward of the University of Cambridge.[1] That the King himself had come to place a higher value than ever on More's administrative capabilities had meanwhile been made clear by his appointment for life on 30 September 1525 as Chancellor of the Duchy (and also of the County Palatine) of Lancaster, an office which soon (in January 1526) entailed his resignation from the Under-Treasurership of the Exchequer.[2] And More only abandoned the duchy office when appointed Chancellor of England on 25 October 1529.

Wolsey's handling of the parliament of 1523 had scarcely had the effect of popularizing his foreign intentions. Even so, what with the Scottish war (on which nearly 100,000 marks had been spent by the end of the year) and the launching of Suffolk's army into France in September, the Cardinal's immediate need of money was so pressing that he was soon driven into far more questionable excesses: without waiting for the first instalment of the parliamentary subsidies (due in February 1524), he overrode the Commons' stipulation that their grant should be spread over four years and, in October 1523, issued commissions for the whole of it to be collected at once *by anticipation*; and when, less than two years later, the tax of 1523 had yielded scarcely more than £150,000, and the Crown was in worse straits for funds than ever, he ignored the need for a parliament altogether and levied a graduated income-tax at 3s. 4d. in the £ on the laity and at twice that rate on the clergy—the Amicable Grant of 1525—simply by prerogative. It was now that the discontents already vocal in 1523 came to a head in the country at large: in face of sometimes only sullen, sometimes quite open, resistance, the new imposition had to be abandoned.

---

[1] A. B. Emden, *A Biographical Register of the University of Oxford to A.D. 1500*, vol. ii, p. 1306.

[2] R. Somerville, op. cit., i. 393. Only three months before this appointment, More had been given for life the office of duchy steward in Essex, Herts., and Middlesex (ibid., 606).

All along, but with ever greater force, it was being realized that the Cardinal's foreign policy was itself at fault and not worth all the heavy outlay. Whereas, under cover of Suffolk's excursion in the autumn of 1523 to within forty miles of Paris, Charles V had been enabled to recover Milan, Genoa, and Tournai, Henry VIII had gained nothing of French territory for himself. And the victory of the imperial forces at Pavia (24 February 1525), where Francis I was taken prisoner, was so complete that Charles could disregard altogether the claims of his English ally to be restored to the lands of France once won by Edward III and Henry V. Although the King and Wolsey were at first keen to exploit the great French disaster by an invasion of Normandy in May 1525, the situation left them no real option but peace, and soon Wolsey was driven to construct an Anglo-French alliance which matured in 1527. His policy of foreign intervention had proved futile and when parliament next met, in 1529, was in ruins. So now, partly on account also of his unforgivable failure to promote Henry's divorce from Queen Katherine (the King's Great Cause), was Wolsey's own career as Legate and as Lord Chancellor.

It was his former servant, Sir Thomas More, who was chosen to succeed him in the custody of the Great Seal. And so it came about that the first parliament to meet after Wolsey's dismissal — the Reformation Parliament of 1529-36 — was opened by him who had been Speaker for the Commons in its predecessor. More, therefore, was not only the first Speaker to become Chancellor of England, but also, that being the case, the first to act as Speaker, successively, in each of the two Houses of Parliament.[1]

[1] For some further remarks on More's career as Chancellor and his last days, see the Appendix.

CHAPTER 12

Conclusion

WHEN once the Commons had got into the habit of meeting outside the parliament-chamber where the King and Council deliberated with the Lords Spiritual and Temporal, the need would obviously arise for some exchange of views between the Houses. This occasionally resulted in delegations holding joint discussions. But when the two Houses did not have recourse to this procedure of 'intercommuning', other convenient means of communication were available. Messages from the Lords to the Commons might be conveyed by an important royal official, with perhaps a few of the peers at his back. Proposals from the Commons seem normally to have been delivered by a small deputation of members. Such are bound to have had a spokesman, and he at first is likely to have been chosen merely on each occasion as it arose. In fact, evidence that the Commons used the services of a single spokesman for the duration of a parliament does not appear until the end of Edward III's reign; and there seems good reason to believe that this practice actually began in the Good Parliament of 1376. There soon emerged, however, a regular office, the office of Speaker; and an important contribution to its establishment was made when the Chancellor, at the opening of parliament, began to order the Commons to elect one of their number to perform the office. Such a command was first formally recorded in 1384, and it was not long before it became quite usual.

It was the King who summoned parliament, and its principal concern was to answer his demands. Because the Speaker's responsibility was to convey and explain the Commons' reaction to those demands and also any proposals or views of their own, he was likely to be cognizant of antecedent discussions. On this account and by reason of his distinctive and officially recognized position, he became potentially a royal agent. This being so, the Crown was almost bound to interest itself in his election, even, sooner or later, to the point of actual interference, whether open or concealed. Each one of these two inherent possibilities was, in fact, fulfilled in the course of time. But whenever, in the medieval period, this was the case, there is cause to believe that it was normally by the Commons'

333

tolerance, and that it was always possible for them to retrench. Though the Speaker might assist the government in the Lower House and even come to be paid a royal reward (taking shape before the end of the fifteenth century as an almost regular fee), it was never forgotten that he was primarily the Commons' mouth-piece, and that to them was his chief responsibility. (Supremely, we think of Sir Thomas More in 1523.) The election of the Speaker could be so genuine as to lead to a contest decided by votes (as in 1420); it was possible for the Commons' free choice to result in what was effectively royal disapproval (as in 1399); and a change of Speaker was not out of the question if, in the course of duty, he acted beyond or contrary to the Commons' intention (as in 1413). In a time of crisis, when political passions ran high, a Speaker might be chosen who represented a movement hostile to the King or his administration (as in 1411, 1449, and 1450). Fragmentary though this evidence is, it suggests that at least until the middle of the fifteenth century the Lower House exercised a real choice in elect-ing its Speaker, that his election was not normally a cut-and-dried affair.

However, to say all of this is not to contradict the view that the Commons, in electing a Speaker, might have acted as a general rule in a way calculated to suit the Crown. And if collaboration in ex-pediting parliamentary business was at a premium, an accommoda-tive attitude on the part of the Commons in their Speaker's election was likely, in ordinary circumstances, to be as much to their advan-tage as to the King's. Prudence and self-interest would often prompt the Commons to choose as leader one of their number known to enjoy the King's confidence and goodwill: to do so was in itself to make a friendly gesture, and a wise choice doubtless turned to the credit of the House. But, in any case, the most able men among the knights of the shire in the Commons, those best qualified to dis-charge the Speaker's duties with efficiency and decorum, were bound to include those who had made good in the King's service and were known to, and respected by, the politically influential. Most of the medieval Speakers were, in fact, royal retainers; many of whom be-longed to the King's Household, sometimes holding office there or in some branch of the central executive. Royal retainers, however, though a majority of the early Speakers were, they were not of one type. There was a fairly wide variety. Which is not to say that certain trends cannot be discerned in the Commons' preference. We can best discover what qualifications were looked for in a Speaker, and which

of these are likely to have been considered most important, by dis-
covering what the Speakers were when elected into office.

The first question naturally to arise relates to the Speaker's previous parliamentary experience. That this was not an absolutely
essential qualification is quite evident. A Speaker might be elected
who had not previously been a member of the House. But this certainly did not happen in more than nine out of the seventy-one parliaments meeting between 1376 and 1523 for which the Speaker's name
is known. This calculation, moreover, ignores the gaps in the electoral returns, which are especially embarrassing under the Yorkists
and the first two Tudors; and it would be fairly safe even to halve the
number of these occurrences. It was very rare for a Speaker to be a
newcomer to the House. In the case of more than a few of the
Speakers, their parliamentary experience was considerable. Sometimes, it was even quite intensive: for example, when Bussy became
Speaker in 1394, he had sat without a break in the previous five parliaments; John Russell, when Speaker in 1423, had similarly attended
each of the last six meetings; William Burley, when Speaker in 1445,
had been elected to every one of the preceding nine parliaments.
Former service in the House was doubtless of some importance as a
qualification. None the less, it can hardly have been one of the
determining factors in any Speaker's election.

And if this was so, how much less of a qualification was earlier
experience of the Speakership itself? During the period under review,
it occurred on average roughly only once in three parliaments that
the Speaker had held the office on a previous occasion. Even when
one or more former Speakers had been returned to parliament, the
Commons were just as liable as not to choose somebody else. And,
as is only to be expected, instances of election to the Speakership in
successive parliaments were much more unusual than elections of
men simply with earlier experience of the office. If a Speaker in one
parliament happened to secure re-election to the next—and this was
very far from certain—the odds were generally against his being re-
elected as Speaker. In the period, 1376–1523, only the following
were Speakers in two or more parliaments running: John Gildsburgh (in 1380), Sir John Bussy (1397–8), Thomas Chaucer (1407,
1410, 1411), Roger Flore (1416, 1417, 1419), William Tresham
(1439–40, 1442), John Say (1463–5, 1467–8), and William Allington
(1472–5, 1478). The establishment of a link between even no more
than two successive parliaments through a re-elected Speaker was on
the whole quite an infrequent occurrence: as will have been seen, it

did not happen so once between, for example, 1419 and 1439, or between 1442 and 1467, and after 1478 it did not happen again for nearly seventy years. Of election to the Speakership in three parliaments running there are only two instances in the medieval period: those of Thomas Chaucer under Henry IV and Roger Flore under Henry V. And yet, infrequent though re-election was in our period, it proved much less so than in the sixteenth and seventeenth centuries. Twice only under the Tudors did the same Speaker act in successive parliaments: Sir John Baker held office in Henry VIII's last parliament and Edward VI's first, and Sir John Puckering in the parliaments of 1585 and 1586. It was not until the Hanoverians, in fact, that the Speaker's re-election became something of a custom.

Very many of the knights of the shire, from among whom the medieval Commons invariably chose their Speakers, were men of substance, standing high among the landed gentry of their own region. A fair number were ambitious to enhance their power, wealth and status, and frequently did so in practice by taking service with the titular nobility and/or by obtaining advancement in the royal administration, preferably at Court, always a potential source of quick and lucrative preferment. In general, the Speakers of the medieval period convincingly exemplify this characteristic of their class.

Although, at that time, tenure of appointments was subject to favouritism, graft and political shifts, presumably at least some correlation existed between executive ability, backed by personal drive, and official promotion. If so much be conceded, then the medieval Commons, in electing their Speakers, may be credited with some concern to take administrative talent and energy into account. This was particularly the case if these qualities were to be found in men already engaged in royal service.

When the King's Council included a substantial commoner element, as under Richard II and in the first half of Henry IV's reign, and again under the Yorkists and Tudors, and such councillors were returned to parliament, the Commons might well elect one of these as Speaker. Under Richard II there was Bussy (in 1397-8); under Henry IV, Doreward (1399), Savage (January 1404) and Sturmy (October 1404); under Edward IV, Say (1463-5, 1467-8), Allington (1478); under Richard III, Catesby (1484); under Henry VII, Lovell (1485-6), Empson (1491-2), Dudley (1504); and under Henry VIII, Englefield (1510), Neville (1515), and More (1523), to go no further. Obviously, after 1461 the choice of a royal councillor as Speaker achieved a high probability. But, because there were exceptions, it can hardly be insisted that the Commons elected a councillor *qua* councillor. The same competence which attracted royal notice might well do the same in the Lower House. In any case, there were places nearer the throne than seats at the council-board (which is not, of course, to say that councillors did not sometimes occupy them, too).

Among those usually very close to the King were the officials of his Household and also the select band of the knights of his Chamber. Tiptoft was one of these personal henchmen when made Speaker in the parliament of 1406, before its dissolution being promoted Treasurer of the Household (the first layman to hold this office). Sir Walter Beauchamp, Sir John Tyrell, Sir John Popham and Sir Thomas Lovell all at some time occupied this post of senior financial official of the Household, though Tyrell was the only one to be actually in office when elected Speaker (in 1437). When made Speaker in 1449, John Say was a gentleman-usher of Henry VI's Chamber. His successor at Coventry ten years later, Thomas Tresham, was then an esquire of the Chamber (unless he had already become Controller of the Household). When elected Speaker in Henry VII's first parliament, Lovell was Treasurer of the Chamber. There were also the officials of the households of the royal children when these were too young to have independent control of their staff. Under Henry IV, Savage, Speaker in 1401 and 1404, in between whiles was steward of the household of Henry, the royal heir-apparent. At the same time, his successor at Coventry in 1404, Sturmy, had been serving the King's elder daughter in the same capacity. For obvious reasons, such officers were not required under Henry V and Henry VI, nor yet under Edward IV for a fair while. But Allington, Speaker in the 1470's, was one of the 'tutors' and councillors of the young Prince of Wales, in whose service he ended life as Chancellor of the Duchy of Cornwall. Englefield, Speaker in 1497, was similarly then a member of the entourage of Arthur Tudor. Meanwhile, when Speaker in 1455, the later Lord Wenlock had only recently terminated his duties as Chamberlain to Henry VI's Queen. Incidentally, Wenlock was the third of the Speakers to attain the peerage, the first two being Sir John Tiptoft and Sir Walter Hungerford, both of whom had taken their seats as barons in 1426. Wenlock owed his promotion to the Upper House in 1461 to Edward IV.

Some other Speakers were in receipt of fees and liveries as members of the royal Household, but when elected by the Commons were better known for administrative activities organized outside it. Of course, no Speaker could possibly have been supplied by any of the three secretarial departments of the Crown—the Chancery and the offices of Privy Seal and Signet—where the staff was normally not even eligible for membership of the Lower House. In the Exchequer, however, was ample room for the type of lay administrative and legal expert to which belonged so many of the medieval Speakers, and, over the years, a fair number of Exchequer officials sat in the Commons as knights of the shire or burgesses. Roger Hunt, Speaker in 1420 and 1433, became a Baron of the Exchequer, but this was not until some five years after his second spell as Speaker. In fact, no acting Exchequer official was called upon to serve as Speaker until, at Reading in 1453, the Commons elected Thomas Thorpe, the Treasurer's Remembrancer, who when still Speaker became a Baron. No other member of the Exchequer staff became Speaker until Say, the Under-Treasurer, in 1463. But Say, who held other offices under the Crown, had relinquished his Exchequer post before his re-election as Speaker in 1467, so that twenty years elapsed before, in Edward IV's last parliament (1483), another Exchequer official was elected: again it was the Under-Treasurer of the day, John Wood (who three months later followed the Earl of Essex as Treasurer). Both of Wood's two immediate successors in the Speakership, Catesby and Lovell, held office in the Exchequer, the former as Chancellor and Chamberlain, the latter simply as Chancellor. No other Exchequer official secured election as Speaker, however, until 1523, when once more it was the Under-Treasurer: Sir Thomas More. Of all these Speakers with a connexion with the Exchequer, Thorpe alone had consistently made his career in the department, and not even of him could it be said that his long tenure of office there supplied the Commons with the reason for electing him. All the rest concurrently held some other more significant office or offices elsewhere. For example, Say, when Speaker in both 1463–5 and 1467–8, was the Chancellor of the Duchy of Lancaster, having then held this post continuously since 1450.

Of all the several branches of the royal administration, it was the Duchy of Lancaster with which the medieval Speakers tended predominantly to be linked. The choice of Sir Thomas Hungerford, Chief Steward of the Duchy of Lancaster estates south of Trent, in Edward III's last parliament, and of Sir John Bussy, Chief Steward of the duchy estates north of Trent, in certainly three (possibly all) of the last four of Richard II's parliaments, might be taken to reflect the Commons' appreciation on those occasions of the importance of the political rôle or interest of John of Gaunt. But after 1399, when Gaunt's heir had seized the throne, the political status of the upper officials of the duchy as such was significantly enhanced. For the duchy became a royal possession: moreover, not absorbed into the common stock of Crown lands, it continued to be separately administered by the Lancastrians as their own private inheritance, with the result that its leading officials were linked to the King in a special, sometimes intimate, relationship. (The creation of trusts in duchy estates by Henry V and Henry VI to assist the fulfilment of their wills, involved the appointment of duchy officials as royal executors.) And the traditional, distinctive organization of the duchy still persisted under the Yorkists and Tudors, notwithstanding its annexation to the Crown by Edward IV in 1461. If, therefore, after 1399 the Commons elected a Speaker from among the duchy hierarchy, they were choosing a royal servant of a special sort. In fact, members of the council of the duchy—chief of whom were the Chamberlain, the Chancellor, the Chief Stewards for the estates north and south of Trent respectively, the Receiver-General and the Attorney-General—were not even ever elected to parliament under Henry IV, with the sole exception of Sir John Pelham who, when Chief Steward for the south parts, sat for Sussex in 1406 and 1407. And it was only under Henry V, who at the outset of his first regnal year almost completely transformed the composition of the duchy council, that the repeated return of one and another of its members to the Lower House made possible the not infrequent election to the Speakership of a highly placed duchy official. At Leicester in 1414, the new Chief Steward of the duchy estates south of Trent, Sir Walter Hungerford, was Speaker. Later, in 1417 and 1419 was chosen Hungerford's 'opposite number' for the northern territories: Roger Flore, the Oakham lawyer who had already been Speaker in 1416. And Flore, still occupying his Chief Stewardship, was for a fourth time leader of the Lower House in the first parliament meeting (in 1422) after Henry V's death. In the meantime, Roger Hunt, who was Hungerford's deputy-steward in the south in 1415–16, had become Speaker in 1420 after defeating John Russell, one of the legal advisers to the duchy council since 1403, in the only known medieval contest for the Speakership. But neither of these two lawyers was a member of the *corps d'élite* of the duchy administration, and when Russell was elected Speaker in Henry VI's second parliament (in 1423) he was no more than the local duchy steward in Gloucestershire, having ceased to be even one of the legal advisers to the duchy council. Russell's earliest successor in the Speakership with duchy associations, Sir Richard Vernon, who headed the Commons at Leicester in 1426, was similarly only one of a great number of local duchy officials in his capacity as steward and master-forester in the lordship of the High Peak. In fact, the first member of the duchy council itself to attain the Speakership after Flore in 1422 was his successor in the Chief Stewardship for the northern parts: John Tyrell, who was elected by the Commons in 1431 and again in 1437 (by which date he was also Treasurer of Henry VI's Household). His successor in the parliaments of 1439-40, 1442, 1447, and 1449-50, William Tresham, was all through these years connected with the duchy administration, as legal adviser, as steward of some of the duchy estates in the hands of Henry V's feoffees, and as one of Henry VI's feoffees (also acting as their chancellor). But it was only in the last of these parliaments that, in his capacity as Chancellor of the Duchy (a post for which he had been earmarked ever since 1442), he was an *ex officio* member of the duchy council when Speaker. William's son, Thomas Tresham, Speaker at Coventry in 1459, followed his father in all his duchy appointments, save that he never reached the chief executive office of the Chancellorship. That post had been given in reversion to John Say when he was Speaker in 1449, and on William Tresham's murder in the following year it was Say who came into possession. As well off under Edward IV as under Henry VI, Say was still Chancellor of the Duchy when Speaker in the successive parliaments of 1463-5 and 1467-8. But although during the next sixty years three of Say's successors in the Speakership had custody of the duchy seal, their tenure of office as Speaker did not once coincide with it. (These were John Mordaunt, Speaker in 1487, Chancellor of the Duchy in 1504; Richard Empson, Speaker in 1491-2, Chancellor in 1505-9; Sir Thomas More, Speaker in 1523, Chancellor in 1525-9.) In fact, after Sir John Say's last Speakership ended in 1468, the only highly placed duchy official of the day to preside in the Commons before Sir Thomas Audley, the Attorney-General of the Duchy, was elected Speaker at the beginning of the Reformation Parliament (1529), was Empson who, when Speaker in Henry VII's fourth parliament, occupied that same duchy office.

Obviously, when electing a royal servant as their Speaker, the medieval Commons followed no consistent policy of discriminating between the different branches of the royal administration. What was generally convenient and agreeable was to choose some royal servant who was *affairé* and competent. Very many of the medieval Speakers, however, possessed one other important qualification: experience as men of law.

Sir Peter de la Mare (able to cite statutes and actually producing a book of statutes in the parliament-chamber in 1376) and other of the earliest Speakers (Sir Thomas Hungerford, Sir John Bussy, and John Doreward) who were similarly the stewards of great magnates or monasteries, are likely to have been trained lawyers. But it was not until the reign of Henry V that the lawyer-Speakers as a type made their effective *début*. In Henry V's first parliament (1413) the Commons chose an apprentice-at-law, William Stourton, a former Recorder of Bristol. They then did without a lawyer in the next four parliaments. But their election of lawyers (starting with Roger Flore's three successive elections in 1416–19) in seven out of the next eight parliaments (1416–23) created a tendency which before very long became a fairly regular practice. In the century between Henry VI's coronation (1429) and the Reformation Parliament, those Speakers who were lawyers by training and profession outnumbered, in a proportion of roughly three to one, those who were not. From 1432 to 1447 (in eight successive parliaments), from 1484 to 1512 (in ten successive parliaments), the Speaker was always a lawyer. Even those few Speakers who were politically colourless and whose careers were quite humdrum or unspectacular—Stourton (1413), Baynard (1421), Bowes (1435) and Green (1460)—had at least their membership of the legal profession to recommend them to the Lower House.

Speaking generally, lawyers were an indispensable element in later medieval English society. Professional skill in a vernacular law of great complexity and the legal outlook itself were always at a premium. Eventually they became so among the Commons, one of whose chief functions—petitioning for reforms—being largely legislative in intention, demanded legal knowledge to be most effectively discharged. The recognition by the Lower House of the value of its legal element, in the frequent election of lawyers to the Speakership, suggests that the old prejudice against lawyers serving as M.P.s (expressed by the Commons in 1372, by the King in 1404) had virtually disappeared. Not only that. It would also seem to argue for a greater degree of sophistication in the transaction of the Commons' own business. And the contribution of the lawyer-Speakers to the development of the procedure of the House and to the extension of their own office, although unrecorded, may well have been substantial.

However, as will have been realized, the later medieval Commons mainly elected to the Speakership not just lawyers, but lawyers experienced in working for the Crown. Their engagement by the King was a sign of an ability which in itself, presumably, gave the Commons some promise of competence in the handling of their affairs. At the same time, the choice of a Speaker from this category was generally all too likely to profit the Crown. This was especially so when, as had happened before the end of the fifteenth century, much of the legislative work of parliament became 'officially inspired'. No single reason will explain why, under the Tudors, the Commons quite automatically came to elect into the Chair lawyers in Crown employment, career-lawyers, more than a few of whom became judges of the Bench. But, certainly, the ability to steer government bills was one compelling reason why lawyers then monopolized the Chair. The Commons' habit became so engrained that when Sir Edward Seymour was elected in 1673, he was the first Speaker for over a century and a half who was not a lawyer.

It was not long before Seymour was involved in another but more serious breach with long-established custom touching the Speakership. This was in 1679. The House gave up Seymour when Charles II rejected him, but refused to accept the King's own nominee. Royal control, as distinct from royal influence, over the Speaker's election was never thereafter reasserted. And so the Speaker ceased to be what he had been almost from the first (apart from some few exceptions confined to the medieval period), namely, an employee of the Crown. The most important chronic dilemma facing the Speaker so far—to whom should he be the more dutiful servant, to the Commons or to the King?—was thus resolved. Another problem, prospectively more basic still—should the Speaker's theoretical impartiality be guaranteed by his own independence of any political party?—was left for the nineteenth century to settle. A notable contribution to this development, however, had already been supplied by the vote to the Speaker in 1790 of a fixed salary of £6,000 a year in place of the old system of remuneration by fees and sinecure offices.

There was hardly a single medieval Speaker who was not actively involved in politics, and all were partisans to some extent. A considerable number of them are known to have been attached to one or other of the great magnates, not all of whom were unquestionably loyal to the Crown. Such connexions were frequently important. Now and then they were very important, witness the case of De la Mare (the Earl of March's steward) in 1376, of Chaucer (Bishop

Beaufort's cousin and agent) in the second half of Henry IV's reign, of Tyrell (the Duke of Gloucester's retainer) in 1427, 1431, and 1437, of Oldhall (the Duke of York's chamberlain) in 1450, of Thorpe (the Duke of Somerset's adherent) in 1453, of Strangeways (a friend of the Nevilles) in 1461–2. But most of the medieval Speakers, like all of the Tudor and early Stuart Speakers, were (whether the King's nominees or not) royal servants of a sort, ready to do among the Commons what they could to further the King's interests. None the less, there is evidence enough to suggest that what would be a natural tendency on the part of most of the medieval Speakers was liable to be offset by the Commons if their mood was critical of the royal administration, suspicious of its policy, or hostile to its demands. Need we do more than recall More's uneasy predicament in 1523? None was more alive than he to the traditions of the medieval Commons or more conscious, King's servant though he was, of the rôle which his office as Speaker required him to play.

One important problem remains to be discussed: when did the Speaker become *also* the moderator of the proceedings in the Commons' own House and preside over it (which, unquestionably, he did in mid-Tudor times)? It was not, of course, the Speaker's original and primary function to control the Commons: that function was to stand in the parliament-chamber and there 'speak' what the Commons wanted him to say. (This duty to the Commons involved him in a duty to parliament as a whole, and it is worth bearing in mind that 'the Speaker for the Commons' was sometimes alternatively described as 'Speaker of Parliament'.) It may be difficult to imagine that Sir Peter de la Mare, when once elected Speaker in 1376, did not continue to exercise that influence on the Commons' proceedings which had prompted the Commons to make him their Speaker in the first place. But we do not know that his appointment gave him any authority, and fresh means, to control the Commons in their discussions. Nor do we know what methods were used by Sir John Bussy, Speaker in Richard II's latest parliaments, to do the King service in the Lower House. We only know that the services Bussy rendered there were regarded at the time as important and valuable to the King. We may, however, fairly ask ourselves at this point, why did Archbishop Arundel fear that Sir John Cheyne's continuance as Speaker in Henry IV's first parliament (in 1399) might do the Church a serious disservice, if Cheyne's office was to act as the Commons' spokesman in the parliament-chamber and to do no more? We may also ask, why did some of the early Speakers show concern to have

z

all ambiguities removed from the 'charge' presented at the beginning of a parliament? It could, of course, be argued that if a request for the 'charge' to be clarified were made at all, it would be up to the Speaker to make it, for the request could only be made in the parliament-chamber, and the Speaker alone of the Commons had any right to speak there. However, as early as 1384 the Chancellor, at the very opening of parliament, had begun to order the Commons, not only to elect a Speaker, but to do so forthwith (so that his services would be available as soon as possible, not simply when the Commons had something to communicate). It may therefore be not unreasonable to suppose that when the Speaker was concerned about the 'charge', it was because it was his duty to ensure that the Commons considered the 'charge' promptly as well as effectively, and in order that, when he himself spoke the Commons' answers to the 'points' of the 'charge' he would be in a position to do this satisfactorily in every way. Such evidence as this, however, creates no more at best than a supposition that the early Speakers may have been afforded openings to 'direct and guide' the Commons' own proceedings. When does this supposition achieve greater validity?

For some time the evidence remains inconclusive. That in the first half of the fifteenth century (as well as later) the Speakers not infrequently took advantage of their tenure of office to present petitions of their own, and that during this period (from late in Henry V's reign) other private petitions were sometimes specifically addressed to the Speaker and Commons together, possibly suggests that the Speaker was already able to affect the passage of private bills. But then, early in the second half of the century, appears clear evidence (and with increasing frequency) that the Speaker had it in his power to expedite the promotion of bills of that sort: corporate bodies are known to have paid the Speaker a fee (or given him a present) to procure his favour towards the bills they wished to promote. (From 1475 comes an instance of a Speaker needing to be persuaded not to oppose a private bill.) The good offices for which the Speaker was recompensed, usually in advance, were such as could hardly have been performed except in the Lower House itself. And the same may be said of the 'diligence' exercised by the Speaker on behalf of the Crown, expressly for which he was being regularly and handsomely rewarded under Edward IV and later. The first, although for a long time isolated, payment of such royal monetary rewards had been made, however, as early as 1435.

There is good reason to believe that the Speaker's performance of these services for the King and others depended upon his control of the Lower House in virtue of his office. What Abbot Wheathampstead of St Albans believed his local enemy, Sir Thomas Charlton, had secured by his election as Speaker in 1454, was *regimen domus inferioris*. Perhaps the abbot's fears had moved him to exaggerate. No objection, however, can be raised against the remarks which the Chancellor, Bishop Russell of Lincoln, had intended to make at the opening of Edward V's first parliament in 1483: what the Chancellor wrote was that among the Commons *alle ys directed* by the Speaker; and, from what is said elsewhere in the passage where these words occur, it may reasonably be inferred that this *alle* included acting for the Commons as *president in ther consultacions* and as the one who *makithe the questions*. It would appear that we are mainly indebted to Bishop Russell on two grounds: (*a*) for confirming Abbot Wheathampstead's estimate of the authority of the Speaker of a generation earlier, and (*b*) for disclosing, to some extent, how the Speaker came by and exercised his authority. The latter service is obviously the greater. For what we are given to understand for the first time is that the Speaker presided over the Commons. Moreover, we are given an inkling of how he was able as chairman to influence the passage of bills; 'making the questions' quite possibly provided opportunity to determine the order in which bills were entertained, and also to interpret the 'voice' of the House. Except that the Speaker occupied the Chair, 'made the questions', and kept a register of attendances and licensed members to be absent or depart (duties laid upon him in 1515 by statute), we know nothing of how *in detail* the Speaker did his work in the Commons' own House during the period under review. It is none the less clear that before the end of the fifteenth century the Speaker's total function was much more varied and significant than originally: it had come to include a responsibility to 'direct' the proceedings of the House. He was not only the Commons' spokesman in the Upper House, but also occupied the Chair in their own. The Speaker's duty to the Commons had become twofold.

It would appear that it was chiefly because of this, that the Speaker's function became more significantly twofold in another sense. By serving the Lower House in an amplified rôle, he had been made better able to serve the King also, as his agent there. And that he actually did so may be gathered from the fact that he was regularly paid a substantial royal fee from Edward IV's accession onwards. In this connexion, we may reflect upon the possibility that more work was being thrown upon his shoulders by the growing number and importance of government bills. But it must be remembered, too, that there were always liable to be occasions when the Commons needed handling with care and circumspection. Some measure of the greater importance attached by the royal government to this 'handling' is provided by the increasing royal interest manifested in the Speaker's office, especially during the second half of the fifteenth century. Not only is the Speaker now a well fee-ed servant of the Crown; it would seem that royal nomination begins to lie behind his election by the Commons.

The very emergence of the Speaker's office had been a sign of a quickening sense of corporateness among the Commons. Its development, during the first century and a half of its history, had contributed to their growing constitutional and political importance. If, by the end of that period, the Crown had already learned how to use the Speaker's office, this was because it wished to take advantage of that growing importance.

Additional Notes on some of the Speakers
(arranged alphabetically)

Richard Baynard (1421)

Baynard's lands were in the east of Essex, where he held a few manors on either side of the long estuary of the Blackwater.

In January 1398 he was one of the feoffees to whom Walter Lord Fitz-Walter conveyed his reversionary interests in such of the family estates as were held by his father's widow. (The latter was soon to marry Edward of Norwich (elder son of the Duke of York) whom, in Henry IV's first parliament, Lord FitzWalter charged with murdering Thomas of Woodstock.) When FitzWalter died in 1406, Baynard acted as feoffee to *his* widow, who then married Hugh Lord Burnell but died in 1409. He was also a feoffee to FitzWalter's second son and eventual heir, the Lord FitzWalter who was taken prisoner at the battle of Baugé in March 1421, was first summoned to parliament in 1429, and died in 1431 (*CPR, 1396–9*, 351; *1422–9*, 211; *1429–36*, 208–11; *CCR, 1405–9*, 446; *1422–9*, 260; *1429–35*, 154).

Richard Baynard's mother, Katherine, sometime between his father's death in 1375 and 1380, married John Hende, a clothier and draper who, an alderman of London from 1379, was mayor in 1391–2 and 1404–5. Hende's loans to Henry IV totalled over £14,500 (an average of over £1,000 a year) and those to Henry V over £3,500. Baynard was one of his stepfather's feoffees in his considerable estates in Essex and Kent, even after his mother's death and when Hende had married again. When Baynard was Speaker, Hende had been dead for over three years (he died in the summer of 1418) (A. Steel, *The Receipt of the Exchequer*, 86, 195, et passim; *CCR, 1405–9*, 259; *1409–13*, 221; *1413–19*, 375, 478; *1419–22*, 798).

Although an escheator in 1399–1400, Baynard served on no other royal commission until after being returned to parliament for Essex in 1406. In February 1407 he became a J.P. and held office until June 1410. Perhaps Baynard had made some mark in the parliament of 1406: for when, on the day of its dissolution, the Commons requested that both Houses should be represented at the engrossment of the parliament-roll, he was one of the ten knights of the shire chosen for this duty (*Rot. Parl.*, iii. 585). From November 1413 until April 1419 he was again a J.P. in Essex. But otherwise his royal commissions were infrequent and generally not important. Some of his private connexions, however, were significant: in 1412 he was one of a syndicate who as mortgagees secured an interest in some of the estates of the Earl of Oxford (Richard de Vere) on account of loans totalling some £733; in 1415 he arbitrated between the abbot and the town authorities at Colchester; he was a feoffee-to-uses on behalf of Thomas Lord Morley (a member of the royal Council at his death in 1416), and, of course, for the FitzWalters as well as for many of the gentry in Essex and East Anglia.

Appointed to the commission of the peace for Essex in February 1422, Baynard remained a J.P. until his death in the winter of 1433-4. In July 1422 he shared a royal grant of the wardship of the heir of Thomas Coggeshall of Essex with Bishop Beaufort, John Leventhorpe (Receiver-General of the Duchy of Lancaster) and others. Again elected to parliament in 1423, he was then appointed as escheator in Essex and Herts. During the first session of this parliament he acted as the spokesman of a small deputation to the Upper House, expressing the Commons' gratitude that the Chancellor should have told them of the progress of negotiations regarding the liberation of James I of Scotland and his marriage with Joan, Bishop Beaufort's niece, and asking that they should be kept informed of developments. Incidentally, a reference to the roll of this parliament might in 1440 have taken much of the stuffing out of that one of the charges, made by the Duke of Gloucester against Cardinal Beaufort, in which the duke stated that, although the conditional liberation of James I was presumed to have been effected *by auctorite of parlement*, he himself had *herd full notable men of the Lower Hous saye that they never hard of it amonges them* (*Rot. Parl.*, iv. 199; *Letters and Papers illustrative of the Wars of the English in France, Henry VI*, ed. J. Stevenson (R.S.), vol. ii, part 2, p. 444). Baynard was re-elected to parliament in 1425. He was also returned in 1427, when again he headed a deputation to the Upper House, this time to announce the election as Speaker of one of his own feoffees, Sir John Tyrell, a friend of the Duke of Gloucester (*Rot. Parl.*, iv. 317). It was with Tyrell, now Treasurer of the Household, that Baynard was last elected to parliament in 1433. He died in January following and was buried in the chancel of the abbey-church at Colchester.

Sir Walter Beauchamp (1416)

Sir Walter's grandfather, Sir John, had been one of the knights of the King's Chamber at the end of Edward III's reign; and Sir John's brother, Roger Beauchamp of Bletsoe (Beds.) and Lydiard Tregoze (Wilts.), who was Chamberlain to Edward III in the last year of his reign, had been summoned to parliament as Lord Beauchamp from 1363 until his death in 1380. Sir Walter's father, Sir William of Powick, who was still alive in 1416, had been sheriff of Worcestershire in 1401-2 and of Gloucestershire in 1403-4 and 1413-14, and M.P. for Worcestershire in 1407, 1413, and 1414.

Walter married Elizabeth, one of the two daughters and coheirs of Sir John de la Roche and his wife, Willelma, the daughter and heir of Sir

Robert de la Mare of Fisherton Delamere (Wilts.) and Offley (Herts.). In 1377 Elizabeth's father had been given by Edward III an annuity of 100 marks which both Richard II and Henry IV had confirmed. M.P. for Wilts. on eight occasions between 1381 and 1399, he had died in September 1400. His widow died in 1410.

Only ten days after Henry IV's coronation Walter had secured a grant of £40 a year for life from the royal revenues of Gloucestershire. In June–July 1402 he attended the King's daughter Blanche when she journeyed to Heidelberg to be married to Lewis of Bavaria. Most probably he fought with the Household contingent at the battle of Shrewsbury on 21 July 1403, four weeks later being granted by the King's own warrant a debt of £20 owing to Sir Henry Percy (Hotspur) and forfeited by the dead rebel leader. In June 1405 he was almost certainly with Henry IV, coping with the rebellions in the north-east, where, at Newcastle upon Tyne on 16 July, he was given the keepership of the royal forest of Braden for life, *vice* his wife's uncle, Sir John Dallingridge, then a knight of the King's Chamber. He was first made a J.P. in Wiltshire in February 1410.

In March 1419, when *bailli* of Rouen, Sir Walter was granted by Henry V, to hold in tail male, the castle of Beausault (forfeited by a 'rebel' Norman seigneur, Sir Jean de Montmorency), in return for homage and the annual render of a sword. Beauchamp came home with Henry V on 1 February 1421, by which time he was Treasurer of the King's Household, and was present at Queen Katherine's coronation some three weeks later. No longer Treasurer of the Household, he probably did not go back to France until May 1422 when, following the birth of Henry of Windsor, the Queen rejoined her husband. By then Sir Walter was Steward of Katherine's Household. Returning to England, almost certainly with Henry V's body and in the Queen's entourage, Sir Walter was made a member of the royal Council set up in the parliament of 1422.

Doubtless Beauchamp now became busy as one of the late King's executors specially appointed to administer his will. A long drawn-out task, it was still far from completed when he died. His own family had an interest in the royal will, or rather in the terms of an autograph codicil sealed on 9 June 1421. This expressed Henry's wish that Sir Walter's sister Elizabeth should be given for her lifetime lands worth £200 a year, on condition that she married within a year of his death as agreed by her mother, Thomas Beaufort (Duke of Exeter), Sir Walter, and his cousin, Sir Ralph Butler, half of the lands being then entailed on her issue. If she did not marry but lived chaste, she might have lands worth 200 marks a year, these reverting on her death to Henry's feoffees. She did in fact marry (later than had been specified, but before November 1425) the choice of her advisers: Thomas Swynford, grandson of Katherine Swynford and a nephew of the Duke of Exeter and Cardinal Beaufort. Her brother, Sir Walter, may well have been drawn by this alliance into opposing the Protector, Gloucester, to whom the Beauforts were hostile. But he was also connected with another important nobleman who was out of sympathy with Gloucester: his distant kinsman, Richard Beauchamp, Earl of Warwick, for whom, in a dispute (for precedence) with the Earl Marshal, he acted as chief councillor and spokesman in the parliament of 1425. Meanwhile, Sir Walter had been dropped from the King's Council when its composition was modified in the parliament of 1423-4. It was doubtless Warwick's influence as Henry VI's governor which secured Sir Walter's appointment by the Council on 8 May 1428 as one of the group of four knights and four esquires authorized to wait upon the boy-king under the earl's supervision, with a personal fee of 100 marks a year. It was as a Knight of the Body that he attended Henry VI's coronation in November 1429, his elder son (William) receiving knighthood on the vigil of the ceremony. By this time Sir Walter was also acting as master of the King's horses. He died soon after, either at the very end of 1429 or early in 1430, and was buried at Steeple Lavington (Wilts.).

Sir John Bussy (1394, 1397, 1397-8)

Bussy's main estates were in the valley of the Witham, in and about Hougham, and in the Trent valley, near Newark; and he also held lands close to the Wash, in Rutland, and also (*jure uxoris*) in Yorkshire. His wife was Maud, daughter and heir of Sir Philip Neville of Scotton (Lincs.). Bussy was her third husband when he married her in 1382. Not long after this he was knighted and joined the retinue of John of Gaunt. In December 1382 he first became a J.P. in Kesteven and a year later took office as sheriff of Lincolnshire (1383-4). He was again sheriff in 1385-6 and 1390-1. He was M.P. for Lincolnshire in 1383 (twice), 1388, 1390 (twice), 1391, 1393, 1394, 1395, and 1397 (twice), in the last eleven years of his life quite monopolizing one of the two county seats. In 1387-8, when John of Gaunt was in Spain, Bussy supported the Lords Appellant in their opposition to Richard II and his party, which included the Earl of Suffolk, with whom he himself had so far been friendly. In December 1391, however, he was retained by the King for life with an annuity of 40 marks. This connexion did not weaken his ties with John of Gaunt who by the summer of 1394 had made him Chief Steward of his estates north of Trent, an office Bussy retained until the spring of 1398. Meanwhile, in 1397, Bussy's royal fee was raised by half, and later in the same year he not only received an additional £100 a year as a member of the King's Council but also, after his great success as Speaker in the autumn parliament, profited by various grants of the forfeited property (including lands) of the magnates condemned in the parliament. Immediately following the last act of the parliamentary commission set up at Shrewsbury in January 1398—the revocation in March 1399 of the permission given to the banished Henry of Bolingbroke and the Duke of Norfolk to take possession of any inheritance through their attorneys-general—Bussy was one of a small group of royal councillors given custody of the Mowbray lands.

When Richard II went to Ireland in May 1399, Bussy stayed behind to assist the government of the Duke of York, and the story of the brief remainder of his life is chiefly one of what happened to this administration after Bolingbroke's return from exile in France. Arrested with the Treasurer (the Earl of Wiltshire) and Sir Henry Green in Bristol castle, Bussy was executed with them on 29 July, following a 'judgement' which, confirmed in Henry IV's first parliament, involved his estates in forfeiture. At the time of this parliamentary confirmation, Henry IV declared that by way of conquest he would disinherit none but these three, who had been guilty of all the evil that had befallen the realm. For this *droiturel juggement* against their late Speaker, the Commons thanked the new King; and they thanked God, too, that He had sent them *tiel Roy et Governour.*

William Catesby (1484)

Catesby's reputation for influence over Richard III was, if we may believe the *Croyland Chronicle*, particularly exemplified following the death of the Queen (Anne Neville) in March 1485. A rumour was current that the King proposed to marry his niece, Elizabeth, Edward IV's eldest daughter, and soon after the Queen's death Richard had to deny the truth of it to the chief citizens of London. Those in the royal Council most hostile to the proposal were Radcliffe and Catesby, *quorum sententiis vix unquam Rex ipse ausus fuit resistere.* This Croyland source goes on to relate that they told Richard to his face that even the northerners (whose affection he enjoyed) would charge him with procuring the death of his Queen, a daughter and heir of Warwick the Kingmaker, in order to enter an incestuous relationship, and that he must disavow any such scheme. The chronicle alleged further that Catesby and his colleague were afraid of the vengeance Elizabeth of York would take on them, if she were made Queen, for the death of those members of her mother's family (her uncle, Earl Rivers, and her stepbrother, Sir Richard Grey) executed nearly two years before (*Rerum Anglicarum Scriptorum Veterum* (Oxford, 1684), i. 572). Radcliffe and Catesby were related: they shared Lord Scrope as a father-in-law. Neither of the two men survived the fall of Richard III. Catesby was executed, his remains being entombed at Ashby St Legers. Radcliffe was killed at Bosworth. Viscount Lovell, however, escaped to sanctuary at Colchester. Lord Zouche, Catesby's brother-in-law, also got away.

Catesby's will, dated 25 August 1485, expressed his disappointment at the failure of his wife's uncle (Lord Stanley) to secure him clemency; but he was still hoping that Henry Tudor would be generous to his children, *for he is callid a full gracious prince, and I never offended hym by my good and free will, for, God I take to my juge, I have ever lovid hym.* There was perhaps more ground for such optimism than at first meets the eye: Catesby's wife and Henry were cousins. (Her mother, Elizabeth, was a daughter of Sir Oliver St John by Margaret, daughter and eventual heir of Sir John de Beauchamp of Bletsoe (Beds.). This Margaret, after Sir Oliver's death, married

John Beaufort, Duke of Somerset, by whom she became mother of Lady Margaret Beaufort, whose son by Edmund Tudor was Henry VII. Margaret (née Beauchamp) had died in 1482–3 when her heir was John St John, her son by her first husband.) This relationship, however, went for nothing, and Catesby's estates (including even the entails) were forfeited following an Act of Attainder, against him and other of Richard III's supporters at Bosworth, passed in the first of Henry VII's parliaments. Despite the fact that Catesby's heir, George, was son-in-law to Sir Richard Empson, one of Henry's 'great projectors' (and Speaker in 1491–2), it was not until ten years had passed that Catesby's attainder was reversed (in 1495), and even then there were some severe limitations applied to the recovery. Catesby's widow did not quite live to see this *act of adnullacion and restitucion* in her son's favour: she had died on 8 October 1494.

Sir Thomas Charlton (1454)

Save that Thomas Charlton was re-appointed to the commission of the peace for Middlesex, nothing is known of his activities during the year that followed his Speakership (1454–5). It is not even known whether he was drawn into the battle of St Albans (near as it was fought to his own home at South Mimms), or whether he sat for Middlesex in the parliament that followed it (for the Middlesex returns have been lost). He had his contacts among members of *both* sides. Although probably still a member of Henry VI's Household, his kinship with the Countess of Salisbury was something which the Abbot of St Albans regarded as important; and it is worth noting that in December 1455, at the earliest opportunity the Yorkists had to make sheriffs of their own choosing after their victory at St Albans, they appointed Charlton as sheriff of Bedfordshire and Buckinghamshire. This suggests that, at any rate at this time and to that extent, he was trusted by them. But he kept out of trouble even in 1459, and he clearly had nothing to fear from the Lancastrians when, as M.P. for Middlesex, he attended the parliament of Coventry (in November) and at the end of the session was appointed a commissioner of array for resisting the Yorkists. He was, however, at least wavering in his allegiance when, a fortnight after the Yorkist victory at Northampton in July 1460, he acted as a justice of oyer and terminer at the London Guildhall in the company of the Earls of Salisbury and Warwick. (This impression is confirmed by his re-election to the autumn parliament, which, summoned in Henry VI's name, was used to register the recent Yorkist triumph.) Certainly, he soon committed himself and was with the Earl of Warwick's army when it was defeated by Queen Margaret's forces in the second battle of St Albans on 17 February 1461. There Charlton was captured and, his life being spared, was taken northwards as a prisoner to York (*Calendar of State Papers, Venetian*, vol. i (1202–1509), p. 99). He was probably liberated after Edward IV's victory at Towton, six weeks later.

But he seems now to have been incapable of profiting by Edward's accession, and, though he remained a J.P. in Middlesex, almost all that is known of him down to his death on 26 February 1465 is of a private nature. It mainly relates in fact to the settlement on feoffees of his lands in Middlesex, Essex, Bedfordshire, and Cambridgeshire, and also of some property in Southwark. (Chief among the feoffees were his cousins, the Frowykes.) That his estates were of considerable value is clear from the fact that his executors paid 1,000 marks to the Exchequer for the right to administer the wardship of his heir, Richard, for no more than five years (CFR, *1461-71*, 151; CCR, *1468-76*, 118). A supporter of Richard III, Charlton's heir was attainted of treason by Henry VII and underwent forfeiture (*VCH, Beds.*, ii. 231).

Sir John Cheyne (1399)

Before sitting in 1399, Cheyne had already been M.P. for Gloucestershire in 1390, 1393, and 1394. In October 1379 as a royal retainer he had been given a lease of the estates of the alien priory of Beckford (Glos.). He was confirmed in possession for life in 1381 and held the property virtually rent-free from 1383 (when his royal annuity of 100 marks was made a charge on what he owed as farm to the Exchequer). Further concessions by Richard II and Henry IV augmented these alien priory possessions of Cheyne's, the rents being similarly absorbed by additional royal annuities, so that during the first half of Henry IV's reign Cheyne's income from monastic estates was worth (even by Exchequer calculations) over £230 a year. Apart from serving Richard II in the diplomatic field, Cheyne was captain of the castle of Marck in the March of Calais from October 1384 to January 1386, was a knight of the King's Chamber by 1389, and went with Richard to Ireland in 1394. What indiscretions occasioned his condemnation for treason in 1398 are not known: it is possible that he had favoured the Lords Appellant ten years earlier. Although forced by Archbishop Arundel's hostility to resign the Speakership in 1399, Cheyne by no means forfeited the goodwill of Henry IV, who confirmed and added to his existing royal emoluments and allowed him to retain his hold on his alien priory estates. In fact, by mid-June 1400 Cheyne was a member of the King's Council and continued to act as such until certainly 1407, being among those councillors nominated in parliament in 1404 and 1406. He once more fell foul of Archbishop Arundel in 1404 when in the parliament at Coventry he strongly supported a proposal to confiscate the temporalities of the Church put forward by the knights of the shire. But Henry IV found him too useful to repudiate. Cheyne's most important work for Henry IV, as for Richard II, was in foreign affairs: in 1401-2 he assisted in the negotiations for the marriage of the King's elder daughter, Blanche, with Lewis of Bavaria, son of the anti-Kaiser, Rupert III; in 1404 he twice went to France to confer with Charles VI and the Burgundians; between November 1406 and August 1408 he accompanied Dr

Henry Chichele, the future primate, in an embassy to Charles VI and the Roman Curia, the main object of which was to bring an end to the Papal Schism; in 1410 and 1411 he again visited France, on each occasion to renew truces. He died sometime between November 1413 and April 1414 and was buried at Beckford. The terms of his will suggest that he had repented of his Lollardy.

Richard Empson (1491-2)

Sir Robert Somerville gives Empson much of the credit for the tightening up of the administration of the Duchy of Lancaster during this period, Empson's policy as Chancellor of the Duchy being to increase its feudal revenues, *approve* rents from leases, and enclose common lands. While still Attorney-General he also occupied a number of local duchy stewardships: from 1486 at Long Buckby and in what appertained to Peverel's fee in Northants.; from 1492 at Kenilworth and in all other duchy lands in Warwickshire (jointly with Sir Reginald Bray, then Chancellor of the Duchy); from 1493 at Ascot and Deddington in Oxfordshire (again with Bray); and from 1503 at Sutton and Potton (Beds.). When himself Chancellor of the Duchy, Empson added to these in 1507 the stewardship of the lordship of Higham Ferrers and all its members in Northants., Huntingdonshire, and Cambridgeshire (op. cit., i. 590n., 561, 631, 593, 587). Duchy affairs by no means monopolized, of course, Empson's administrative capabilities. Throughout the second half of Henry VII's reign he was a member of the King's *council learned*, of the Court of Requests, and of the Council in the Star Chamber (*EHR*, liv. 440), and was listed in Perkin Warbeck's proclamation of 1495 among those 'caitiffs and villains of birth' so objectionably employed as councillors by Henry VII (Bacon, *Henry VII*, ed. J. R. Lumby, p. 142). It was the oppressive financial administration in which he co-operated with Dudley which brought about his disgrace and made recovery impossible. Henry VII trusted him to the last and appointed him an executor of his will. But Henry VIII was all too ready to throw him over, and on 1 October 1509 Empson was tried and convicted of treason at Northampton and remanded to the Tower. The charges against him were his use of illegal imprisonment for the levying of extra-judicial fines, his refusal of pardons to outlaws unless they paid excessive fines, his usurpation of the jurisdiction of the common law courts, his especially harsh judicial conduct at Coventry (where he was Recorder), and his illegal policy towards Crown tenants and other landowners (wrongfully determining estates to be held in chief, and preventing royal wards who had come of age from suing livery of seisin until they had paid large fines, a simple breach of *Magna Carta*). Together attainted by parliament in January 1510, Empson and Dudley were both executed at Tower Hill on 17 August following. Both attainders were reversed in the second parliament of the reign.

Sir John Gildsburgh (1380)

In addition to his own family's estates in and near Wennington (half-way between London and Tilbury) and what he held of the De Bohuns, Gildsburgh *jure uxoris* enjoyed possession of a large cluster of estates near Bury St Edmunds and of manors in the Colne valley (held of the De Veres). Despite all these holdings Gildsburgh was never sheriff or escheator; and he was not appointed as a J.P. in Essex until May 1376, although he then continued in office for the rest of his life. He was among the local J.P.s sent to restore order at Brentwood (Essex) on 30 May 1381 when the earliest rising in the Peasants' Revolt took place. When the serfs there murdered three of John Bampton's clerks, the commissioners fled, Gildsburgh among them, probably to London (A. Réville, *Le Soulèvement des Travailleurs d'Angleterre en 1381*, lxxi). On the appearance of the King and his retinue at Chelmsford, Gildsburgh received a writ from the Chancery authorizing him to recover all his goods seized during the rising, without hindrance from any royal officials busy attaching the forfeited property of rebels (*CPR, 1381–5*, 24). In December 1381 he was put on the Essex commission ordered to suppress all movements of disturbance.

After twice acting as Speaker in 1380, Gildsburgh again represented Essex in parliament in 1383, 1385, and 1388 (the 'Merciless Parliament'). In 1384 he served on John of Gaunt's expedition to Scotland, presumably in the retinue of Thomas of Woodstock. From January 1387, he shared in a royal grant of certain property in Essex, Kent, and London, belonging to the Hospital of Montjoux in Savoy (sequestered by the Crown as the possessions of schismatics), at an annual rent of £40 payable in the Exchequer; and it seems likely that he supported the aristocratic party, hostile to Richard II, led by Thomas of Woodstock at that time and during the 'Merciless Parliament'. Although M.P. in this parliament, Gildsburgh did not long survive it. He was dead by October 1389. His widow (a second wife) subsequently married Sir John Deyncourt, the steward of the household of the Duke of Lancaster, with whom she was buried in the London Greyfriars. Gildsburgh himself was buried at Wennington with his first wife. His feoffees, by a settlement made during the second session of the 'Merciless Parliament', included the former Speakers, Sir Thomas Hungerford and Sir Richard de Waldegrave.

John Green (1460)

Under Edward IV, Green remained a J.P. of the *quorum* in Essex. Otherwise, he served on few royal commissions, but on 2 February 1462 he and his brother William were entrusted for life with the office of steward in all the lordships in Essex, Suffolk, and Cambridgeshire, forfeited by John de Vere, Earl of Oxford, who was executed on 26 February (following his condemnation by the Court of the Constable on a charge of arranging for a Lancastrian landing on the east coast); this office was extended on

1 March to cover all estates held to the late earl's use. John Green is referred to in the patent as 'King's servant' (*CPR, 1461–7*, 139, 142). By February 1469 he was acting as deputy for the Earl of Warwick in the office of Chief Steward of the Duchy of Lancaster (R. Somerville, op. cit., i. 431), a connexion which helps to explain how, in 1470, he soon came to be regarded as a reliable agent in Essex by the Lancastrian government of the Readeption. This is not to say that Green assumed a rôle likely to endanger himself personally. Admittedly, he took out a royal pardon when Edward IV recovered the throne. But neither he nor his brother was then dropped from the commission of the peace in Essex to which the Lancastrian administration had re-appointed them, and John continued to sit on the bench until his death. This occurred on 1 May 1473. John was buried at Gosfield where his 'brass' still remains. His widow Edith (née Rolf) survived until 1497. One of their daughters (Agnes) had married Sir William Fynderne, the son of one of the Lancastrians attainted in 1461, who himself fought as a Lancastrian at Barnet in 1471, forfeited what family lands remained unforfeited by his father, but recovered his place under Henry VII. Another married daughter was the wife of Henry Tey. A third daughter became Abbess of the Dominican nuns of Dartford.

Sir Thomas Hungerford (1377)

Hungerford's parliamentary career extended from 1357 to 1393, during which time he sat in sixteen parliaments, most of them under Richard II, representing Wiltshire eleven times, Somerset four times, and on one occasion (at Salisbury in 1384) both counties simultaneously. He was sheriff of Wiltshire from 1355 to 1360, and also escheator during the first two of these five years. From 1361 he was normally a J.P. in Wiltshire and from 1374 in Somerset too. No later than 1362 he became deputy to Lord Burghersh, a close friend of the Black Prince, in his stewardship of the prince's honours of Wallingford and St Valery in the Thames valley, parcels of the Duchy of Cornwall. This indirect link with the royal heir-apparent probably ended with Lord Burghersh's death in 1369. Hungerford was one of Burghersh's feoffees and executors, by no means to his own detriment. He acted in the same capacity for William Edington, Treasurer of the Exchequer (1345–56), Chancellor of England (1356–63), and Bishop of Winchester (1346–66); during this prelate's last years Hungerford was the steward of the lands of his see. He was also steward of the city of Salisbury for Bishop Wyvill, continuing in office under each of his three successors (Erghum, Waltham, and Metford). Appointed chief steward of the Duchy of Lancaster south of Trent in 1375, he remained as such a member of the duchy council during John of Gaunt's absence in Spain and Aquitaine between 1386 and 1389, only retiring from office in 1393. He died on 3 December 1397 and was buried in the chapel of the manor-house of Farleigh (Somerset), which he had been licensed by Richard II in 1383 to fortify as a castle.

Sir Walter Hungerford (1414)

Before his election as Speaker in 1414 Hungerford had already been M.P. for Wiltshire in 1401, 1404, 1407, and 1413, and for Somerset in 1410. His first wife, Katherine Peverell, through her mother was a kinswoman of the Earl of Devon. This marriage brought Hungerford considerable estates, especially in Somerset, Devon, and Cornwall, and his lands were also greatly augmented by his second marriage (sometime between 1429 and 1439) with Eleanor, Countess of Arundel, her estates being mainly in Dorset, Wiltshire, and Gloucestershire. By 1421 his eldest son (Robert) was married to the heir of Lord Botreaux and his third son (Edmund) to a granddaughter and coheir of Lord Burnell. In November 1399 Sir Walter had been given a lease for life of the royal castle and manor of Marlborough, and shortly afterwards he shared a gift from Henry IV of £200 from the lands of the late Duchess of Norfolk, 'to recompense him for his great expenses in the King's service after his last coming to England'. Early in January 1400 at Windsor castle he was arrested by a group of Richard II's friends among the nobility (when they were hoping to seize King Henry and his sons) and was taken along with them to Cirencester, where the townspeople broke up the rebellion. In the year (1405–6) in which he went to Sweden as the Princess Philippa's chamberlain, he was sheriff of Wiltshire, where he had been a J.P. since 1401. He was also made a J.P. in Somerset in 1408. Henry V made Sir Walter the Chief Steward of the Duchy of Lancaster estates south of Trent and in Wales on 5 April 1413, and he retained this office until May 1437, even after his appointment as Duchy Chamberlain in February 1425. The Chamberlainship, a dignity with which was associated the presidency of the duchy council, he held until 1444, when his son Edmund succeeded him. Within three weeks of his being appointed Steward of the King's Household on 24 July 1415, Sir Walter went on Henry V's first expedition to France with a big retinue of 20 men-at-arms and 60 archers; and it was he who on the eve of the battle of Agincourt expressed a wish that the army had another 10,000 archers, a remark with which the King himself vehemently disagreed. In July 1416 Hungerford was made one of the two Admirals of the fleet which, under the Duke of Bedford, won a great victory in the Seine. A year later he again accompanied Henry V to Lower Normandy, this time with a retinue three times what it had been in 1415. Many military, administrative, and diplomatic responsibilities now came his way. So did recognition and reward. He was at Alençon in November 1417 when given for life the constableship of Windsor castle and the custody of its forest and parks (offices he retained until 1438). In 1418 he was made captain of Cherbourg and in 1422 of Château Gaillard. His grants of forfeited property in Normandy were considerable, and in 1421 he was elected a Knight of the Garter. He now soon gave up his Stewardship of the Household, but was still in France with Henry V at the latter's death in August 1422. Then returning to England, he became a member of the new royal Council, which he remained until certainly after Henry VI came of age. Hungerford was again Steward of the Household from April 1424 until March 1426, when, having recently been created a peer, he became Treasurer of the Exchequer. By this appointment his official stipends were raised by £500 a year, and he held office as Treasurer until displaced by the Duke of Gloucester's contrivance in February 1432 (when Lord Cromwell was required to give up the office of King's Chamberlain and Lord Tiptoft the Stewardship of the Household). Hungerford was not again called upon to fill any high office, but he remained a member of the King's Council and was influential there if only because of his position as a feoffee and executor of Henry V and his membership of the administration of the Duchy of Lancaster. He was one of the English embassy to the great Congress of Arras in 1435. When this peace conference failed, and the Duke of Burgundy went over to Charles VII of France, Hungerford fully approved of an anti-Burgundian policy, raised a force of over 400 men-at-arms and archers for service in France, and also, both then and later, contributed loans towards military expenses. In 1439 he was engaged in making overtures for peace with France, but this proved to be his last employment as a diplomat: the diplomacy of defeat and withdrawal can hardly have been congenial. From 1444 he excused himself from chapter-meetings of the Order of the Garter, and it is doubtful whether after 1445 he attended either parliament or the Council. He died at Farleigh Hungerford on 9 August 1449. He was buried in the nave of Salisbury Cathedral, where he had founded a chantry (in addition to others established at Farleigh and in the chapel of St Stephen in the palace of Westminster).

Sir Thomas Lovell (1485–6)

Although Lovell did not again act as Speaker after 1486, he sat in the parliaments of 1491–2 (for Middlesex), 1495 (Norfolk), and 1497 (Middlesex), and possibly in all others which met under Henry VII and, before Lovell's death, under Henry VIII (except that of 1523, when he was reported to be *right sick*). Early in Henry VII's reign his influence had been increased by appointment to a number of subsidiary offices, some of them in the provincial administrations of the Crown: in February 1486 he was a joint-commissioner for royal mines; and then, all in 1489, he acquired the posts of constable of the castle, and steward of the honour, of Wallingford, constable of Nottingham castle, steward and keeper of the forest and parks of Sherwood, and steward of the Duchy of Lancaster lands in Norfolk, Suffolk, and Cambridgeshire. He had been knighted for his services at the battle of Stoke in 1487 and was to be made a knight-banneret at Blackheath in 1497. In the meantime, in 1492, he had been promoted from the office of Treasurer of the Chamber to be Treasurer of the Household (Richardson, op. cit., 485). Reported by the Spanish ambassador in

1498 as one of the half-dozen most influential men in England (*Cal. S.P., Spanish, 1485–1509*, 163), Lovell was described in 1499 as 'the King's chief financier' (ibid., *Venetian, 1202–1509*, 285). Already, in 1495, Perkin Warbeck's proclamation had included him among *those caitiffs and villains of birth which by subtile inventions, and pilling of the people, have been the principal finders, occasioners, and counsellors of the misrule and mischief now reigning in England*, apart from whom Henry VII *hath none in favour and trust about his person* (Bacon, *History of the Reign of Henry VII*, ed. J. R. Lumby (Cambridge, 1902), p. 142); and the Cornish rebels in 1497 demanded his surrender as partly responsible for the recent heavy taxation. In fact, Lovell was an extremely able, hard-working civil servant. Created Knight of the Garter in 1503, he was appointed by Henry VII as one of the executors of his will. Henry VIII not only continued him in office as Treasurer of the Household, Chancellor of the Exchequer, and member of the Privy Council, but also made him Warden and Chief Justice of the forests south of Trent (Feb. 1510), Constable of the Tower (Sept. 1512), and Master of the King's Wards (June 1513). By about 1516 Lovell began to withdraw from an active share in the formulation of royal policy and soon ceased to interfere in the government (J. S. Brewer, *The Reign of Henry VIII*, vol. i, p. 258). He was now aged about seventy, but his retirement was almost certainly due to his dislike of Wolsey's foreign policy (only partly on account of its financial implications). None the less, he retained the Treasurership of the Household and most of his other offices until his death on 25 May 1524, although perhaps, even in general, honorifically. After a memorable funeral, he was buried in the nunnery at Halliwell, to which he had been a great benefactor.

Sir Thomas More (1523)

When More was Chancellor, he gave great satisfaction on the legal side of his office, being wonderfully expeditious in conducting pleas in equity. But, in the great dispute over the divorce of Queen Katherine, his conscientious inability to support King Henry was resented. It was really on account of this matter and also because of Henry's claim to be Supreme Head of the English Church that More resigned the Great Seal on 16 May 1532. Inconclusively attacked in parliament in February 1534 as a friend of Elizabeth Barton ('the Holy Maid of Kent'), he was committed to the Tower in April following, for refusing to take any oath that would impugn the Pope's authority or admit the justice of the royal divorce. At the same time he was ready to accept the Act of Succession vesting the crown in the issue of Anne Boleyn. (This was merely to offer to recognize the Princess Elizabeth as heir whether legitimate or illegitimate.) In November 1534 More was attainted of misprision of treason, but after parliament had conferred upon the King the title of Supreme Head and made its denial high treason, he was tried on an indictment for treason in Westminster Hall on 1 July 1535. He was then condemned. At his execution at Tower Hill on 6 July, he declared: 'I die the King's servant, but God's first.' Refusing to admit any usurpation of the right of the Roman See, he justly asserted that he died for *the common corps of Christendom*. Beatified by the Roman Catholic Church on 29 October 1886, he was canonized on 19 May 1935.

Sir William Oldhall (1450-1)

In Easter term 1452, Oldhall was indicted in the King's Bench of armed conspiracy at Westminster in July and September 1451, at Fotheringhay in November following, at Hitchen (Herts.), Westminster and Hounslow in February 1452 (part of the rising which culminated at Dartford), and again at Westminster in April (in a plot to raise the Welsh border, for which a fellow-conspirator, John Sharp of Brentford, was hanged at Tyburn a year later). In March 1453, when in sanctuary, Oldhall was outlawed. Meanwhile, in December 1452, Oldhall's goods and chattels (including all the building material at his places in Herts.) had been given to Walter Burgh, an esquire of the Household and M.P. for Downton in 1450-1, who had been 'beaten up' in the London streets earlier in the year, as a punishment for accusing Oldhall of helping himself to Somerset's effects when the duke's house was pillaged in December 1450. In May 1453, following Oldhall's attainder at the Reading parliament, Somerset himself was granted his manors of Hunsdon and East Wick (Herts.). Soon after the first battle of St Albans, Oldhall was acquitted in the King's Bench of all charges of treason preferred in 1452, and in the parliament of 1455 his condemnation at Reading was also reversed. Eventually, under York's Protectorate, he recovered his lands. Whether Oldhall again became Chamberlain to the Duke of York is not known, but he remained in touch with the duke and members of his household. In August 1458 he acted as host at Hunsdon to York's brother-in-law, Viscount Bourchier, and Bourchier's brother, the Archbishop of Canterbury, and in July 1459 was plotting (in London) the Yorkist insurrection which collapsed in the Rout of Ludford on 12 October. He was again attainted in the parliament at Coventry, all his real and personal property being first granted to the Duke of Buckingham and then taken over by a group of royal receivers of forfeitures. Meanwhile, Oldhall had made himself scarce, possibly in Ireland with the Duke of York who only returned to England after his supporters' victory at Northampton in July 1460. Himself back in London with the duke in October, Oldhall secured a parliamentary reversal of the attainder passed at Coventry. There can hardly have been time for him to get his estates back once again before his death, which occurred in London between 17 and 20 November. He was buried in Whittington College. His will provided for bequests to the Duke of York's two elder sons (Edward and Edmund) and also to Archbishop Bourchier and Thomas Young (the Bristol lawyer), both of whom were among his executors. (Justice Yelverton of the King's Bench was another.) Sir William's heir was his daughter Mary, whose husband was Walter Gorges of Wroxhall (Somerset), with whom her father had violently quarrelled.

Sir James Pickering (1378, 1383)

Before being Speaker at Gloucester in 1378, Pickering had already been an M.P. four times: for Westmorland in 1362 and 1365, for Cumberland in 1368, and for Westmorland again in Richard II's first parliament (1377). He also represented Westmorland in 1378, 1379, and 1382, and then Yorkshire in 1383, 1384, 1388, 1390, and 1397. He had long been associated with the Cliffords, being a retainer of Roger Lord Clifford, whom he served as under-sheriff of Westmorland in 1365-7, 1368-9, and 1371-6. He was appointed as a J.P. in both Cumberland and Westmorland in 1373 and, although soon excluded from the commission of the peace in Cumberland, remained a J.P. in Westmorland even when, during the years 1376-80, he acted as a J.P. in the West Riding of Yorkshire. Early in 1378 Pickering complained to the King's Council that when he was absent from home as M.P. in the previous year Sir Thomas de Roos and his sons had ambushed some of his men and tenants near Kendal, killing two and wounding six; and royal commissions of enquiry were set up in both Westmorland and Yorkshire.

Between his Speakerships in 1378 and 1383 Pickering served on a number of local royal commissions in Westmorland and the West Riding of Yorkshire. He was escheator in Yorkshire from November 1379 to February 1381. In November 1382, for long but unrewarded services in Scotland and elsewhere under Edward III, he successfully requested Richard II for the custody of a small estate near Selby (then in royal control), the petition being handed by the King personally to the Chancellor with orders to draw up the necessary patent in due form. A few days later Pickering was again appointed escheator in Yorkshire. Before the end of his year of office (1382-3), he was busy administering the will of Sir William de Windsor, by which he and his fellow-executors were involved in long and difficult exchanges with the Exchequer over Windsor's accounts both as Lieutenant of Ireland and custodian of Cherbourg in Normandy. Meanwhile, in 1386, he was appointed by the Duke of Gloucester (as Constable of England) to take depositions bearing on the armorial dispute between Lord Scrope and Sir Robert Grosvenor. In 1389-90 Pickering was sheriff of Yorkshire. During his term of office he was retained by Richard II as a 'King's knight', undertaking to serve in time of war with a retinue of 20 men-at-arms and 100 archers in return for an annuity of 40 marks; and at the end of his shrievalty he was once more appointed as escheator for Yorkshire (1390-1). He was again sheriff of Yorkshire in 1393-4 and in 1397-8, dying during, or shortly after, this last term of office.

Sir Arnald Savage (1401, 1404)

By 1401 Savage had already been three times M.P. for Kent: twice in 1390 and again in 1391. He had been sheriff of Kent in the year after the Peasants' Revolt (1381–2) and was intermittently a J.P. in the county from 1384. He accompanied Richard II's first military expedition, the invasion of Scotland in 1385, during which he was knighted. In the following year (1385–6) he was sheriff again and so was responsible for the election by which Geoffrey Chaucer became M.P. (for Kent) in October 1386. His serving in 1387 with a retinue of 29 men-at-arms and 36 archers in the maritime force put under the orders of the Earl of Arundel (to clear the Channel) did his reputation no harm. Although probably still a knight of the King's Chamber, Savage did not accompany Richard II to Ireland in 1399. Consequently, he was on hand to be commissioned by the Council on 10 September to enquire into the whereabouts of the chattels of Roger Walden, intruded by Richard II into the see of Canterbury instead of Archbishop Arundel (who had now returned from exile with Bolingbroke and been reinstated in the primacy). By this time Savage was on good terms with his Kentish neighbour, Lord Cobham, being one of his feoffees-to-uses. Like Archbishop Arundel, Cobham too had been banished in Richard's last parliament for his membership of the parliamentary commission of 1386 and his share in the condemnation of Richard's supporters during the 'Merciless Parliament' of 1388. Evidently, Savage was not without influential friends at the outset of the Lancastrian régime.

Savage was steward of Prince Henry's household in December 1401, but by April 1403 had been replaced by Sir John Stanley. Stubbs' view of the significance of Savage's election as Speaker in January 1404 appears to rest on the assumption that it was only during this parliament that he was made a member of the King's Council. Between his Speakerships, Savage, as a member of the entourage of the young prince, had at first been kept busy by the rebellion in Wales, but he had been M.P. in the autumn parliament of 1402 and was then also much preoccupied as one of the royal Council (*Archaeologia Cantiana*, lxx, pp. 78–9). Re-appointed a councillor during the second session of the long parliament of 1406, Savage continued to act as such, possibly until the Council was re-shaped early in 1410. He was included in October 1408, May and September 1409, in embassies to France. Meanwhile, he had acted in 1407 as a trustee for Sir Nicholas Hawberk, one of the knights of the King's Chamber (whose widow, the Baroness Cobham, soon married the Lollard, Sir John Old-castle), and, in 1408, as an executor to John Gower, the poet. Savage's own life ended on 29 November 1410. He was buried at Bobbing.

Sir John Say (1449, 1463–5, 1467–8)

Sir John Say appears to have held aloof from the disaffection of 1469 but, when Edward IV fled to Flanders in September 1470 and Henry VI was

restored, gave his support to the government of the Readeption: he continued to be a J.P. in Herts. and in February 1471 was confirmed in the
keepership of the privy palace at Westminster; moreover, when Edward
had recovered the throne, Say needed a general pardon and, although he
was able to secure it on 8 June 1471, two days later was superseded as
Chancellor of the Duchy of Lancaster. That he sat in the next parliament
for Tavistock implies a reduction of his influence (even locally in Herts.),
and so does the limitation of his exemption from the Act of Resumption of
1473 to his royal grants under the seal of the Duchy of Lancaster. By the
end of 1475, however, he was again a member of the royal Council and
back at the Exchequer as Under-Treasurer. Less than a year later (October
1476) he was made Keeper of the Great Wardrobe of the Household, and
immediately following the death of his successor in the Chancellorship of
the Duchy of Lancaster (November 1477) he also recovered this office (in
a grant for life). He was still holding this collection of posts when, shortly
after serving once again as M.P. for Herts., he died on 12 April 1478. He
was buried at Broxbourne where his 'brass' depicts him wearing the
Yorkist collar of suns and roses. In his will he remembered Edward IV
and also Henry VI *in whos service I was brought up and preferred*. The overseer
of the will was William Lord Hastings, the King's Chamberlain, whom Say
described as his *singuler and speciall goode lorde*. The most important of his
executors were John Russell, Bishop of Rochester and Keeper of the Privy
Seal, and John Morton, the future Cardinal, who was then Master of the
Rolls. His connexion with the Bourchiers had been an important aspect
of Sir John Say's career, and after his death it still continued to bear fruit
in the lives of members of his family: his granddaughter (Mary), for
example, married Henry Bourchier, second Earl of Essex, a grandson of
the first earl and a nephew of Edward IV's Queen, Elizabeth Wydeville.

William Stourton (1413)

William Stourton was M.P. for Somerset in 1401, 1402, and 1404, for
Wiltshire in 1407, and for Dorset in 1410 and 1413. He had first been
appointed a J.P. in Dorset in 1389, in Wiltshire in 1394, in Somerset in
1401, and in Cornwall in 1405. His royal commissions under Henry IV
had been very numerous indeed. Evidently Stourton was also well
thought of locally as a legal adviser and agent: he constantly acted for the
Dean and Chapter of Wells and the Abbot of Glastonbury, sometimes for
the civic authorities at Salisbury. By March 1407 (perhaps even as early
as 1401) he was Recorder at Bristol. As long ago as 1386 he had received
a lease for life of the royal castle and park at Mere which, after some
trouble at first, he retained under Henry IV. Then, in 1400, he was given
a lease of the manor of Knowle following its forfeiture by John, Earl of
Salisbury. In May 1409 he shared with Sir Walter Hungerford a royal
grant of the custody of the temporalities of the then vacant Cluniac priory
of Monkton Farleigh (Wilts.), a house founded by the family of Henry IV's

first wife, Mary de Bohun, and consequently under the King's patronage: owing to a dispute over Henry's right to appoint the new prior, this grant involved Hungerford and Stourton in nothing but trouble with the Exchequer. Stourton's relations with this department were evidently on a sounder footing by November 1412 when he and his brother John secured the wardship of the estates of their late brother-in-law, Sir John Beauchamp of Bletsoe, for which, soon after Henry V's accession, they agreed to pay £100. William Stourton did not long survive his Speakership: he died on 18 September 1413 and was buried in the Carthusian priory at Witham (near Frome in Selwood). The wardship of William's son and heir, John, was given by the Crown to his brother John and Chief Justice Hankford. Stourton's heir became Treasurer of Henry VI's Household in 1446 and was created Baron Stourton in 1448.

Sir James Strangeways (1461–2)

If Strangeways was re-elected to parliament in 1463, which is not improbable (although the Yorkshire returns are not extant), he was not made Speaker again. In the meantime, he was evidently busy helping Warwick and other members of the Neville family to deal with Lancastrian disaffection in the north-east. During the parliament itself he and Warwick's brother, John Lord Montagu, in executing a commission to arrest Humphrey Neville (a nephew of the second Earl of Westmorland) who had been attainted in 1461 but had managed to escape from the Tower and get away to Northumberland, were instructed to decide for themselves whether to offer him a royal pardon. In the spring of 1464 Strangeways was associated with Warwick, Montagu, and their brother George (the Chancellor) in negotiations for a peace and close alliance with Scotland; and he was present when, after their return, the Great Seal was restored to George Neville at York. Strangeways and other members of this party were similarly engaged with the Scots in 1465 (at Alnwick) and in 1466 (at Newcastle). Meanwhile, in February 1465, Warwick had appointed Sir James as his deputy-steward in the Duchy of Lancaster lordship of Pickering. Exempted from the Resumption Act of 1467, in November 1468 Strangeways was made sheriff of Yorkshire, receiving in advance a royal 'reward' of £340. His year of office was one of great turbulence in his bailiwick, largely engineered by the now totally disaffected Warwick and culminating in Edward IV's temporary imprisonment at Middleham. The next year (1470) witnessed other rebellions, one in Lincolnshire, where the rising was led by Sir Robert Welles (son of Lord Welles, who in 1468 had married Strangeways' daughter Margaret and was now executed by the King for Sir Robert's treason), and then another, equally unsuccessful, led by Warwick himself, in which Strangeways' younger son Robert was involved. Sir James himself kept out of trouble. His abstention may have annoyed Warwick, and, when the earl restored Henry VI in 1470, Strangeways was not included by the new government in its commissions of the peace in the North and West Ridings. Edward IV soon after his restoration used Strangeways' services again in Scottish negotiations and continued to do so for a year or two longer (until 1474); he also re-established him as a J.P. in the North Riding, his latest re-appointment falling in 1477. By this time, however, Sir James was ceasing to be very active, and he died in the summer of 1480. His second wife, Elizabeth, daughter of Henry Eure of Bradley (Durham) and widow of Sir William Bulmer of Wilton (near Redcar), died in March 1482. His son and heir, Sir Richard, died in April 1488. The latter's heir, James, despite his having served Richard III as a Knight of the Body, had safely weathered the transition from Yorkist to Tudor rule and, after succeeding to the family property, was sheriff of Yorkshire in 1492-3 and 1508-9. This Sir James, the Speaker's grandson, died in 1521. (In the *DNB* article on the Speaker, the two Sir Jameses have been confused.)

Sir William Sturmy (1404)

Before his Speakership Sturmy had been an M.P. in seven different parliaments (including those of 1399 and 1401), representing in turn each of the three counties in which he held lands (Wilts., Hants., and Devon). He was sitting for Devon when Speaker in 1404, but he sat most frequently for Wiltshire, and it was for this county that, after 1404, he was to sit again in 1413, 1414, 1417, and 1422. Although Sturmy had been a retainer of Richard II, Henry IV soon (in November 1399) made him a J.P. in Wiltshire and in 1401, after his temporary appointment as a royal councillor, in Hampshire as well. In the year after his Speakership, Sturmy was negotiating with the Teutonic Knights at Marienburg (from August to October 1405), with the local authorities at Lübeck, Hamburg, Bremen, and other Hanseatic ports on the way back, and then finally with representatives of the whole Hanse at Dordrecht. He spent most of 1407 in inconclusive negotiations in Prussia and the Low Countries. It was sometime before the summer of 1412 that Sturmy was appointed overseer of the estates of Henry IV's Queen (Joan of Navarre), whose seneschal of household was Sir Hugh Luttrell of Dunster, Sturmy's stepdaughter's husband. He continued to be connected with Queen Joan in the reign of Henry V. The latter renewed Sturmy's royal annuities and in 1418 employed him in diplomacy again, to arrange a marriage between the Duke of Bedford and Jacqueline of Hainault (who eventually married the Duke of Gloucester). The only time when Sturmy was sheriff was in 1418-19 when he held office in Wiltshire. It was at Henry V's instance that he was restored in 1420 to the hereditary wardenship of Savernake forest, of which he had been deprived by the Duke of Gloucester in 1417. He last sat in parliament in 1422. But although now (at the beginning of Henry VI's reign) his royal annuities were again confirmed and he remained a J.P., he seems no longer to have been very active. He died on 22 March 1427, being buried in the Trinitarian priory of Easton (in

Savernake forest) of which he was the patron. He was an ancestor of Jane Seymour, Henry VIII's third Queen and the mother of Edward VI.

Thomas Thorpe (1453)

It seems highly probable that Thorpe secured his release from the Fleet prison before the end of the parliament of 1453–4. He was evidently not deprived of his office as Baron of the Exchequer, being paid his terminal fee on 17 July 1454 (E 403/798, mem. 11). Shortly afterwards he came to terms with the Duke of York over the question of damages, although a year later £210 was still outstanding (CCR, 1454–61, 108–9). Following Somerset's return to influence early in 1455, Thorpe was granted for life the office of Chancellor of the Exchequer (24 March), still continuing in the office of Baron. It was along with Somerset that he was accused by the Yorkists of embezzling the letters they sent to the King from Ware on the eve of the battle of St Albans (21 May 1455), to explain the motive of their insurrection, and also of preventing a personal interview with the King on the day of the battle itself, the effect of which was to make a fight inevitable (Rot. Parl., v. 280–2). Thorpe escaped with his life (Paston Letters, iii. 28), but during the following parliament itself was held partly responsible for the battle. A proposal to deprive him of all his offices failed when the King rejected it during the first session. It did, however, succeed during the second session, probably after York became Protector (Rot. Parl., v. 332–3, no. 9; 342, no. 23). Only by paying York 500 marks did Thorpe then escape a surrender of his lands to the duke, pending a completion of payment of the damages awarded against him in 1453–4 (CCR, 1454–61, 108–9). After these reverses it took some time before Thorpe got back into station: although appointed for life as Keeper of the Privy Wardrobe in the Tower on 16 November 1457, it was only on 12 September 1458 that he recovered office as a Baron of the Exchequer, being then, however, appointed Second Baron (not Third, as before) (CPR, 1452–61, 392; 458, 477). By this time he had attached himself more closely to the young Somerset (Henry Beaufort) who was now taking his father's place in the Lancastrian party. In the spring of 1459 when the Court was preparing for a 'show-down', Thorpe was busy collecting munitions of war at the Tower (Privy Seal warrants for issue, E 404/71/3, no. 77) and after the Yorkist defeat at Ludford was with Henry VI at Coventry when parliament met in November. He was still unable to recover the office of Chancellor of the Exchequer, but soon afterwards (8 January 1460) was confirmed in his post as Second Baron, being now granted it during good behaviour and not (as before) at royal pleasure (CPR, 1452–61, 549). In March 1460 he was one of the Exchequer officials appointed to act as receivers of revenues from the estates of attainted Yorkists and himself profited at their expense. He was taken prisoner at the battle of Northampton (16 July) and kept in custody, first in the Newgate and then the Marshalsea prison. On the day of the second

battle of St Albans (17 February 1461), he escaped, presumably intending
to join the Queen's army, but was caught by Londoners in Harringay
Park and beheaded (*Rot. Parl.*, vi. 294). His estates were sequestrated by
Edward IV, under whom his son Roger (who had fought with Somerset
at Wakefield in December 1460 when the Duke of York was killed)
enjoyed poor fortune. Not until Henry VII's first parliament did Roger
secure rehabilitation (ibid.).

Sir John Tiptoft (1406)

Soon after his Speakership, Tiptoft married, as his first wife, Philippa, a
daughter and coheir of Sir John Talbot of Richard's Castle (Herefordshire). She was the widow of Edward III's last Chamberlain, Sir Robert
de Assheton (who had died in 1384) and also of Sir Matthew de Gurney,
an old campaigner of the French wars. Gurney died (in September 1406)
leaving no heir to succeed to estates for the mere reversion to which
Henry IV's youngest son Humphrey in 1407 was prepared to pay
5,000 marks and Henry V ten years later (after Philippa's death) £4,000.
Tiptoft's second marriage, in 1422, was to Joyce, a daughter and coheir of
Edward Lord Charlton of Powys, a half-sister of Edmund, Earl of March,
a niece of the Dowager Duchesses of Clarence and York, and a coheir (as
was Richard, Duke of York) to the lands of her maternal uncle, Edmund
Holland, Earl of Kent (nephew of Richard II), who had died in 1408.

Tiptoft's grants from Henry IV included the wardship of the heirs of
Sir Robert Shardelow and John de Tuddenham (both of Suffolk); in
1405, a grant for life of two manors in Leicestershire forfeited by Sir
Ralph Hastings who had been executed at Durham for his part in the
northern rising of Archbishop Scrope and the Earl Marshal, a shared gift
of the Earl Marshal's clothes, armour and saddles, an additional annuity of
£20 from the fee-farm of Norwich, and the stewardship of the Mortimer
lordship of Bottisham (Cambs.); and, in the year of his Speakership, a
grant of £150 and estates in Carmarthenshire and Cardiganshire, all forfeited by Rees ap Griffith, a Welsh supporter of Owen Glendower, together with the forestership of Waybridge and Sapley in Huntingdonshire. These last concessions were made, expressly, notwithstanding
Tiptoft's enjoyment of royal annuities and grants worth £150 a year.

When Tiptoft was in his first half-year as Treasurer of the Household,
he was also appointed Chief Butler of England. But Thomas Chaucer (his
successor in the Speakership), who had been given the Chief Butlership
for life in 1402, recovered it in December 1407. Towards the end of his
first half-year as Treasurer of the Exchequer (on 23 May 1409) Tiptoft
received a special reward of 200 marks, in addition to the ancient fee of
100 marks a year and the annual incremental fee of £300 attached to the
office. Additional grants of royal revenues received by him while occupying the office amounted to nearly a further £200 a year, and Tiptoft
retained most of these under Henry V.

The salient points of Tiptoft's career following his dismissal from the Treasurership of the Exchequer in 1409 are as follows. After a long period of inactivity and Henry V's reduction in 1413 of his considerable income as a royal annuitant to £120, he was appointed on 8 May 1415 as Seneschal of Aquitaine instead of Thomas Beaufort, Earl of Dorset, and retained this office for the next eight years at an annual fee of £500. He came home from Gascony early in 1416 and, during the visit of the Emperor Sigismund to England in the following summer, acted as his Steward of Household. When Sigismund returned to the continent, Tiptoft remained in his entourage as Henry V's confidential diplomatic agent. Although he was considered for the post of 'knight-constable' of the expeditionary force with which Henry V again invaded France in 1417, his services were employed instead at the General Council in Constance, where his main job was to secure the military help promised by Sigismund in the Treaty of Canterbury. Joining Henry V in Lower Normandy, Tiptoft was appointed on 1 November 1417 as President of the Exchequer and other judicial tribunals in Normandy and also as Treasurer-General, with his administrative base at Caen, and he held these offices until May 1419. In 1420-1 he administered the Gascon seneschalship in person. On the accession of Henry VI in 1422 he became a member of the minority Council approved by parliament and was at first one of its most assiduous attenders. He remained a royal councillor, with hardly a break, until his death, having been made a peer early in 1426. Later in this year he was made Steward of the King's Household and retained office for nearly six years. In this capacity he accompanied Henry VI to France in 1430 and was there again in 1431. He vacated his office as head of the royal Household on 1 March 1432, when Gloucester also contrived a change in the major offices of state. Tiptoft remained a member of the Council and still attended it (and parliament, too) but he now lost something of his former influence on affairs. In 1437 he participated in negotiations, regarding trade, with Flanders and the Hanse, and in 1439 for an alliance with the Archbishop of Cologne. He died late in January 1443. His son and heir (John), who six years later married a daughter of the Earl of Salisbury (the widow of Henry, Duke of Warwick) and was shortly afterwards created Earl of Worcester, soon became a Yorkist and remained one until his execution during the Lancastrian Readeption in 1470.

Sir Thomas Tresham (1459)

Tresham was among the Lancastrian gentry who joined Queen Margaret and her son after their landing at Weymouth on 14 April 1471; and when, on 27 April, Edward IV issued proclamations declaring Margaret, Prince Edward, and their adherents to be notorious traitors and rebels and ordering no one to assist them, Tresham was one of those adherents named in the writs. He was with the Lancastrian army that was cut to pieces at Tewkesbury on 4 May and, although he fled the field and took sanctuary in the abbey, he was taken out for trial by the Duke of Gloucester (as Constable) and the Duke of Norfolk (as Marshal), condemned, and beheaded. He was buried in the monastic church. In the parliament which met in 1472 he was posthumously attainted, and all his lands were once again declared forfeit. All profits from these were at first appropriated to the Household, later to the building of Edward IV's new chapel for the Order of the Garter at Windsor, until in Henry VII's first parliament (1485) Tresham's son and heir, John, secured an annulment of the attainder and recovered possession.

Sir Richard Waldegrave (1381-2)

Already returned as M.P. for Suffolk in 1376, 1377, and 1378, Waldegrave sat after 1382 in all but three of the next eleven parliaments (for the last time in 1390). Originating at Walgrave in Northants., where he still held a number of estates, Sir Richard lived at Bures St Mary, the home of his wife's family, and most of his property was hereabouts in the Stour valley. Before his Speakership, he had served on a number of royal commissions in Suffolk and Essex. These included the detested commission to investigate under-assessments and evasions of the triple poll-tax which 'triggered off' the Peasants' Revolt. His own property does not appear to have suffered much in the great rising, but he helped in the enquiry about damage done to manors held by the King's mother in Essex and, while Speaker, was included among the commissioners authorized to suppress disorders in Suffolk. Here, in December 1382, he was first made a J.P., serving this office until the end of the reign of Richard II but not under Henry IV. In 1385 he shared a grant of the administration of the temporalities of the see of Norwich, sequestrated by the Crown following Bishop Despenser's disastrous crusade in Flanders in 1383. Later in the same year he was a member of the royal retinue in Richard II's ineffectual expedition to Scotland. His attitude in the prolonged political crisis of 1386-8 may well have been equivocal, for he remained a J.P. throughout and sat in each of the three parliaments which met in this period. But it was only after Richard II reasserted himself in 1389 that Waldegrave, as a member of syndicates, profited from royal grants of estates forfeited as a result of the condemnations of the 'Merciless Parliament'. In November 1393, as a 'King's knight', he was made a member of the royal Council with a fee of 100 marks a year, augmented by an annuity of £40. He was still a councillor at the end of 1397. All the same, in November 1397 he took out a general pardon for all offences against the Crown, including treasons. Nothing is known of Waldegrave's actions during the revolution of 1399, and he seems now to have retired into a decent obscurity, although membership of a trust administering some of the Bohun estates in Essex continued to keep him in touch with Archbishop Arundel until his death on 2 May 1410.

Sir Thomas Waweton (1425)

Under Henry VI Waweton did not serve as a J.P. in Bedfordshire until 1435, but he was sheriff in the joint bailiwick of Bedfordshire and Buckinghamshire in 1422–3, 1428–9, and 1432–3. In the second of these terms of office (1428–9) there was serious upset in Bedfordshire arising out of differences, first, between the Duke of Norfolk and the Earl of Huntingdon and, then, between Huntingdon and his brother-in-law, the Earl of Stafford (whose wife and the Duchess of Norfolk were sisters), so much so that the Protector (Gloucester) hurried down from London to investigate. In 1429 Waweton himself made trouble in Buckinghamshire by brushing aside the result of a normal parliamentary election, having already illegally interfered in the election for Huntingdonshire along with many other 'invaders' from Bedfordshire (see my book, *The Commons in the Parliament of 1422*, pp. 17–21). In 1437 and again in 1439 he was actively involved in riots at the sessions for the peace in Bedfordshire as a supporter of Lord Grey of Ruthin against Lord Fanhope, and as a result of the second offence was suspended from his office of J.P. for nearly five years. Restored as J.P. in November 1443, he was again dropped in June 1448, although he lived on for more than another two years. He is known to have been still alive in August 1450. Waweton's third wife, Alana, daughter of Sir Simon Felbrigge, K.G., and widow of Sir William Tyndale of Dean (Northants.), whom he had probably married in 1427, was, however, a widow when she died in 1458 (Bridges, *Northants.*, op. cit., ii. 338).

Sir John Wenlock (1455–6)

Within about two years of being Speaker, Wenlock became a member of the King's Council. He is known to have been present at one of its meetings held at the London Blackfriars on 4 March 1458, and on 26 August following was ordered to attend at Westminster about a fortnight later. Meanwhile in May he had been appointed, along with the Earls of Salisbury and Warwick and Viscount Bourchier, to treat at Calais with commissaries of Duke Philip of Burgundy about breaches of the Anglo-Burgundian truce; late in August he was preparing to go to Antwerp, presumably on similar business. This mission afforded an opportunity for discussing the possibility of a series of marriages between the sons of Henry VI and the Dukes of York and Somerset and daughters of the Count of Charolais (Burgundy's heir) and the Dukes of Bourbon and Guelders, or, alternatively, between these English boys and daughters of Charles VII, the Duke of Orleans, and the Count of Maine. It was Wenlock who seemingly offered these last proposals to the representatives of Charles VII at Rouen in December 1458 and January 1459. Both sets of offers were politely but firmly turned down. That a Yorkist marriage abroad was even projected suggests the dynastic drift in York's intentions at this time, and Wenlock's part in the business presupposes some closeness of contact with him and Duke Richard. If this were actually so, it would go far to explain how in 1459 Wenlock came to be completely committed to active membership of the Yorkist party. At its dispersal following the Rout of Ludford on 12 October 1459 Wenlock fled with the Nevilles and York's eldest son, Edward, first to Devon and then (via Guernsey) to Calais. For his treason in taking arms against King Henry he was attainted in the Coventry parliament and incurred forfeiture of his estates. 500 marks were soon to be offered as a reward for his capture, half of the sum promised for the capture of any one of the traitor peers. Returning with the refugees at Calais in June 1460, he assisted Salisbury in besieging the Tower. When the Yorkists won control by the battle of Northampton, Wenlock rejoined the King's Council, was restored to his estates, and, on 14 November, was granted for life the office of Chief Butler. He was with York's heir at Ludlow at the time of Duke Richard's death and probably assisted him in his victory at Mortimer's Cross. On 8 February 1461 he was made a Knight of the Garter. Seven weeks later he fought at Ferrybridge and Towton. He now became a regular member of Edward IV's Council and was summoned as a peer to the first Yorkist parliament, on the day of the issue of his writ of summons being made Chamberlain of the Duchy of Lancaster for life; and on the last day of the parliament he was appointed Treasurer of Ireland (jointly with Sir Richard FitzEustace). He retained the office of Chief Butler. He now profited extensively from grants of royal wardships and custodies of estates, especially those forfeited by prominent Lancastrians. Chief Justice Fortescue's lands in Middlesex, to which were later added those in Wiltshire and Somerset, were given him for keeps. He helped in the Yorkist reduction of the North in 1462. But his principal services to Edward IV were in the diplomatic field, and from 1461 until his death never a year passed but what he went overseas on ambassadorial business, the early purpose of which was to upset the Lancastrians' calculations of foreign assistance. In much of this work Wenlock was closely associated with the Earl of Warwick; and he became a member of his private council and eventually shared in his intrigues with the exiled Lancastrians. But in April 1470, when Warwick's rebellion proved unsuccessful and he fled to Calais, Wenlock (then acting as the earl's deputy in command) refused him entry, and was immediately made by Edward IV Lieutenant of Calais and the Marches. None the less he soon played Edward false, joined the alliance between Warwick and his own former mistress, Queen Margaret, and accompanied the latter back to England in April 1471. Put in charge of the Lancastrian centre-battle facing Edward at Tewkesbury on 4 May, he fell in the fighting and was buried in the abbey nearby. His lands were of course once again forfeited, most of them falling into the possession of the then Chancellor, Bishop Rotherham of Lincoln, to the exclusion of Wenlock's heir, a distant kinsman, Thomas Lawley of Much Wenlock. (By neither of his marriages did he have children of his own.)

Index

Abergavenny, George (Neville), 2nd baron, 317; George, 3rd baron, 317

Adam of Usk (chronicler), 11–12

Admiral, office of, 357

Admiralty, commissaries-general, 293; Court of, 322; office of vice-admiral, 293

Adrian VI, pope, 233

Agincourt (1415), battle of, 80, 161, 164, 172, 236, 357

Aire, R., 269

Aiscough, William, bishop of Salisbury, 224, 241

Albany, duke of, see under Stuart

Alcock, John, bishop of Rochester, 285

Aldbrough, William, 1st baron, 162; William, son of, 162n.

Alençon, 357

Aliceholt (Hants.), forest of, 160

Allington, John, 284, 289n.; Mary (Cheyne), wife of, 284n.; William (Speaker, 1429–30), 197–9; William (Speaker, 1472–5, 1478), 67, 81, 94–5, 113, 199n., 283–9, 335–7

Alnwick (Northumberland), 364

Alnwick, William, bishop of Lincoln, 179

Alphonso V (Portugal), 243

Alred, Richard, 267

Amadas, Robert, 320n.

Ampthill (Beds.), 259

Ancient Method and Manor of holding Parliaments in England (Henry Elsynge), 43

Angers (Fr.), settlement of, 281–2

Anjou, 50

Anne, queen of Richard II, 106, 129

Anne, queen of Richard III, 281, 351

Anne, second queen of Henry VIII, 359

Anonimalle Chronicle, 4, 10, 11, 14–17, 19–21, 28, 42n., 44, 77, 84, 119

Anstey, John, 284, 289

Antwerp, 370

Aquitaine, 133, 247, 356; office of lieutenant, 248; office of seneschal, 171, 208, 368

Arc, Joan of, see under Joan of Arc

Argentan (Fr.), 243

Argentine, family of, 197

Arras (1435), Congress of, 211, 236, 358

Arras (1482), Treaty of, 290

Arthur (Tudor), Prince of Wales, 300n., 301, 305, 307, 310, 337

Articuli super Cartas (1301), 5

Artois, 212, 315

Arundel, earls of, see under FitzAlan

Arundel, Eleanor, countess of, 357

Arundel, Thomas, bishop of Ely, later archbishop of York and then of Canterbury, 9, 12, 47–8, 54, 69, 131, 134, 137, 139, 146, 148, 151, 153, 155–6, 171, 343, 353, 362, 369

Ascot (Oxon.), 354

Ashby St Legers (N'hants.), 294, 351

Assheton, Sir Robert de, 367

Attainder (1465, 1485), acts of, 276, 352

Attorney-General, King's, office of, 94–5, 170, 171n., 207

Audley, James (Tuchet), 5th lord, 190n., 263; Sir Thomas (Speaker, 1529–33), 115, 340

Austria, Philip, archduke of, 305

Avignon, 141

Ayssheton, Nicholas, 108n.

Ayton (1497), Treaty of, 306

Babbington (Notts.), 312

Babthorpe, Sir Robert, 203

Bacon, Sir Francis, 307–8

Baker, Sir John (Speaker, 1545–7, 1547–1552), 115, 336

Baltic, 129, 144

Bamborough (Northumberland), 260

Bampton, John, 355

Banbury (Oxon), 153

Barking (Essex), 249n.

Barnet (1471), battle of, 112, 232n., 283, 292, 356

Barnwell All Saints (N'hants.), 248n.

Barton ('the Holy Maid of Kent'), Elizabeth, 359

Bassingbourne (Cambs.), 289n.

Bath, Order of the, 112, 279, 291, 308

Bathe, Sir Thomas, 93

Baugé (1421), battle of, 172, 175, 186, 198–199, 347

Bavaria, Lewis, duke of, 145, 150n., 349, 353

Bayeux, 236